JAPANESE HISTORY AND CULTURE FROM ANCIENT TO MODERN TIMES:

SEVEN BASIC BIBLIOGRAPHIES

JAPANESE HISTORY AND CULTURE FROM ANCIENT TO MODERN TIMES:

SEVEN BASIC BIBLIOGRAPHIES

John W. Dower with Timothy S. George

Second Edition
Revised and Updated

Markus Wiener Publishers
PRINCETON

A NOTE ON THE TITLE AND HALF-TITLE DESIGNS

The designs used on the title and half-title pages are Japanese *mon* or crests. The basic square design motif is known as the "mesh" *(meyui,* literally "eye tie"), and derives from procedures used in an expensive traditional dyeing process to create a dappled effect. An almost identical variant on the same square pattern is the "nail puller" *(kuginuki),* based on an old carpenter's tool and carrying connotations of deriving leverage and strength from small sources.

Second edition, revised and updated, 1995.

For information write to:
  Markus Wiener Publishers
  114 Jefferson Road, Princeton, NJ 08540

Library of Congress Cataloging-in-Publication Data

Dower, John W.
    Japanese history & culture from ancient to modern times: seven basic
bibliographies/John W. Dower, Timothy S. George.—2nd revised and updated ed.
    Includes bibliographical references and index.
    ISBN 1-55876-097-0 hardcover
    ISBN 1-55876-098-9 paperback
    1. Japan—History—Bibliography.   I. George, Timothy S.   II. Title.
III. Title: Japanese history and culture from ancient to modern times.
Z3306.D69   1994
[DS835]
016.952—dc20   94-48170
                                                                          CIP

This book has been composed in Romance by CMF Graphic Design

Cover design by Cheryl Mirkin

Markus Wiener Publishers books are printed on acid-free paper
and meet the guidelines for permanence and durability of the
Committee on Production Guidelines for Book Longevity
of the Council on Library Resources
Manufactured in the United States of America

CONTENTS

4. JAPAN & THE CRISIS IN ASIA, 1931-1945: 'PRIMARY' MATERIALS IN ENGLISH   347

5. OCCUPIED JAPAN & THE COLD WAR IN ASIA   373

PREFACE TO THE FIRST EDITION

As a graduate student in the late 1960s, I recall being impressed by the passing comment of a senior scholar. Until recently, he said, he had been pretty much able to keep abreast of Western scholarship about the Far East, but that was becoming more difficult. Today, almost twenty years later, we can only marvel at a time when it was possible for academics to still dream about being conversant with the gamut of scholarly writings about China and Japan. In the Japan field, the articles and books that have been published since the 1950s in English alone are so numerous, in fact, that even the bibliographers appear to have abandoned hope of keeping up.

How else can one account for the fact that even now the best known general bibliographic surveys of Western writings about Japanese history and culture still date from between the 1950s and early 1970s? The pioneer Harvard listing by Hugh Borton and his colleagues appeared in 1954. Bernard Silberman's useful annotated bibliography was published in 1962. Naomi Fukuda's union catalog of Western books on Japan is dated 1968, and the two multi-volume cumulative bibliographies covering all Asia issued by the Association of Asian Studies cover publications through 1970. Most of the more recent bibliographic guides to scholarship on Japan have been of a specialized, attenuated, or annual nature—valuable indeed, but still making it necessary for a generation of students, teachers, and scholars to compile their own working bibliographies.

This present publication is the unexpected offspring of such a private endeavor, having its origin in personal bibliographies compiled over the years to guide students into the flourishing but poorly marked terrain of historical studies of Japan. History is the most catholic and generous of scholarly fields—bridging the humanities and social sciences, as it necessarily does, and weaving together such diverse concerns as personality and economic forces, ideologies and institutions, the gentle arts and the exercise of unbridled violence. The bibliographies of Japanese history offered here are thus multidisciplinary in content and wide-ranging in their topical as well as chronological focus. At the same time, they inevitably reflect personal pedagogic concerns, and the criteria of selection and organization require explanation.

1. Every effort has been made to maintain and enhance the practical, "working" nature of this guide. Thus, the classroom origins of the volume have been preserved in a manner that will enable teachers to lift out parts of the whole as basic reading lists for the most common survey courses pertaining to Japan: the ancient and medieval periods to 1600; early modern and modern Japan (1600-1945); diplomacy, imperialism, and war from the 1850s to 1945; and the Allied occupation of Japan (1945-1952). In addition, each of these major bibliographies is bro-

ken down into numerous topical sections to facilitate quick identification of specific concerns, and cumbersome cross-referencing has been kept to an absolute minimum by repeating the same reference wherever it is topically pertinent.

2. Entries under every section or subsection tend to be clustered in ways that are internally logical. Grand overviews are listed together, for example, as are articles and books focusing on essentially the same subject. Where chronology is relevant within any section, references dealing with earlier events naturally precede those concerning later periods. Subjective evaluation undeniably colors such organization to a minor degree, and even whimsy may come into play on occasion. To anyone immersed in history, however, it is much more rational and convenient to have sources grouped in accordance with thematic affinity, as opposed to purely mechanical conventions such as authors in alphabetical order. The bibliography is designed to keep jumping around to a minimum.

3. The difficulty of Oriental languages always is evoked as one of the greatest barriers to Western comprehension of the East, and no one can deny the importance of understanding other peoples through their native tongue. At the same time, however, it must be noted that much of the "primary" record through which we can better understand Japanese history is accessible in English. The great classics of ancient and medieval literature are now available in excellent translations; the minor classics are gradually finding their translators; and translation of modern Japanese literature has become a small cottage industry. Most of the basic legal codes and "house laws" from early times on have been rendered into English, as has a great variety of religious texts. In the modern period, the Japanese themselves produced literally millions of pages in Western languages in the form of books, magazines, newspapers, yearbooks, documents submitted to international organizations, and sheer propaganda. Their diplomatic exchanges with foreign nations beginning in the mid-nineteenth century, along with the voluminous reports of British and American diplomats concerned with Japan, are now widely accessible. The crisis years between World War One and World War Two saw Japan, China, and the Western nations produce a veritable deluge of English-language material. This wide range of "primary" materials in English is of immense value to students, teachers, and scholars alike, and special care has been taken to introduce the most important of such sources here for every period of Japanese history. For 1931 to 1945, a separate bibliography is devoted exclusively to such materials.

4. On more technical matters, it should be noted that Japanese as well as Western authors of cited English-language publications are listed with given name first and surname second, thus keeping the treatment of authors' names consistent throughout. It has not been possible to place macrons over the "long" vowels in Japanese names.

5. The bibliographies are generally up-to-date through 1985, and include materials scheduled for publication early in 1986. Special effort has been made to itemize not only articles from the basic scholarly journals that deal with Japan, but also especially useful essays that appear in edited volumes. Selectivity—and plain

oversight—are naturally most conspicuous at the article and essay level, and worthy scholarly contributions have undoubtedly been overlooked. I can only hope their number is relatively small and their authors will be understanding. In passing, I might note that the selective process has extended to exclusion of some of my own publications.

Over the course of the years I have shared bibliographies with William Wray and learned of many sources from him that might otherwise have been neglected. Carol Gluck, James O'Brien, and Martin Collcutt kindly read portions of earlier drafts of this volume and offered helpful addenda. Julie Bogle not only typed the ever expanding draft of the manuscript, but also provided invaluable library assistance in clarifying and correcting imprecise references. Lee Tablewski assisted in the final design of the manuscript, and Markus Wiener, the publisher, tolerated innumerable revisions with unfailing patience. My thanks to these individuals and others who contributed to this compilation.

I presume this will be the last of the survey bibliographies of Japanese history and culture to emanate from file cards in a private study. Certainly I hope that is the case, for like anyone in the Japan field I look forward to the day when we will have available a multi-volume and truly comprehensive computer-based bibliography of writings on Japan in Western languages. Until then, it will be gratifying if this guide enables other teachers and researchers to "keep up" with greater ease— and, at the same time, suggests some useful ways to organize our thinking about Japan.

JOHN W. DOWER

Madison, Wisconsin
March 11, 1986

PREFACE TO THE SECOND EDITION

It is even more difficult now than in 1986 to keep up with English-language publications on Japan. This new edition is the result of a continuing attempt to do so. Several useful bibliographies have appeared since the first edition, but there is still no comprehensive, up-to-date bibliography of Japanese history and culture in either printed or electronic form. Frank Shulman's extensively annotated (and therefore necessarily highly selective) bibliography appeared in 1989. The Association for Asian Studies slowly continues to compile its comprehensive annual listings covering all of Asia, which as of this writing cover publications through 1988. Most other new works have been devoted to specialized topics. Scholars must still compile their own working bibliographies; this book began as such and is intended to help others jump-start their own.

The second edition retains the structure and content of the first, and adds mostly materials published since 1986. Macrons and an index of names (of authors, editors, translators, and persons mentioned in titles) have been added. The new material testifies to the considerable growth of the field over the past eight years. There are many more translations of literature, especially from the Heian and medieval periods, and a number of works have appeared in the field of business history. There are also signs that postwar Japan is beginning to be treated as history rather than being left as the exclusive domain of the political scientists and economists. This trend will likely necessitate a new section in the next edition.

Our thanks to the librarians at the Widener and Harvard-Yenching Institute libraries at Harvard University, at Hamilton Library's Asia Collection at the University of Hawaii, at the International House of Japan, and at the Institute of Social Science, Institute of Oriental Culture, and General Library of the University of Tokyo. We also thank Yang Daqing for his research assistance, Cheryl Mirkin for her page layout work, and Markus Wiener for his patience through many delays.

The research for this revised edition was done not only by surveying file cards in library catalogs, but also with the aid of computer searches made possible by on-line library catalogs. Anyone with a computer, modem, and telephone line can now access many such catalogs, including those of the University of California, Harvard, Stanford, Michigan, Cambridge, and Oxford, directly or through the Internet. There is still, however, no comprehensive computer-based bibliography on Japan that would obviate the need for scholars to search library catalogs and stacks. We will be gratified if this guide continues to point the way for such hands-on searches.

JOHN W. DOWER
TIMOTHY S. GEORGE

November 1, 1994

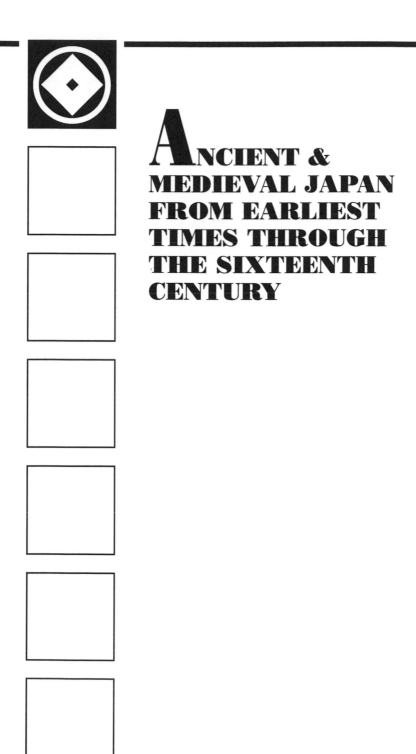

ANCIENT & MEDIEVAL JAPAN FROM EARLIEST TIMES THROUGH THE SIXTEENTH CENTURY

Ancient & Medieval Japan from Earliest Times Through the Sixteenth Century

GENERAL WORKS: HISTORICAL OVERVIEWS

KŌDANSHA ENCYCLOPEDIA OF JAPAN. 1983: Kōdansha. Eight volumes plus Index volume and 1986 Supplement. Contains over 10,000 articles, including major essays (with bibliographic references) by contemporary scholars on all aspects of Japanese history and culture. See especially the long "History of Japan" entry in volume 3.

JAPAN: AN ILLUSTRATED ENCYCLOPEDIA. 1993: Kōdansha. Two-volume version of the *Kōdansha Encyclopedia of Japan*, lavishly illustrated.

CAMBRIDGE HISTORY OF JAPAN. Cambridge University Press. Collections of essays by leading scholars, both western and Japanese.

> Delmer M. Brown, ed. Volume 1, ANCIENT JAPAN (1993)
> Volume 2, HEIAN JAPAN (forthcoming)
> Kōzō Yamamura, ed. Volume 3, MEDIEVAL JAPAN (1990)
> John Whitney Hall, ed. Volume 4, EARLY MODERN JAPAN (1991)
> Marius B. Jansen, ed. Volume 5, THE NINETEENTH CENTURY (1989)
> Peter Duus, ed. Volume 6, THE TWENTIETH CENTURY (1988).

CAMBRIDGE ENCYCLOPEDIA OF JAPAN. 1993: Cambridge University Press.

ENCYCLOPEDIA OF ASIAN HISTORY. 1988: Charles Scribner's Sons. Four volumes.

Dorothy Perkins. ENCYCLOPEDIA OF JAPAN: JAPANESE HISTORY AND CULTURE, FROM ABACUS TO ZŌRI. 1991: Facts on File.

Ryūsaku Tsunoda, Wm. Theodore DeBary & Donald Keene, eds. SOURCES OF JAPANESE TRADITION. 1958: Columbia University Press. Also published in two paperback volumes (1964: Columbia University Press).

David J. Lu, ed. SOURCES OF JAPANESE HISTORY. Volume 1. 1974: McGraw-Hill.

George B. Sansom. JAPAN: A SHORT CULTURAL HISTORY. Revised edition. 1943: Appleton. The classic English- language study of premodern Japanese culture.

_____. A HISTORY OF JAPAN TO 1334. 1958: Stanford University Press.

_____. A HISTORY OF JAPAN, 1334-1615. 1961: Stanford University Press.

_____. A HISTORY OF JAPAN, 1615-1867. 1963: Stanford University Press.

John W. Hall. JAPAN: FROM PREHISTORY TO MODERN TIMES. 1970: Delacorte.

_____. GOVERNMENT AND LOCAL POWER IN JAPAN, 500 TO 1700: A STUDY BASED ON BIZEN PROVINCE. 1966: Princeton University Press.

Conrad Shirokauer. A BRIEF HISTORY OF JAPANESE CIVILIZATION. 1993: Harcourt Brace Jovanovich.

Edwin O. Reischauer. JAPAN: THE STORY OF A NATION. 4th edition. 1990: McGraw-Hill. Revision of the author's JAPAN, PAST AND PRESENT. Strongest on the modern period.

_____ & John K. Fairbank. EAST ASIA: THE GREAT TRADITION. 1960: Houghton Mifflin.

John K. Fairbank, Edwin O. Reischauer & Albert M. Craig. EAST ASIA: TRADITION AND TRANSFORMATION. 1989: Houghton Mifflin. Updated and abridged version of preceding work, plus chapters on the modern period.

Edwin O. Reischauer & Albert M. Craig. JAPAN: TRADITION AND TRANS-FORMATION. 1989: Houghton Mifflin. Contains same chapters on premodern Japan as preceding work.

Mikiso Hane. PREMODERN JAPAN: A HISTORICAL SURVEY. 1991: Westview Press.

Arthur E. Tiedemann, ed. AN INTRODUCTION TO JAPANESE CIVILIZA-TION. 1974: Heath. Both chronological and topical essays by leading scholars.

Conrad Totman. JAPAN BEFORE PERRY: A BRIEF SYNTHESIS. 1981: University of California Press.

H. Paul Varley. JAPANESE CULTURE: A SHORT HISTORY. 3rd edition. 1984: University of Hawaii Press.

Richard J. Pearson, ed. ANCIENT JAPAN. 1992: G. Braziller.

Hugh Cortazzi. THE JAPANESE ACHIEVEMENT: A SHORT HISTORY OF JAPAN AND ITS CULTURE. 1990: St. Martin's.

Robert S. Ellwood, Jr. AN INVITATION TO JAPANESE CIVILIZATION. 1980: Wadsworth.

Milton Walter Meyer. JAPAN: A CONCISE HISTORY. Third edition. 1993: Rowman & Littlefield.

James Murdoch. A HISTORY OF JAPAN. 3 volumes. 1923-1926; reprinted 1949, 1964: Ungar. Outdated, but occasionally useful for detail.

Mitsusada Inoue. INTRODUCTION TO JAPANESE HISTORY BEFORE THE MEIJI RESTORATION. 1962: Kokusai Bunka Shinkōkai.

Takeo Yazaki. SOCIAL CHANGE AND THE CITY IN JAPAN: FROM EARLIEST TIMES THROUGH THE INDUSTRIAL REVOLUTION. 1968: Japan Publications.

Susan B. Hanley & Arthur P. Wolf, eds. FAMILY AND POPULATION IN EAST ASIAN HISTORY. 1985: Stanford University Press.

William D. Wray. JAPAN'S ECONOMY: A BIBLIOGRAPHY OF ITS PAST AND PRESENT. 1989: Markus Wiener.

Yosaburō Takekoshi. ECONOMIC ASPECTS OF THE HISTORY OF THE CIVILIZATION OF JAPAN. 3 volumes. 1930: Macmillan. Poorly presented, but contains interesting detail.

Ryōsuke Ishii. A HISTORY OF POLITICAL INSTITUTIONS IN JAPAN. C. Kiley, transl. 1980: University of Tokyo Press.

Hyōe Murakami, ed. GREAT HISTORICAL FIGURES OF JAPAN. 1978: Japan Culture Institute.

Ronald L. Tarnstrom. THE WARS OF JAPAN. 1992: Trogen Books.

W. G. Beasley & E. G. Pulleyblank, eds. HISTORIANS OF CHINA AND JAPAN. 1961: Oxford University Press. Covers history-writing in Japan beginning with the six national histories.

Jeffrey P. Mass. ANTIQUITY AND ANACHRONISM IN JAPANESE HISTORY. 1992: Stanford University Press. Thoughtful essays on problems and trends in the field of pre-Tokugawa Japanese history, emphasizing especially the Kamakura period.

GENERAL WORKS: SOCIO-CULTURAL & INTELLECTUAL OVERVIEWS

Kurt Singer. MIRROR, SWORD AND JEWEL: THE GEOMETRY OF JAPANESE LIFE. 1981: Kōdansha International.

Ruth F. Benedict. THE CHRYSANTHEMUM AND THE SWORD: PATTERNS OF JAPANESE CULTURE. 1946: Houghton Mifflin. A famous and controversial analysis, based on wartime studies by the U.S. Office of War Information.

Yasusuke Murakami. *"Ie* Society as a Pattern of Civilization," *Journal of Japanese Studies* 10.2 (1984), 279-363. See also commentaries on this article in *Journal of Japanese Studies* 11.1.

Robert J. Smith. JAPANESE SOCIETY: TRADITION, SELF, AND THE SOCIAL ORDER. 1984: Cambridge University Press.

_____ & Richard K. Beardsley. JAPANESE CULTURE: ITS DEVELOP-MENT AND CHARACTERISTICS. 1962: Aldine.

Takie Sugiyama Lebra. JAPANESE PATTERNS OF BEHAVIOR. 1976: University of Hawaii Press.

_____, ed. JAPANESE SOCIAL ORGANIZATION. 1992: University of Hawaii Press.

_____ & William P. Lebra, eds. JAPANESE CULTURE AND BEHAVIOR: SELECTED READINGS. 1974: University of Hawaii Press.

John W. Hall & Richard K. Beardsley, eds. TWELVE DOORS TO JAPAN. 1965: McGraw-Hill. Disciplinary approaches to Japan.

Eichirō Ishida. JAPANESE CULTURE: A STUDY OF ORIGINS AND CHARACTERISTICS. Teruko Kachi, transl. 1974: University of Hawaii Press.

Edwin O. Reischauer. THE JAPANESE TODAY: CHANGE AND CONTINU-ITY. 1988: Belknap. Revised version of THE JAPANESE (1977).

Peter N. Dale. THE MYTH OF JAPANESE UNIQUENESS. 1986: Croom Helm.

Harumi Befu. JAPAN: AN ANTHROPOLOGICAL INTRODUCTION. 1971: Chandler.

Bernard S. Silberman, ed. JAPANESE CHARACTER AND CULTURE: A BOOK OF SELECTED READINGS. 1962: University of Arizona Press.

Martin Collcutt. CULTURAL ATLAS OF JAPAN. 1988: Phaidon.

Hyōe Murakami & Edward G. Seidensticker, eds. GUIDES TO JAPANESE CULTURE. 1977: Japan Culture Institute.

John S. Brownlee. POLITICAL THOUGHT IN JAPANESE HISTORICAL WRITING: FROM KOJIKI (712) TO TOKUSHI YORON (1712). 1991: Wilfrid Laurier University Press.

Nyozekan Hasegawa. THE JAPANESE CHARACTER: A CULTURAL PROFILE. 1965: Kōdansha International.

Yoshihiko Ikegami, ed. THE EMPIRE OF SIGNS: SEMIOTIC ESSAYS ON JAPANESE CULTURE. Foundations of Semiotics, vol. 8. 1991: J. Benjamins.

Charles A. Moore, ed. THE JAPANESE MIND: ESSENTIALS OF JAPANESE PHILOSOPHY AND CULTURE. 1967: University of Hawaii Press.

Hajime Nakamura. WAYS OF THINKING OF EASTERN PEOPLES: INDIA, CHINA, TIBET, JAPAN. 1964: University of Hawaii Press.

_____. A HISTORY OF THE DEVELOPMENT OF JAPANESE THOUGHT FROM 592 TO 1868. 1967: University of Tokyo.

David Pollack. THE FRACTURE OF MEANING: JAPAN'S SYNTHESIS OF CHINA FROM THE EIGHTH THROUGH THE EIGHTEENTH CENTURIES. 1986: Princeton University Press.

Ivan Morris. THE NOBILITY OF FAILURE: TRAGIC HEROES IN THE HISTORY OF JAPAN. 1976: Holt, Rinehart & Winston.

Emiko Ohnuki-Tierney. THE MONKEY AS MIRROR: SYMBOLIC TRANS-FORMATIONS IN JAPANESE HISTORY AND RITUAL. 1987: Princeton University Press.

_____. RICE AS SELF: JAPANESE IDENTITIES THROUGH TIME. 1993: Princeton University Press.

Carl Steenstrup. A HISTORY OF LAW IN JAPAN UNTIL 1868. 1991: E. J. Brill.

Masayoshi Sugimoto & David L. Swain. SCIENCE AND CULTURE IN
    TRADITIONAL JAPAN, A.D. 600-1854. 1978: Massachusetts
    Institute of Technology Press.

Hideomi Tuge. HISTORICAL DEVELOPMENT OF SCIENCE AND TECH-
    NOLOGY IN JAPAN. 1968: Kokusai Bunka Shinkōkai.

Shigeru Nakayama. A HISTORY OF JAPANESE ASTRONOMY; CHINESE
    BACKGROUND AND WESTERN IMPACT. 1969: Harvard
    University Press.

Alan Kennedy. JAPANESE COSTUME: HISTORY AND TRADITION. 1990:
    A. Biro.

Lucy Seligman. "The History of Japanese Cuisine," *Japan Quarterly* 41.2
    (1994), 165-180. Includes chronological chart of "Japanese Food
    through the Ages."

Edwina Palmer. "Land of the Rising Sun: The Predominant East-West Axis
    among the Early Japanese," *Monumenta Nipponica* 46.1 (1991), 69-90

GODS & HEROES: THE MYTHIC WORLD

KOJIKI ("Records of Ancient Matters," A.D. 712)

- Donald L. Philippi, transl. *KOJIKI*: A JAPANESE CLASSIC. 1968:
  University of Tokyo Press.

- Basil Hall Chamberlain, transl. *KOJIKI*, OR RECORDS OF
  ANCIENT MATTERS. 1932: Routledge & Kegan Paul. Originally
  published in 1882 as a supplement to *Transactions, Asiatic Society of
  Japan.*

- Fuminobu Murakami. "Incest and Rebirth in *Kojiki*," *Monumenta
  Nipponica* 43.4 (1988), 455-463.

- Hitomi Tonomura. "Positioning Amaterasu: A Reading of the *Kojiki*,"
  Japan Foundation Newsletter 22.2 (1994), 12-17.

NIHONGI (or NIHON SHOKI: "Chronicles of Japan," A.D. 720)

- William G. Aston, transl. *NIHONGI*, CHRONICLES OF JAPAN
  FROM THE EARLIEST TIMES TO A.D. 697. 1896; reprinted 1956:
  Allen & Unwin.

Delmer M. Brown. "The Early Evolution of Historical Consciousness," in Delmer M. Brown ed. CAMBRIDGE HISTORY OF JAPAN, Volume 1: ANCIENT JAPAN (1993: Cambridge University Press), 504-548.

Tarō Sakamoto. THE SIX NATIONAL HISTORIES OF JAPAN. John S. Brownlee, transl. 1991: University of British Columbia Press.

Masaharu Anesaki. "Japanese Mythology," in Louis H. Gray, ed. MYTHOLOGY OF ALL RACES (1964: Cooper Square), volume 8, 205-400.

E. Dale Saunders. "Japanese Mythology," in Samuel Noah Kramer, ed. MYTHOLOGIES OF THE ANCIENT WORLD (1961: Doubleday), 409-442.

Juliet Piggot. JAPANESE MYTHOLOGY. New revised edition. 1982: Harper & Row.

Post Wheeler. THE SACRED SCRIPTURES OF THE JAPANESE. 1952: Schuman.

Joseph Campbell. THE MASKS OF GOD: ORIENTAL MYTHOLOGY. 1962: Viking.

Taryō Ōbayashi. "The Origins of Japanese Mythology," *Acta Asiatica* 31 (1977), 1-23.

_____. "Origins of Japanese Mythology," in Joseph Pittau, ed. FOLK CULTURES OF JAPAN AND EAST ASIA. (1966: Monumenta Nipponica Monographs), 1-15.

_____. "The Origin of the Universe, 1," *The East* 12.1 (1976), 8-15.

_____. "The Origin of the Universe, 2," *The East* 12.2 (1976), 9-13.

_____. "The Structure of the Pantheon and the Concept of Sin in Ancient Japan," *Diogenes* 98 (1977), 117-132.

_____. "The Ancient Myths of Korea and Japan," *Acta Asiatica* 61 (1991), 68-82.

Joseph M. Kitagawa. "Prehistoric Background of Japanese Religion," *History of Religions* 2 (1963), 292-328.

_____. "The Japanese *Kokutai* (National Community) in Myth and History," *History of Religions* 13 (1973), 209-226.

_____. "A Past of Things Present: Notes on Major Motifs of Early Japanese
Religions," *History of Religions* 20 (1980), 27-42.

Atsuhiko Yoshida. "Japanese Mythology and the Indo-European Trifunctional
System," *Diogenes* 98 (1977), 93-116.

Toshio Akima. "The Origins of the Grand Shrine of Ise and the Cult of the Sun
Goddess Amaterasu Ōmikami," *Japan Review* 4 (1993), 141-198.

Daniel C. Holtom. "The Storm God Theme in Japanese Mythology," *Sociologius*
6.1 (1956), 44-56.

Cornelius Ouwehand. "Some Notes on the God Susa-no-o," *Monumenta
Nipponica* 14.3-4 (1958-1959), 384-407.

Manabu Waida. "Sacred Kingship in Early Japan: A Historical Introduction,"
History of Religions 15 (1976), 319-342.

Y. T. Hosoi. "The Sacred Tree in Japanese Prehistory," *History of Religions* 16
(1976), 95-119.

John C. Pelzel. "Human Nature in the Japanese Myths," in Albert M. Craig &
Donald Shively, eds. PERSONALITY IN JAPANESE HISTORY
(1970: University of California Press), 29-59.

Allan G. Grapard. "Visions of Excess and Excesses of Vision: Women and
Transgression in Japanese Myth," *Japanese Journal of Religious Studies*
18.1 (1991).

Donald L. Philippi, transl. SONGS OF GODS, SONGS OF HUMANS: THE
EPIC TRADITION OF THE AINU. 1979: Princeton University Press.

Joseph M. Kitagawa. "Ainu Myths," in Joseph M. Kitagawa & Charles H. Long,
eds. MYTHS AND SYMBOLS: STUDIES IN HONOR OF MIRCEA
ELIADE (1969: University of Chicago Press), 309-323

PREHISTORY: THE LINGUISTIC & ARCHEOLOGICAL RECORD

J. Edward Kidder, Jr. "The Earliest Societies in Japan," in Delmer M. Brown, ed.
CAMBRIDGE HISTORY OF JAPAN, Volume 1: ANCIENT JAPAN
(1993: Cambridge University Press), 48-107.

Gordon T. Bowles. "Origin of Japanese People," KŌDANSHA ENCYCLO-
PEDIA OF JAPAN 4: 33-35.

Takashi Okazaki. "Japan and the Continent," in Delmer M. Brown ed.
CAMBRIDGE HISTORY OF JAPAN, Volume 1: ANCIENT JAPAN
(1993: Cambridge University Press), 268-316.

"Symposium: Japanese Origins," *Journal of Japanese Studies* 2.2 (1976),
295-436. Essays by Roy Andrew Miller, Bruno Lewin, and Shichirō
Murayama on historical linguistics, and by Richard Pearson on
archeological finds.

Taryō Ōbayashi. "The Ethnological Study of Japan's Ethnic Culture:
A Historical Survey," *Acta Asiatica* 61 (1991), 1-23. A historiographical survey of research on the ethnic origins of the Japanese, with an
excellent bibliography of works in Japanese.

Edwin O. Reischauer & Albert M. Craig. JAPAN: TRADITION AND TRANS-
FORMATION (1989: Houghton Mifflin), chapter 1.

Roy Andrew Miller. "The Relevance of Historical Linguistics for Japanese
Studies," *Journal of Japanese Studies* 2.2 (1976), 335-388.

_____. ORIGINS OF THE JAPANESE LANGUAGE. 1980: University of
Washington Press.

_____. THE JAPANESE LANGUAGE. 1967: University of Chicago Press.

_____. "The Origins of Japanese," *Monumenta Nipponica* 29.1 (1974), 93-102.
Review of Murayama Shichirō & Ōbayashi Taryō, *Nihongo no Kigen*,
1973.

Bruno Lewin. "Japanese and Korean: The Problems and History of a Linguistic
Comparison," *Journal of Japanese Studies* 2.2 (1976), 389-412.

Shichirō Murayama. "The Malayo-Polynesian Component in the Japanese
Language," *Journal of Japanese Studies* 2.2 (1976), 413-436.

Lajos Kazar. "Uralic-Japanese Language Comparison," *Ural-Altaishe Jahrbucker*
48-49 (1976), 127-150.

Susumu Ōno. THE ORIGIN OF THE JAPANESE LANGUAGE. 1970:
Kokusai Bunka Shinkōkai. Criticized in R.A. Miller review,
Monumenta Nipponica 26. 3-4 (1971), 455-469.

Isao Komatsu. THE JAPANESE PEOPLE: ORIGINS OF THE PEOPLE AND THE LANGUAGE. 1962: Kokusai Bunka Shinkōkai.

Peter Bleed. "Prehistory," KŌDANSHA ENCYCLOPEDIA OF JAPAN 3: 158-160.

C. Melvin Aikens & Takayasu Higuchi. PREHISTORY OF JAPAN. 1981: Academic.

Fumiko Ikawa-Smith. EARLY PALEOLITHIC OF SOUTH AND EAST ASIA. 1974: Mouton.

Chester S. Chard. NORTHEAST ASIA IN PREHISTORY. 1974: University of Wisconsin Press.

Jonathan Edward Kidder, Jr. JAPAN BEFORE BUDDHISM. 2nd edition. 1959: Thames & Hudson.

_____. ANCIENT JAPAN. 1965: John Day.

_____. THE BIRTH OF JAPANESE ART. 1965: Praeger.

_____. "Jōmon Culture," KŌDANSHA ENCYCLOPEDIA OF JAPAN 4: 72-74.

_____. PREHISTORIC JAPANESE ARTS: JŌMON POTTERY. 1968: Kōdansha International.

_____. THE JŌMON POTTERY OF JAPAN. 1957: Artibus Asiae.

THE RISE OF A GREAT TRADITION: JAPANESE ARCHEOLOGICAL CERAMICS FROM THE JŌMON THROUGH HEIAN PERIODS (10,500 B.C.-A.D. 1185). 1990: Japan Society.

Vadime Elisseeff. ANCIENT CIVILIZATIONS: JAPAN. 1974: Barrie & Jenkins. Translated from the French.

Kiyotari Tsuboi. "Issues in Japanese Archeology," *Acta Asiatica* 63 (1992), 1-20.

Richard K. Beardsley. "Japan Before History: A Survey of the Archeological Record," *Far Eastern Quarterly* 14 (1955), 317-346. Reprinted in John A. Harrison, ed. JAPAN (1972: University of Arizona Press), 149-178.

Richard J. Pearson, ed. WINDOWS ON THE JAPANESE PAST: STUDIES IN ARCHEOLOGY AND PREHISTORY. 1986: Center for Japanese Studies, University of Michigan.

_____. "The Contribution of Archeology to Japanese Studies," *Journal of Japanese Studies* 2.2 (1976), 305-327.

_____. "Paleo-environment and Human Settlement in Japan and Korea," *Science* 197 (1977), 1239-1245.

Yoshinori Yasuda. "Monsoon Fluctuations and Cultural Changes During the Last Glacial Age in Japan," *Japan Review* 1 (1990), 113-152.

Kazurō Hanihara. "Dual Structure Model for the Population History of the Japanese," *Japan Review* 2 (1991), 1-33.

_____. "Current Trends in Physical Anthropology in Japan," *Japan Review* 3 (1992), 131-139.

Michio Okamura. "The Achievements of Research into the Japanese Paleolithic," *Acta Asiatica* 63 (1992), 21-39. Includes a useful bibliography of Japanese works.

Kōichi Mori & Kazuto Matsufuji. "Paleolithic Forest Dwellers Surmised," *Japan Quarterly* 35.3 (1988), 242-247.

Mizuno Yū. "The Origins of the Japanese Race," *The East* 10.4 (1974), 37-44.

Charles T. Keally. "The Earliest Cultures in Japan," *Monumenta Nipponica* 27.2 (1972), 143-148.

Takeru Akazawa & C. Melvin Aikens, eds. PREHISTORIC HUNTER-GATHERERS IN JAPAN: NEW RESEARCH METHODS. 1986. University Museum, University of Tokyo, Bulletin no. 27.

Sōsuke Sugihara & Mitsumori Tozawa. "Pre-ceramic Age in Japan," *Acta Asiatica* 1 (1960), 1-28.

Harumi Befu & Chester S. Chard. "Preceramic Cultures in Japan," *American Anthropologist* 62.4 (1960), 815-849.

Richard E. Morlar. "Chronometric Dating in Japan," *Arctic Anthropology* 14.2 (1967), 180-212.

C. G. Turner. "Dental Evidence of the Origins of the Ainu and Japanese,"
    Science 193 (1976), 911-913.

Kazurō Hanihara. "Emishi, Ezo, and Ainu: An Anthropological Perspective,"
    Japan Review 1 (1990), 35-48.

Kiyotari Tsuboi, ed. RECENT ARCHEOLOGICAL DISCOVERIES IN JAPAN.
    Gina L. Barnes, transl. 1987: Centre for East Asian Cultural Studies
    (Tokyo) and UNESCO (Paris).

Gina L. Barnes, ed. HOABINHAN, JŌMON, YAYOI, EARLY KOREAN
    STATES: BIBLIOGRAPHIC REVIEWS OF FAR EASTERN
    ARCHEOLOGY, 1990. 1990: Oxbow Books for East Asian
    Archeology Network.

Johannes Maringer. "Clay Figurines of the Jōmon Period: A Contribution to the
    History of Ancient Religion in Japan," *History of Religions* 14 (1974),
    129-139.

R. Tsunoda & L. Carrington Goodrich, transl. JAPAN IN THE CHINESE
    DYNASTIC HISTORIES: LATER HAN THROUGH MING
    DYNASTIES. 1951: P. D. & Ione Perkins.

Kōmei Sasaki. "The Wa People and Their Culture in Ancient Japan: The
    Cultures of Swidden Cultivation and Padi-Rice Cultivation," *Acta
    Asiatica* 61 (1991), 24-46. Useful bibliography of Japanese works on
    the "Wa" people and early agriculture.

Makoto Sahara. "Rice Cultivation and the Japanese," *Acta Asiatica* 63 (1992),
    40-63. Extensive bibliography of Japanese works.

Peter Bleed. "Yayoi Cultures of Japan," *Arctic Anthropology* 9.2 (1972), 1-20.

Erika Kaneko. "Japan: A Review of Yayoi Burial Practices," *Asian Perspectives*
    9 (1966), 1-26.

Jonathan Edward Kidder, Jr. "Yoshinogari and the Yamatai Problem,"
    Transactions, Asiatic Society of Japan, 4th series, 6 (1991), 115-140.

Mark Hudson & Gina L. Barnes. "Yoshinogari: A Yayoi Settlement in Northern
    Kyūshū," *Monumenta Nipponica* 46.2 (1991), 211-235.

Joan R. Piggott. "Sacral Kingship and Confederacy in Early Izumo," *Monumenta
    Nipponica* 44.1 (1989), 45-74.

PROTOHISTORY: THE GREAT TOMBS & THE INVASION CONTROVERSY

Primary Sources

Delmer M. Brown. "The Early Evolution of Historical Consciousness," in Delmer M. Brown ed. CAMBRIDGE HISTORY OF JAPAN, Volume 1: ANCIENT JAPAN (1993: Cambridge University Press), 504-548.

R. Tsunoda & L. Carrington Goodrich, transl. JAPAN IN THE CHINESE DYNASTIC HISTORIES: LATER HAN THROUGH MING DYNASTIES. 1951: P. D. & Ione Perkins.

Tarō Sakamoto. THE SIX NATIONAL HISTORIES OF JAPAN. John S. Brownlee, transl. 1991: University of British Columbia Press.

KOJIKI ("Records of Ancient Matters," A.D. 712)

- Donald L. Philippi, transl. *KOJIKI*: A JAPANESE CLASSIC. 1968: Princeton University Press.

- Basil Hall Chamberlain, transl. *KOJIKI*, OR RECORDS OF ANCIENT MATTERS. 1932: Routledge & Kegan Paul.

NIHONGI (or NIHON SHOKI: "Chronicles of Japan," A.D. 720)

- William G. Aston, transl. *NIHONGI*, CHRONICLES OF JAPAN FROM THE EARLIEST TIMES TO A.D. 697. 1896; reprinted 1956: Allen & Unwin.

SHOKU NIHONGI (official historical sequel to NIHONGI, covering years 697-791)

- J. B. Snellen, transl. "*SHOKU NIHONGI*, Chronicles of Japan, Continued, A.D. 697-791," *Transactions, Asiatic Society of Japan*, 2nd series, 11 (1934), 151-239; 14 (1937), 209-278.

FUDOKI (8th-century local records)

- Michiko Yamaguchi Aoki. *IZUMO FUDOKI*. 1971: Monumenta Nipponica Monographs.

- Atsuharu Sakai. "The *Hitachi Fudoki* or Records of Customs and Land of Hitachi," *Cultural Nippon* 8.2 (1940), 145-185; 8.3 (1940), 109-156; and 8.4 (1940), 137-186.

- Mark C. Funke. "Hitachi no Kuni Fudoki," *Monumenta Nipponica* 49.1 (1994), 1-29.

TAKAHASHI UJIBUMI (local chronicle, A.D. 792)

- Douglas Edward Mills. "The *Takahasi Ujibumi*," *Bulletin of the School of Oriental and African Studies* 16.1 (1954), 113-133.

The Great Tombs

Gina Lee Barnes. "Kofun (Tomb Mounds)," KŌDANSHA ENCYCLOPEDIA OF JAPAN 4: 244-246.

"Studies on Ancient Japanese History." Special Issue of *Acta Asiatica* 31 (1977). Includes articles on mythology, tombs, Yamato state & Korea, and Ritsuryō legal structure.

Ken Amakasu. "The Significance of the Formation and Distribution of *Kofun*," *Acta Asiatica* 31 (1977), 24-50.

Hiroshi Tsude. "The Kofun Period and State Formation," *Acta Asiatica* 63 (1992), 64-86.

Sōkichi Tsuda. "On the Stages of the Formation of Japan as a Nation, and the Origin of Belief in the Perpetuity of the Imperial Family," *Philosophical Studies of Japan* 4 (1963), 49-78.

Hiroshi Mizuo. "Patterns of Kofun Culture," *Japan Quarterly* 16.1 (1969), 71-77.

Jonathan Edward Kidder, Jr. EARLY JAPANESE ART: THE GREAT TOMBS AND TREASURES. 1964: Thames & Hudson.

_____. EARLY BUDDHIST JAPAN. 1972: Thames & Hudson.

_____. "The Newly Discovered Takamatsuzuka Tomb," *Monumenta Nipponica* 27.3 (1972), 245-251.

_____. "The Fujinoki Tomb and Its Grave Goods," *Monumenta Nipponica* 42.1 (1987), 57-87.

_____. "The Fujinoki Sarcophagus," *Monumenta Nipponica* 44.4 (1989), 415-460.

_____. "Saddle Bows and Rump Plumes: More on the Fujinoki Tomb,"
        Monumenta Nipponica 45.1 (1990), 75-85.

Shichirō Murayama & Roy Andrew Miller. "The Inariyama Tumulus Sword
        Inscription," *Journal of Japanese Studies* 5.2 (1979), 405-438.

Joan R. Piggott. "Sacral Kingship and Confederacy in Early Izumo," *Monumenta
        Nipponica* 44.1 (1989), 45-74.

The "Horse-Rider" Thesis & the Invasion Controversy

Namio Egami. "Mounted Nomadic Peoples," in Hyōe Murakami & Edward
        Seidensticker, eds. GUIDES TO JAPANESE CULTURE (1977: Japan
        Culture Institute), 130-134.

_____. "Light on Japanese Cultural Origins from Historical Archeology and
        Legend," in Robert J. Smith & Richard K. Beardsley, eds. JAPANESE
        CULTURE: ITS DEVELOPMENT AND CHARACTERISTICS
        (1962: Aldine), 11-16.

_____. "The Formation of the People and the Origin of the State in Japan,"
        Memoirs of the Tōyō Bunko 23 (1964), 35-70.

_____. THE BEGINNINGS OF JAPANESE ART. 1973: Weatherhill.

[Namio Egami] See summary in Ledyard, *Journal of Japanese Studies* 1.2
        (1975), especially p. 222 (the "8 points").

[Namio Egami] For summary and discussion of the invasion thesis, see Eichirō
        Ishida, JAPANESE CULTURE: A STUDY OF ORIGINS AND
        CHARACTERISTICS (1974: University of Hawaii Press), 86-88.

Gari Ledyard. "Horse-Rider Theory," KŌDANSHA ENCYCLOPEDIA OF
        JAPAN 3: 229-230.

_____. "Galloping Along with the Horseriders: Looking for the Founders of
        Japan," *Journal of Japanese Studies* 1.2 (1975), 217-254.

Toshio Akima. "The Myth of the Goddess of the Undersea World and the Tale
        of Empress Jingū's Subjugation of Silla," *Japanese Journal of Religious
        Studies* 20.2-3 (1993), 95-185. Takes issue with Egami and Ledyard.

20 JAPANESE HISTORY & CULTURE FROM ANCIENT TO MODERN TIMES

John H. Douglas. "The Horsemen of Yamato," *Science News* 113.22 (1978), 364-366.

Walter Edwards. "Event and Process in the Founding of Japan: The Horserider Theory in Archeological Perspective," *Journal of Japanese Studies* 9.2 (1983), 265-295.

J. Edward Kidder, Jr. "The Archeology of the Early Horse-Riders in Japan," *Transactions, Asiatic Society of Japan*, 3nd series, 20 (1986), 89-123.

Takashi Okazaki. "Japan and the Continent," in Delmer M. Brown ed. CAMBRIDGE HISTORY OF JAPAN, Volume 1: ANCIENT JAPAN (1993: Cambridge University Press), 268-316.

Reinier H. Hesselink. "The Introduction of the Art of Mounted Archery into Japan," *Transactions, Asiatic Society of Japan*, 4th series, 6 (1991), 27-47.

Taryō Ōbayashi. "The Ancient Myths of Korea and Japan," *Acta Asiatica* 61 (1991), 68-82.

PROTOHISTORY:
EMERGENCE OF THE IMPERIAL STATE

Delmer M. Brown, ed. CAMBRIDGE HISTORY OF JAPAN. Volume 1, ANCIENT JAPAN. 1993: Cambridge University Press.

Edwin O. Reischauer & Albert M. Craig. JAPAN: TRADITION AND TRANSFORMATION (1989: Houghton Mifflin), chapter 1.

John W. Hall. GOVERNMENT AND LOCAL POWER IN JAPAN, 500-1700: A STUDY BASED ON BIZEN PROVINCE. 1966: Princeton University Press.

George B. Sansom. A HISTORY OF JAPAN TO 1334. 1958: Stanford University Press.

Robert Karl Reischauer. EARLY JAPANESE HISTORY (c. 40 B.C.-A.D. 1169). 2 volumes. 1937: Princeton University Press. An adaptation of Katsumi Kuroita, *Kōtei Kokushi no Kenkyū* (1931).

Lars Vargö. SOCIAL AND ECONOMIC CONDITIONS FOR THE FORMA-
TION OF THE EARLY JAPANESE STATE. 1982: Institute of
Oriental Languages, Stockholm University.

The Korean Influence

Jon Carter Covell & Alan Covell. JAPAN'S HIDDEN HISTORY: KOREAN
IMPACT ON JAPANESE CULTURE. 1984: Hollym International.

Wontack Hong. RELATIONSHIP BETWEEN KOREA AND JAPAN IN
EARLY PERIOD: PAEKCHE AND YAMATO WA. 1988:
Ilsimsa.

Taryō Ōbayashi. "The Ancient Myths of Korea and Japan," *Acta Asiatica* 61
(1991), 68-82.

Gari Ledyard. "Yamatai," KŌDANSHA ENCYCLOPEDIA OF JAPAN
8: 305-307.

Takashi Okazaki. "Japan and the Continent," in Delmer M. Brown ed.
CAMBRIDGE HISTORY OF JAPAN, Volume 1: ANCIENT JAPAN
(1993: Cambridge University Press), 268-316.

Benjamin H. Hazard. "Korea and Japan, Premodern Relations (to 1875),"
KŌDANSHA ENCYCLOPEDIA OF JAPAN 4: 276-279.

Kunio Hirano. "The Yamato State and Korea in the Fourth and Fifth Centuries,"
Acta Asiatica 31 (1977), 51-82.

James K. Ash. "Korea in the Making of the Early Japanese State," *Journal of
Social Sciences and Humanities* (1971).

Yasukazu Suematsu. "Japan's Relations with the Asian Continent and the Korean
Peninsular (Before 950 A.D.)," *Cahiers d'histoire Mondiale* (*Journal of
World History*) 4.3 (1958), 671-687.

Tadashi Nishitani. "The Kaya Tumuli: Windows on the Past," *Japan Foundation
Newsletter* 21.3 (1993), 1-6.

George B. Sansom. "An Outline of Recent Japanese Archeological Research in
Korea in its Bearing Upon Early Japanese History," *Transactions,
Asiatic Society of Japan*, 2nd series, 6 (1929), 5-19.

KŌDANSHA ENCYCLOPEDIA OF JAPAN. See also entries on "Hata Family," "Kaya (Mimana)," "Kikajin," and "Wani."

Yamato State / Ritsuryō

Delmer M. Brown. "The Yamato Kingdom," in Delmer M. Brown ed. CAMBRIDGE HISTORY OF JAPAN, Volume 1: ANCIENT JAPAN (1993: Cambridge University Press), 108-162.

Cornelius J. Kiley. "State and Dynasty in Archaic Yamato," *Journal of Asian Studies* 33.1 (1973), 25-49.

_____. "Uji and Kabane in Ancient Japan," *Monumenta Nipponica* 32.3 (1977), 365-376.

_____. "Uji-Kabane System," KŌDANSHA ENCYCLOPEDIA OF JAPAN 8: 131-137.

_____. "Ritsuryō System," KŌDANSHA ENCYCLOPEDIA OF JAPAN 6: 322-332.

Bruce Loyd Batten. "State and Frontier in Early Japan: The Imperial Court and Northern Kyūshū, 645-1185." 1989: Ph.D. dissertation in History, Stanford University.

_____. "Foreign Threat and Domestic Reform: Emergence of the *Ritsuryō* State," *Monumenta Nipponica* 41.2 (1986), 199-219.

Mitsusada Inoue. "The Ritsuryō System in Japan," *Acta Asiatica* 31 (1977), 83-112.

_____, with Delmer M. Brown. "The Century of Reform," in Delmer M. Brown ed. CAMBRIDGE HISTORY OF JAPAN, Volume 1: ANCIENT JAPAN (1993: Cambridge University Press), 163-220.

Alan L. Miller. "Ritsuryō Japan: The State as Liturgical Community," *History of Religions* 11 (1971), 98-121.

Joan R. Piggott. "Sacral Kingship and Confederacy in Early Izumo," *Monumenta Nipponica* 44.1 (1989), 45-74.

John Young. THE LOCATION OF YAMATAI: A CASE STUDY IN JAPANESE HISTORIOGRAPHY, 720-1945. 1957: Johns Hopkins.

Gina Lee Barnes. PROTOHISTORIC YAMATO: ARCHEOLOGY OF THE
FIRST JAPANESE STATE. Michigan Papers in Japanese Studies,
No. 17; and Anthropological Papers, Museum of Anthropology,
Univeristy of Michigan, No. 78. 1988: published jointly by University
of Michigan, Center for Japanese Studies; and Museum of Anthro-
pology, University of Michigan.

John A. Harrison. NEW LIGHT ON EARLY AND MEDIEVAL JAPANESE
HISTORIOGRAPHY. 1960: University of Florida Press.

Richard J. Miller. ANCIENT JAPANESE NOBILITY: THE KABANE
RANKING SYSTEM. 1974: University of California Press.

_____. "A Study of the Development of a Centralized Japanese Government
Prior to the Taika Reform (A.D. 645)." 1953: Ph.D. dissertation in
History, University of California.

_____. JAPAN'S FIRST BUREAUCRACY: A STUDY OF EIGHTH-CEN-
TURY GOVERNMENT. 1978: *Cornell University East Asia Papers.*

J. I. Crump. "Borrowed T'ang Titles and Offices in the Yōrō Code," *Occasional
Papers of the Center for Japanese Studies, University of Michigan* 2
(1952), 35-58.

George B. Sansom. "Early Japanese Law and Administration," *Transactions,
Asiatic Society of Japan*, 2nd series, 9 (1932), 67-110 & 11 (1934),
117-150.

J. Edward Kidder. "Asuka History (mid-6th century to 710)," KŌDANSHA
ENCYCLOPEDIA OF JAPAN 3: 161-163.

E. Patricia Tsurumi. "The Male Present Versus the Female Past: Historians and
Japan's Ancient Female Emperors," *Bulletin of Concerned Asian
Scholars* 14.4 (1983), 71-75.

Gary L. Ebersole. RITUAL POETRY AND THE POLITICS OF DEATH IN
EARLY JAPAN. 1989: Princeton University Press. Addresses the
Taika era (645-710).

Ancient Economy

Dana Robert Morris. "Peasant Economy in Early Japan, 650-950." 1980: Ph.D.
dissertation in History, University of California.

William Wayne Farris. POPULATION, DISEASE AND LAND IN EARLY
JAPAN, 645-900. 1985: Harvard- Yenching Institute Monograph
Series.

Kōzō Yamamura. "The Decline of the Ritsuryō System: Hypotheses on
Economic and Institutional Change," *Journal of Japanese Studies* 1.1
(1974), 3-38.

Ancient Cities

Paul Wheatley & Thomas See. FROM COURT TO CAPITAL: A TENTATIVE
INTERPRETATION OF THE ORIGINS OF THE JAPANESE URBAN
TRADITION. 1978: University of Chicago Press. See also the review
by R.A. Miller in *Journal of Japanese Studies* 5.1 (1979), 211-234.

Takeo Yazaki. SOCIAL CHANGE AND THE CITY IN JAPAN: FROM
EARLIEST TIMES THROUGH THE INDUSTRIAL REVOLUTION.
1968: Japan Publications.

Richard A. Ponsonby-Fane. IMPERIAL CITIES: THE CAPITALS OF JAPAN
FROM THE OLDEST TIMES UNTIL 1229. 1979 reprint by University
Publications of America of 2 long essays published prior to World War
Two: "Ancient Capitals and Palaces of Japan" and "The Capital and
Palace of Heian."

Kiyotari Tsuboi. "The Excavation of Ancient Palaces and Capitals," *Acta
Asiatica* 63 (1992), 87-98.

THE NARA (710-794) & HEIAN (794-1185) PERIODS:
SECONDARY SOURCES

George B. Sansom. A HISTORY OF JAPAN TO 1334. 1958: Stanford
University Press.

_____. JAPAN: A SHORT CULTURAL HISTORY. Revised edition. 1943:
Appleton. See especially pp. 107-184 ("Nara"), and 185-269
("The Heian Period").

Edwin O. Reischauer & Albert M. Craig. JAPAN: TRADITION AND
TRANSFORMATION (1989: Houghton Mifflin), chapter 1.

Ivan J. Morris. THE WORLD OF THE SHINING PRINCE: COURT LIFE IN
    ANCIENT JAPAN. 1960: Oxford University Press; 1994: Kōdansha.

Kōjirō Naoki. "The Nara State," in Delmer M. Brown ed. CAMBRIDGE
    HISTORY OF JAPAN, Volume 1: ANCIENT JAPAN (1993:
    Cambridge University Press), 221-267.

Torao Toshiya. "Nara Economic and Social Institutions," in Delmer M. Brown
    ed. CAMBRIDGE HISTORY OF JAPAN, Volume 1: ANCIENT
    JAPAN (1993: Cambridge University Press), 415-452.

Edwin A. Cranston. "Asuka and Nara Culture: Literacy, Literature, and Music,"
    in Delmer M. Brown ed. CAMBRIDGE HISTORY OF JAPAN,
    Volume 1: ANCIENT JAPAN (1993: Cambridge University Press),
    453-503.

Rizō Takeuchi. "Nara History (710-794)," KŌDANSHA ENCYCLOPEDIA OF
    JAPAN 3: 163-165.

Kiyotari Tsuboi & Migaku Tanaka. THE HISTORIC CITY OF NARA:
    AN ARCHEOLOGICAL APPROACH. David W. Hughes & Gina L.
    Barnes, transl. 1991: UNESCO and the Centre for East Asian Cultural
    Studies, Tokyo.

Joan Rita Piggott. "Tōdaiji and the Nara Imperium." 1987: Ph.D. dissertation in
    History, Stanford University.

_____. "Sacral Kingship and Confederacy in Early Izumo," *Monumenta
    Nipponica* 44.1 (1989), 45-74.

_____. "*Mokkan*: Wooden Documents from the Nara Period," *Monumenta
    Nipponica* 45.4 (1990), 449-470.

Ronald P. Toby. "Why Leave Nara? Kammu and the Transfer of the Capital,"
    Monumenta Nipponica 40.3 (1985), 330-347.

G. Cameron Hurst III. "Heian History (794-1185)," KŌDANSHA ENCYCLO-
    PEDIA OF JAPAN 3: 165-169.

_____. "Regency Government," KŌDANSHA ENCYCLOPEDIA OF JAPAN
    6: 286-288.

H. Paul Varley. "The Age of the Court Nobles," in Arthur Tiedemann, ed.
    AN INTRODUCTION TO JAPANESE CIVILIZATION (1974: Heath),
    33-59.

Robert K. Reischauer. EARLY JAPANESE HISTORY (c. 40 B.C.-A.D. 1167). 2 volumes. 1937: Princeton University Press.

Karl F. Friday. "The Taming of the Shrewd: The Conquest of the Emishi and Northern Japan," *Japan Foundation Newsletter* 21.6 (1994), 17-22.

Bruce Loyd Batten. "State and Frontier in Early Japan: The Imperial Court and Northern Kyūshū, 645-1185." 1989: Ph.D. dissertation in History, Stanford University.

_____. "Provincial Administration in Early Japan: From *Ritsuryō kokka* to *Ōchō kokka*," *Harvard Journal of Asiatic Studies* 53.1 (1993), 103-134.

John W. Hall & Jeffrey P. Mass, eds. MEDIEVAL JAPAN: ESSAYS IN INSTITUTIONAL HISTORY. 1974: Yale University Press. See especially pp. 3-124, containing five essays on "Court and *Shōen* in Heian Japan."

John W. Hall. "Kyoto As Historical Background," in Hall & Mass, MEDIEVAL JAPAN (1974: Yale University Press), 3-38.

Nicolas B. Fiévé. "Urban Evolution in *Heiankyō*: A Study of the Iconogaphic Sources," *Japan Forum* 4.1 (1992), 91-107; 4.2 (1992), 285-304.

G. Cameron Hurst III. "The Structure of the Heian Court: Some Thoughts on the Nature of 'Familial Authority' in Heian Japan," in Hall & Mass, MEDIEVAL JAPAN (1974: Yale University Press), 39-59.

_____. "The Development of the *Insei*: A Problem in Japanese History and Historiography," in Hall & Mass, MEDIEVAL JAPAN (1974: Yale University Press), 60-90.

_____. "*Insei*," KŌDANSHA ENCYCLOPEDIA OF JAPAN 3: 314-315.

_____. "The Reign of Go-Sanjō and the Revival of Imperial Power," *Monumenta Nipponica* 27.1 (1972), 65-84.

_____. *INSEI*: ABDICATED SOVEREIGNS IN THE POLITICS OF LATE HEIAN JAPAN, 1086-1185. 1976: Columbia University Press.

Richard Ponsonby-Fane. KYOTO THE OLD CAPITAL OF JAPAN (794-1869). 1956 reprint of 1931 work: Ponsonby Memorial Society.

_____. THE FORTUNES OF THE EMPERORS: STUDIES IN REVOLU-
TION, EXILE, ABDICATION, USURPATION, AND DEPOSITION
IN ANCIENT JAPAN. 1979 reprint of 6 articles published prior to
World War Two: University Publications of America.

Rose Hempel. THE GOLDEN AGE OF JAPAN, 794-1192. 1983: Rizzoli.
A translation of *Japan zur Heian Zeit*.

Ross Bender. "The Hachiman Cult and the Dōkyō Incident," *Monumenta
Nipponica* 34.2 (1979), 125-154.

Shigeki Kaizuka. "Confucianism in Ancient Japan," *Cahiers d'histoire Mondiale
(Journal of World History)* 5.1 (1959), 41-58.

Takashi Okazaki. "Japan and the Continent," in Delmer M. Brown ed.
CAMBRIDGE HISTORY OF JAPAN, Volume 1: ANCIENT JAPAN
(1993: Cambridge University Press), 268-316.

Robert Borgen. "The Japanese Mission to China, 801-806," *Monumenta
Nipponica* 37.1 (1982), 1-28.

_____. SUGAWARA NO MICHIZANE AND THE EARLY HEIAN COURT.
1986: Council on East Asian Studies, Harvard University.

Ivan Morris. "The Deity of Failures," in his THE NOBILITY OF FAILURE
(1976: Holt, Rinehart & Winston), 41-66. About Sugawara no
Michizane, who died in 903 and was "deified" in 987.

_____. "Women of Ancient Japan: Heian Ladies," *History Today* 13.3 (1963),
160-168.

_____. "Marriage in the World of Genji," *Asia* 11 (1968), 54-77.

William McCullough "Japanese Marriage Institutions of the Heian Period,"
Harvard Journal of Asiatic Studies 27 (1967), 103-167. Takes issue
with Ivan Morris.

_____. "Spirit Possession in the Heian Period," in The Japan P. E. N. Club, ed.
STUDIES ON JAPANESE CULTURE, volume 1 (1973: The Japan
P. E. N. Club), 91-98.

Peter Nickerson. "The Meaning of Matrilocality: Kinship, Property, and Politics
in Mid-Heian," *Monumenta Nipponica* 48.4 (1993), 429-467.

Helen McCullough. "Social and Psychological Aspects of Heian Ritual and
     Ceremony," in The Japan P. E. N. Club, ed. STUDIES ON JAPANESE
     CULTURE, volume 2 (1973: The Japan P. E. N. Club), 275-279.

G. Cameron Hurst III. "Michinaga's Maladies," *Monumenta Nipponica* 34.1
     (1979), 101-112.

Liza Dalby. "The Cultured Nature of Heian Colors," *Transactions, Asiatic
     Society of Japan*, 4th series, 3 (1988), 1-19.

Donald Keene. "Feminine Sensibility in the Heian Era," in his LANDSCAPES
     AND PORTRAITS: APPRECIATIONS OF JAPANESE CULTURE
     (1971: Kōdansha International), 11-25.

_____. TRAVELERS OF A HUNDRED AGES: THE JAPANESE AS
     REVEALED THROUGH 1,000 YEARS OF DIARIES. 1989:
     Henry Holt.

Ivo Smits. "The Poem as a Painting: Landscape Poetry in Late Heian Japan,"
     Transactions, Asiatic Society of Japan, 4th series, 6 (1991), 61-86.

Edwin A. Cranston. "The Dark Path: Images of Longing in Japanese Love
     Poetry," *Harvard Journal of Asiatic Studies* 35 (1975), 60-100.

Janet Walker. "Conventions of Love Poetry in Japan and the West," *Journal of
     the Association of Teachers of Japanese* 14.1 (1977), 31-65.

Kenneth Rexroth & Ikuko Atsumi, transl. THE BURNING HEART: WOMEN
     POETS OF JAPAN. 1976: Seabury.

Edith Lorraine Sarra. "The Art of Remembrance, the Poetics of Destiny:
     Self-Writings by Three Women of Heian Japan." 1988: Ph.D. disserta-
     tion in Comparative Literature, Harvard University.

D. E. Mills. "Popular Elements in Heian Literature," *Journal Newsletter of the
     Association of Teachers of Japanese* 3.3 (1966).

Richard H. Okada. FIGURES OF RESISTANCE: LANGUAGE, POETRY,
     AND NARRATING IN *THE TALE OF GENJI* AND OTHER
     MID-HEIAN TEXTS. 1991: Duke University Press.

Jacob Raz. "Popular Entertainment and Politics: The Great *Dengaku* of 1096,"
     Monumenta Nipponica 40.3 (1985), 283-298.

THE COURTLY SOCIETY IN ITS OWN WORDS: PROSE & POETRY IN TRANSLATION

MAN'YŌSHŪ (mid 8th-century poetic anthology)

- Nippon Gakujutsu Shinkōkai (Japan Society for the Promotion of Scientific Research), comp. *MANYŌSHŪ: ONE THOUSAND POEMS*. 1965: Columbia University Press.

- Ian Hideo Levy, transl. THE TEN THOUSAND LEAVES: A TRANSLATION OF *MAN'YŌSHŪ*, JAPAN'S PREMIER ANTHOLOGY OF CLASSICAL POETRY. 1981: University of Tokyo Press & Princeton University Press. A projected 4-volume translation.

- Edwin A. Cranston. "The Ramifying Vein: An Impression of Leaves—A Review of Levy's Translation of the *Man'yōshū*," *Journal of Japanese Studies* 9.1 (1983), 97-138.

- _____. "*Man'yōshū*," KŌDANSHA ENCYCLOPEDIA OF JAPAN 5: 102-111.

- Ian Hideo Levy. HITOMARO AND THE BIRTH OF JAPANESE LYRICISM. 1984: Princeton University Press.

- Paula Doe. A WARBLER'S SONG IN THE DUSK: THE LIFE AND WORK OF ŌTOMO YAKAMOCHI (718-785). 1982: University of California Press.

- Peter Nosco. "*Man'yōshū* Studies in Tokugawa Japan," *Transactions, Asiatic Society of Japan*, 4th series, 1 (1986), 109-146.

UTA NO SHIKI (KAKYŌ HYŌSHIKI) (poetic criticism and guide by Fujiwara no Hamanari, 772)

- Judith Rabinovitch. "Wasp Waists and Monkey Tails: A Study and Translation of Hamanari's *Uta no Shiki* (*The Code of Poetry*, 772), Also Known as *Kakyō Hyōshiki* (*A Formulary for Verse Based on the Canons of Poetry*)," *Harvard Journal of Asiatic Studies* 51.2 (1991), 471-560.

KINKAFU (collection of Japanese songs dated 981)

- Noah S. Branner, "The *Kinkafu* Collection," *Monumenta Nipponica* 23.3-4 (1968), 229-320.

Donald L. Philippi, transl. THIS WINE OF PEACE, THIS WINE OF
LAUGHTER—A COMPLETE ANTHOLOGY OF JAPAN'S EARLI-
EST SONGS. 1968: Grossman.

Burton Watson, transl. JAPANESE LITERATURE IN CHINESE. 2 volumes.
1975: Columbia University Press.

Robert H. Brower & Earl Miner. JAPANESE COURT POETRY. 1961:
Stanford University Press. Covers to the fifteenth century.

Edwin A. Cranston, transl. A WAKA ANTHOLOGY. Volume I: THE GEM-
GLISTENING CUP. 1994: Stanford University Press.

Elizabeth Markham, transl. *SAIBARA*: JAPANESE COURT SONGS OF THE
HEIAN PERIOD. 1983: Cambridge University Press.

NIHON RYŌIKI (Buddhist stories from the 5th to 9th centuries)

- Kyōko Motomochi Nakamura, transl. MIRACULOUS STORIES
  FROM THE JAPANESE BUDDHIST TRADITION: THE *NIHON
  RYŌIKI* OF THE MONK KYŌKAI. 1973: Harvard University
  Press.

DAINIHONKOKU HOKEKYŌKENKI (129 Buddhist tales collected in the 11th
century)

- Yoshiko K. Dykstra, transl. MIRACULOUS TALES OF THE
  LOTUS SUTRA FROM ANCIENT JAPAN: THE *DAINIHONKOKU
  HOKEKYŌKENKI* OF PRIEST CHINGEN. 1983: University of
  Hawaii Press.

KOKINSHŪ (early 10th-century "official" poetic anthology; more formally
known as KOKIN WAKASHŪ)

- Laurel Rasplica Rodd & Mary Catherine Henkenius, transl.
  KOKINSHŪ: A COLLECTION OF POEMS ANCIENT AND
  MODERN. 1984: Princeton University Press.

- Helen McCullough, transl. *KOKIN WAKASHŪ*: THE FIRST
  IMPERIAL ANTHOLOGY OF JAPANESE POETRY, WITH *TOSA
  NIKKI* AND *SHINSEN WAKA*. 1985: Stanford University Press.

- _____. BROCADE BY NIGHT: *KOKIN WAKASHŪ* AND THE
  COURT STYLE IN JAPANESE CLASSICAL POETRY. 1985:
  Stanford University Press.

ISE MONOGATARI

- Helen McCullough, transl. TALES OF ISE: LYRICAL EPISODES FROM TENTH-CENTURY JAPAN. 1968: Stanford University Press.

- Frits Vos. A STUDY OF THE *ISE-MONOGATARI*, WITH THE TEXT ACCORDING TO THE *DEN-TEIKA-NIPPON* AND AN ANNOTATED TRANSLATION. 2 volumes. 1957: Mouton.

- H. Jay Harris, transl. THE TALES OF ISE. 1972: Tuttle.

- Richard Bowring. "The *Ise monogatari*: A Short Cultural History," *Harvard Journal of Asiatic Studies* 52.2 (1992), 401-480.

TOSA NIKKI (by Ki no Tsurayuki, ca. 935)

- Earl Miner, transl. JAPANESE POETIC DIARIES. 1969: University of California Press.

- Helen McCullough, transl. *KOKIN WAKASHŪ*: THE FIRST IMPERIAL ANTHOLOGY OF JAPANESE POETRY, WITH *TOSA NIKKI* AND *SHINSEN WAKA*. 1985: Stanford University Press.

HEICHŪ MONOGATARI (mid-10th century, based on the life of poet Taira Sadabumi, d. 923)

- Susan Downing Videen. TALES OF HEICHŪ. 1989: Council on East Asian Studies, Harvard University.

TAKETORI MONOGATARI (mid-10th century)

- Donald Keene, transl. "*Taketori Monogatari* (Tale of the Bamboo Cutter)," *Monumenta Nipponica* 11.1 (1955), 1-28.

- Tzvetana Kristeva. "The Pattern of Signification in the *Taketori Monogatari*: The 'Ancestor' of all *Monogatari*," *Japan Forum* 2.2 (1990), 253-259.

YAMATO MONOGATARI (10th century)

- Mildred Tahara, transl. TALES OF YAMATO: A TENTH-CENTURY POEM-TALE. 1980: University of Hawaii Press.

SHŌMONKI (Japan's earliest war chronicle, concerning events culminating in 940)

- Judith N. Rabinovitch, transl. *SHŌMON KI*: THE STORY OF MASAKADO'S REBELLION. 1986: Monumenta Nipponica Monographs.

- Giuliana Stramigioli. "Preliminary Notes on the *Masakado-ki* and the Taira no Masakado Story," *Monumenta Nipponica* 28.3 (1973), 261-294.

KAGERŌ NIKKI (ca. 974, covering the previous two decades)

- Edward C. Seidensticker, transl. THE GOSSAMER YEARS: A DIARY BY A NOBLEWOMAN OF HEIAN JAPAN. 1964: Tuttle.

- Joshua S. Mostow. "The Amorous Statesman and the Poetess: The Politics of Autobiography and the *Kagerō Nikki*," *Japan Forum* 4.2 (1992), 305-315.

SAMBŌE (or SAMBŌEKOTOBA) (by Minamoto no Tamenori, ca. 984)

- Edward Burt Kamens. "The Three Treasures: A Study and Translation of Minamoto no Tamenori's 'Sambōe'." 1982: Ph.D. dissertation in East Asian Languages and Literatures, Yale University.

OCHIKUBO MONOGATARI (ca. 980)

- Wilfrid Whitehouse, transl. *OCHIKUBO MONOGATARI*, OR THE TALE OF THE LADY OCHIKUBO: A TENTH-CENTURY JAPANESE NOVEL. 1965: Hokuseidō.

GENJI MONOGATARI (by Murasaki Shikibu, ca. 1006)

- Arthur Waley, transl. THE TALE OF GENJI. 1960: Random House.

- E. Seidensticker, transl. THE TALE OF GENJI. 1976: Knopf. See reviews by Edwin Cranston in *Journal of Japanese Studies* 4.1 (1978), 1-26, and Helen McCullough in *Monumenta Nipponica* 32.1 (1977), 93-110.

- _____. GENJI DAYS. 1978: Kōdansha International. A diary kept by Seidensticker while he was translating Lady Murasaki's classic work.

- Helen Craig McCullough, transl. GENJI AND HEIKE: SELECTIONS FROM "THE TALE OF GENJI" AND "THE TALE OF THE HEIKE." 1994: Stanford University Press.

- William J. Puette. THE *TALE OF GENJI* BY MURASAKI SHIKIBU: A READER'S GUIDE. 1992: Tuttle. In addition to discussion of the novel itself, includes maps, information on Heian court life, etc.

- Andrew Pekarik, ed. UKIFUNE: LOVE IN THE TALE OF GENJI. 1982: Columbia University Press.

- Marian Ury. "The Real Murasaki," *Monumenta Nipponica* 38.2 (1983), 175-190.

- David Pollack. "The Informing Image: 'China' in *Genji Monogatari*," *Monumenta Nipponica* 38.4 (1983), 359-376.

- Doris G. Bargen. "Spirit Possession in the Context of Dramatic Expressions of Gender Conflict: The Aoi Episode of the *Genji*," *Harvard Journal of Asiatic Studies* 48.1 (1988), 95-130.

- _____. "The Search for Things Past in the *Genji monogatari*," *Harvard Journal of Asiatic Studies* 51.1 (1991), 199-232. Compares Murasaki Shikibu and Marcel Proust.

- Richard H. Okada. FIGURES OF RESISTANCE: LANGUAGE, POETRY, AND NARRATING IN *THE TALE OF GENJI* AND OTHER MID-HEIAN TEXTS. 1991: Duke University Press.

- Ivan Morris, ed. & transl. THE TALE OF GENJI SCROLL. 1971: Kōdansha International.

- Miyeko Murase. ICONOGRAPHY OF THE TALE OF GENJI: *GENJI MONOGATARI EKOTOBA*. 1984: Weatherhill.

- Janet Emily Goff. NOH DRAMA AND THE TALE OF GENJI: THE ART OF ALLUSION IN FIFTEEN CLASSICAL PLAYS. 1991: Princeton University Press.

- Royall Tyler. "The *Nō* Play *Matsukaze* as a Transformation of *Genji monogatari*," *Journal of Japanese Studies* 20.2 (1994), 377-422.

- Richard Bowring. MURASAKI SHIKIBU: THE TALE OF GENJI. 1988: Cambridge University Press.

- Norma Field. THE SPLENDOR OF LONGING IN THE *TALE OF GENJI*. 1987: Princeton University Press.

- Haruo Shirane. THE BRIDGE OF DREAMS: A POETICS OF "THE TALE OF GENJI." 1987: Stanford University Press.

- _____. "The Aesthetics of Power: Politics in *The Tale of Genji*," *Harvard Journal of Asiatic Studies* 45.2 (1985), 615-647.

- Mark Morris. "Desire and the Prince: New Work on *Genji monogatari* —A Review Article," *Journal of Asian Studies* 49.2 (1990), 291-304. Reviews above books by Bowring, Field, and Shirane.

- Janet Goff. "The Pleasure of Reading the *Genji*," *Journal of Japanese Studies* 17.2 (1991), 345-358. Another review of Bowring, Field, and Shirane.

- Marian Ury. "Tales of *Genji*," *Harvard Journal of Asiatic Studies* 51.1 (1991), 263-308.

- I. J. McMullen. GENJI GAIDEN: THE ORIGINS OF KUMAZAWA BANZAN'S COMMENTARY ON THE TALE OF GENJI. 1991: Ithaca Press, Oxford Oriental Institute.

MURASAKI SHIKIBU NIKKI (Diary of Lady Murasaki, ca. 1010)

- Richard Bowring. MURASAKI SHIKIBU: HER DIARY AND POETIC MEMOIRS: A TRANSLATION AND STUDY. 1982: Princeton University Press.

MAKURA NO SŌSHI (by Sei Shōnagon, early 11th century)

- Ivan Morris, transl. & ed. THE PILLOW BOOK OF SEI SHŌNAGON. 1991: Columbia University Press.

- Arthur Waley, transl. THE PILLOW BOOK OF SEI SHŌNAGON. 1953: Grove.

- Tzvetana Kristeva. "The Pillow Hook: The *Pillow Book* as an 'Open Work'," *Japan Review* 5 (1994), 15-54.

IZUMI SHIKIBU NIKKI (early 11th century)

- Edwin Cranston, transl. THE IZUMI SHIKIBU DIARY. 1969: Harvard University Press.

- Earl Miner, transl. JAPANESE POETIC DIARIES. 1969: California University Press.

- Jane Hirshfield with Mariko Aratani, trans. THE INK DARK MOON: LOVE POEMS BY ONO NO KOMACHI & IZUMI SHIKIBU. 1988: Scribner.

- Janet A. Walker. "The *Izumi Shikibu Nikki* As a Work of Courtly Literature," *The Literary Review* 23.4 (1980), 463-480.

ŌKAGAMI ("history" covering years 850-1025)

- Helen Craig McCullough, transl. *ŌKAGAMI: THE GREAT MIRROR*. 1980: Princeton University Press & University of Tokyo Press.

- Joseph K. Yamagiwa, transl. THE *ŌKAGAMI*: A JAPANESE HISTORICAL TALE. 1967: Allen & Unwin.

- _____ & Edwin O. Reischauer. TRANSLATIONS FROM EARLY JAPANESE LITERATURE (1951: Harvard University Press), 271-374.

EIGA MONOGATARI ("history" of the great Fujiwara leader Michinaga)

- Helen Craig McCullough & William H. McCullough, transl. A TALE OF FLOWERING FORTUNES. 2 volumes. 1979: Stanford University Press.

- Karen Brazell. "Three Tales of Michinaga," *Journal of Japanese Studies* 10.1 (1984), 185-196.

SANUKI NO SUKE NIKKI (ca. 1010)

- Jennifer Brewster, transl. THE EMPEROR HORIKAWA DIARY. 1977: University of Hawaii Press.

SARASHINA NIKKI (ca. 1059)

- Ivan Morris, transl. AS I CROSSED A BRIDGE OF DREAMS: RECOLLECTIONS OF A WOMAN IN ELEVENTH- CENTURY JAPAN. 1971: Dial.

HAMAMATSU CHŪNAGON MONOGATARI (11th century)

- Thomas H. Rohlich, transl. A TALE OF ELEVENTH-CENTURY JAPAN: *HAMAMATSU CHŪNAGON MONOGATARI*. 1983: Princeton University Press.

MUTSU WAKI (account of mid 11th-century military campaign; predecessor of the "war chronicles" of the feudal period)

- Helen C. McCullough, transl. "A Tale of Mutsu," *Harvard Journal of Asiatic Studies* 25 (1964-1965), 178-211.

TSUTSUMI CHŪNAGON MONOGATARI (10 stories, attributed largely to 11th and 12th centuries)

- Robert L. Backus, transl. THE RIVERSIDE COUNSELOR'S STORIES: VERNACULAR FICTION OF LATE HEIAN JAPAN. 1985: Stanford University Press.

- Umeyo Hirano, transl. THE *TSUTSUMI CHŪNAGON MONOGATARI*: A COLLECTION OF 11TH CENTURY SHORT STORIES OF JAPAN. 1976: Hokuseidō.

- Edwin O. Reischauer & Joseph Yamagiwa, transl. TRANSLATIONS FROM EARLY JAPANESE LITERATURE (1951: Harvard University Press), 137-267.

- Oscar Benl. *"Tsutsumi Chūnagon Monogatari,"* *Monumenta Nipponica* 3.1 (1940), 144-164.

- Arthur Waley, transl. THE LADY WHO LOVED INSECTS. 1929: Blackmore.

TORIKAEBAYA MONOGATARI (12th century)

- Rosette F. Willig. THE CHANGELINGS: A CLASSICAL JAPANESE COURT TALE. 1983: Stanford University Press.

- Gregory M. Pflugfelder. "Strange Fates: Sex, Gender, and Sexuality in *Torikaebaya Monogatari,*" *Monumenta Nipponica* 47.3 (1992), 347-368.

KONJAKU MONOGATARI (collection of 1,080 stories from China, India, and Japan; early 12th century)

- Marian Ury, transl. TALES OF TIMES NOW PAST: SIXTY-TWO STORIES FROM A MEDIEVAL JAPANESE COLLECTION. 1979: University of California Press.

- Susan Wilber Jones, transl. AGES AGO: THIRTY-SEVEN TALES FROM THE *KONJAKU MONOGATARI* COLLECTION. 1959: Harvard University Press.

- Robert H. Brower. "The *Konzyaku Monogatarisyū*: An Historical and Critical Introduction, with Annotated Translations of Seventy-Eight Tales." 1952: Ph.D. dissertation in History, University of Michigan.

- W. Michael Kelsey. *KONJAKU MONOGATARI-SHŪ*. 1982: Twayne.

- Yoshiko Kurata Dykstra, transl. THE KONJAKU TALES. INDIAN SECTION: FROM A MEDIEVAL JAPANESE COLLECTION. 1986: Intercultural Research Institute, Kansai University of Foreign Studies.

- Hitomi Tonomura, "Black Hair and Red Trousers: Gendering the Flesh in Medieval Japan," *American Historical Review* 99.1 (1994), 129-154. On gender and sexuality in *Konjaku Monogatari*.

RYŌJIN HISHŌ (collection edited by emperor Go-Shirakawa, 1127-1192)

- Yung-Hee Kim, transl. SONGS TO MAKE THE DUST DANCE: THE *RYŌJIN HISHŌ* OF TWELFTH-CENTURY JAPAN. 1994: University of California Press.

- Yasuhiko Moriguchi & David Jenkins, transl. THE DANCE OF THE DUST ON THE RAFTERS: SELECTIONS FROM *RYŌJIN-HISHŌ*. 1990: Broken Moon Press.

SHIKISHI NAISHINNO SHŪ (poems by Princess Shikishi daughter of Go-Shirakawa, ca. 1153-1201)

- Hiroaki Satō, transl. STRING OF BEADS: COMPLETE POEMS OF PRINCESS SHIKISHI. 1993: University of Hawaii Press.

KENREIMON'IN UKYŌ NO DAIBU SHŪ (early 13th century)

- Philip Tudor Harries, transl. THE POETIC MEMOIRS OF LADY DAIBU. 1980: Stanford University Press.

- James G. Wagner. "The *Kenreimon'in Ukyō no Daibu Shū*," *Monumenta Nipponica* 31.1 (1976), 1-28.

FEUDAL JAPAN & THE WARRIOR SOCIETY: Overviews

Edwin O. Reischauer & Albert M. Craig. JAPAN: TRADITION AND TRANSFORMATION (1989: Houghton Mifflin), chapter 2.

Peter Duus. FEUDALISM IN JAPAN. 1969: Knopf; 1993: McGraw Hill.

_____. "Feudalism," KŌDANSHA ENCYCLOPEDIA OF JAPAN 3: 263-267.

Edwin O. Reischauer. "Japanese Feudalism," in Rushton Coulborn, ed.
FEUDALISM IN HISTORY (1956: Princeton University Press), 26-48.

William Wayne Farris. HEAVENLY WARRIORS: THE EVOLUTION OF
JAPAN'S MILITARY, 500-1300. 1992: Council on East Asian
Studies, Harvard University.

Karl F. Friday. HIRED SWORDS: THE RISE OF PRIVATE WARRIOR
POWER IN EARLY JAPAN. 1992: Stanford University Press.
Focuses on Heian period.

_____. "Teeth and Claws: Provincial Warriors and the Heian Court,"
Monumenta Nipponica 43.2 (1988), 153-185.

Stephen R. Turnbull. SAMURAI WARRIORS. 1987: Blandford Press.

Anthony J. Bryant. THE SAMURAI: WARRIORS OF MEDIEVAL JAPAN,
940-1600. 1989: Osprey.

H. Paul Varley. WARRIORS OF JAPAN, AS PORTRAYED IN THE WAR
TALES. 1994: University of Hawaii Press.

_____. "The Age of the Military Houses," in Arthur Tiedemann, ed.
AN INTRODUCTION TO JAPANESE CIVILIZATION (1974: Heath),
61-95.

Jeffrey P. Mass & William B. Hauser, eds. THE BAKUFU IN JAPANESE
HISTORY. 1986: Stanford University Press.

John W. Hall. GOVERNMENT AND LOCAL POWER IN JAPAN, 500-1700:
A STUDY BASED ON BIZEN PROVINCE. 1966: Princeton
University Press.

_____. "Feudalism in Japan—A Reassessment," *Comparative Studies in
Science and History* 5.1 (1962). Reprinted in John W. Hall & Marius
B. Jansen, eds. STUDIES IN THE INSTITUTIONAL HISTORY OF
EARLY MODERN JAPAN (1968: Princeton University Press), 15-51.

Ryōsuke Ishii. "Japanese Feudalism," *Acta Asiatica* 35 (1978), 1-29.

Motohisa Yasuda. "History of the Studies of the Formation of Japanese *Hōken*
System (Feudalism)," *Acta Asiatica* 8 (1965), 74-100.

Conrad Totman. "English Language Studies of Medieval Japan: An Assessment," *Journal of Asian Studies* 38.3 (1979), 541-551.

Archibald Lewis. KNIGHTS AND SAMURAI: FEUDALISM IN NORTHERN FRANCE AND JAPAN. 1974: Harper.

Louis Frederic. DAILY LIFE IN JAPAN IN THE AGE OF THE SAMURAI, 1185-1603. 1972: Praeger.

Yoshiaki Shimizu, ed. JAPAN: THE SHAPING OF DAIMYŌ CULTURE, 1185-1868. 1988: G. Braziller.

Susumu Ishii. "The Formation of *Bushi* Bands (*Bushidan*)," *Acta Asiatica* 49 (1985), 1-14.

Keiji Nagahara. "The Medieval Origins of the *Eta-Hinin*," *Journal of Japanese Studies* 5.2 (1979), 385-403.

FEUDAL JAPAN & THE WARRIOR SOCIETY:
The Kamakura Period (1185-1333)

Minoru Shinoda. "Kamakura History (1185-1333)," KŌDANSHA ENCYCLO-PEDIA OF JAPAN 3: 169-172.

_____. THE FOUNDING OF THE KAMAKURA SHŌGUNATE, 1180-1185—WITH SELECTED TRANSLATIONS FROM THE *AZUMA KAGAMI*. 1960: Columbia University Press. See especially 15-39 and 136-144 for a concise overview of the origins of warrior government.

Martin Collcutt. "Religion in the Formation of the Kamakura Bakufu: As Seen through the *Azuma Kagami*," *Japan Review* 5 (1994), 55-86.

George B. Sansom. A HISTORY OF JAPAN TO 1334. 1958: Stanford University Press.

Keiji Nagahara. "The Social Structure of Early Medieval Japan," *Hitotsubashi Journal of Economics* 1 (1960), 90-97.

John W. Hall & Jeffrey P. Mass, eds. MEDIEVAL JAPAN: ESSAYS IN INSTITUTIONAL HISTORY. 1974: Yale University Press; 1988: Stanford University Press. Reviewed by Keiji Nagahara in *Journal of Japanese Studies* 1.2 (1975), 437-445.

Jeffrey P. Mass. "The Kamakura Bakufu," in Kōzō Yamamura, ed.
CAMBRIDGE HISTORY OF JAPAN, Volume 3: MEDIEVAL JAPAN
(1990: Cambridge University Press), 46-88.

———. WARRIOR GOVERNMENT IN EARLY MEDIEVAL JAPAN:
A STUDY OF THE KAMAKURA BAKUFU, SHUGO & JITŌ. 1974:
Stanford University Press. Reviewed by Kōzō Yamamura in *Journal of
Japanese Studies* 1.2 (1975), 451-459.

———. THE DEVELOPMENT OF KAMAKURA RULE, 1180-1250:
A HISTORY WITH DOCUMENTS. 1979: Stanford University Press.
Reviewed by Dan F. Henderson in *Journal of Japanese Studies* 9.2
(1983), 367-373.

———. "The Missing Minamoto in the Twelfth-Century Kantō," *Journal of
Japanese Studies* 19.1 (1993), 121-145.

———. "The Emergence of the Kamakura Bakufu," in Hall & Mass,
MEDIEVAL JAPAN (1974: Yale University Press), 127-156.

———. "The Origins of Kamakura Justice," *Journal of Japanese Studies* 3.2
(1977), 299-322.

———. "Jitō Land Possession in the Thirteenth Century: The Case of Shitaji
Chūbun," in Hall & Mass, MEDIEVAL JAPAN (1974: Yale University
Press), 157-183.

———. LORDSHIP AND INHERITANCE IN EARLY MEDIEVAL JAPAN:
A STUDY OF THE KAMAKURA SŌRYŌ SYSTEM. 1989: Stanford
University Press.

———. ANTIQUITY AND ANACHRONISM IN JAPANESE HISTORY.
1992: Stanford University Press. Thoughtful essays on problems and
trends in the field of pre-Tokugawa Japanese history, emphasizing
especially the Kamakura period.

———, ed. COURT AND BAKUFU IN JAPAN: ESSAYS IN KAMAKURA
HISTORY. 1982: Yale University Press.

——— & William Hauser, eds. THE BAKUFU IN JAPANESE HISTORY.
1985: Stanford University Press.

Akio Yoshie. "The Kamakura *Bakufu* as a Legitimate Public Authority," *Acta
Asiatica* 49 (1985), 15-33.

Akiko Hirota. "Ex-Emperor Go-Toba: A Study in Personality, Politics and Poetry." 1989: Ph.D. dissertation in East Asian Languages and Cultures, UCLA.

John Brownlee. "Crisis as Reinforcement of the Imperial Institution: The Case of the Jōkyū Incident, 1221," *Monumenta Nipponica* 30.2 (1975), 193-202.

Kyotsu Hori. "The Economic and Political Effects of the Mongol Wars," in Hall & Mass, MEDIEVAL JAPAN (1974: Yale University Press), 184-198.

Nakaba Yamada. GHENKO: THE MONGOL INVASION OF JAPAN. 1916: Smith, Elder.

Susumu Ishii. "The Decline of the Kamakura Bakufu," Jeffrey P. Mass & Hitomi Tonomura, transl., in Kōzō Yamamura, ed. CAMBRIDGE HISTORY OF JAPAN, Volume 3: MEDIEVAL JAPAN (1990: Cambridge University Press), 128-174.

Carl Steenstrup. "Pushing the Papers of Kamakura: The Nitty-gritticists versus the Grand Sweeper," *Monumenta Nipponica* 35.3 (1980), 337-346.

FEUDAL JAPAN & THE WARRIOR SOCIETY:
The Ashikaga / Muromachi (1333-1568)
& Azuchi / Momoyama (1568-1600) Periods

Martin C. Collcutt. "Muromachi History (1333-1568)," KŌDANSHA ENCYCLOPEDIA OF JAPAN 3: 172-177.

_____. "Kings of Japan? The Political Authority of the Ashikaga Shōguns," *Monumenta Nipponica* 37.4 (1982), 523-530.

George Elison. "Azuchi-Momoyama History (1568-1600)," KŌDANSHA ENCYCLOPEDIA OF JAPAN 3: 177-185.

John Whitney Hall. "The Muromachi Bakufu," in Kōzō Yamamura, ed. CAMBRIDGE HISTORY OF JAPAN, Volume 3: MEDIEVAL JAPAN (1990: Cambridge University Press), 175-230.

_____. "Foundations of the Modern Japanese Daimyō," *Journal of Asian Studies* 20.3 (1961). Reprinted in John W. Hall & Marius Jansen, eds. STUDIES IN THE INSTITUTIONAL HISTORY OF EARLY MODERN JAPAN (1968: Princeton University Press), 65-77.

George B. Sansom. A HISTORY OF JAPAN, 1334-1615. 1961: Stanford University Press.

Andrew Edmund Goble. "Go-Daigo and the Kemmu Restoration." 1987: Ph.D. dissertation in History, Stanford University.

H. Paul Varley. IMPERIAL RESTORATION IN MEDIEVAL JAPAN. 1971: Columbia University Press. Covers the Kemmu Restoration and aftermath, 1333-1392.

_____. THE ŌNIN WAR: HISTORY OF ITS ORIGINS AND BACK-GROUND WITH A SELECTIVE TRANSLATION OF THE CHRONI-CLE OF ŌNIN. 1967: Columbia University Press. Analysis of the great civil war of 1467-1477, which ushered in the period of "high feudalism."

Kenneth Alan Grossberg. JAPAN'S RENAISSANCE: THE POLITICS OF THE MUROMACHI BAKUFU. 1981: Council on East Asian Studies, Harvard University. Reviewed by Peter Arneson in *Journal of Japanese Studies* 9.2 (1983), 385-391.

_____. "From Feudal Chieftain to Secular Monarch," *Monumenta Nipponica* 31.1 (1976), 29-50.

Prescott B. Wintersteen, Jr. "The Early Muromachi Bakufu in Kyoto," in Hall & Mass, MEDIEVAL JAPAN (1974: Yale University Press), 201-209.

_____. "The Muromachi Shugo and Hanzei," in Hall & Mass, MEDIEVAL JAPAN (1974: Yale University Press), 210-220.

Akira Imatani. "Muromachi Local Government: *Shugo* and *kokujin*," Suzanne Gay, transl., in Kōzō Yamamura, ed. CAMBRIDGE HISTORY OF JAPAN, Volume 3: MEDIEVAL JAPAN (1990: Cambridge University Press), 231-259.

_____, with Kōzō Yamamura. "Not for Lack of Will or Wile: Yoshimitsu's Failure to Supplant the Imperial Lineage," *Journal of Japanese Studies* 18.1 (1992), 45-77.

Suzanne Gay. "The Kawashima: Warrior-Peasants of Medieval Japan," *Harvard Journal of Asiatic Studies* 46.1 (1986), 81-119.

John W. Hall & Takeshi Toyoda, eds. JAPAN IN THE MUROMACHI AGE. 1976: University of California Press. Contains 18 essays on political, economic, cultural, and religious developments. Reviewed by Mary E. Berry in *Journal of Japanese Studies* 4.1 (1978), 187-198.

Hitomi Tonomura. "Forging the Past: Medieval Counterfeit Documents," *Monumenta Nipponica* 40.1 (1985), 69-96.

_____. COMMUNITY AND COMMERCE IN LATE MEDIEVAL JAPAN: THE CORPORATE VILLAGES OF TOKUCHIN-HO. 1992: Stanford University Press.

Wendell Cole. KYOTO IN THE MOMOYAMA PERIOD. 1967: University of Oklahoma Press.

George Elison & Bardwell L. Smith, eds. WARLORDS, ARTISTS, AND COMMONERS: JAPAN IN THE SIXTEENTH CENTURY. 1981: University of Hawaii Press. Includes essays on urban autonomy in Sakai, painting, linked-verse poetry, music, song and the performing arts, the tea ceremony, and the great unifier Toyotomi Hideyoshi. See also the useful bibliographic essay on "Japanese Society and Culture in the Momoyama Era" (pp. 245-279), and the review of this book by Barbara Ruch in *Journal of Japanese Studies* 8.2 (1982), 369-382.

John Hall, Keiji Nagahara & Kōzō Yamamura, eds. JAPAN BEFORE TOKU-GAWA: POLITICAL CONSOLIDATION AND ECONOMIC GROWTH, 1500-1650. 1981: Princeton University Press. Contains 11 essays on the period of daimyō warfare and unification.

Keiji Nagahara & Kōzō Yamamura. "Shaping the Process of Unification: Technological Progress in Sixteenth- and Seventeenth-Century Japan," *Journal of Japanese Studies* 14.1 (1988), 77-109.

Peter Judd Arneson. THE MEDIEVAL JAPANESE DAIMYŌ: THE ŌUCHI FAMILY'S RULE OF SUŌ AND NAGATO. 1979: Yale University Press. Covers period from 1333-1573.

Keiji Nagahara. "The Lord-Vassal System and Public Authority (*Kōgi*): The Case of the *Sengoku Daimyō*," *Acta Asiatica* 49 (1985), 34-45.

David L. Davis. "*Ikki* in Late Medieval Japan," in Hall & Mass, MEDIEVAL JAPAN (1974: Yale University Press), 221-247. Concerns peasant uprisings.

Naohiro Asao. "The Sixteenth-Century Unification," Bernard Susser, transl., in John Whitney Hall, ed. CAMBRIDGE HISTORY OF JAPAN, Volume 4: EARLY MODERN JAPAN (1991: Cambridge University Press), 40-95.

Osamu Wakita. "The Social and Economic Consequences of Unification," James L. McClain, transl., in John Whitney Hall, ed. CAMBRIDGE HISTORY OF JAPAN, Volume 4: EARLY MODERN JAPAN (1991: Cambridge University Press), 96-127.

_____. "The Emergence of the State in Sixteenth-Century Japan: From Oda to Tokugawa," *Journal of Japanese Studies* 8.2 (1982), 343-367.

_____. "The Kokudaka System: A Device for Unification," *Journal of Japanese Studies* 1.2 (1975), 297-320.

Kōzō Yamamura. "From Coins to Rice: Hypotheses on the *Kandaka* and *Kokudaka* Systems," *Journal of Japanese Studies* 14.2 (1988), 341-367.

Michael P. Birt. "Samurai in Passage: The Transformation of the Sixteenth-Century Kantō," *Journal of Japanese Studies* 11.2 (1985), 369-399.

Neil McMullin. BUDDHISM AND THE STATE IN SIXTEENTH-CENTURY JAPAN. 1984: Princeton University Press. Examines policies of the first great unifier, Oda Nobunaga (1534-1582).

Kun Anthony Namkung. "The Aesthetics of Power: Noh and Society in the Unification of Japan." 1986: Ph.D. dissertation in History, University of California.

Mary Elizabeth Berry. THE CULTURE OF CIVIL WAR IN KYOTO. 1994: University of California Press. Covers the "warring states" period from 1467 to 1568.

_____. HIDEYOSHI. 1982: Harvard University Press.

_____. "Public Peace and Private Attachment: The Goals and Conduct of Power in Early Modern Japan," *Journal of Japanese Studies* 12.2 (1986), 237-271.

George Elison. "Hideyoshi, the Bountiful Minister," in Elison & Smith, WARLORDS, ARTISTS & COMMONERS (1981: University of Hawaii Press), 223-244.

Walter Dening. THE LIFE OF TOYOTOMI HIDEYOSHI (1536-1598). 1906: Hokuseidō.

Adriana Boscaro, transl. 101 LETTERS OF HIDEYOSHI. 1975: Monumenta Nipponica Monographs.

Giuliana Stramigioli. "Hideyoshi's Expansionist Policy on the Asiatic Mainland," *Transactions, Asiatic Society of Japan*, 3rd series, 3 (1954), 74-116.

Arthur L. Sadler. "The Naval Campaign in the Korean War of Hideyoshi (1592-1598)," *Transactions, Asiatic Society of Japan*, 2nd series, 14 (1937), 179-208.

Yoshi S. Kuno. JAPANESE EXPANSION ON THE ASIATIC CONTINENT. 2 volumes. 1937-1940: University of California Press. See volume 1 for Hideyoshi's invasion of Korea.

Homer B. Hulbert. THE HISTORY OF KOREA. 2 volumes. 1905: The Methodist Publishing House. See volume 1 for Hideyoshi's invasion.

Shōsaku Takagi. " 'Hideyoshi's Peace' and the Transformation of the *Bushi* Class: The Dissolution of the Autonomy of the Medieval *Bushi*," *Acta Asiatica* 49 (1985), 46-77.

Conrad Totman. TOKUGAWA IEYASU: SHŌGUN. 1983: Heian International. Based on *Ieyasuden* (The Biography of Ieyasu) by Kōya Nakamura.

FEUDAL JAPAN & THE WARRIOR SOCIETY:
The "Christian Century" (1549-1650)

Francois Caron & Joost Schouten. A TRUE DESCRIPTION OF THE MIGHTY KINGDOMS OF JAPAN AND SIAM. 1986: Siam Society (facsimile of 1671 London edition translated by Roger Manley); 1935: Argonaut Press (reprint of 1663 English edition).

Charles R. Boxer. THE CHRISTIAN CENTURY IN JAPAN, 1549-1650. 1951: University of California Press.

_____. THE GREAT SHIP FROM AMACON: ANNALS OF MACAO AND THE OLD JAPAN TRADE, 1555-1640. 1959: Centro de Estudos Historicos Ultramarinos.

_____. PAPERS ON PORTUGUESE, DUTCH, AND JESUIT INFLUENCES IN SIXTEENTH- AND SEVENTEENTH- CENTURY JAPAN. 1979: University Publications of America reprint.

_____. A PORTUGUESE EMBASSY TO JAPAN (1644-1647) and THE EMBASSY OF CAPTAIN GONCALO DE SIQUIERIA DE SOUZA TO JAPAN IN 1644-7. 1979: University Publications of America reprint.

_____. PORTUGUESE MERCHANTS AND MISSIONARIES IN FEUDAL JAPAN 1543-1640. 1986: Variorum Reprints.

_____ & J. S. Cummins. THE DOMINICAN MISSION IN JAPAN (1602-1622) AND LOPE DE VEGA. 1963: Archivum Fratrum Praedictorum.

Michael Cooper, S.J. "Christianity," KŌDANSHA ENCYCLOPEDIA OF JAPAN 1: 306-310.

_____, ed. THEY CAME TO JAPAN: AN ANTHOLOGY OF EUROPEAN REPORTS ON JAPAN, 1543-1640. 1965: University of California Press.

_____, transl. & ed. THIS ISLAND OF JAPON: JOAO RODRIGUES' ACCOUNT OF 16TH-CENTURY JAPAN. 1973: Kōdansha International.

_____. THE SOUTHERN BARBARIANS: THE FIRST EUROPEANS IN JAPAN. 1971: Kōdansha International.

W. Michael Mathes. "A Quarter Century of Trans-Pacific Diplomacy: New Spain and Japan, 1592-1617," *Journal of Asian History* 24.1 (1990), 1-29.

THE DESHIMA DAGREGISTERS: THEIR ORIGINAL TABLES OF CONTENTS. Seven volumes covering 1641-1760, with more planned to cover through 1800. 1986- : Leiden Centre for the History of European Expansion.

Paul van der Velde & Rudolph Bachofner. THE DESHIMA DIARIES: MAR-
GINALIA, 1700-1740. 1992: Japan-Netherlands Institute (Tokyo).

Anthony Farrington, ed. THE ENGLISH FACTORY IN JAPAN, 1613-1623.
2 volumes. 1991: The British Library.

Derek Massarella. A WORLD ELSEWHERE: EUROPE'S ENCOUNTER
WITH JAPAN IN THE SIXTEENTH AND SEVENTEENTH
CENTURIES. 1990: Yale University Press.

_____. "The Early Career of Richard Cocks (1566-1624), Head of the English
East India Company's Factory in Japan (16133-1623)," *Transactions,
Asiatic Society of Japan*, 3rd series, 20 (1985), 1-46.

_____ & Izumi K. Tyler. "The Japonian Charters: The English and Dutch
Shuinjō," *Monumenta Nipponica* 45.2 (1990), 189-205.

Donald Lach. JAPAN IN THE EYES OF EUROPE: THE SIXTEENTH
CENTURY. 1968: University of Chicago Press.

George Elison. "The Cross and the Sword: Patterns of Momoyama History," in
George Elison & Bardwell L. Smith, eds. WARLORDS, ARTISTS &
COMMONERS (1981: University of Hawaii Press), 55-86.

_____. DEUS DESTROYED: THE IMAGE OF CHRISTIANITY IN EARLY
MODERN JAPAN. 1973: Harvard University Press.

Jurgis Elisonas [formerly George Elison]. "Christianity and the Daimyō," in John
Whitney Hall, ed. CAMBRIDGE HISTORY OF JAPAN, Volume 4:
EARLY MODERN JAPAN (1991: Cambridge University Press),
301-372.

David Reid. NEW WINE: THE CULTURAL SHAPING OF JAPANESE
CHRISTIANITY. 1991: Asian Humanities Press.

George B. Sansom. "Christianity in Japan, 1549-1614," in his THE WESTERN
WORLD AND JAPAN (1962: Knopf), 115-133.

Richard H. Drummond. A HISTORY OF CHRISTIANITY IN JAPAN. 1971:
William Eerdmans.

Otis Cary. A HISTORY OF CHRISTIANITY IN JAPAN: ROMAN
CATHOLIC, GREEK ORTHODOX AND PROTESTANT MISSIONS.
1909: Revell. Reprinted in 1976; covers 1549 to the 20th century.

Frederick Vincent Williams. THE MARTYRS OF NAGASAKI. 1956:
    Academy Library Guild.

Hubert Cheslik. "The Great Martyrdom in Edo, 1623," *Monumenta Nipponica*
    10.1-2 (1955), 1-44.

J. F. Moran. THE JAPANESE AND THE JESUITS: ALESSANDRO VALIG-
    NANO IN SIXTEENTH-CENTURY JAPAN. 1993: Routledge.

Mary Ann Harrington. JAPAN'S HIDDEN CHRISTIANS. 1993: Loyola
    University Press.

Peter Nosco. "Secrecy and the Transmission of Tradition: Issues in the Study of
    the 'Underground' Christians," *Japanese Journal of Religious Studies*
    20.1 (1993), 3-29.

Christal Whelan. "Religion Concealed: The Kakure Kirishitan on Narushima,"
    Monumenta Nipponica 47.3 (1992), 369-387.

Montague Paske-Smith, ed. JAPANESE TRADITIONS OF CHRISTIANITY:
    BEING SOME OLD TRANSLATIONS FROM THE JAPANESE,
    WITH BRITISH CONSULAR REPORTS OF THE PERSECUTIONS
    OF 1868-1872. 1930: Kōbe.

Henry Smith II, ed. LEARNING FROM "SHŌGUN": JAPANESE HISTORY
    AND WESTERN FANTASY. 1980: Program in Asian Studies,
    University of California, Santa Barbara. A scholarly response to
    SHŌGUN, the popular novel by James Clavell.

LAND, LABOR & COMMERCE BEFORE 1600

Conrad Totman. THE GREEN ARCHIPELAGO: FORESTRY IN PRE-
    INDUSTRIAL JAPAN. 1989: University of California Press.

Elizabeth S. Satō. "Shōen," KŌDANSHA ENCYCLOPEDIA OF JAPAN
    7: 155-158.

_____. "The Early Development of the Shōen," in John Hall & Jeffrey Mass,
    eds. MEDIEVAL JAPAN (1974: Yale University Press), 91-108.

_____. "Ōyama Estate and Insei Land Policies," *Monumenta Nipponica* 34.1
    (1979) 73-100.

Kyōhei Ōyama. "Medieval *Shōen*," Martin Collcutt, transl., in Kōzō Yamamura, ed. CAMBRIDGE HISTORY OF JAPAN, Volume 3: MEDIEVAL JAPAN (1990: Cambridge University Press), 89-127.

Cornelius J. Kiley. "Estate and Property in the Late Heian Period," in Hall & Mass, MEDIEVAL JAPAN (1974: Yale University Press), 109-124.

Jeffrey P. Mass. "Patterns of Provincial Inheritance in Late Heian Japan," *Journal of Japanese Studies* 9.1 (1983), 67-95.

_____. LORDSHIP AND INHERITANCE IN EARLY MEDIEVAL JAPAN: A STUDY OF THE KAMAKURA SŌRYŌ SYSTEM. 1989: Stanford University Press.

Peter J. Arneson. "The Struggle for Lordship in Late Heian Japan: The Case of Aki," *Journal of Japanese Studies* 10.1 (1984), 101-141.

Kōzō Yamamura. "The Decline of the Ritsuryō System: Hypotheses on Economic & Institutional Change," *Journal of Japanese Studies* 1.1 (1974), 3-37.

_____ et al. "Workshop Papers on the Economic and Institutional History of Medieval Japan," *Journal of Japanese Studies* 1.2 (1975), 255-346.

_____. "Tara in Transition: A Study of a Kamakura Shōen," *Journal of Japanese Studies* 7.2 (1981), 349-391.

Keiji Nagahara. "Landownership Under the Shōen Kokugaryō System," *Journal of Japanese Studies* 1.2 (1975), 269-296.

_____. "The Decline of the *Shōen* System," Michael P. Birt, transl., in Kōzō Yamamura, ed. CAMBRIDGE HISTORY OF JAPAN, Volume 3: MEDIEVAL JAPAN (1990: Cambridge University Press), 260-300.

_____. "The Medieval Peasant," Suzanne Gay, transl., in Kōzō Yamamura, ed. CAMBRIDGE HISTORY OF JAPAN, Volume 3: MEDIEVAL JAPAN (1990: Cambridge University Press), 301-343.

Thomas Keirstead. THE GEOGRAPHY OF POWER IN MEDIEVAL JAPAN. 1992: Princeton University Press.

_____. "The Theater of Protest: Petitions, Oaths, and Rebellion in the *Shōen*," *Journal of Japanese Studies* 16.2 (1990), 357-388.

_____. "Fragmented Estates: The Breakup of the *Myō* and the Decline of the *Shōen* System," *Monumenta Nipponica* 40.3 (1985), 311-330.

James Kanda. "Methods of Land Transfer in Medieval Japan," *Monumenta Nipponica* 33.4 (1978), 379-405.

Ryōsuke Ishii. "On Japanese Possession of Real Property—A Study of Chigyō in the Middle Ages," *Japan Annual of Law and Politics* 1 (1952), 149-162.

Kan'ichi Asakawa, ed. THE DOCUMENTS OF IRIKI, ILLUSTRATIVE OF THE DEVELOPMENT OF THE FEUDAL INSTITUTION IN JAPAN. 1955: Japan Society for the Promotion of Science.

_____. LAND & SOCIETY IN MEDIEVAL JAPAN. 1965: Japan Society for the Promotion of Science. Introduction by J. W. Hall and Rizō Takeuchi. Contains 7 essays by the pioneer of English-language studies of Japanese feudal structures.

John H. Wigmore & D. B. Simmons. NOTES ON LAND TENURE AND LOCAL INSTITUTIONS IN OLD JAPAN. 1891; reprinted 1979 by University Publications of America.

Kristina Kade Troost. "Common Property and Community Formation: Self-Governing Villages in Late Medieval Japan, 1300-1600." 1990: Ph.D. dissertation in History and East Asian Languages, Harvard University.

Hitomi Tonomura. "Forging the Past: Medieval Counterfeit Documents," *Monumenta Nipponica* 40.1 (1985), 69-96.

_____. COMMUNITY AND COMMERCE IN LATE MEDIEVAL JAPAN: THE CORPORATE VILLAGES OF TOKUCHIN-HO. 1992: Stanford University Press.

Haruko Wakita. "Towards a Wider Perspective on Medieval Commerce," *Journal of Japanese Studies* 1.2 (1975), 321-345.

_____. "Marriage and Property in Premodern Japan from the Perspective of Women's History," *Journal of Japanese Studies* 10.1 (1984), 73-99.

John W. Hall & Takeshi Toyoda, eds. JAPAN IN THE MUROMACHI AGE. 1976: University of California Press.

Mitsuru Miyagawa & Cornelius J. Kiley. "From Shōen to Chigyō: Proprietary Lordship and the Structure of Local Power," in Hall & Toyoda, JAPAN IN THE MUROMACHI AGE (1976: University of California Press), 89-106.

Keiji Nagahara & Kōzō Yamamura. "Village Communities and Daimyō Power," in Hall & Toyoda, JAPAN IN THE MUROMACHI AGE (1976: University of California Press), 107-124.

Takeshi Toyoda, Hiroshi Sugiyama & V. Dixon Morris. "The Growth of Commerce and the Trades," in Hall & Toyoda, JAPAN IN THE MUROMACHI AGE (1976: University of California Press), 129-144.

V. Dixon Morris. "Sakai: From Shōen to Port City," in Hall & Toyoda, JAPAN IN THE MUROMACHI AGE (1976: University of California Press), 145-158.

Takeo Tanaka & Robert Sakai. "Japan's Relations with Overseas Countries," in Hall & Toyoda, JAPAN IN THE MUROMACHI AGE (1976: University of California Press), 159-178.

John W. Hall, Keiji Nagahara & Kōzō Yamamura, eds. JAPAN BEFORE TOKUGAWA: POLITICAL CONSOLIDATION & ECONOMIC GROWTH, 1500-1650. 1981: Princeton University Press. Contains essays on land control and commerce under the warring daimyō and late 16th-century unifiers, urbanization, and overall economic growth.

Delmer M. Brown. MONEY ECONOMY IN MEDIEVAL JAPAN: A STUDY IN THE USE OF COINS. 1951: Yale University Press.

Kōzō Yamamura. "The Growth of Commerce in Medieval Japan," in Kōzō Yamamura, ed. CAMBRIDGE HISTORY OF JAPAN, Volume 3: MEDIEVAL JAPAN (1990: Cambridge University Press), 344-395.

_____. "The Development of Za in Medieval Japan," Business History Review 47.4 (1973), 438-465.

Shōji Kawazoe. "Japan and East Asia," G. Cameron Hurst III, transl., in Kōzō Yamamura, ed. CAMBRIDGE HISTORY OF JAPAN, Volume 3: MEDIEVAL JAPAN (1990: Cambridge University Press), 396-446.

Chaiwat Khamchoo & E. Bruce Reynolds, eds. THAI-JAPANESE RELATIONS IN HISTORICAL PERSPECTIVE. 1988: Institute of Asian Studies, Chulalongkorn University.

Y. T. Wang. OFFICIAL RELATIONS BETWEEN CHINA AND JAPAN, 1368-1549. 1953: Harvard University Press.

Katsumi Mori. "International Relations Between the 10th and 16th Century and the Development of the Japanese International Consciousness," *Acta Asiatica* 2 (1961), 69-93.

_____. "The Beginnings of Overseas Advance of Japanese Merchant Ships," *Acta Asiatica* 23 (1972), 1-24.

Kwan-wai So. JAPANESE PIRACY IN MING CHINA DURING THE 16TH CENTURY. 1975: Michigan State University Press.

Benjamin H. Hazard. "The Formative Years of the *Wakō*," *Monumenta Nipponica* 22.3-4 (1967), 260-277.

Yosaburō Takekoshi. THE STORY OF THE WAKŌ: JAPANESE PIONEERS IN THE SOUTHERN REGIONS. Hideo Watanabe, transl. 1940: Kenkyūsha.

FEUDAL CULTURE BEFORE 1600

H. Paul Varley. "Cultural Life in Medieval Japan," in Kōzō Yamamura, ed. CAMBRIDGE HISTORY OF JAPAN, Volume 3: MEDIEVAL JAPAN (1990: Cambridge University Press), 447-499.

Barbara Ruch. "The Other Side of Culture in Medieval Japan," in Kōzō Yamamura, ed. CAMBRIDGE HISTORY OF JAPAN, Volume 3: MEDIEVAL JAPAN (1990: Cambridge University Press), 500-543.

Daisetz T. Suzuki. ZEN AND JAPANESE CULTURE. 1959: Pantheon. Includes chapters on swordsmanship, Confucianism, haiku, tea ceremony, and attitudes toward nature.

George B. Sansom. JAPAN: A SHORT CULTURAL HISTORY. Revised edition. 1943: Appleton.

Martin Collcutt. FIVE MOUNTAINS: THE RINZAI ZEN MONASTIC INSTITUTION IN MEDIEVAL JAPAN. 1980: Council on East Asian Studies, Harvard University.

Marian Ury. POEMS OF THE FIVE MOUNTAINS: AN INTRODUCTION TO THE LITERATURE OF THE ZEN MONASTERIES. 1992: Center for Japanese Studies, University of Michigan.

William R. LaFleur. THE KARMA OF WORDS: BUDDHISM AND THE LITERARY ARTS IN MEDIEVAL JAPAN. 1983: University of California Press.

Royall Tyler. "Buddhism in Noh," *Japanese Journal of Religious Studies* 14.1 (1987), 19-52.

Steven D. Carter, ed. LITERARY PATRONAGE IN LATE MEDIEVAL JAPAN. 1992: Center for Japanese Studies, University of Michigan.

Neil McMullin. BUDDHISM AND THE STATE IN SIXTEENTH-CENTURY JAPAN. 1985: Princeton University Press.

H. Paul Varley. "Ashikaga Yoshimitsu and the World of Kitayama: Social Change and Shōgunal Patronage in Early Muromachi Japan," in John W. Hall & Takeshi Toyoda, eds. JAPAN IN THE MUROMACHI AGE (1976: University of California Press), 183-204.

John M. Rosenfield. "The Unity of the Three Creeds: A Theme in Japanese Ink Painting of the Fifteenth Century," in Hall & Toyoda, JAPAN IN THE MUROMACHI AGE (1976: University of California Press), 205-226.

Teiji Itō & Paul Novograd. "The Development of Shoin-Style Architecture," in Hall & Toyoda, JAPAN IN THE MUROMACHI AGE (1976: University of California Press), 227-240.

Robert N. Huey. "The Medievalization of Poetic Practice," *Harvard Journal of Asiatic Studies* 50.2 (1990), 651-668.

Earl Miner. "Waka: Features of Its Constitution and Development," *Harvard Journal of Asiatic Studies* 50.2 (1990), 669-706.

Mark Morris. "Waka and Form, Waka and History," *Harvard Journal of Asiatic Studies* 46.2 (1986), 551-610.

Makoto Ōoka. THE COLORS OF POETRY: ESSAYS ON CLASSIC JAPANESE VERSE. 1991: Katydid Books.

Steven D. Carter. THE ROAD TO KOMATSUBARA: A CLASSICAL READING OF THE *RENGA HYAKUIN*. 1987: Council on East Asian Studies, Harvard University.

Donald Keene. "The Comic Tradition in Renga," in Hall & Toyoda, JAPAN IN
    THE MUROMACHI AGE (1976: University of California Press),
    241-278.

_____. "A Neglected Chapter: Courtly Fiction of the Kamakura Period,"
    Monumenta Nipponica 44.1 (1989), 1-30.

_____. TRAVELERS OF A HUNDRED AGES: THE JAPANESE AS
    REVEALED THROUGH 1,000 YEARS OF DIARIES. 1989:
    Henry Holt.

H. Mack Horton. "Saiokuken Sōchō and the Linked-Verse Business,"
    Transactions, Asiatic Society of Japan, 4th series, 1 (1986), 45-78.

_____. "Renga Unbound: Performative Aspects of Japanese Linked Verse,"
    Harvard Journal of Asiatic Studies 53.2 (1993), 443-512.

Barbara Ruch. "Medieval Jongleurs and the Making of a National Literature,"
    in Hall & Toyoda, JAPAN IN THE MUROMACHI AGE (1976:
    University of California Press), 279-310.

Toshihide Akamatsu & Philip Yampolsky. "Muromachi Zen and the Gozan
    System," in Hall & Toyoda, JAPAN IN THE MUROMACHI AGE
    (1976: University of California Press), 313-330.

Stanley Weinstein. 'Rennyō and the Shinshū Revival," in Hall & Toyoda,
    JAPAN IN THE MUROMACHI AGE (1976: University of California
    Press), 331-350.

George Elison & Bardwell L. Smith, eds. WARLORDS, ARTISTS &
    COMMONERS: JAPAN IN THE SIXTEENTH CENTURY. 1981:
    University of Hawaii Press. Includes essays on painting, poetry and
    song, music, and tea.

Margaret H. Childs. "*Chigo Monogatari*: Love Stories or Buddhist Sermons?"
    Monumenta Nipponica 35.2 (1980), 127-152.

Frederick Graham Kavanagh. "Twenty Representative Muromachi-Period Prose
    Narratives: An Analytic Study." 1985: Ph.D. dissertation in Asian
    Languages and Literature, University of Hawaii.

Chieko Irie Mulhern. "*Otogi-zōshi*: Short Stories of the Muromachi Period,"
    Monumenta Nipponica 29.2 (1974), 181-198.

_____. "Cinderella and the Jesuits: An *Otogi-zōshi* Cycle as Christian Literature," *Monumenta Nipponica* 34.4 (1979), 409-448.

Jacqueline Pigeot. "Enumeration in the *Otogi Zōshi* and Its Meaning," *Japan Foundation Newsletter* 18.3 (1991), 1-7.

James T. Araki. "*Otogi-zōshi* and *Nara-ehon*: A Field of Study in Flux," *Monumenta Nipponica* 36.1 (1981), 1-20.

Kakuzō Okakura. THE BOOK OF TEA: A JAPANESE HARMONY OF ART, CULTURE AND THE SIMPLE LIFE. 2nd edition. 1935: Angus & Robertson; 1989: Kōdansha International.

F. G. Notehelfer. "On Idealism and Realism in the Thought of Okakura Tenshin," *Journal of Japanese Studies* 16.2 (1990), 309-353.

Beatrice M. Bodart. "Tea and Counsel: The Political Role of Sen Rikyū," *Monumenta Nipponica* 32.1 (1977), 49-74.

Paul Varley & Isao Kumakura, eds. TEA IN JAPAN: ESSAYS ON THE HISTORY OF CHANOYU. 1989: University of Hawaii Press.

Robert Walker Kramer. "The Tea Cult in History." 1985: Ph.D. dissertation in Far Eastern Languages and Civilizations, University of Chicago.

Susan Matisoff. THE LEGEND OF SEMIMARU, BLIND MUSICIAN OF JAPAN. 1978: Columbia University Press.

James Araki. THE BALLAD-DRAMA OF MEDIEVAL JAPAN. 1964: University of California Press.

Donald Keene. NŌ AND BUNRAKU: TWO FORMS OF JAPANESE THEATRE. 1990: Columbia University Press.

_____ & Hiroshi Kaneko. NŌ: THE CLASSICAL THEATRE OF JAPAN. 1966: Kōdansha International.

Kunio Komparu. THE NOH THEATER: PRINCIPLES & PERSPECTIVES. 1983: Weatherhill.

C. Andrew Gerstle. "The Concept of Tragedy in Japanese Drama," *Japan Review* 1 (1990), 49-72.

Michele Marra. THE AESTHETICS OF DISCONTENT: POLITICS AND
      RECLUSION IN MEDIEVAL JAPANESE LITERATURE. 1991:
      University of Hawaii Press.

Margaret Helen Childs, transl. RETHINKING SORROW: REVELATORY
      TALES OF LATE MEDIEVAL JAPAN. 1991: Center for Japanese
      Studies, University of Michigan.

_____. "The Influence of the Buddhist Practice of *Sange* on Literary Form:
      Revelatory Tales," *Japanese Journal of Religious Studies* 14.1 (1987),
      53-66.

MEDIEVAL LITERATURE
(EXCEPT WAR CHRONICLES) IN TRANSLATION

Edwin A. Cranston, transl. A WAKA ANTHOLOGY. Volume I: THE GEM-
      GLISTENING CUP. 1994: Stanford University Press.

Steven D. Carter, transl. WAITING FOR THE WIND: THIRTY-SIX POETS
      OF JAPAN'S LATE MEDIEVAL AGE. 1989: Columbia University
      Press. *Waka* from ca. 1250-1500.

KENREIMON'IN UKYŌ NO DAIBU SHŪ (12th-13th century)

   • Philip Tudor Harries, transl. THE POETIC MEMOIRS OF LADY
     DAIBU. 1980: Stanford University Press.

   • James G. Wagner. "The *Kenreimon'in Ukyō no Daibu Shū*,"
     Monumenta Nipponica 31.1 (1976), 1-28.

UJI SHŪI MONOGATARI (early 13th century)

   • D. E. Mills, transl. A COLLECTION OF TALES FROM UJI:
     A STUDY AND TRANSLATION OF *UJI SHŪI MONOGATARI*.
     1970: Cambridge University Press.

   • John S. Foster, transl. *"Uji Shūi Monogatari,"* *Monumenta Nipponica*
     20.1-2 (1965) 135-208. Translation of 55 tales.

HŌJŌKI (written in 1212 by Kamo no Chōmei, 1153-1216)

- Arthur L. Sadler, transl. THE TEN FOOT SQUARE HUT AND TALES OF THE HEIKE. 1918 and 1921; reprint edition, 1972: Tuttle.

- Thomas Blenman Hare. "Reading Kamo no Chōmei," *Harvard Journal of Asiatic Studies* 49.1 (1989), 173-228.

MUMYŌSHŌ (written in the early 13th century by Kamo no Chōmei)

- Hilda Katō. THE *MUMYŌSHŌ* OF KAMO NO CHŌMEI AND ITS SIGNIFICANCE IN JAPANESE LITERATURE. 1968: University of British Columbia.

- Michele Marra. "*Mumyōzōshi*: Introduction & Translation," *Monumenta Nipponica* 39.2 (1984), 115-146.

HOSSHINSHŪ (Kamo no Chōmei's tales of wandering monks, early 13th century)

- Rajyashree Pandey. "*Suki* and Religious Awakening: Kamo no Chōmei's *Hosshinshū*," *Monumenta Nipponica* 47.3 (1992), 299-321.

GUKANSHŌ (written in 1219 by Jien, 1155-1225)

- Delmer Brown & Ichirō Ishida. THE FUTURE AND THE PAST: A TRANSLATION AND STUDY OF THE *GUKANSHŌ*, AN INTERPRETATIVE HISTORY OF JAPAN WRITTEN IN 1219. 1978: University of California Press.

- J. Rahder. "Miscellany of Personal Views of an Ignorant Fool (Guk/w/anshō)," *Acta Orientalia* 15 (1936), 173-230.

- H. Paul Varley. "The Place of *Gukanshō* in Japanese Intellectual History," *Monumenta Nipponica* 34.4 (1979), 479-488.

SHOGAKU HYAKUSHU (a sequence of 100 poems by Teika Fujiwara, 1162-1241)

- Roselee Bundy. "Poetic Appreticeship: Fujiwara Teika's *Shogaku Hyakushu*," *Monumenta Nipponica* 45.2 (1990), 157-188.

KINDAI SHŪKA (another collection of poems by Fujiwara Teika)

- Robert H. Brower & Earl Miner, transl. FUJIWARA TEIKA'S "SUPERIOR POEMS OF OUR TIME." 1967: Stanford University Press.

MATSURA NO MIYA MONOGATARI (late 12th-century fiction by Fujiwara Teika)

  • Wayne P. Lammers, transl. THE TALE OF MATSURA: FUJIWARA TEIKA'S EXPERIMENT IN FICTION. 1992: University of Michigan Press.

HYAKUNIN ISSHŪ (famous popular anthology of "100 poems by 100 poets," editorship attributed to Fujiwara Teika in the year 1200)

  • Tom Galt, transl. THE LITTLE TREASURY OF ONE HUNDRED PEOPLE, ONE POEM EACH. 1984: Princeton University Press.

  • Robert H. Brower. FUJIWARA TEIKA'S HUNDRED-POEM SEQUENCE OF THE SHŌJI ERA, 1200. 1978: Monumenta Nipponica Monographs (originally published in 1976 in *Monumenta Nipponica* 31.3 and 31.4).

  • Peter Morse. HOKUSAI: ONE HUNDRED POETS. 1989: Cassell. Includes English translation of *Hyakunin isshū* by Clay MacCauley.

EIGA NO ITTEI (poetic treatise by Fujiwara Tameie, 1198-1275)

  • Robert H. Brower. "The Foremost Style of Poetic Composition: Fujiwara Tameie's *Eiga no Ittei*," *Monumenta Nipponica* 42.4 (1987), 391-429.

KOKON CHOMONJŪ (stories compiled in 1254 by Tachibana Narisue)

  • Yoshiko K. Dykstra. "Notable Tales Old and New: Tachibana Narisue's *Kokon Chomonjū*," *Monumenta Nipponica* 47.4 (1992), 469-493.

BEN NO NAISHI NIKKI (poetic diary of the daughter of Fujiwara Nobuzane, describing life at the court of the mid-13th century emperor Go-Fukakusa)

  • Shirley Yumiko Hulvey. "The Nocturnal Muse: A Study and Partial Translation of *Ben no Naishi nikki*, a Thirteenth Century Poetic Diary." 1989: Ph.D. dissertation in Oriental Languages, University of California.

  • _____. "The Nocturnal Muse: *Ben no Naishi Nikki*," *Monumenta Nipponica* 44.4 (1989), 391-413.

SHASEKISHŪ (late 13th-century collection of Buddhist *setsuwa*, or "tale literature")

- Robert E. Morrell. SAND AND PEBBLES (*SHASEKISHŪ*): THE TALES OF MUJŪ ICHIEN, A VOICE FOR PLURALISM IN KAMAKURA BUDDHISM. 1985: University of New York Press.

UTATANE (written in the mid-13th century by the nun Abutsu, d. 1283)

- John R. Wallace. "Fitful Slumbers: Nun Abutsu's *Utatane*," *Monumenta Nipponica* 43.4 (1988), 391-416.

IZAYOI NIKKI (recounting journey from Kyoto to Kamakura by the nun Abutsu, d. 1283, ca. 1277-1280)

- Edwin O. Reischauer & Joseph Yamagiwa. TRANSLATIONS FROM EARLY JAPANESE LITERATURE (1951: Harvard University Press), 1-135.

Herbert Plutschow & Hideichi Fukuda, transl. FOUR JAPANESE TRAVEL DIARIES OF THE MIDDLE AGES. 1981: *Cornell University East Asia Papers*. Translations of "Takakura-in Itsukushima Gokō Ki" (25-44); "Shinshō Hōshi Nikki" (45-60); "Miyako no Tsuto" (61-76); "Zenkōji Kikō" (77-86).

KINGYOKU UTA-AWASE (a poetry contest ca. 1304 between Kyōgoku Tamekane, 1254-1332, and retired emperor Fushimi, 1265-1317)

- Robert N. Huey. "The Kingyoku Poetry Contest," *Monumenta Nipponica* 42.3 (1987), 299-330.

- _____. "Kyōgoku Tamekane and Poetry in the Late Kamakura Period." 1985: Ph.D. dissertation in Asian Languages, Stanford University.

FUSHIMI-IN NIJŪBAN UTA-AWASE (a poetry contest held ca. 1303-1308)

- Robert N. Huey. "*Fushimi-in Nijūban Uta-awase*," *Monumenta Nipponica* 48.2 (1993), 167-203.

ISE DAIJINGŪ SANKEIKI (14th century)

- Arthur L. Sadler, transl. THE *ISE DAIJINGŪ SANKEIKI*, OR DIARY OF A PILGRIM TO ISE. 1940: Meiji Japan Society.

TOWAZUGATARI ("autobiography" of former imperial concubine, covering 1271-1306)

- Karen Brazell, transl. THE CONFESSIONS OF LADY NIJŌ. 1973: Doubleday-Anchor.

- _____. "*Towazugatari*: Autobiography of a Kamakura Court Lady," *Harvard Journal of Asiatic Studies* 31 (1971), 220-233.

TSUREZUREGUSA (of Yoshida Kenkō, written ca. 1330-1332)

- Donald Keene, transl. ESSAYS IN IDLENESS: THE *TSUREZUREGUSA* OF KENKŌ. 1967: Columbia University Press.

- George B. Sansom, transl. "The *Tsurezuregusa* of Yoshida Kaneyoshi," *Transactions, Asiatic Society of Japan*, 1st series, 39 (1911), 1-146.

- Linda H. Chance. "An Aesthetics of Formlessness: Kenkō's *Tsurezuregusa* and the *Zuihitsu* Genre of Japanese Prose." 1990: Ph.D. dissertation in East Asian Languages and Cultures, UCLA.

JINNŌ SHŌTŌKI ("Record of the Legitimate Succession of the Divine Emperors" by Kitabatake Chikafusa, 1293-1354)

- H. Paul Varley, transl. A CHRONICLE OF GODS AND KINGS: *JINNŌ SHŌTŌKI* OF KITABATAKE CHIKAFUSA. 1980: Columbia University Press.

SHŌTETSU MONOGATARI (poetic miscellany by a follower of Shōtetsu, 1381-1459)

- Robert H. Brower, transl. CONVERSATIONS WITH SHŌTETSU. 1992: University of Michigan Press.

SHIRAKAWA KIKŌ (travel record written in 1468 by the *renga* master Sōgi, 1421-1502)

- Steven D. Carter. "Sōgi in the East Country: *Shirakawa Kikō*," *Monumenta Nipponica* 42.2 (1987), 167-209.

MISCELLANEOUS *OTOGI ZŌSHI* TALES

- Royall Tyler, transl. JAPANESE FOLK TALES. 1987: Pantheon.

- Virginia Skord, transl. TALES OF TEARS AND LAUGHTER: SHORT FICTION OF MEDIEVAL JAPAN. 1991: University of Hawaii Press. A collection of 13 *otogi-zōshi*.

• _____. "*Monogusa Tarō:* From Rags to Riches and Beyond," *Monumenta Nipponica* 44.2 (1989), 171-198.

• Margaret H. Childs. "Didacticism in Medieval Short Stories: *Hatsuse Monogatari* and *Akimichi,*" *Monumenta Nipponica* 42.3 (1987), 253-288.

• _____. RETHINKING SORROW: REVELATORY TALES OF LATE MEDIEVAL JAPAN. 1991: Center for Japanese Studies, University of Michigan.

NŌ THEATER AND *KYŌGEN*

• Donald Keene, transl. TWENTY PLAYS OF THE *NŌ* THEATRE. 1970: Columbia University Press.

• _____ & Hiroshi Kaneko. *NŌ*: THE CLASSICAL THEATER OF JAPAN. 1966: Kōdansha International.

• Arthur Waley, transl. THE *NŌ* PLAYS OF JAPAN. 1911: Allen & Unwin.

• J. Thomas Rimer & Masakazu Yamazaki, transl. ON THE ART OF THE *NŌ* DRAMA: THE MAJOR TREATISES OF ZEAMI. 1984: Princeton University Press. The nine major treatises of Zeami Motokiyo (1363-1443), the great master of the *Nō* theater.

• Michiko Yusa. "*Riken no Ken*: Zeami's Theory of Acting and Theatrical Appreciation," *Monumenta Nipponica* 42.3 (1987), 330-345.

• Royall Tyler. "Buddhism in Noh," *Japanese Journal of Religious Studies* 14.1 (1987), 19-52.

• _____. JAPANESE NŌ DRAMAS. 1992: Penguin.

• _____. "The *Nō* Play *Matsukaze* as a Transformation of *Genji monogatari,*" *Journal of Japanese Studies* 20.2 (1994), 377-422.

• Chifumi Shimazaki, transl. WARRIOR GHOST PLAYS FROM THE JAPANESE NOH THEATRE. 1993: Cornell University Press.

• Shelley Fenno Quinn. "How to Write a Noh Play: Zeami's *Sandō,*" *Monumenta Nipponica* 48.1 (1993), 53-88.

- Mae J. Smethurst. THE ARTISTRY OF AESCHYLUS AND ZEAMI: A COMPARATIVE STUDY OF GREEK TRAGEDY AND NŌ. 1989: Princeton University Press.

- Janet Emily Goff. NOH DRAMA AND THE TALE OF GENJI: THE ART OF ALLUSION IN FIFTEEN CLASSICAL PLAYS. 1991: Princeton University Press.

- Kun Anthony Namkung. "The Aesthetics of Power: Noh and Society in the Unification of Japan." 1986: Ph.D. dissertation in History, University of California.

- Carol Ann Morley. TRANSFORMATION, MIRACLES, AND MISCHIEF: THE MOUNTAIN PRIEST PLAYS OF KYŌGEN. 1993: Cornell University Press.

- Carolyn Martha Haynes. "Parody in the Maikyōgen and Monogurui Kyōgen." 1988: Ph.D. dissertation in East Asian Literature, Cornell University.

- _____. "Parody in Kyōgen: Makura Monogurui and Tako," *Monumenta Nipponica* 39.3 (1984), 261-280.

- Ury Eppstein. "The Stage Observed: Western Attitudes toward Japanese Theatre," *Monumenta Nipponica* 48.2 (1993), 147-166.

THE "WAY OF THE WARRIOR":
General Accounts of Samurai Values & Practices

Martin C. Collcutt. "Bushidō," KŌDANSHA ENCYCLOPEDIA OF JAPAN 1: 221-223.

R. Tsunoda et al., SOURCES OF JAPANESE TRADITION (1958: Columbia University Press), chapters 15-24.

Harold Bolitho. "The Myth of the Samurai," in Alan Rix & Ross Mouer, eds. JAPAN'S IMPACT ON THE WORLD (1984: Japanese Studies Association of Australia), 1-9.

H. Paul Varley. SAMURAI. 1970: Delacorte.

_____. WARRIORS OF JAPAN, AS PORTRAYED IN THE WAR TALES. 1994: University of Hawaii Press.

Ivan Morris. THE NOBILITY OF FAILURE: TRAGIC HEROES IN THE HISTORY OF JAPAN. 1975: Holt, Rinehart & Winston.

William Wayne Farris. HEAVENLY WARRIORS: THE EVOLUTION OF JAPAN'S MILITARY, 500-1300. 1992: Council on East Asian Studies, Harvard University.

Karl F. Friday. HIRED SWORDS: THE RISE OF PRIVATE WARRIOR POWER IN EARLY JAPAN. 1992: Stanford University Press.

_____. "Teeth and Claws: Provincial Warriors and the Heian Court," *Monumenta Nipponica* 43.2 (1988), 153-185.

_____. "Valorous Butchers: The Art of War during the Golden Age of the Samurai," *Japan Forum* 5.1 (1993), 1-19.

Anthony J. Bryant. THE SAMURAI: WARRIORS OF MEDIEVAL JAPAN, 940-1600. 1989: Osprey.

Louis Frederic. DAILY LIFE IN JAPAN IN THE AGE OF THE SAMURAI, 1185-1603. 1972: Praeger.

Kenneth Dean Butler. "The *Heike Monogatari* and the Japanese Warrior Ethic," *Harvard Journal of Asiatic Studies* 29 (1969), 93-108.

Tadashi Hasegawa. "The Early Stages of the *Heike Monogatari*," *Monumenta Nipponica* 22.1-2 (1967), 65-81.

Stephen R. Turnbull. THE SAMURAI: A MILITARY HISTORY. 1977: Macmillan.

_____. THE BOOK OF THE SAMURAI: THE WARRIOR CLASS OF JAPAN. 1982: Arco.

_____. BATTLES OF THE SAMURAI. 1987: Arms and Armour Press.

_____. SAMURAI WARRIORS. 1987: Blandford Press.

_____. SAMURAI WARLORDS: THE BOOK OF THE DAIMYŌ. 1989: Blandford Press; 1992: Firebird Books.

Richard Storry. THE WAY OF THE SAMURAI. 1978: Putnam.

Captain F. Brinkley. SAMURAI: THE INVINCIBLE WARRIORS. 1975: Ohara.

Michael Gibson. THE SAMURAI OF JAPAN. 1969: Wayland.

Ronald L. Tarnstrom. THE WARS OF JAPAN. 1992: Trogen Books.

Daisetz T. Suzuki. ZEN AND JAPANESE CULTURE. 1959: Pantheon. See especially chapters 4 ("Zen and the Samurai"), and 5-6 ("Zen and Swordmanship").

Joe Hyams. ZEN IN THE MARTIAL ARTS. 1979: Tarcher.

Winston L. King. ZEN AND THE WAY OF THE SWORD: ARMING THE SAMURAI PSYCHE. 1993: Oxford University Press.

Inazō Nitobe. BUSHIDŌ, THE SOUL OF JAPAN. 1905: Putnam.

Jack Seward. HARA-KIRI: JAPANESE RITUAL SUICIDE. 1968: Tuttle.

John Allyn. THE FORTY-SEVEN RŌNIN STORY. 1970: Tuttle.

Kailen Nukariya. THE RELIGION OF THE SAMURAI. 1913: Luzac.

Takuan Sōhō. THE UNFETTERED MIND: WRITINGS OF THE ZEN MASTER TO THE SWORD MASTER. William Scott Wilson, transl. 1986: Kōdansha International.

Fumiko Miyazaki. "Religious Life of the Kamakura Bushi: Kumagai Naozane and His Descendants," *Monumenta Nipponica* 47.4 (1992), 435-467.

Tōru Sagara. "The Spiritual Strength and Independence in Bushidō," *Acta Asiatica* 23 (1973), 91-106.

Robert N. Bellah. "Bushidō," in his TOKUGAWA RELIGION (1957: Free Press), 90-106.

Tasuke Kawakami. "Bushidō in Its Formative Period," *Annals of the Hitotsubashi Academy* 3 (1952), 65-83.

Noel Perrin. GIVING UP THE GUN: JAPAN'S REVERSION TO THE SWORD, 1543-1879. 1979: Godine.

Caryl Callahan. "Tales of Samurai Honor: Saikaku's *Buke Giri Monogatari*," *Monumenta Nipponica* 34.1 (1979), 1-20. Tales by a famous 17th-century satirist.

Saikaku Ihara. IHARA SAIKAKU: TALES OF SAMURAI HONOR *(BUKE GIRI MONOGATARI)*. Caryl Callahan, transl. 1982: Monumenta Nipponica Monographs.

_____. COMRADE LOVES OF THE SAMURAI. E. Powys Mathers, transl. 1981: Tuttle.

Musashi Miyamoto. A BOOK OF FIVE RINGS: THE CLASSIC GUIDE TO STRATEGY. Victor Harris, transl. 1974: Overlook. A translation of *Go Rin no Sho* by Musashi Miyamoto, Japan's greatest swordsman, written shortly before his death in 1645.

Thomas F. Cleary. THE JAPANESE ART OF WAR: UNDERSTANDING THE CULTURE OF STRATEGY. 1991: Shambala.

Tsunetomo Yamamoto. *HAGAKURE*: THE BOOK OF THE SAMURAI. William Scott Wilson, transl. 1979: Kōdansha International. A translation of a classic statement of the "way of death," written in 1716.

William R. LaFleur. "Death and Japanese Thought: The Truth and Beauty of Impermanence", in Frederick Holck, ed. DEATH AND EASTERN THOUGHT: UNDERSTANDING DEATH IN EASTERN RELIGIONS AND PHILOSOPHIES (1974: Abingdon), 226-256.

Winston King. "Practicing Dying: The Samurai-Zen Death Techniques of Suzuki Shōsan," in Frank Reynolds & Earle Waugh, eds. RELIGIOUS ENCOUNTERS WITH DEATH (1977: Pennsyvalnia State University), 143-158.

THE "WAY OF THE WARRIOR":
War Tales in Translation

KONJAKU MONOGATARI (popular tales collected in early 12th century)

• William Ritchie Wilson, transl. "The Way of the Bow and Arrow: The Japanese Warrior in *Konjaku Monogatari*," *Monumenta Nipponica* 28.2 (1973), 177-234.

SHŌMONKI (Japan's earliest war chronicle, concerning events culminating in 940)

- Judith N. Rabinovitch, transl. *SHŌMONKI:* THE STORY OF MASAKADO'S REBELLION. 1986: Monumenta Nipponica Monographs.

- Giuliana Stramigioli. "Preliminary Notes on the *Masakado-ki* and the Taira no Masakado Story," *Monumenta Nipponica* 28.3 (1978), 261-293.

MUTSU WAKI (mid 11th-century campaign)

- Helen C. McCullough, transl. "A Tale of Mutsu," *Harvard Journal of Asiatic Studies* 25 (1964-5), 178-211.

HŌGEN MONOGATARI (conflict of 1156)

- William R. Wilson, transl. *HŌGEN MONOGATARI*, TALE OF THE DISORDER IN HŌGEN. 1971: Monumenta Nipponica Monographs.

HEIJI MONOGATARI (conflict of 1159-1160)

- Edwin O. Reischauer & Joseph Yamagiwa, transl. TRANSLATIONS FROM EARLY JAPANESE LITERATURE (1951: Harvard University Press), 377-457.

- Marisa Chalitpatananggune. "*Heiji Monogatari*: A Study and Annotated Translation of the Oldest Text." 1987: Ph.D. dissertation in Oriental Languages, University of California.

HEIKE MONOGATARI (the epic clash of the Taira and Minamoto clans, 1180-1185)

- Arthur L. Sadler, transl. THE TEN FOOT SQUARE HUT AND TALES OF THE HEIKE. 1972: Tuttle. Abridged version of translation originally published in *Transactions, Asiatic Society of Japan* volumes of 1918 and 1921.

- Hiroshi Kitagawa & Bruce T. Tsuchida, transl. THE TALE OF THE HEIKE. 2 volumes. 1975: University of Tokyo Press.

- Helen Craig McCullough, transl. THE TALE OF THE HEIKE. 1988: Stanford University Press.

AZUMA KAGAMI (about the founding of the Kamakura Shōgunate)

- Minoru Shinoda. THE FOUNDING OF THE KAMAKURA SHŌGUNATE, 1180-1185—WITH SELECTED TRANSLATIONS FROM THE *AZUMA KAGAMI*. 1960: Columbia University Press.

- Martin Collcutt. "Religion in the Formation of the Kamakura Bakufu: As Seen through the *Azuma Kagami*," *Japan Review* 5 (1994), 55-86.

- William McCullough, transl. "The *Azuma Kagami* Account of the Shōkyū War," *Monumenta Nipponica* 23.1-2 (1968), 102-155.

SHŌKYŪKI (the abortive war against the Bakufu led by Emperor Go-Toba)

- William McCullough, transl. "*Shōkyūki*: An Account of the Shōkyū War of 1221," *Monumenta Nipponica* 19.1-2 and 19.3-4 (1964), 163-215, 420-455

- John S. Brownlee. "The Shōkyū War and the Political Rise of the Warriors," *Monumenta Nipponica* 24.1-2 (1969), 59-77

TAIHEIKI (the great chronicle about the 14th century transition from Kamakura to Ashikaga rule)

- Helen C. McCullough, transl. THE *TAIHEIKI*: A CHRONICLE OF MEDIEVAL JAPAN. 1959: Columbia University Press.

SOGA MONOGATARI (c. 1340; a tale of the Soga brothers' late-12th century quest to avenge their father's murder)

- Thomas J. Cogan, transl. THE TALE OF THE SOGA BROTHERS. 1987: University of Tokyo Press.

- Laurence Richard Kominz. "The Soga Revenge Story: Tradition and Innovation in Japanese Drama." 1985: Ph.D. dissertation in East Asian Languages and Cultures, Columbia University.

ŌNINKI (civil upheaval of 1467-1477 that led to the "Period of Warring States")

- H. Paul Varley. THE ŌNIN WAR: HISTORY OF ITS ORIGINS AND BACKGROUND, WITH A SELECTIVE TRANSLATION OF THE CHRONICLES OF ŌNIN. 1967: Columbia University Press.

GIKEIKI (15th-century account of Minamoto Yoshitsune, the tragic hero of the 12th century)

• Helen C. McCullough, transl. YOSHITSUNE: A FIFTEENTH-CENTURY JAPANESE CHRONICLE. 1965: Stanford University Press.

THE "WAY OF THE WARRIOR":
Warrior Laws & Codes of Conduct

William Scott Wilson, transl. IDEALS OF THE SAMURAI: WRITINGS OF JAPANESE WARRIORS. 1982: Ohara. Translations of family codes or clan precepts (*kakun*) dating from approximately 1250 to 1600.

Jeffrey Mass. THE DEVELOPMENT OF KAMAKURA RULE, 1180-1250: A HISTORY WITH DOCUMENTS. 1979: Stanford University Press.

J. C. Hall. "Japanese Feudal Laws (*Go Seibai Shikimoku*)," *Transactions, Asiatic Society of Japan*, 1st series, 34 (1906), 1-44.

Carl Steenstrup. HŌJŌ SHIGETOKI (1198-1261) AND HIS ROLE IN THE HISTORY OF POLITICAL AND ETHICAL IDEAS IN JAPAN. 1979: Curzon Press (Scandinavian Institute of Asian Studies Monograph Series 41). Includes translations of "Letter to Nagatoki" (139-157) and "Gokurakuji Letter" (158-198).

_____. "The Legal System of Japan at the End of the Kamakura Period," in Brian E. McKnight, ed. LAW AND THE STATE IN TRADITIONAL EAST ASIA: SIX STUDIES ON THE SOURCES OF EAST ASIAN LAW (1987: University of Hawaii Press), 73-110.

John Brownlee. "*Jikkinshō*: A Miscellany of Ten Maxims," *Monumenta Nipponica* 29.2 (1974), 121-162.

Delmer M. Brown. "The Japanese *Tokusei* of 1297," *Harvard Journal of Asiatic Studies* 12 (1949), 188-206.

Kenneth A. Grossberg & Nobuhisa Kanamoto, transl. THE LAWS OF THE MUROMACHI BAKUFU. 1981: Monumenta Nipponica Monographs. Annotated translation of *Kemmu Shikimoku* (1336) and *Muromachi Bakufu Tsuikahō*.

J. C. Hall. "Japanese Feudal Laws, II (*Kemmu Shikimoku*)," *Transactions, Asiatic Society of Japan*, 1st series, 36 (1908), 3-25.

David John Lu. *"Kemmu Shikimoku,"* in his SOURCES OF JAPANESE HISTORY (1974: McGraw-Hill), volume 1, 150-152.

Carl Steenstrup. *"Sata Mirensho*: A Fourteenth-Century Law Primer," *Monumenta Nipponica* 35.4 (1980), 337-346.

_____. "The Imagawa Letter: A Muromachi Warrior's Code of Conduct Which Became a Tokugawa Schoolbook," *Monumenta Nipponica* 28.3 (1973), 295-316.

David John Lu. "Seventeen-Article Injunction of Asakura Toshikage, c. 1480," in his SOURCES OF JAPANESE HISTORY (1974: McGraw-Hill), volume 1, 171-174.

Carl Steenstrup. "Hōjō Sōun's Twenty-One Articles: The Code of Conduct of the Odawara Hōjō," *Monumenta Nipponica* 29.3 (1974), 283-303.

David John Lu. "Hōjō Sōun's Twenty-One Article Injunction for His Vassals, c. 1495," in his SOURCES OF JAPANESE HISTORY (1974: McGraw-Hill), volume 1, 174-175.

_____. "Takeda Shingen's House Law," in his SOURCES OF JAPANESE HISTORY (1974: McGraw-Hill), volume 1, 175-176. Also a complete translation by W. Rohl in *Oriens Extremus* 6 (1959), 210-235, totaling 99 articles.

_____. "The Hundred Article Code of Chōsokabe, 1597," in his SOURCES OF JAPANESE HISTORY (1974: McGraw-Hill), volume 1, 177-181.

James Murdoch. "Testament of Ieyasu," in his A HISTORY OF JAPAN (1925-1926: Ungar), volume 3, 796-814.

S. Gubbins, transl. "A Samurai Manual," *Transactions and Proceedings of the Japan Society, London* 9 (1910), 140-151.

J. C. Hall, transl. "Teijō's Family Instruction (1763): A Samurai's Ethical Bequest to His Posterity," *Transactions and Proceedings of the Japan Society, London* 14 (1915), 128-156.

Donald Keene, transl. CHŪSHINGURA. 1971: Columbia University Press.

Arthur L. Sadler, transl. THE BEGINNER'S BOOK OF BUSHIDŌ BY DAIDŌJI YŪZAN *(BUDŌ SHOSHINSHŪ)*. 1941: Kokusai Bunka Shinkōkai.

Tsunetomo Yamamoto. *HAGAKURE*: THE BOOK OF THE SAMURAI. William Scott Wilson, transl. 1979: Kōdansha International. A translation of a classic statement of the "way of death," written in 1716.

Kathryn Sparling, transl. THE WAY OF THE SAMURAI: YUKIO MISHIMA ON *HAGAKURE* IN MODERN LIFE. 1977: Basic Books.

Arai Hakuseki. THE SWORD BOOK IN *HONCHŌ GUNGIKŌ* OF ARAI HAKUSEKI & THE BOOK OF *SAME* [Shark Skin]: *KŌ HI SEI GI* OF INABA TSURIO. Henri L. Joly & Hogitarō Inada, transl. & ed. 1913; reprinted by Tuttle.

Musashi Miyamoto. A BOOK OF FIVE RINGS: THE CLASSIC GUIDE TO STRATEGY. Victor Harris, transl. 1974: Overlook.

Walter Dening. JAPAN IN DAYS OF YORE. 1976: East-West Publications.

Ernest W. Clement. "Instructions of a Mito Prince to His Retainers," *Transactions, Asiatic Society of Japan*, 1st series, 26 (1898), 115-153.

THE "WAY OF THE WARRIOR": The Martial Arts

Oscar Ratti & Adele Westbrook. SECRETS OF THE SAMURAI: A SURVEY OF THE MARTIAL ARTS OF FEUDAL JAPAN. 1974: Tuttle.

John J. Donohue. THE FORGE OF THE SPIRIT: STRUCTURE, MOTION, AND MEANING IN THE JAPANESE MARTIAL TRADITION. 1991: Garland. An anthropological survey of Japan's martial arts tradition.

Stephen Turnbull. THE LONE SAMURAI AND THE MARTIAL ARTS. 1990: Firebird Books.

Joe Hyams. ZEN IN THE MARTIAL ARTS. 1979: Tarcher.

Takuan Sōhō. THE UNFETTERED MIND: WRITINGS OF THE ZEN MASTER TO THE SWORD MASTER. William Scott Wilson, transl. 1986: Kōdansha International.

Donn F. Draeger. CLASSICAL BUJUTSU. 1973: Weatherhill.

_____. CLASSICAL BUDŌ. 1974: Weatherhill.

_____ & Robert W. Smith. COMPREHENSIVE ASIAN FIGHTING ARTS. 1980: Kōdansha International.

_____ & Gordon Warner. JAPANESE SWORDSMANSHIP: TECHNIQUE AND PRACTICE. 1982: Weatherhill.

Winston L. King. ZEN AND THE WAY OF THE SWORD: ARMING THE SAMURAI PSYCHE. 1993: Oxford University Press.

Kanzan Satō. THE JAPANESE SWORD. 1983: Kodansha International.

Charles R. Watrall. THE ARTS OF THE JAPANESE SWORD. 1974: Norman Mackenzie Art Gallery.

Basil W. Robinson. THE ARTS OF THE JAPANESE SWORD. 1961: Tuttle.

John M. Yumoto. THE SAMURAI SWORD: A HANDBOOK. 1959: Tuttle.

L. J. Anderson. JAPANESE ARMOUR. 1968: Lionel Leventhal.

Masaaki Hatsumi. NINJUTSU: HISTORY AND TRADITION. 1981: Unique.

Donn F. Draeger. NINJUTSU: THE ART OF INVISIBILITY. 1977: Lotus Press.

Stephen Turnbull. NINJA: THE TRUE STORY OF JAPAN'S SECRET WARRIOR CULT. 1992: Firebird Books.

Bruce A. Haines. KARATE'S HISTORY AND TRADITIONS. 1968: Tuttle.

John Stevens, transl. & ed. AIKIDŌ: THE SPIRITUAL DIMENSION. 1985: Kōdansha International. Consists partly of writings by Ueshiba Morihei (1883-1969), the founder of *aikidō*.

P. L. Cuyler. SUMŌ: FROM RITE TO SPORT. 1979: Weatherhill.

RELIGION: General Works
[See items marked * for more detailed bibliographies]

*Joseph M. Kitagawa. RELIGION IN JAPANESE HISTORY. 1990: Columbia University Press.

*____. "The Religions of Japan," in Charles J. Adams, ed. A READER'S GUIDE
TO THE GREAT RELIGIONS (1965: Free Press), 161-190.

_____. "Religions of Japan," in Wing-tsit Chan, et al., THE GREAT ASIAN
RELIGIONS (1969: Macmillan), 231-305.

_____. ON UNDERSTANDING JAPANESE RELIGION. 1987: Princeton
University Press. A collection of essays.

*H. Byron Earhart. JAPANESE RELIGION: UNITY AND DIVERSITY.
3rd edition. 1982: Wadsworth.

_____, ed. RELIGION IN THE JAPANESE EXPERIENCE: SOURCES AND
INTERPRETATIONS. 1974: Dickenson.

Ichirō Hori, ed. JAPANESE RELIGION: A SURVEY BY THE AGENCY FOR
CULTURAL AFFAIRS. 1972: Kōdansha International.

Wm. Theodore DeBary. "Religion," in Arthur Tiedemann, ed. AN INTRO-
DUCTION TO JAPANESE CIVILIZATION (1974: Heath), 309-328.

Masaharu Anesaki. HISTORY OF JAPANESE RELIGION. 1930; reprint
edition, 1963: Tuttle.

_____. RELIGIOUS LIFE OF THE JAPANESE PEOPLE. 1961: Kokusai
Bunka Shinkōkai.

Ian Reader, Esben Andreason, & Finn Stefansson. JAPANESE RELIGIONS:
PAST AND PRESENT. 1993: University of Hawaii Press.

Ryūsaku Tsunoda, Wm. Theodore DeBary & Donald Keene, eds. SOURCES
OF JAPANESE TRADITION. 1958: Columbia University Press.
See especially chapters 2 (early Shintō), 5 (Nara Buddhism), 6-8 (Heian
Buddhism), 10-13 (Buddhism and Shintō in the Medieval Period).

Alfred Bloom. "Japan: Religion of a Sacred People in a Sacred Land," in
W. Richard Comstock, ed. RELIGION AND MAN (1971: Harper &
Row), 336-394.

Peter Nosco, ed. THE EMPEROR SYSTEM AND RELIGION IN JAPAN.
Japanese Journal of Religious Studies 17.2-17.3 (1990). Special
double issue.

Fumiko Miyazaki. "Religious Life of the Kamakura Bushi: Kumagai Naozane
and His Descendants," *Monumenta Nipponica* 47.4 (1992), 435-467.

Masahide Bitō. "Thought and Religion, 1550-1700," Kate Wildman Nakai, transl., in John Whitney Hall, ed. CAMBRIDGE HISTORY OF JAPAN, Volume 4: EARLY MODERN JAPAN (1991: Cambridge University Press), 373-424.

Winston Bradley Davis. JAPANESE RELIGION AND SOCIETY: PARADIGMS OF STRUCTURE AND CHANGE. 1992: State University of New York Press.

Mark R. Mullins, Susumu Shimazono, & Paul L. Swanson, eds. RELIGION AND SOCIETY IN MODERN JAPAN: SELECTED READINGS. 1993: Asian Humanities Press.

Neil McMullin. "Historical and Historiographical Issues in the Study of Pre-Modern Japanese Religions," *Japanese Journal of Religious Studies* 16.1 (1989), 3-40.

Mark J. Hudson & Simon Kaner, eds. "Archeological Approaches to Ritual and Religion in Japan," *Japanese Journal of Religious Studies* 19.2-19.3 (1992). Special double issue.

RELIGION: Shintō

Takashi Matsumae. "Early Kami Worship," in Delmer M. Brown ed. CAMBRIDGE HISTORY OF JAPAN, Volume 1: ANCIENT JAPAN (1993: Cambridge University Press), 317-358.

Allan G. Grapard. "Shintō," KŌDANSHA ENCYCLOPEDIA OF JAPAN 7: 125-132.

_____. "The Shintō of Yoshida Kanetomo," *Monumenta Nipponica* 47.1 (1992), 27-58.

_____. *"Yuiitsu Shintō Myōbō Yōshū," Monumenta Nipponica* 47.2 (1992), 137-161. Translation of Yoshida Kanetomo's ca. 1485 work.

_____. THE PROTOCOL OF THE GODS: A STUDY OF THE KASUGA CULT IN JAPANESE HISTORY. 1992: University of California Press. A study of the relations between Shintō and Buddhism, centering on Kasuga Shrine and Kōfukuji.

Royall Tyler, transl. THE MIRACLES OF THE KASUGA DEITY. 1990: Columbia University Press.

Toshio Kuroda. "Shintō in the History of Japanese Religion," *Journal of Japanese Studies* 7.1 (1981), 1-21.

Genchi Katō. A STUDY OF SHINTŌ: THE RELIGION OF THE JAPANESE NATION. 1926: Barnes & Noble.

Sokyō Ono with William P. Woodard. SHINTŌ, THE KAMI WAY. 1962: Tuttle.

Robert J. Smith. ANCESTOR WORSHIP IN CONTEMPORARY JAPAN. 1974: Stanford University Press. See especially chapters 1 and 2.

Keiji Iwata. "The Evolution of the *Kami* Cult," *Acta Asiatica* 61 (1991), 47-67.

D. C. Holtom. "The Meaning of *Kami*," *Monumenta Nipponica* 3.1 and 3.2 (1940), 1-26, 392-413; and *Monumenta Nipponica* 4.2 (1941), 351-394.

_____. THE NATIONAL FAITH OF JAPAN: A STUDY IN MODERN SHINTŌ. 1938: Dutton.

Jean Herbert. SHINTŌ: THE FOUNTAINHEAD OF JAPAN. 1967: Allen & Unwin.

Floyd Hiatt Ross. SHINTŌ, THE WAY OF JAPAN. 1965: Beacon.

Tsunetsugu Muraoka. STUDIES IN SHINTŌ THOUGHT. 1964: Japanese National Commission for UNESCO.

Joseph W. Mason. THE MEANING OF SHINTŌ: THE PRIMEVAL FOUNDATIONS OF CREATIVE SPIRIT IN MODERN JAPAN. 1935: Dutton.

Joseph J. Spae. SHINTŌ MAN. 1972: Oriens Institute for Religious Research.

Mark Teeuwen. "Attaining Union with the Gods: The Secret Books of Watarai Shintō," *Monumenta Nipponica* 48.2 (1993), 225-245.

Haruki Kageyama. THE ARTS OF SHINTŌ. 1973: Weatherhill.

Toshio Akima. "The Origins of the Grand Shrine of Ise and the Cult of the Sun Goddess Amaterasu Ōmikami," *Japan Review* 4 (1993), 141-198.

Kenzō Tange & Teiji Itoh. ISE: PROTOTYPE OF JAPANESE ARCHITECTURE. 1965: Massachusetts Institute of Technology Press.

Shōji Okada. "The Development of State Ritual in Ancient Japan," *Acta Asiatica* 51 (1987), 22-41.

Donald L. Philippi, transl. *NORITO*: A NEW TRANSLATION OF THE ANCIENT JAPANESE RITUAL PRAYERS. 1959: Kokugakuin. Reissued, with new preface by Joseph M. Kitagawa, as NORITO: A TRANSLATION OF THE ANCIENT JAPANESE RITUAL PRAYERS (1990: Princeton University Press).

Genchi Katō & Hikoshirō Hoshino, transl. *KOGOSHŪI*: GLEANINGS FROM ANCIENT STORIES. 1926: Barnes & Noble. Memorial presented in 807, revealing Shintō rites and customs.

Felicia Bock, transl. *ENGI-SHIKI*: PROCEDURES OF THE ENGI ERA. 2 volumes. 1970, 1972: Monumenta Nipponica Monographs. A valuable translation of Shintō prayers as recorded in the 9th century.

_____. "The Great Feast of the Enthronement," *Monumenta Nipponica* 45.1 (1990), 27-38.

_____. "The Enthronement Rites: The Text of the *Engishiki*, 927," *Monumenta Nipponica* 45.3 (1990), 307-337.

Nicola Liscutin. "*Daijōsai*, The Great Festival of Tasting the New Fruits: Some Aspects of Its History and Meaning," *Transactions, Asiatic Society of Japan*, 4th series, 5 (1990), 25-52.

Karl Florenz. "Ancient Japanese Rituals," *Transactions, Asiatic Society of Japan*, 1st series, 27 (1900), 1-112.

Robert S. Ellwood. THE FEAST OF KINGSHIP: ACCESSION CEREMONIES IN ANCIENT JAPAN. 1973: Monumenta Nipponica Monographs.

D. C. Holtom. THE JAPANESE ENTHRONEMENT CEREMONIES, WITH AN ACCOUNT OF THE IMPERIAL REGALIA. 1928; reprint edition, 1972: Monumenta Nipponica Monographs.

RELIGION: Buddhism

Kōyū Sonoda, with Delmer M. Brown. "Early Buddha Worship," in Delmer M.
Brown ed. CAMBRIDGE HISTORY OF JAPAN, Volume 1:
ANCIENT JAPAN (1993: Cambridge University Press), 359-414.

Hajime Nakamura. "Buddhism," KŌDANSHA ENCYCLOPEDIA OF JAPAN
1: 176-180.

Joseph M. Kitagawa. "The Buddhist Transformation in Japan," *History of
Religions* 4 (1965), 319-336.

Heinrich Dumoulin. UNDERSTANDING BUDDHISM: KEY THEMES.
Transl. & adapted by Joseph S. O'Leary. 1993: Weatherhill.

Daigan & Alicia Matsunaga. FOUNDATION OF JAPANESE BUDDHISM.
2 volumes. 1974, 1976: Buddhist Books International.

Alicia Matsunaga. THE BUDDHIST PHILOSOPHY OF ASSIMILATION:
THE HISTORICAL DEVELOPMENT OF THE HONJI-SUIJAKU
THEORY. 1969: Monumenta Nipponica Monographs.

Ryūsaku Tsunoda et al. SOURCES OF JAPANESE TRADITION. 1958:
Columbia University Press. See chapters 5 (Nara), 6 (Tendai), 7 and 8
(Esoteric), 10 (Pure Land), 11 (Nichiren), and 12 (Zen).

Charles Eliot. JAPANESE BUDDHISM. 1935; reprint edition, 1959:
Routledge & Kegan Paul.

E. Dale Saunders. BUDDHISM IN JAPAN. 1964: University of Pennsylvania
Press.

Kenneth W. Morgan, ed. THE PATH OF THE BUDDHA. 1956: Ronald.
See especially 307-363.

Shōko Watanabe. JAPANESE BUDDHISM: A CRITICAL APPRAISAL.
1968: Kokusai Bunka Shinkōkai.

Wm. Theodore DeBary, ed. THE BUDDHIST TRADITION IN INDIA, CHINA,
AND JAPAN. 1969: Modern Library.

Diana Y. Paul. WOMEN IN BUDDHISM: IMAGES OF THE FEMININE IN
THE MAHAYANA TRADITION. 1985: Stanford University Press.

Michele Marra. "The Buddhist Mythmaking of Defilement: Sacred Courtesans in Medieval Japan," *Journal of Asian Studies* 52.1 (1993), 49-65.

J. H. Kamstra. ENCOUNTER OR SYNCRETISM: THE INITIAL GROWTH OF JAPANESE BUDDHISM. 1967: Brill.

Marinus Willem de Visser. ANCIENT BUDDHISM IN JAPAN: SUTRAS AND CEREMONIES IN THE SEVENTH AND EIGHTH CENTURIES A.D. AND THEIR HISTORY IN LATER TIMES. 2 volumes. 1935: Brill.

Shinshō Hanayama. "Prince Shōtoku and Japanese Buddhism," *Philosophical Studies of Japan* 4 (1963), 23-48.

Edwin O. Reischauer, transl. ENNIN'S DIARY: THE RECORD OF A PILGRIMAGE TO CHINA IN SEARCH OF THE LAW. 1955: Ronald.

_____. ENNIN'S TRAVELS IN T'ANG CHINA. 1955: Ronald.

Roy Andrew Miller. THE FOOTPRINTS OF THE BUDDHA: AN EIGHTH-CENTURY OLD JAPANESE POETIC SEQUENCE. 1975: American Oriental Society.

Fumihiko Seki. "Annen: The Philospher Who Japanized Buddhism," *Acta Asiatica* 66 (1994), 69-86.

Kyōko Motomochi Nakamura, transl. MIRACULOUS STORIES FROM THE JAPANESE BUDDHIST TRADITION. THE *NIHON RYŌIKI* OF THE MONK KYŌKAI. 1973: Harvard University Press.

Yoshito S. Hakeda. KŪKAI: MAJOR WORKS. 1972: Columbia University Press.

Thomas Blenman Hare. "Reading, Writing and Cooking: Kūkai's Interpretive Strategies," *Journal of Asian Studies* 49.2 (1990), 253-273. A post-structuralist analysis.

Richard Karl Payne. "Feeding the Gods: The Shingon Fire Ritual." 1985: Ph.D. dissertation in History and Phenomenology of Religions, Graduate Theological Union.

Paul L. Swanson, ed. "Tendai Buddhism in Japan," *Japanese Journal of Religious Studies* 14.2-14.3 (1987). Special double issue on Tendai.

Paul Groner. SAICHŌ: THE ESTABLISHMENT OF THE JAPANESE
    TENDAI SCHOOL. 1984: University of California Press.

Michael Saso. TANTRIC ART AND MEDITATION: THE TENDAI
    TRADITION. 1991: University of Hawaii Press.

Allan A. Andrews. THE TEACHINGS ESSENTIAL FOR REBIRTH:
    A STUDY OF GENSHIN'S ŌJŌYŌSHŪ. 1973: Monumenta
    Nipponica Monographs.

Fernando G. Gutierrez. "Emakimono Depicting the Pains of the Damned,"
    Monumenta Nipponica 22.3-4 (1967), 278-289.

William Edward Deal. "Ascetics, Aristocrats, and the Lotus Sutra:
    The Construction of the Buddhist Universe in Eleventh Century Japan".
    1988: Ph.D. dissertation in the Study of Religion, Harvard University.

_____. "The Lotus Sutra and the Rhetoric of Legitimization in Eleventh-Century
    Japanese Buddhism," Japanese Journal of Religious Studies 20.4
    (1993), 261-295.

Yoshiko K. Dykstra, transl. MIRACULOUS TALES OF THE LOTUS SUTRA
    FROM ANCIENT JAPAN: THE DAINIHONKOKU HOKEKYŌKENKI
    OF PRIEST CHINGEN. 1983: University of Hawaii Press.

George J. Tanabe, Jr. & Willa Jane Tanabe, eds. THE LOTUS SUTRA IN
    JAPANESE CULTURE. 1989: University of Hawaii Press.

Kazuo Ōsumi. "Cultural Life in Medieval Japan," (translated, adapted, &
    expanded by James C. Dobbins), in Kōzō Yamamura, ed.
    CAMBRIDGE HISTORY OF JAPAN, Volume 3: MEDIEVAL JAPAN
    (1990: Cambridge University Press), 544-582.

Robert E. Morrell, transl. SAND AND PEBBLES (SHASEKISHŪ):
    THE TALES OF MUJŪ ICHIEN, A VOICE FOR PLURALISM IN
    KAMAKURA BUDDHISM. 1985: State University of New York
    Press.

_____. EARLY KAMAKURA BUDDHISM: A MINORITY REPORT.
    1987: Asian Humanities Press.

George J. Tanabe, Jr. MYŌE THE DREAMKEEPER: FANTASY AND
    KNOWLEDGE IN EARLY KAMAKURA BUDDHISM. 1992:
    Council on East Asian Studies, Harvard University.

Janet R. Goodwin. "Building Bridges and Saving Souls: The Fruits of Evangelism in Medieval Japan," *Monumenta Nipponica* 44.2 (1989), 137-149.

_____. "Alms for Kasagi Temple," *Journal of Asian Studies* 46.4 (1987), 827-841.

_____. ALMS AND VAGABONDS: BUDDHIST TEMPLES AND POPULAR PATRONAGE IN MEDIEVAL JAPAN. 1994: University of Hawaii Press.

Harper Coates & Ryugaku Ishizuka, transl. & ed. HŌNEN, THE BUDDHIST SAINT: HIS LIFE AND TEACHING. 5 volumes. 1925: Society for the Publication of Sacred Books of the World.

Alfred Bloom. SHINRAN'S GOSPEL OF PURE GRACE. 1965: University of Arizona Press.

Daisetz T. Suzuki. SHIN BUDDHISM. 1970: Harper & Row.

_____, ed. COLLECTED WRITINGS ON SHIN BUDDHISM. 1974: Harper & Row.

Shinran. THE *KYŌGYŌSHINSHŌ*. Daisetz T. Suzuki, transl. 1954: English Publication Bureau.

_____. *TANNISHŌ*: A TRACT DEPLORING HERESIES OF FAITH. 1962: Higashi Honganji.

Kōshō Yamamoto. THE PRIVATE LETTERS OF SHINRAN SHŌNIN. 1963: Darin Bunko.

_____. THE OTHER POWER. 1965: Darin Bunko.

Luis O. Gomez. "Shinran's Faith and the Sacred Name of Amida," *Monumenta Nipponica* 38.1 (1983), 73-84.

James C. Dobbins. "From Inspiration to Institution: The Rise of Sectarian Identity in Jōdo Shinshū," *Monumenta Nipponica* 41.3 (1986), 331-343.

Masaharu Anesaki. NICHIREN, THE BUDDHIST PROPHET. 1949: Harvard University Press.

Laurel Rasplica Rodd. NICHIREN: A BIOGRAPHY. 1978: Center for Asian Studies, Arizona State University.

Philip Yampolsky, ed. SELECTED WRITINGS OF NICHIREN. Burton Watson, et al., transl. 1990: Columbia University Press.

Michele Marra. "The Development of *Mappō* Thought in Japan," in two parts: *Japanese Journal of Religious Studies* 15.2 (1988), 25-54; 15.4 (1988), 287-305.

Willy Vande Walle. "Japan: From Petty Kingdom to Buddha Land," *Japan Review* 5 (1994), 87-101. How medieval Buddhist leaders, especially Nichiren, came to see their geographically peripheral country as favored by the gods.

Kenneth A. Marcure. "The *Danka* System," *Monumenta Nipponica* 40.1 (1985), 39-67. On affiliation of families with temples.

William R. LaFleur. LIQUID LIFE: ABORTION AND BUDDHISM IN JAPAN. 1992: Princeton University Press.

_____. THE KARMA OF WORDS: BUDDHISM AND THE LITERARY ARTS IN MEDIEVAL JAPAN. 1983: University of California Press.

James H. Sanford, William R. LaFleur, & Masatoshi Nagatomi, eds. FLOWING TRACES: BUDDHISM IN THE LITERARY AND VISUAL ARTS OF JAPAN. 1992: Princeton University Press.

Richard B. Pilgrim. BUDDHISM AND THE ARTS OF JAPAN. Second revised & enlarged edition. 1993: Anima Books.

Donald F. McCallum. ZENKŌJI AND ITS ICON: A STUDY IN MEDIEVAL JAPANESE RELIGIOUS ART. 1994: Princeton University Press.

Royall Tyler. "Buddhism in Noh," *Japanese Journal of Religious Studies* 14.1 (1987), 19-52.

Margaret H. Childs. "*Chigo Monogatari*: Love Stories or Buddhist Sermons?" *Monumenta Nipponica* 35.2 (1980), 127-151.

James H. Sanford. "Mandalas of the Heart: Two Prose Works by Ikkyū Sōjun," *Monumenta Nipponica* 35.3 (1980), 273-298.

_____. "The Abominable Tachikawa Skull Ritual," *Monumenta Nipponica* 46.1 (1991), 1-20.

Takeshi Umehara. "The Japanese View of the 'Other World': Japanese Religion in World Perspective," *Japan Review* 2 (1991), 161-190. Explains how Buddhism became "funeral Buddism" in Japan.

Neil McMullin. BUDDHISM AND THE STATE IN SIXTEENTH-CENTURY JAPAN. 1985: Princeton University Press.

RELIGION: Zen

*James L. Gardner. ZEN BUDDHISM: A CLASSIFIED BIBLIOGRAPHY OF WESTERN-LANGUAGE PUBLICATIONS THROUGH 1990. 1991: Wings of Fire Press.

*Patricia Armstrong Vessie. ZEN BUDDHISM: A BIBLIOGRAPHY OF BOOKS AND ARTICLES IN ENGLISH, 1892-1975. 1976: University Microfilms International.

*Ruth Fuller Sasaki. "A Bibliography of Translations of Zen (Ch'an) Works," *Philosophy East and West* 10 (1960-1961), 149-166.

Trevor Legget, transl. THREE AGES OF ZEN: SAMURAI, FEUDAL, AND MODERN. 1993: Tuttle. A collection of writings on Zen, from the Kamakura period to the present.

Daisetz T. Suzuki. Suzuki (1890-1966) was the pioneer interpreter of Zen to the West. His books in English include ZEN BUDDHISM and ZEN AND JAPANESE CULTURE, and many other titles.

Heinrich Dumoulin. A HISTORY OF ZEN BUDDHISM. 1963: Random House. Translated from the German.

Martin Collcutt. FIVE MOUNTAINS: THE RINZAI ZEN MONASTIC INSTI-TUTIONS IN MEDIEVAL JAPAN. 1981: Harvard University Press.

_____. "Zen and the *Gozan*," in Kōzō Yamamura, ed. CAMBRIDGE HISTORY OF JAPAN, Volume 3: MEDIEVAL JAPAN (1990: Cambridge University Press), 583-652.

Alan W. Watts. THE WAY OF ZEN. 1957: Vintage Books.

Nancy Wilson Ross, ed. THE WORLD OF ZEN. 1960: Random House.

Philip Kapleau, comp. & ed. THE THREE PILLARS OF ZEN: TEACHING, PRACTICE, ENLIGHTENMENT. 1964: Beacon.

Mircea Eliade. FROM PRIMITIVES TO ZEN. 1967: Collins.

Isshū Miura & Ruth Fuller Sasaki. ZEN DUST: THE HISTORY OF THE KŌAN AND KŌAN STUDY IN RINZAI (LIN-CHI) ZEN. 1967: Harcourt Brace & World.

_____. THE ZEN KŌAN: ITS HISTORY AND USE IN RINZAI ZEN. 1965: Harcourt Brace & World.

John Stevens. THREE ZEN MASTERS: IKKYŪ, HAKUIN, RYŌKAN. 1993: Kōdansha.

Philip B. Yampolsky, transl. THE ZEN MASTER HAKUIN: SELECTED WRITINGS. 1985: Columbia University Press.

Kenneth Kraft. ELOQUENT ZEN: DAITŌ AND EARLY JAPANESE ZEN. 1992: University of Hawaii Press.

Masao Abe. A STUDY OF DŌGEN: HIS PHILOSOPHY AND RELIGION. Steven Heine, ed. 1992: State University of New York Press.

Carl Bielefeldt. DŌGEN'S MANUALS OF ZEN MEDITATION. 1988: University of California Press.

William R. LaFleur, ed. DŌGEN STUDIES. 1985: University of Hawaii Press.

Hee-Jin Kim. DŌGEN KIGEN—MYSTICAL REALIST. 1984: University of Arizona Press.

Reihō Masunaga, transl. A PRIMER OF SŌTŌ ZEN: A TRANSLATION OF DŌGEN'S *SHŌBŌGENZŌ ZUIMONKI.* 1971: University of Hawaii Press.

Bernard Faure. "The Daruma-shū, Dōgen, and Sōtō Zen," *Monumenta Nipponica* 42.1 (1987), 25-55.

William M. Bodiford. SŌTŌ ZEN IN MEDIEVAL JAPAN. 1993: University of Hawaii Press.

Marian Ury. POEMS OF THE FIVE MOUNTAINS: AN INTRODUCTION TO THE LITERATURE OF THE ZEN MONASTERIES. 1992: Center for Japanese Studies, University of Michigan.

Takuan Sōhō. THE UNFETTERED MIND: WRITINGS OF THE ZEN
     MASTER TO THE SWORD MASTER. William Scott Wilson, transl.
     1986: Kōdansha International.

Eshin Nishimura. UNSUI: A DIARY OF ZEN MONASTIC LIFE. Bardwell L.
     Smith, ed. 1973: University of Hawaii Press. Charming illustrations.

Jan Fontein & Money L. Hickman. ZEN PAINTING AND CALLIGRAPHY.
     1970: Boston Museum of Fine Arts.

John Stevens. "Brushstrokes of Enlightenment: The Interpretation and
     Appreciation of Zen Art," *Transactions, Asiatic Society of Japan*, 4th
     series, 1 (1986), 79-107.

H. Neill McFarland. DARUMA: THE FOUNDER OF ZEN IN JAPANESE
     ART AND POPULAR CULTURE. 1987: Kōdansha International.

RELIGION: Folk Religion

Ichirō Hori. FOLK RELIGION IN JAPAN: CONTINUITY & CHANGE.
     1968: University of Chicago Press.

_____. "On the Concept of *Hijiori* (Holy Man)," *Numen* 5 (1958), 128-160,
     199-232.

_____. "Rites of Purification and Orgy in Japanese Folk Religion,"
     Philosophical Studies of Japan 9 (1969), 61-78.

Hitoshi Miyake. "Folk Religion," in Ichirō Hori, ed. JAPANESE RELIGION
     (1972: Kōdansha International), 121-143.

Joseph Pittau, ed. FOLK CULTURES OF JAPAN AND EAST ASIA. 1966:
     Monumenta Nipponica Monographs.

Tokihiko Otō. FOLKLORE IN JAPANESE LIFE AND CUSTOMS. 1963:
     Kokusai Bunka Shinkōkai. Useful for illustrations.

Carmen Blacker. "Japan," in Michael Loewe & Carmen Blacker, eds.
     ORACLES AND DIVINATION (1981: Shambhala), 63-86.

_____. THE CATALPA BOW: A STUDY OF SHAMANISTIC PRACTICES
     IN JAPAN. 1975: Allen & Unwin.

William P. Fairchild. "Shamanism in Japan," *Folklore Studies* 21 (1962), 1-122.

Hisako Kamata. "'Daughters of the Gods': Shaman Priestesses in Japan and Okinawa," in Pittau, ed. FOLK CULTURES OF JAPAN AND EAST ASIA (1966: Monumenta Nipponica Monographs), 56-73.

Robert J. Smith. ANCESTOR WORSHIP IN CONTEMPORARY JAPAN. 1974: Stanford University Press. See especially chapter 1, "The Historical Perspective" (6-38); and chapter 2, "Spirits, Ghosts, and Gods" (39-68).

C. Ouwehand. NAMAZU-E AND THEIR THEMES: AN INTERPRETIVE APPROACH TO SOME ASPECTS OF JAPANESE FOLK RELIGION. 1964: Brill.

Geoffrey Bownas. JAPANESE RAINMAKING AND OTHER FOLK PRACTICES. 1963: Allen & Unwin.

U. A. Casal. THE FIVE SACRED FESTIVALS OF ANCIENT JAPAN: THEIR SYMBOLISM AND HISTORICAL DEVELOPMENT. 1967: Monumenta Nipponica Monographs.

Fanny Hagin Mayer, transl. JAPANESE FOLK FESTIVALS. 1970: Miura.

Anne-Marie Bouchy. "The Cult of Mount Atago and the Atago Confraternities," *Journal of Asian Studies* 46.2 (1987), 279-303.

Michael Czaja. GODS OF MYTH AND STONE: PHALLICISM IN JAPAN-ESE FOLK RELIGION. 1974: Weatherhill.

Donald Richie & Kenkichi Itō. THE EROTIC GODS: PHALLICISM IN JAPAN. 1967: Zufushinsha.

Genchi Katō. "A Study of the Development of Religious Ideas Among the Japanese People as Illustrated by Japanese Phallicism," *Transactions, Asiatic Society of Japan*, 2nd series, 2, Supplement (1924), 1-70.

Edmund Buckley. "Phallicism in Japan," in Lee Alexander Stone, ed. THE STORY OF PHALLICISM, volume 1 (1927: Pascal Covici), 287-325.

FOLKTALES & FOLKLORE
[See also the numerous articles on Japanese folklore and folktales in the
journal *Folklore Studies*, later renamed *Asian Folklore Studies*]

Kunio Yanagita. THE YANAGITA KUNIO GUIDE TO THE JAPANESE
FOLK TALE. Fanny Hagin Mayer, ed. and transl. 1986: University of
Indiana Press.

Hiroko Ikeda. A TYPE AND MOTIF INDEX OF JAPANESE FOLKLORE.
1971: Tiedeakatemia.

Hayao Kawai. THE JAPANESE PSYCHE: MAJOR MOTIFS IN THE FAIRY
TALES OF JAPAN. Transl. Hayao Kawai & Sachiko Reece. 1988:
Spring Publications, Dallas, Texas.

Joanne P. Algarin. JAPANESE FOLK LITERATURE: A CORE COLLEC-
TION & REFERENCE GUIDE. 1982: R. R. Bowker.

Keigo Seki. "Types of Japanese Folktales," *Asian Folklore Studies* 25 (1966),
1-20.

_____, ed. FOLKTALES OF JAPAN. 1963: University of Chicago Press.

Royall Tyler. JAPANESE FOLK TALES. 1987: Pantheon.

Fanny Hagin Mayer, transl. ANCIENT TALES IN MODERN JAPAN:
AN ANTHOLOGY OF JAPANESE FOLK TALES. 1985: University
of Indiana Press. 343 folk tales from the *Meii*, the standard Japanese
collection.

_____. "Available Japanese Folk Tales," *Monumenta Nipponica* 24.3 (1969),
235-247.

Richard M. Dorson. STUDIES IN JAPANESE FOLKLORE. 1963: University
of Indiana Press. Volume 17 of University of Indiana Folklore Series.

_____. FOLK LEGENDS OF JAPAN. 1962: Tuttle.

Kunio Yanagida. JAPANESE FOLK TALES: A REVISED SELECTION.
1960: Kadokawa.

Garrett Bang, transl. MEN FROM THE VILLAGE DEEP IN THE MOUN-
TAINS AND OTHER JAPANESE FOLK TALES. 1973: Macmillan.

Shio Sakanishi, transl. JAPANESE FOLK PLAYS: THE INK SMEARED
LADY AND OTHER KYŌGEN. 1960: Tuttle.

Patia R. Isaku. MOUNTAIN STORM, PINE BREEZE: FOLK SONG IN
JAPAN. 1984: University of Arizona Press.

Donald L. Philippi, transl. SONGS OF GODS, SONGS OF HUMANS: THE
EPIC TRADITION OF THE AINU. 1979: Princeton University Press.

Carl Etter. AINU FOLKLORE: TRADITIONS AND CULTURE OF THE
VANISHING ABORIGINES OF JAPAN. 1949: Wilcox & Follett.

Frances Carpenter. PEOPLE FROM THE SKY: AINU TALES FROM
NORTHERN JAPAN. 1972: Doubleday.

LITERATURE

*Japan P. E. N. Club. JAPANESE LITERATURE IN EUROPEAN
LANGUAGES: A BIBLIOGRAPHY. 2nd edition. 1961; Supplement,
1964: The Japan P. E. N. Club.

*Japan P. E. N. Club, comp. JAPANESE LITERATURE IN FOREIGN
LANGUAGES, 1945-1990. 1990: Japan Book Publishers Association.

*Claire Zebroski Mamola. JAPANESE WOMEN WRITERS IN ENGLISH
TRANSLATION: AN ANNOTATED BIBLIOGRAPHY. 2 vols.
1989, 1992: Garland.

Donald Keene. JAPANESE LITERATURE: AN INTRODUCTION FOR
WESTERN READERS. 1955: Grove.

_____. "Literature," in Arthur Tiedemann, ed. AN INTRODUCTION TO
JAPANESE CIVILIZATION (1974: Heath), 375-421.

_____. THE PLEASURES OF JAPANESE LITERATURE. 1988: Columbia
University Press.

_____. SEEDS IN THE HEART: JAPANESE LITERATURE FROM
EARLIEST TIMES TO THE LATE SIXTEENTH CENTURY.
1993: Henry Holt.

Edwin A. Cranston. "Literature," KŌDANSHA ENCYCLOPEDIA OF JAPAN
5: 28-41.

Shūichi Katō. A HISTORY OF JAPANESE LITERATURE: THE FIRST
THOUSAND YEARS. David Chibbett, transl. 1979: Kōdansha
International. First volume of a 3-volume series.

Jin'ichi Konishi. A HISTORY OF JAPANESE LITERATURE. Aileen Gatten &
Nicholas Teele, transl.; Earl Miner, ed. Princeton University Press.
A projected 5-volume survey.

Vol. 1: THE ARCHAIC AND ANCIENT AGES. 1984.
Vol. 2: THE EARLY MIDDLE AGES. 1986.
Vol. 3: THE HIGH MIDDLE AGES. 1991.

Edward Putzar. JAPANESE LITERATURE: A HISTORICAL OUTLINE.
1973: University of Arizona Press. An adaptation of Sen'ichi
Hisamatsu, ed., *Nihon Bungaku* (1960).

J. Thomas Rimer. A READER'S GUIDE TO JAPANESE LITERATURE:
FROM THE EIGHTH CENTURY TO THE PRESENT. 1988:
Kōdansha International.

Kokusai Bunka Shinkōkai, ed. INTRODUCTION TO CLASSIC JAPANESE
LITERATURE. 1948: Kokusai Bunka Shinkōkai.

Earl Miner, Hiroko Odagiri & Robert E. Morrell. THE PRINCETON COMPAN-
ION TO CLASSICAL JAPANESE LITERATURE. 1985: Princeton
University Press. See also the review by Edwin A. Cranston in *Harvard
Journal of Asiatic Studies* 53.1 (1993), 188-231.

Earl Miner, ed. PRINCIPLES OF CLASSICAL JAPANESE LITERATURE.
1985: Princeton University Press.

_____. AN INTRODUCTION TO JAPANESE COURT POETRY. 1968:
Stanford University Press.

Helen Craig McCullough, comp. CLASSICAL JAPANESE PROSE:
AN ANTHOLOGY. 1990: Stanford University Press.

Donald Keene, comp. ANTHOLOGY OF JAPANESE LITERATURE: FROM
THE EARLIEST ERA TO THE MID- NINTEENTH CENTURY.
1955: Grove.

Aileen Gatten & Anthony Hood Chambers, eds. NEW LEAVES: STUDIES
AND TRANSLATIONS OF JAPANESE LITERATURE IN HONOR
OF EDWARD SEIDENSTICKER. 1993: University of Michigan
Press.

Steven D. Carter, transl. TRADITIONAL JAPANESE POETRY:
AN ANTHOLOGY. 1991: Stanford University Press.

Hiroaki Satō & Burton Watson, transl. FROM THE COUNTRY OF EIGHT
ISLANDS: AN ANTHOLOGY OF JAPANESE POETRY. 1981:
Doubleday; 1986: Columbia University Press.

Herbert E. Plutschow. CHAOS AND COSMOS: RITUAL IN EARLY AND
MEDIEVAL JAPANESE LITERATURE. 1990: E. J. Brill.

E. V. Gatenby. CLOUD-MEN OF YAMATO, BEING AN OUTLINE OF
MYSTICISM IN JAPANESE LITERATURE. 1929: J. Murray.

Michele Marra. THE AESTHETICS OF DISCONTENT: POLITICS AND
RECLUSION IN MEDIEVAL JAPANESE LITERATURE. 1991:
University of Hawaii Press.

_____. REPRESENTATIONS OF POWER: THE LITERARY POLITICS OF
MEDIEVAL JAPAN. 1993: University of Hawaii Press.

Shōichi Sakae. "The Autobiography in Japan," Teruko Craig, transl., *Journal of
Japanese Studies* 11.2 (1985), 357-368.

Yaeko Satō Habein. THE HISTORY OF THE JAPANESE WRITTEN
LANGUAGE. 1984: Columbia University Press & University of
Tokyo Press.

Christopher Seeley. A HISTORY OF WRITING IN JAPAN. 1991: E. J. Brill.

ART & MUSIC

GENSHOKU: NIHON NO BIJUTSU, 30 volumes. 1970: Kōdansha. This
lavish collection of "Japanese Art in Full-Color Reproductions,"
arranged topically rather than chronologically, includes brief English
identification of plates at the back of each volume.

Penelope Mason. HISTORY OF JAPANESE ART. 1993: Harry N. Abrams.

Robert Treat Paine & Alexander Soper. THE ART AND ARCHITECTURE OF JAPAN. 1955: Penguin. A standard narrative history, but not lavishly illustrated.

Hugo Munsterberg. THE ARTS OF JAPAN: AN ILLUSTRATED HISTORY. 1957: Tuttle. See also other works by Munsterberg.

Peter Swann. A CONCISE HISTORY OF JAPANESE ART. 1958: Kōdansha International.

John W. Dower. THE ELEMENTS OF JAPANESE DESIGN. 1971: Weatherhill.

THE HEIBONSHA SURVEY OF ART. Jointly published by John Weatherhill, Inc. and Heibonsha, this 30-volume adaptation of Heibonsha's popular *Nihon no Bijutsu* series is the best English-language overview of Japanese art history. Authors and titles are as follows:

1. Itsuji Yoshikawa. Major Themes in Japanese Art
2. Namio Egami. The Beginnings of Japanese Art
3. Yasutada Watanabe. Shintō Art: Ise and Izumo Shrines
4. Sciichi Mizuno. Asuka Buddhist Art: Hōryū-ji
5. Tsuyoshi Kobayashi. Nara Buddhist Art: Tōdai-ji
6. Ryōichi Hayashi. The Silk Road and the Shōsō-in
7. Minoru O-oka. Temples of Nara and Their Art
8. Takaaki Sawa. Art in Japanese Esoteric Buddhism
9. Toshio Fukuyama. Heian Temples: Byōdō-in and Chūson-ji
10. Saburō Ienaga. Painting in the Yamato Style
11. Hisashi Mori. Sculpture of the Kamakura Period
12. Ichimatsu Tanaka. Japanese Ink Painting: Shūbun to Sesshū
13. Kiyoshi Hirai. Feudal Architecture of Japan
14. Tsuguyoshi Doi. Momoyama Decorative Painting
15. T. Hayashi, M. Nakamura & S. Hayashiya. Japanese Art and the Tea Ceremony
16. Seiroku Noma. Japanese Costume and Textile Arts
17. Yūzō Yamane. Momoyama Genre Painting
18. Hiroshi Mizuo. Edo Painting: Sōtatsu and Kōrin
19. Yoshitomo Okamoto. The Namban Art of Japan
20. Naomi Ōkawa. Edo Architecture: Katsura and Nikkō
21. Teiji Itoh. Traditional Domestic Architecture of Japan
22. Seiichirō Takahashi. Traditional Woodblock Prints of Japan

23. Yoshiho Yonezawa & Chū Yoshizawa. <u>Japanese Painting in the Literati Style</u>
24. Michiaki Kawakita. <u>Modern Currents in Japanese Art</u>
25. Tōru Terada. <u>Japanese Art in World Perspective</u>
26. Kageo Muraoka & Kichiemon Okamura. <u>Folk Arts and Crafts of Japan</u>
27. Yūjirō Nakata. <u>The Art of Japanese Calligraphy</u>
28. Masao Hayakawa. <u>Garden Art of Japan</u>
29. Tsugio Mikami. <u>The Art of Japanese Ceramics</u>
30. Saburō Ienaga. <u>Japanese Art: A Cultural Appreciation</u>

William P. Malm. SIX HIDDEN VIEWS OF JAPANESE MUSIC. 1986: University of California Press.

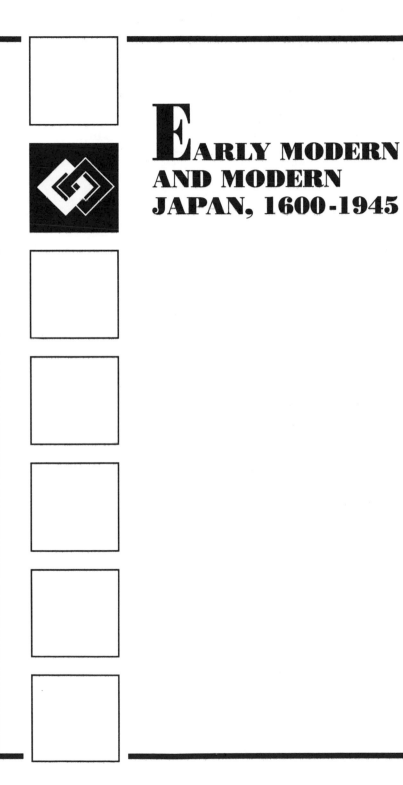

EARLY MODERN AND MODERN JAPAN, 1600-1945

Early Modern and Modern Japan, 1600-1945

GENERAL WORKS

KŌDANSHA ENCYCLOPEDIA OF JAPAN. 1983: Kōdansha. Eight volumes plus Index volume and 1986 Supplement. Contains over 10,000 articles, including major essays (with bibliographic references) by contemporary scholars on all aspects of Japanese history and culture. See especially the long "History of Japan" entry in volume 3.

CAMBRIDGE HISTORY OF JAPAN. Cambridge University Press. Collections of essays by leading scholars, both western and Japanese. See: Volume 4, EARLY MODERN JAPAN (1991), Volume 5, THE NINETEENTH CENTURY (1989), and Volume 6, THE TWENTIETH CENTURY (1988).

CAMBRIDGE ENCYCLOPEDIA OF JAPAN. 1993: Cambridge University Press.

Janet E. Hunter, comp. CONCISE DICTIONARY OF MODERN JAPANESE HISTORY. 1984: University of California Press.

ENCYCLOPEDIA OF ASIAN HISTORY. 1988: Charles Scribner's Sons. Four volumes.

Dorothy Perkins. ENCYCLOPEDIA OF JAPAN: JAPANESE HISTORY AND CULTURE, FROM ABACUS TO ZŌRI. 1991: Facts on File.

Kenneth B. Pyle. THE MAKING OF MODERN JAPAN. 1978: Heath.

Peter Duus. THE RISE OF MODERN JAPAN. 1976: Houghton Mifflin.

Mikiso Hane. MODERN JAPAN: A HISTORICAL SURVEY. 2nd edition. 1992: Westview Press.

_____. PEASANTS, REBELS AND OUTCASTES: THE UNDERSIDE OF MODERN JAPAN. 1982: Pantheon.

Conrad Totman. JAPAN BEFORE PERRY: A SHORT HISTORY. 1981: University of California Press.

_____. EARLY MODERN JAPAN. 1993: University of California Press. Covers 1568 to 1868.

Janet Hunter. THE EMERGENCE OF MODERN JAPAN: AN INTRODUC-
TORY HISTORY SINCE 1853. 1989: Longman.

John W. Dower. "E. H. Norman, Japan, and the Uses of History," in Dower, ed.
ORIGINS OF THE MODERN JAPANESE STATE: SELECTED
WRITINGS OF E. H. NORMAN (1975: Pantheon), 3-101.

Jon Halliday. A POLITICAL HISTORY OF JAPANESE CAPITALISM.
1975: Pantheon.

Edwin O. Reischauer & John K. Fairbank. EAST ASIA: THE GREAT
TRADITION. 1960: Houghton Mifflin.

John K. Fairbank, Edwin O. Reischauer & Albert M. Craig. EAST ASIA:
THE MODERN TRANSFORMATION. 1965: Houghton Mifflin.

_____. EAST ASIA: TRADITION AND TRANSFORMATION. 1989:
Houghton Mifflin. Revised and abridged version of preceding two
works.

Edwin O. Reischauer & Albert M. Craig. JAPAN: TRADITION AND
TRANSFORMATION. 1989: Houghton Mifflin. Japan sections from
preceding survey text.

_____. JAPAN: THE STORY OF A NATION. 4th edition. 1990:
McGraw-Hill.

Edwin O. Reischauer. THE JAPANESE TODAY: CHANGE AND CONTINU-
ITY. 1988: Belknap. Revised version of THE JAPANESE (1977).

John W. Hall. JAPAN: FROM PREHISTORY TO MODERN TIMES. 1970:
Delacorte. Strongest on premodern.

_____ & Richard Beardsley, eds. TWELVE DOORS TO JAPAN. 1965:
McGraw-Hill. A disciplinary approach.

Hugh Borton. JAPAN'S MODERN CENTURY. 2nd edition. 1973: Ronald.

W. G. Beasley. THE RISE OF MODERN JAPAN. 1990: St. Martin's.

Barry Williams. MODERN JAPAN. 1987: Longman.

Kōichi Kishimoto. POLITICS IN MODERN JAPAN: DEVELOPMENT AND
ORGANIZATION. 3rd edition. 1988: Japan Echo.

Gavan McCormack & Yoshio Sugimoto, eds. THE JAPANESE TRAJECTORY: MODERNIZATION AND BEYOND. 1988: Cambridge University Press.

Marius B. Jansen. JAPAN AND CHINA: FROM WAR TO PEACE, 1894-1972. 1975: Rand-McNally.

_____. JAPAN AND ITS WORLD: TWO CENTURIES OF CHANGE. 1984: Princeton University Press.

Richard Storry. A HISTORY OF MODERN JAPAN. 1965: Penguin.

Arthur Tiedemann, ed. AN INTRODUCTION TO JAPANESE CIVILIZATION. 1974: Heath. Contains both historical overviews and topical essays by leading scholars.

H. Paul Varley. JAPANESE CULTURE: A SHORT HISTORY. 3rd edition. 1984: University of Hawaii Press.

Takeshi Ishida. JAPANESE POLITICAL CULTURE: CHANGE AND CONTINUITY. 1989: Transaction.

Barrington Moore, Jr. SOCIAL ORIGINS OF DICTATORSHIP AND DEMOCRACY. 1966: Beacon.

Jean-Pierre Lehmann. THE ROOTS OF MODERN JAPAN. 1982: St. Martin's.

James B. Crowley, ed. MODERN EAST ASIA: ESSAYS IN INTERPRETATION. 1970: Harcourt Brace & World.

Jon Livingston, Joe Moore & Felicia Oldfather, eds. THE JAPAN READER, 1: IMPERIAL JAPAN, 1800-1945. 1973: Pantheon.

_____. THE JAPAN READER, 2: POSTWAR JAPAN. 1973: Pantheon.

The Developing Economies. Special issues on "The Modernization of Japan" in the December publications for 1965, 1966, & 1967, by Japanese scholars.

Seiichi Tōbata, ed. THE MODERNIZATION OF JAPAN. 1966: The Institute of Asian Economic Affairs. Articles from the journal The Developing Economies.

Robert E. Ward & Dankwart Rustow, eds. POLITICAL MODERNIZATION IN JAPAN & TURKEY. 1964: Princeton University Press.

Cyril E. Black, et al., eds. THE MODERNIZATION OF JAPAN AND RUSSIA:
A COMPARATIVE STUDY. 1975: Free Press.

Princeton University Press Series on "Studies in the Modernization of Japan,"
1965-1971:

Marius B. Jansen, ed. CHANGING JAPANESE ATTITUDES
TOWARD MODERNIZATION. 1965.

William W. Lockwood, ed. THE STATE & ECONOMIC ENTER-
PRISE IN JAPAN. 1965.

Ronald P. Dore, ed. ASPECTS OF SOCIAL CHANGE IN MODERN
JAPAN. 1967.

Robert E. Ward, ed. POLITICAL DEVELOPMENT IN MODERN
JAPAN. 1968.

Donald Shively, ed. TRADITION AND MODERNIZATION IN
JAPANESE CULTURE. 1971.

James W. Morley, ed. DILEMMAS OF GROWTH IN PREWAR
JAPAN. 1971.

Sheldon Garon. "Rethinking Modernization and Modernity in Japanese History:
A Focus on State-Society Relations," *Journal of Asian Studies* 53.2
(1994), 346-366.

Harry Wray & Hilary Conroy, eds. JAPAN EXAMINED: PERSPECTIVES
ON MODERN JAPANESE HISTORY. 1983: University of Hawaii
Press. 46 issue-oriented essays by leading scholars.

Sue Henny & Jean-Pierre Lehmann, eds. THEMES AND THEORIES IN
MODERN JAPANESE HISTORY: ESSAYS IN MEMORY OF
RICHARD STORRY. 1988: Athlone.

Albert M. Craig, ed. JAPAN: A COMPARATIVE VIEW. 1979: Princeton
University Press.

Tetsuo Najita. JAPAN: THE INTELLECTUAL FOUNDATIONS OF
MODERN JAPANESE POLITICS. 1974; 1980: University of Chicago
Press.

_____ & J. Victor Koschmann, eds. CONFLICT IN MODERN JAPANESE
HISTORY: THE NEGLECTED TRADITION. 1982: Princeton
University Press. Eighteen essays focusing on the period from the
mid-19th century through the 1920s.

Masao Miyoshi & H. D. Harootunian, eds. POSTMODERNISM AND JAPAN.
1989: Duke University Press.

Karel Van Wolferen. THE ENIGMA OF JAPANESE POWER: PEOPLE AND
POLITICS IN A STATELESS NATION. 1989: Knopf.

Irwin Scheiner, ed. MODERN JAPAN: AN INTERPRETIVE ANTHOLOGY.
1974: University of California Press.

Ryūsaku Tsunoda, Wm. Theodore DeBary & Donald Keene, eds. SOURCES OF
JAPANESE TRADITION. 1958: Columbia University Press.
Documentary intellectual history; 2 volumes in the paperback edition.

David J. Lu, ed. SOURCES OF JAPANESE HISTORY. 2 volumes. 1974:
McGraw-Hill. Wide range of primary materials.

Donald Keene, ed. ANTHOLOGY OF JAPANESE LITERATURE: FROM
THE EARLIEST ERA TO THE MID-NINETEENTH CENTURY.
1955: Grove.

_____. MODERN JAPANESE LITERATURE: AN ANTHOLOGY. 1956:
Grove.

Michiko Y. Aoki & Margaret B. Dardess, eds. AS THE JAPANESE SEE IT:
PAST AND PRESENT. 1981: University of Hawaii Press.

John W. Dower. JAPAN IN WAR AND PEACE: SELECTED ESSAYS. 1994:
The New Press.

John Hunter Boyle. MODERN JAPAN: THE AMERICAN NEXUS. 1993:
Harcourt Brace Jovanovich.

Donald Richie. THE HONORABLE VISITORS. 1994: Tuttle. Fascinating
stories of visits to Japan by Ulysses S. Grant, Rudyard Kipling, Charlie
Chaplin, and others.

TOKUGAWA: GENERAL

John Whitney Hall, ed. CAMBRIDGE HISTORY OF JAPAN, Volume 4:
    EARLY MODERN JAPAN. 1991: Cambridge University Press.

Chie Nakane & Shinzaburō Ōishi, eds. TOKUGAWA JAPAN: THE SOCIAL
    AND ECONOMIC ANTECEDENTS OF MODERN JAPAN. Transl.
    ed. Conrad Totman. 1990: University of Tokyo Press.

E. H. Norman. "People Under Feudalism," *Bulletin of Concerned Asian Scholars*
    9.2 (1977), 56-61.

_____. ORIGINS OF THE MODERN JAPANESE STATE: SELECTED
    WRITINGS OF E. H. NORMAN. J. W. Dower, ed. 1975: Pantheon.
    See especially 321-357 on "Late Feudal Society."

John W. Hall. "E. H. Norman on Tokugawa Japan," *Journal of Japanese Studies*
    3.2 (1977), 365-374.

_____. "The Nature of Traditional Society: Japan," in Robert E. Ward &
    Dankwart A. Rustow, eds. POLITICAL MODERNIZATION IN
    JAPAN AND TURKEY (1964: Princeton University Press), 14-41.

_____. "Tokugawa Japan, 1800-1853," in James B. Crowley, ed. MODERN
    EAST ASIA: ESSAYS IN INTERPRETATION (1970: Harcourt Brace
    & World), 62-94.

_____. "Edo History (1600-1868)," KŌDANSHA ENCYCLOPEDIA OF
    JAPAN 3: 185-192.

_____. "The *Bakuhan* System," in John Whitney Hall, ed. CAMBRIDGE
    HISTORY OF JAPAN, Volume 4: EARLY MODERN JAPAN
    (1991: Cambridge University Press), 128-182.

_____. "Rule by Status in Tokugawa Japan," *Journal of Japanese Studies* 1.1
    (1974), 39-50.

_____. JAPAN: FROM PREHISTORY TO MODERN TIMES (1970:
    Delacorte), chapter 10.

_____ & Marius Jansen, eds. STUDIES IN THE INSTITUTIONAL HISTORY
    OF EARLY MODERN JAPAN. 1968: Princeton University Press. A
    pioneer collection of 21 essays by leading scholars.

George B. Sansom. A HISTORY OF JAPAN, 1615-1867. 1967: Stanford University Press.

_____. THE WESTERN WORLD AND JAPAN: A STUDY IN THE INTER-ACTION OF EUROPEAN AND ASIATIC CULTURES. (1950: Knopf), chapters 9-12.

_____. JAPAN: A SHORT CULTURAL HISTORY. Revised edition (1944: Appleton), chapter 7.

Edwin O. Reischauer & Albert M. Craig. JAPAN: TRADITION AND TRANSFORMATION (1989: Houghton Mifflin), chapter 3.

Yoshiaki Shimizu, ed. JAPAN: THE SHAPING OF DAIMYŌ CULTURE, 1185-1868. 1988: G. Braziller.

Mary Elizabeth Berry. "Public Peace and Private Attachment: The Goals and Conduct of Power in Early Modern Japan," *Journal of Japanese Studies* 12.2 (1986), 237-271.

Conrad Totman. POLITICS IN THE TOKUGAWA BAKUFU, 1600-1843. 1967: Harvard University Press; 1988: University of California Press.

_____. "Tokugawa Japan," in Arthur Tiedemann, ed. AN INTRODUCTION TO JAPANESE CIVILIZATION (1974: Heath), 97-130

_____. JAPAN BEFORE PERRY: A BRIEF SYNTHESIS. 1982: University of California Press.

_____. TOKUGAWA IEYASU: SHŌGUN. 1983: Heian International.

_____. EARLY MODERN JAPAN. 1993: University of California Press. Covers 1568 to 1868.

Arthur L. Sadler. THE MAKER OF MODERN JAPAN: THE LIFE OF TOKUGAWA IEYASU. 1937: Allen & Unwin.

Harold Bolitho. TREASURES AMONG MEN: THE FUDAI DAIMYŌ IN TOKUGAWA JAPAN. 1974: Yale University Press.

_____. "The *Han*," in John Whitney Hall, ed. CAMBRIDGE HISTORY OF JAPAN, Volume 4: EARLY MODERN JAPAN (1991: Cambridge University Press), 183-234.

_____. "The Tempō Crisis," in Marius B. Jansen, ed. CAMBRIDGE HISTORY
OF JAPAN, Volume 5: THE NINETEENTH CENTURY (1989:
Cambridge University Press), 116-167.

_____. "The Dog Shōgun," in Wang Gungwu, ed. SELF AND BIOGRAPHY:
ESSAYS ON THE INDIVIDUAL AND SOCIETY IN ASIA (1975:
Sydney University Press).

Donald H. Shively. "Tokugawa Tsunayoshi, the Genroku Shōgun," in Albert M.
Craig & Donald H. Shively, eds. PERSONALITY IN JAPANESE
HISTORY (1970: University of Californaia Press), 85-126.

Beatrice Bodart-Bailey. "The Laws of Compassion," *Monumenta Nipponica*
40.2 (1985), 163-189. Tokugawa Tsunayoshi's famous laws.

_____. "The Significance of the Chamberlain Government of the Fifth
Tokugawa Shōgun," in Harold Bolitho & Alan Rix, eds. A NORTH-
ERN PROSPECT: AUSTRALIAN PAPERS ON JAPAN (1981:
Japanese Studies Association of Australia), 10-27.

Charles J. Dunn. EVERYDAY LIFE IN TRADITIONAL JAPAN. 1969:
Putnam.

William S. Atwell. "Some Observations on the 'Seventeenth-Century Crisis'
in China and Japan," *Journal of Asian Studies* 45.2 (1986), 223-244.

_____. "A Seventeenth-Century 'General Crisis' in East Asia?" *Modern Asian
Studies* 24.4 (1990), 661-682.

Niels Steensgaard. "The Seventeenth-Century Crisis and the Unity of Eurasian
History," *Modern Asian Studies* 24.4 (1990), 683-697.

Toshio G. Tsukahira. FEUDAL CONTROL IN TOKUGAWA JAPAN: THE
SANKIN KŌTAI SYSTEM. 1966: Council on East Asian Studies,
Harvard University.

Tatsuya Tsuji. "Politics in the Eighteenth Century," Harold Bolitho, transl., in
John Whitney Hall, ed. CAMBRIDGE HISTORY OF JAPAN, Volume
4: EARLY MODERN JAPAN (1991: Cambridge University Press),
425-477.

Lane Robert Earns. "The Development of Bureaucratic Rule in Early Modern
Japan: The Nagasaki Bugyō in the Seventeenth Century." 1987: Ph.D.
dissertation in History, University of Hawaii.

John W. Hall. TANUMA OKITSUGU, 1719-1788: FORERUNNER OF MODERN JAPAN. 1955: Harvard University Press.

Herman Ooms. CHARISMATIC BUREAUCRAT: A POLITICAL BIOGRA- PHY OF MATSUDAIRA SADANOBU, 1758-1829. 1975: University of Chicago Press.

Masato Matsui. "Shimazu Shigehide, 1745-1833: A Case Study of Daimyō Leadership." 1975: Ph.D. dissertation, University of Hawaii.

James L. McClain. KANAZAWA: A SEVENTEENTH-CENTURY JAPANESE CASTLE TOWN. 1982: Yale University Press.

_____. "Castle Towns and Daimyō Authority: Kanazawa in the Years 1583-1630," *Journal of Japanese Studies* 6.2 (1980), 267-299.

Philip C. Brown. CENTRAL AUTHORITY AND LOCAL AUTONOMY IN THE FORMATION OF EARLY MODERN JAPAN: THE CASE OF KAGA DOMAIN. 1993: Stanford University Press.

Luke S. Roberts. "The Petition Box in Eighteenth-Century Tosa," *Journal of Japanese Studies* 20.2 (1994), 423-458.

Herschel Webb. THE JAPANESE IMPERIAL INSTITUTION IN THE TOKUGAWA PERIOD. 1968: Columbia University Press.

Lee A. Butler. "Court and Bakufu in Early 17th Century Japan." 1991: Ph.D. dissertation in History, Princeton University.

Kenneth A. Marcure. "The *Danka* System," *Monumenta Nipponica* 40.1 (1985), 39-67. On affailiation of families with temples.

Dan F. Henderson. CONCILIATION AND JAPANESE LAW: TOKUGAWA AND MODERN. 1965: University of Washington Press.

John C. Hall, "Japanese Feudal Laws III—The Tokugawa Legislation, Parts I-III," *Transactions, Asiatic Society of Japan*, 1st series, 38 (1911), 269-331. Translation of laws for nobility, warriors, and commoners.

_____. "Japanese Feudal Laws IV—The Tokugawa Legislation, Part IV," *Transactions, Asiatic Society of Japan*, 1st series, 41 (1913), 683-804. Translation of the "Edict in 100 Sections," revised in 1790; accompanied by graphic illustrations of methods of torture and execution.

John Henry Wigmore, ed. MATERIAL FOR THE STUDY OF PRIVATE LAW
IN OLD JAPAN. 1964 reprint by University of Tokyo Press of 4 long
articles originally published in 1892.

_____. LAW AND JUSTICE IN TOKUGAWA JAPAN: MATERIALS FOR
THE HISTORY OF JAPANESE LAW AND JUSTICE UNDER THE
TOKUGAWA SHŌGUNATE, 1603-1867. 1968-1986: 20-volume
reprint edition by the Japan Foundation and the University of Tokyo
Press.

Eiko Ikegami. "Disciplining the Japanese: The Reconstruction of Social Control
in Tokugawa Japan." 1989: Ph.D. dissertation in Sociology, Harvard
University.

Torao Haraguchi et al. THE STATUS SYSTEM AND SOCIAL ORGANIZA-
TION OF SATSUMA: A TRANSLATION OF THE *SHŪMON
TEFUDA ARATAME JŌMOKU*. 1975: University of Hawaii Press.

Shunzō Sakamaki. JAPAN AND THE UNITED STATES, 1790-1853. 1973:
Scholarly Resources reprint; originally a Columbia University Ph.D.
dissertation, first published in *Transactions of the Asiatic Society of
Japan*, 1939.

Ronald P. Toby. STATE AND DIPLOMACY IN EARLY MODERN JAPAN:
ASIA IN THE DEVELOPMENT OF THE TOKUGAWA BAKUFU.
1983: Princeton University Press; 1991: Stanford University Press..

_____. "Reopening the Question of *Sakoku*: Diplomacy in the Legitimation of
the Tokugawa Bakufu," *Journal of Japanese Studies* 3.2 (1977),
323-364.

Jurgis Elisonas [formerly George Elison]. "The Inseparable Trinity: Japan's
Relations with China and Korea," in John Whitney Hall, ed.
CAMBRIDGE HISTORY OF JAPAN, Volume 4: EARLY MODERN
JAPAN (1991: Cambridge University Press), 235-300.

_____. "Christianity and the Daimyō," in John Whitney Hall, ed.
CAMBRIDGE HISTORY OF JAPAN, Volume 4: EARLY MODERN
JAPAN (1991: Cambridge University Press), 301-372.

Marius B. Jansen. CHINA IN THE TOKUGAWA WORLD. 1992: Harvard
University Press.

_____. "Japan in the Early Nineteenth Century," in Marius B. Jansen, ed. CAMBRIDGE HISTORY OF JAPAN, Volume 5: THE NINETEENTH CENTURY (1989: Cambridge University Press), 50-115.

Keiji Nagahara. "The Historical Premises for the Modernization of Japan: On the Structure of the Tokugawa Shōgunate," *Hitosubashi Journal of Economics* 3.1 (October 1962), 61-72.

Anne Walthall. "Peripheries: Rural Culture in Tokugawa Japan," *Monumenta Nipponica* 39.4 (1984), 371-392.

Constantine Nomikos Vaporis. "Overland Communication in Tokugawa Japan." 1987: Ph.D. dissertation in East Asian Studies, Princeton University.

Kären Wigen. "The Geographic Imagination in Early Modern Japanese History: Retrospect and Prospect," *Journal of Asian Studies* 51.1 (1992), 3-29. On the importance of geography in Tokugawa history.

TOKUGAWA: ECONOMIC

Sydney Crawcour. "The Premodern Economy," in Arthur E. Tiedemann, ed. AN INTRODUCTION TO JAPANESE CIVILIZATION (1974: Heath), 461-486.

_____. "The Tokugawa Period and Japan's Preparation for Modern Economic Growth," *Journal of Japanese Studies* 1.1 (1974), 113-125.

_____. "The Tokugawa Heritage," in William W. Lockwood, ed. THE STATE AND ECONOMIC ENTERPRISE IN JAPAN (1965: Princeton University Press), 17-44.

_____. "Changes in Japanese Commerce in the Tokugawa Period," in John W. Hall & Marius Jansen, eds. STUDIES IN THE INSTITUTIONAL HISTORY OF EARLY MODERN JAPAN (1968: Princeton University Press), 189-202.

_____. "Economic Change in the Nineteenth Century," in Marius B. Jansen, ed. CAMBRIDGE HISTORY OF JAPAN, Volume 5: THE NINETEENTH CENTURY (1989: Cambridge University Press), 569-617.

Seymour Broadbridge. "Economic and Social Trends in Tokugawa Japan," *Modern Asian Studies* 8.3 (1974), 347-372.

Daniel L. Spencer. "Japan's Pre-Perry Preparation for Economic Growth," *American Journal of Economics and Sociology* 17 (1958), 195-216.

Mark Jason Ravina. "Political Economy and Statecraft in Early Modern Japan." 1991: Ph.D. dissertation in History, Stanford University.

Junnosuke Sasaki. "Some Remarks on the Economic Foundation of Military Service under the Tokugawa Shōgunate System," *Hitotsubashi Journal of Social Studies* 2.1 (1964), 36-53.

Toshio Furushima. "The Village and Agriculture during the Edo Period," James L. McClain, transl., in John Whitney Hall, ed. CAMBRIDGE HISTORY OF JAPAN, Volume 4: EARLY MODERN JAPAN (1991: Cambridge University Press), 478-518.

Thomas C. Smith. THE AGRARIAN ORIGINS OF MODERN JAPAN. 1959: Stanford University Press.

_____. NAKAHARA: FAMILY FARMING AND POPULATION IN A JAPANESE VILLAGE, 1717-1830. 1977: Stanford University Press.

_____. NATIVE SOURCES OF JAPANESE INDUSTRIALIZATION, 1750-1920. 1988: University of California Press. Reviewed by Osamu Saitō in *Journal of Economic History* 49 (1989), 992-999.

_____. "Pre-Modern Economic Growth: Japan and the West," *Past and Present* 60 (1973), 127-160.

_____. "Farm Family By-Employments in Pre-Industrial Japan," *Journal of Economic History* 29.4 (1969), 687-715.

_____. "The Japanese Village in the Seventeenth Century," *Journal of Economic History* 12.1 (1952), 1-20. Reprinted in Hall & Jansen, STUDIES IN THE INSTITUTIONAL HISTORY OF EARLY MODERN JAPAN (1968: Princeton University Press), 263-282.

_____. "The Land Tax in the Tokugawa Period," *Journal of Asian Studies* 18.1 (1958), 3-20. Reprinted in Hall & Jansen, STUDIES IN THE INSTITUTIONAL HISTORY OF EARLY MODERN JAPAN (1968: Princeton University Press), 283-299.

_____. "The Introduction of Western Industry to Japan During the Last Years of the Tokugawa Period," *Harvard Journal of Asian Studies* 11 (1948), 130-152.

_____ & Robert Eng. "Peasant Families and Population Control in Eighteenth-Century Japan," *Journal of Interdisciplinary History* 6.3 (1976), 417-445.

Osamu Saitō. "Infanticide, Fertility, and 'Population Stagnation': The State of Tokugawa Historical Demography," *Japan Forum* 4.2 (1992), 369-381.

Ann Bowman Jannetta. EPIDEMICS AND MORTALITY IN EARLY MODERN JAPAN. 1987: Princeton University Press.

William Donald Johnston. "Disease, Medicine, and the State: A Social History of Tuberculosis in Japan, 1850-1950." 1987: Ph.D. dissertation in History and East Asian Languages, Harvard University.

Susan B. Hanley & Kōzō Yamamura. ECONOMIC AND DEMOGRAPHIC CHANGE IN PREINDUSTRIAL JAPAN, 1600-1868. 1977: Princeton University Press. See the extended reviews of this work by Dana Morris & Stephen Vlastos in *Journal of Asian Studies* 39.2 (1980), 361-368; and by Harold Bolitho in *Harvard Journal of Asiatic Studies* 39 (1979), 443-448.

_____. "A Quiet Transformation in Tokugawa Economic History," *Journal of Asian Studies* 31.2 (1972), 373-384.

Susan B. Hanley. "Tokugawa Society: Material Culture, Standard of Living, and Life-Styles," in John Whitney Hall, ed. CAMBRIDGE HISTORY OF JAPAN, Volume 4: EARLY MODERN JAPAN (1991: Cambridge University Press), 660-705.

_____. "A High Standard of Living in Nineteenth-Century Japan: Fact or Fantasy?" *Journal of Economic History* 43 (1983), 183-192. See also Yasukichi Yasuba, "Standard of Living in Japan Before Industrialization: From What Level Did Japan Begin?", *Journal of Economic History* 46.1 (1986), 217-224; and Susan B. Hanley, "Standard of Living in Nineteenth-Century Japan: Reply to Yasuba," *Journal of Economic History* 46.1 (1986), 225-226.

Kōzō Yamamura. A STUDY OF SAMURAI INCOME AND ENTREPRE-NEURSHIP. 1974: Harvard University Press.

_____. "Pre-Industrial Landholding Patterns in Japan and England," in Albert M. Craig, ed. JAPAN: A COMPARATIVE VIEW (1979: Princeton University Press), 276-323.

_____. "From Coins to Rice: Hypotheses on the *Kandaka* and *Kokudaka* Systems," *Journal of Japanese Studies* 14.2 (1988), 341-367.

Conrad Totman. "Tokugawa Peasants: Win, Lose, or Draw?" *Monumenta Nipponica* 41.4 (1986), 457-476. A basically pessimistic view of Tokugawa peasant life, from an ecological perspective. Includes an excellent bibliography.

Griffith Feeney & Kiyoshi Hamano. "Rice Price Fluctuations and Fertility in Late Tokugawa Japan," *Journal of Japanese Studies* 16.1 (1990), 1-30.

Philip C. Brown. "The Mismeasure of Land: Land Surveying in the Tokugawa Period," *Monumenta Nipponica* 42.2 (1987), 115-155.

_____. "Practical Constraints on Early Tokugawa Land Taxation: Annual Versus Fixed Assessments in Kaga Domain," *Journal of Japanese Studies* 14.2 (1988), 369-401.

Isao Soranaka. "The Kansei Reforms—Success or Failure?", *Monumenta Nipponica* 33.1 (1978), 151-164.

William Chambliss. CHIARAIJIMA VILLAGE: LAND TENURE, TAXATION, AND LOCAL TRADE, 1811-1884. 1965: University of Arizona Press.

R. Varner. "The Organized Peasant: The *Wakamonogumi* in the Edo Period," *Monumenta Nipponica* 32.4 (1977), 459-483.

Anne Walthall. "Village Networks: *Sōdai* and the Sale of Edo Nightsoil," *Monumenta Nipponica* 43.3 (1988), 279-303.

Arne Kalland. FISHING VILLAGES IN TOKUGAWA JAPAN. 1994: Curzon Press.

_____ & Jon Pedersen. "Famine and Population in Fukuoka Domain During the Tokugawa Period," *Journal of Japanese Studies* 10.1 (1984), 31-72.

Yukiko Kawahara. "Local Development in Japan: The Case of Shimane Prefecture from 1800-1930." 1990: Ph.D. dissertation in Oriental Studies, University of Arizona. On government encouragement of the silk industry.

Kären Esther Wigen. "Regional Inversions: The Spatial Contours of Economic Change in the Southern Japanese Alps, 1750-1920." 1990: Ph.D. dissertation in Geography, University of California.

William B. Hauser. ECONOMIC INSTITUTIONAL CHANGE IN TOKU-GAWA JAPAN: OSAKA AND THE KINAI COTTON TRADE. 1974: Cambridge University Press.

Nobuhiko Nakai & James L. McClain. "Commercial Change and Urban Growth in Early Modern Japan," in John Whitney Hall, ed. CAMBRIDGE HISTORY OF JAPAN, Volume 4: EARLY MODERN JAPAN (1991: Cambridge University Press), 519-595.

Gilbert Rozman. URBAN NETWORKS IN CH'ING CHINA AND TOKUGAWA JAPAN. 1974: Princeton University Press.

_____. "Edo's Importance in the Changing Tokugawa Society," *Journal of Japanese Studies* 1.1 (1974), 113-126.

Ryōsuke Ishii. "Loan Repayments in Edo and Osaka," *Japan Foundation Newsletter* 14.6 (1987), 7-8.

Gary P. Leupp. SERVANTS, SHOPHANDS, AND LABORERS IN THE CITIES OF TOKUGAWA JAPAN. 1992: Princeton University Press.

Takeshi Toyoda. A HISTORY OF PRE-MEIJI COMMERCE IN JAPAN. 1969: Kokusai Bunka Shinkōkai.

Charles D. Sheldon. THE RISE OF THE MERCHANT CLASS IN TOKUGAWA JAPAN, 1600-1868. 1958: Augustin.

John G. Roberts. MITSUI: THREE CENTURIES OF JAPANESE BUSINESS. 1973: Weatherhill.

E. S. Crawcour, transl. "Some Observations on Merchants," *Transactions, Asiatic Society of Japan* (1961), 1-139. A translation of Mitsui Takafusa's *Chōnin Kōken Roku*.

J. Mark Ramseyer. "Thrift and Diligence: House Codes of Tokugawa Merchant Families," *Monumenta Nipponica* 34.2 (1979), 209-230.

Ronald P. Toby. "Both a Borrower and a Lender Be: From Village Moneylender to Rural Banker in the Tempō Era," *Monumenta Nipponica* 46.4 (1991), 483-512.

"Studies in the History of Foreign Trade in Early Modern Japan." Special issue of *Acta Asiatica* 30 (1976).

David Luke Howell. "The Capitalist Transformation of the Hokkaidō Fishery, 1672-1935." 1989: Ph.D. dissertation in History, Princeton University.

_____. "Hard Times in the Kantō: Economic Change and Village Life in Late Tokugawa Japan," *Modern Asian Studies* 23.2 (1989), 349-371.

_____. "Proto-Industrial Origins of Japanese Capitalism," *Journal of Asian Studies* 51.2 (1992), 269-286.

Erich Pauer. "The Years Economic Historians Lost: Japan, 1850-1890," *Japan Forum* 3.1 (1991), 1-9.

Robert J. Smith. "Small Families, Small Households, and Residential Instability: Town and City in 'Pre-Modern' Japan," in Peter Laslett, ed. HOUSE-HOLD AND FAMILY IN PAST TIME (1972: Cambridge University Press), 429-471.

_____. "The Domestic Cycle in Selected Commoner Families in Urban Japan, 1757-1858," *Journal of Family History* 3.3 (1978), 219-235.

James Nakamura & Masao Miyamoto. "Social Structure and Population Change: A Comparative Study of Tokugawa Japan and Ch'ing China," *Economic Development and Cultural Change* 30.2 (January 1982), 229-269.

Robert G. Flershem & Yoshiko N. Flershem. "Migratory Fishermen on the Japan Sea Coast in the Tokugawa Period," *Japan Forum* 3.1 (1991), 71-90.

Conrad Totman. THE ORIGINS OF JAPAN'S MODERN FORESTS: THE CASE OF AKITA. 1984: University of Hawaii Press.

_____. THE GREEN ARCHIPELAGO: FORESTRY IN PREINDUSTRIAL JAPAN. 1989: University of California Press.

_____. "Land-Use Patterns and Afforestation in the Edo Period," *Monumenta Nipponica* 39.1 (1984), 1-10.

_____. "Preindustrial River Conservancy," *Monumenta Nipponica* 47.1 (1992), 59-76.

William W. Kelly. WATER CONTROL IN TOKUGAWA JAPAN: IRRIGA-TION ORGANIZATION IN A JAPANESE RIVER BASIN, 1600-1870. 1982: Cornell China-Japan Program.

TOKUGAWA: INTELLECTUAL

R. Tsunoda et al. SOURCES OF JAPANESE TRADITION (1958: Columbia University Press), chapters 15-24.

Ronald P. Dore. EDUCATION IN TOKUGAWA JAPAN. 1965: University of California Press.

_____. "The Legacy of Tokugawa Education," in Marius Jansen, ed. CHANGING JAPANESE ATTITUDES TOWARD MODERNIZA-TION (1965: Princeton University Press), 99-131.

_____. "Talent and Social Order in Tokugawa Japan," in John Hall & Marius Jansen, eds. STUDIES IN THE INSTITUTIONAL HISTORY OF EARLY MODERN JAPAN (1968: Princeton University Press), 349-361.

Richard Rubinger. PRIVATE ACADEMIES OF THE TOKUGAWA PERIOD. 1982: Princeton University Press.

Marleen R. Kassel. "Hirose Tanzō (1782-1856): Educational Theory and Practice in the Late Tokugawa Period." 1990: Ph.D. dissertation in East Asian Languages and Cultures, Columbia University.

_____. "Moral Education in Early-Modern Japan: The Kangien Confucian Academy of Tansō Hirose," *Japanese Journal of Religious Studies* 20.4 (1993), 297-310.

Herbert Passin. SOCIETY AND EDUCATION IN JAPAN (1965: Teachers College and East Asian Institute, Columbia University), chapters 2-3.

Hiroshi Irie. "Apprenticeship Training in Tokugawa Japan," Rolf W. Giebel, transl., *Acta Asiatica* 54 (1988), 1-23.

Young-chin Kim. "On Political Thought in Tokugawa Japan," *Journal of Politics* 23 (1961), 127-145.

John S. Brownlee. POLITICAL THOUGHT IN JAPANESE HISTORICAL WRITING: FROM KOJIKI (712) TO TOKUSHI YORON (1712). 1991: Wilfrid Laurier University Press.

Ichirō Ishida. "Tokugawa Feudal Society and Neo-Confucian Thought," *Pacific Historical Review* 5 (1964), 1-38.

Yoshio Abe. "The Characteristics of Japanese Confucianism," *Acta Asiatica* 33 (1973), 1-21.

_____. "The Development of Neo-Confucianism in Japan, Korea and China," *Acta Asiatica* 17-18 (1969-1970), 16-39.

Robert Cornell Armstrong. LIGHT FROM THE EAST: STUDIES IN JAPANESE CONFUCIANISM. 1914: University of Toronto. Still useful for its capsule biographies.

Masahide Bitō. "Society and Social Thought in the Tokugawa Period," *Japan Society Newsletterr* 9.2.3 (1981), 1-9.

Tasaburō Itō. "The Book Banning Policy of the Tokugawa Shōgunate," *Acta Asiatica* 32 (1972), 36-61.

Naoki Sakai. VOICES OF THE PAST: THE STATUS OF LANGUAGE IN EIGHTEENTH-CENTURY JAPANESE DISCOURSE. 1992: Cornell University Press. Describes the rapid appearance in the late 17th century of a variety of new world views.

Masao Maruyama. STUDIES IN THE INTELLECTUAL HISTORY OF TOKUGAWA JAPAN. 1974: Princeton University Press. Translation by Mikiso Hane of the classic Japanese study.

Tetsuo Najita. "Reconsidering Maruyama Masao's *Studies*," *Japan Interpreter* 11.1 (1976), 97-108.

_____. JAPAN: THE INTELLECTUAL FOUNDATIONS OF MODERN JAPANESE POLITICS. 1974; 1980: University of Chicago Press.

_____. "Political Economism in the Thought of Dazai Shundai (1680-1747)," *Journal of Asian Studies* 31.4 (1972), 821-839.

_____. "Restorationism in the Political Thought of Yamagata Daini (1725-1767)," *Journal of Asian Studies* 31.1 (1971), 17-30.

_____. "History and Nature in Eighteenth-Century Tokugawa Thought," in John Whitney Hall, ed. CAMBRIDGE HISTORY OF JAPAN, Volume 4: EARLY MODERN JAPAN (1991: Cambridge University Press), 596-659.

_____. "Ōshio Heihachirō (1793-1837)," in Albert Craig & Donald Shively, eds. PERSONALITY IN JAPANESE HISTORY (1970: University of California Press), 155-179.

_____. VISIONS OF VIRTUE IN TOKUGAWA JAPAN: THE KAITOKUDŌ
MERCHANT ACADEMY OF OSAKA. 1987: University of Chicago
Press.

_____ & Irwin Scheiner, eds. JAPANESE THOUGHT IN THE TOKUGAWA
PERIOD, 1600-1868: METHODS AND METAPHORS. 1978:
University of Chicago Press. See the extended reviews by Klaus Kracht
in *Journal of Japanese Studies* 6.2 (1980), 331-353; Richard Minear in
Harvard Journal of Asiatic Studies 40 (1980), 285-291; and Harold
Bolitho in *Monumenta Nipponica* 35.1 (1980), 89-98. Also the Bolitho-
Harootunian exchange in *Monumenta Nipponica* 35.3 (1980), 368-374.

George O. Hlawatsch. "The Life of Dazai Shundai, 1680-1747." 1985:
Ph.D. dissertation in History, University of Hawaii.

Peter Nosco, ed. CONFUCIANISM AND TOKUGAWA CULTURE. 1984:
Princeton University Press.

_____. REMEMBERING PARADISE: NATIVISM AND NOSTALGIA IN
EIGHTEENTH-CENTURY JAPAN. 1990: Council on East Asian
Studies, Harvard University.

_____. "*Man'yōshū* Studies in Tokugawa Japan," *Transactions, Asiatic Society
of Japan*, 4th series, 1 (1986), 109-146.

Kate Nakai. "The Naturalization of Confucianism in Tokugawa Japan: The
Problem of Sinocentrism," *Harvard Journal of Asiatic Studies* 40.1
(June 1980), 157-199.

Beatrice Bodart-Bailey. "The Persecution of Confucianism in Early Tokugawa
Japan," *Monumenta Nipponica* 48.3 (1993), 293-314.

Herman Ooms. TOKUGAWA IDEOLOGY: EARLY CONSTRUCTS,
1570-1680. 1985: University of Chicago Press.

_____. " 'Primeval Chaos' and 'Mental Void' in Early Tokugawa Ideology:
Fujiwara Seika, Suzuki Shōsan, and Yamazaki Ansai," *Japanese Journal
of Religious Studies* 13.4 (1986), 245-260.

Makoto Kuroizumi. "The Nature of Early Tokugawa Confucianism," Herman
Ooms, transl., *Journal of Japanese Studies* 20.2 (1994), 331-375.

David Nivison & Arthur Wright, eds. CONFUCIANISM IN ACTION. 1959:
Stanford University Press. See articles on Japan by DeBary, Hall, and
Shively.

W. T. DeBary. NEO-CONFUCIAN ORTHODOXY: THE LEARNING OF
    THE HEART-AND-MIND. 1981: Columbia University Press.

_____ & Irene Bloom, eds. PRINCIPLE AND PRACTICALITY: ESSAYS
    IN NEO-CONFUCIANISM AND PRACTICAL LEARNING. 1979:
    Columbia University Press.

Thomas C. Smith. " 'Merit' As Ideology in the Tokugawa Period," in Ronald
    Dore, ed. ASPECTS OF SOCIAL CHANGE IN MODERN JAPAN
    (1967: Princeton University Press), 71-90.

Albert Craig. "Science and Confucianism in Tokugawa Japan," in Marius Jansen,
    ed. CHANGING JAPANESE ATTITUDES TOWARD MODERNIZA-
    TION (1965: Princeton University Press), 133-160.

Hajime Nakamura. A HISTORY OF THE DEVELOPMENT OF JAPANESE
    THOUGHT FROM 592 TO 1868. 1967: University of Tokyo.

_____. "Suzuki Shōsan, 1599-1655, and the Spirit of Capitalism in Japanese
    Buddhism," *Monumenta Nipponica* 22.1-2 (1967), 1-14.

Robert N. Bellah. TOKUGAWA RELIGION: THE VALUES OF PRE-INDUS-
    TRIAL JAPAN. 1957: Free Press.

Janine Anderson Sawada. CONFUCIAN VALUES AND POPULAR ZEN:
    SEKIMON SHINGAKU IN EIGHTEENTH-CENTURY JAPAN. 1993:
    University of Hawaii Press.

Ken Ishikawa. "Baigan Ishida's *Shingaku* Doctrine," *Philosophical Studies of
    Japan* 6 (1965), 1-30.

J. Robertson. "Rooting the Pine: *Shingaku* Methods of Organization,"
    Monumenta Nipponica 33.4 (1979), 311-322.

Kōjirō Yoshikawa. JINSAI, SORAI, NORINAGA: THREE CLASSICAL
    PHILOLOGISTS IN MID-TOKUGAWA JAPAN. 1983: University of
    Tokyo Press.

Shōeki Andō. THE ANIMAL COURT: A POLITICAL FABLE FROM OLD
    JAPAN. Jeffrey Hunter, transl. 1992: Weatherhill.

Toshinobu Yasunaga, ed. ANDŌ SHŌEKI: SOCIAL AND ECOLOGICAL
    PHILOSOPHER OF EIGHTEENTH-CENTURY JAPAN. 1992:
    Weatherhill. Includes extensive translations of this iconoclastic thinker.

E. H. Norman. ANDŌ SHŌEKI AND THE ANATOMY OF JAPANESE
FEUDALISM. 1949: Special issue of *Transactions, Asiatic Society of
Japan*.

Shūichi Katō. THE LIFE AND THOUGHT OF TOMINAGA NAKAMOTO,
1715-1746: A TOKUGAWA ICONOCLAST. 1967: University of
British Columbia Press.

T. H. Barrett. "Tominaga Our Contemporary," *Journal of the Royal Asiatic
Society*, Third Series, Volume 3, Part 2 (1993), 245-252.

J. R. McEwan. THE POLITICAL WRITINGS OF OGYŪ SORAI. 1962:
Cambridge University Press.

Olof G. Lidin. THE LIFE OF OGYŪ SORAI, A TOKUGAWA CONFUCIAN
PHILOSOPHER. 1973: Scandinavian Institute of Asian Studies
Monograph Series 19.

_____, transl. OGYŪ SORAI: DISTINGUISHING THE WAY *(BENDŌ)*.
1970: Monumenta Nipponica Monographs.

_____. "Ogyū Sorai's 'Political Discussions': A Plea for Reform," *Japan
Foundation Newsletter* 17.4 (1990), 1-14.

_____. "Ogyū Sorai's Civil Society *(Seidan)*," *Japan Review* 5 (1994), 3-13.

Richard Minear, transl. "Ogyū Sorai's *Instructions for Students*: A Translation
and Commentary," *Harvard Journal of Asiatic Studies* 36 (1976), 5-81.

Joseph J. Spae. ITŌ JINSAI: A PHILOSOPHER, EDUCATOR AND
SINOLOGIST OF THE TOKUGAWA PERIOD. 1948: Catholic
University Press.

Kōjirō Yoshikawa. "Itō Jinsai," *Acta Asiatica* 23 (1973), 22-53.

Gregory J. Smits. "The Sages' Scale in Japan: Nakae Tōju (1608-1648) and
Situational Weighing," *Transactions, Asiatic Society of Japan*, 4th series,
5 (1991), 1-25.

Galen M. Fisher. "The Life and Teaching of Nakae Tōju," *Transactions, Asiatic
Society of Japan*, 1st series, 36 (1908), 24-94.

_____. "Kumazawa Banzan, His Life and Ideas," *Transactions, Asiatic Society
of Japan*, 2nd series, 16 (1938), 223-258.

_____, transl. *"Daigaku Wakumon*: A Discussion of Public Questions in the Light of the Great Learning," *Transactions, Asiatic Society of Japan*, 2nd series, 16 (1938), 259-356.

I. J. McMullen. *GENJI GAIDEN*: THE ORIGINS OF KUMAZAWA BANZAN'S COMMENTARY ON THE TALE OF GENJI. 1991: Ithaca Press, Oxford Oriental Institute.

Gino Piovesana. "Miura Baien, 1723-1769, and His Dialectic and Political Ideas," *Monumenta Nipponica* 20.3-4 (1965), 389-421.

Michiko Y. Aoki & Margaret B. Dardess. "The Popularization of Samurai Values: A Sermon by Hosoi Heishū," *Monumenta Nipponica* 31.4 (1976), 400-413; reprinted in Aoki & Dardess, AS THE JAPANESE SEE IT: PAST AND PRESENT (1981: University of Hawaii Press), 59-72.

Mary Evelyn Tucker. "Religious Aspects of Japanese Neo-Confucianism: The Thought of Nakae Tōju and Kaibara Ekken," *Japanese Journal of Religious Studies* 15.1 (1988), 55-69.

_____. "Moral and Spiritual Cultivation in Japanese Neo-Confucianism: The Life and Thought of Kaibara Ekken (1630-1714)." 1985: Ph.D. dissertation in Religion, Columbia University.

Ekiken (Ekken) Kaibara. "THE WAY OF CONTENTMENT" AND "GREATER LEARNING FOR WOMEN." 1913: reprint edition, 1979: University Publications of America. Translations of two famous essays by a Neo-Confucian scholar who lived from 1630 to 1714.

Olaf Graf. KAIBARA EKKEN. 1942: Brill.

Joyce Ackroyd, transl. TOLD ROUND A BRUSHWOOD FIRE: THE AUTO-BIOGRAPHY OF ARAI HAKUSEKI. 1980: Princeton University Press. Hakuseki lived 1657-1725.

_____, transl. LESSONS FROM HISTORY: ARAI HAKUSEKI'S *TOKUSHI YORON*. 1982: University of Queensland Press.

Kate Wildman Nakai. "Apologia pro Vita Sua: Arai Hakuseki's Autobiography," *Monumenta Nipponica* 36.2 (1981), 173-186.

_____. SHŌGUNAL POLITICS: ARAI HAKUSEKI AND THE PREMISES OF TOKUGAWA RULE. 1988: Council on East Asian Studies, Harvard University.

Herman Ooms. "Hakuseki's Reading of History," *Monumenta Nipponica* 39.3 (1984), 333-350.

Shōichi Sakae. "The Autobiography in Japan," Teruko Craig, transl., *Journal of Japanese Studies* 11.2 (1985), 357-368.

Kokei Tomita. A PEASANT SAGE OF JAPAN: THE LIFE AND WORK OF SONTOKU NINOMIYA. 1912: Harvard University Press.

Bob Tadashi Wakabayashi. "In Name Only: Imperial Sovereignty in Early Modern Japan," *Journal of Japanese Studies* 17.1 (1991), 25-57.

Herschel Webb. THE JAPANESE IMPERIAL INSTITUTION IN THE TOKUGAWA PERIOD. 1968: Columbia University Press.

David Earl. EMPEROR AND NATION IN JAPAN: POLITICAL THINKERS OF THE TOKUGAWA PERIOD. 1964: University of Washington Press. Focus on Yoshida Shōin.

Shigeru Matsumoto. MOTOORI NORINAGA, 1730-1801. 1970: Harvard University Press.

Sey Nishimura. "First Steps into the Mountains: Motoori Norinaga's *Uiyamabumi*," *Monumenta Nipponica* 42.4 (1987), 449-493.

_____. "The Way of the Gods: Motoori Norinaga's *Naobi no Mitama*," *Monumenta Nipponica* 46.1 (1991), 21-41.

John S. Brownlee. "The Jeweled Comb-Box: Motoori Norinaga's *Tamakushige*," *Monumenta Nipponica* 43.1 (1988), 35-61.

Tadashi Ōkubo. "The Thoughts of Mabuchi and Norinaga," *Acta Asiatica* 33 (1973), 68-90.

Robert L. Backus. "Tsukada Taihō on the Way and Virtue. Part One: Career and Scholarship;" "Part Two: Attaining the Gates to the Way of the Sage," *Harvard Journal of Asiatic Studies* 50.1 (1990), 5-69; 50.2 (1990), 505-560.

Richard Devine. "Hirata Atsutane and Christian Sources," *Monumenta Nipponica* 36.1 (1981), 37-54.

Tsuguo Tahara. "The *Kokugaku* Thought," *Acta Asiatica* 33 (1973), 54-67.

Harry D. Harootunian. TOWARD RESTORATION: THE GROWTH OF
POLITICAL CONSCIOUSNESS IN TOKUGAWA JAPAN. Revised
edition. 1991: University of California Press.

_____. "The Functions of China in Tokugawa Thought," in Akira Iriye, ed.
THE CHINESE AND THE JAPANESE (1980: Harvard University
Press), 9-36.

_____. THINGS SEEN AND UNSEEN: DISCOURSE AND IDEOLOGY IN
TOKUGAWA NATIVISM. 1988: University of Chicago Press.

_____. "Late Tokugawa Culture and Thought," in Marius B. Jansen, ed.
CAMBRIDGE HISTORY OF JAPAN, Volume 5: THE NINETEENTH
CENTURY (1989: Cambridge University Press), 168-258.

J. Victor Koschmann. THE MITO IDEOLOGY: DISCOURSE, REFORM,
AND INSURRECTION IN LATE TOKUGAWA JAPAN, 1790-1864.
1987: University of California Press.

Bob Tadashi Wakabayashi. ANTI-FOREIGNISM AND WESTERN LEARN-
ING IN EARLY-MODERN JAPAN: THE NEW THESES OF 1825.
1986: Council on East Asian Studies, Harvard University.

_____. "Opium, Expulsion, Sovereignty: China's Lessons for Bakumatsu
Japan," *Monumenta Nipponica* 47.1 (1992), 1-25.

Bonnie Abiko. "Persecuted Patriot: Watanabe Kazan and the Tokugawa
Bakufu," *Monumenta Nipponica* 44.2 (1989), 199-219.

Jennifer Robertson. "Sexy Rice: Plant Gender, Farm Manuals, and Grass-Roots
Nativism," *Monumenta Nipponica* 39.3 (1984), 233-260.

H. Van Straelen. YOSHIDA SHŌIN: FORERUNNER OF THE MEIJI
RESTORATION. 1952: Brill.

Donald Keene. THE JAPANESE DISCOVERY OF EUROPE: HONDA
TOSHIAKI AND OTHER DISCOVERERS, 1720-1830. 1952.
Revised edition. 1969: Stanford University Press.

Carmen Blacker. "Ōhashi Totsuan: A Study in Anti-Western Thought,"
Transactions, Asiatic Society of Japan (1959), 147-168.

Richard T. Chang. FROM PREJUDICE TO TOLERANCE: A STUDY OF
THE JAPANESE IMAGE OF THE WEST, 1826-1864. 1970:
Monumenta Nipponica Monographs.

Christal Whelan. "Religion Concealed: The Kakure Kirishitan on Narushima," *Monumenta Nipponica* 47.3 (1992), 369-387.

Grant K. Goodman. JAPAN: THE DUTCH EXPERIENCE. 1986: Athlone. Revised version of THE DUTCH IMPACT ON JAPAN, 1600-1853 (1967: Brill).

R. van Gulik, et al., eds. IN THE WAKE OF THE LIEFDE: CULTURAL RELATIONS BETWEEN THE NETHERLANDS AND JAPAN, SINCE 1600. 1986: De Bataafsche Leeuw.

George Elison. DEUS DESTROYED: THE IMAGE OF CHRISTIANITY IN EARLY MODERN JAPAN. 1973: Harvard University Press.

Charles R. Boxer. THE CHRISTIAN CENTURY IN JAPAN (1549-1650). 1967: University of California Press.

_____. JAN COMPAIGNE IN JAPAN: AN ESSAY ON THE CULTURAL, ARTISTIC AND SCIENTIFIC INFLUENCE EXERCISED BY THE HOLLANDERS IN JAPAN FROM THE SEVENTEENTH TO THE NINETEENTH CENTURIES. 1950: Martinus Nijhoff.

K. Vos. ASSIGNMENT JAPAN: VON SIEBOLD, PIONEER AND COLLECTOR. 1989: SDU.

Tessa Morris-Suzuki. A HISTORY OF JAPANESE ECONOMIC THOUGHT. 1989: Routledge.

Masayoshi Sugimoto & David L. Swain. SCIENCE AND CULTURE IN TRADITIONAL JAPAN, 600-1854. 1978: Massachusetts Institute of Technology Press.

Keiji Nagahara & Kōzō Yamamura. "Shaping the Process of Unification: Technological Progress in Sixteenth- and Seventeenth-Century Japan," *Journal of Japanese Studies* 14.1 (1988), 77-109.

Shigeru Nakayama. A HISTORY OF JAPANESE ASTRONOMY. 1969: Harvard University Press.

Shuntarō Itō. "The Introduction of Western Cosmology in Seventeenth Century Japan: The Case of Christovão Ferreira (1580-1652)," *Japan Foundation Newsletter* 14.1 (1986), 1-9.

Mark Ravina. "*Wasan* and the Physics that Wasn't: Mathematics in the Tokugawa Period," *Monumenta Nipponica* 48.2 (1993), 205-224.

Hideomi Tuge. HISTORICAL DEVELOPMENT OF SCIENCE AND TECHNOLOGY IN JAPAN. 1961: Kokusai Bunka Shinkōkai.

John Z. Bowers. WESTERN MEDICAL PIONEERS IN FEUDAL JAPAN. 1970: Johns Hopkins.

_____. MEDICAL EDUCATION IN JAPAN: FROM CHINESE MEDICINE TO WESTERN MEDICINE. 1965: Harper & Row.

Timothy Benjamin Mark Screech. "The Western Scientific Gaze and Popular Culture in Late Edo Japan." 1991: Ph.D. dissertation in Fine Arts, Harvard University.

Genpaku Sugita. DAWN OF WESTERN SCIENCE IN JAPAN, OR *RANGAKU KOTOHAJIME*. R. Matsumoto, transl. 1969: Hokuseidō. Originally published in 1815.

Calvin French. SHIBA KŌKAN: ARTIST, INNOVATOR, AND PIONEER IN THE WESTERNIZATION OF JAPAN. 1974: Weatherhill.

Monumenta Nipponica 19.3-4 (1964), 235-419. Special issue devoted to the early Western influence on Japan in such areas as culture, Dutch language, medicine, geography, astronomy, natural history, the physical sciences, military science, shipbuilding, navigation, and art.

J. A. G. Roberts. "Not the Least Deserving: The *Philosophes* and the Religions of Japan," *Monumenta Nipponica* 44.2 (1989), 151-169.

TOKUGAWA: POPULAR CULTURE

Charles J. Dunn. EVERYDAY LIFE IN TRADITIONAL JAPAN. 1969: Putnam.

Gary P. Leupp. SERVANTS, SHOPHANDS, AND LABORERS IN THE CITIES OF TOKUGAWA JAPAN. 1992: Princeton University Press.

Kenneth Porter Kirkwood. RENAISSANCE IN JAPAN: A CULTURAL SURVEY OF THE SEVENTEENTH CENTURY. New edition. 1970: Tuttle.

C. Andrew Gerstle, ed. 18TH CENTURY JAPAN: CULTURE AND
SOCIETY. 1989: Allen & Unwin.

H. D. Harootunian. "Late Tokugawa Culture and Thought," in Marius B. Jansen,
ed. CAMBRIDGE HISTORY OF JAPAN, Volume 5: THE NINE-
TEENTH CENTURY (1989: Cambridge University Press), 168-258.

Oliver Statler. JAPANESE INN. 1961: Secker & Warburg.

Donald H. Shively. "Popular Culture," in John Whitney Hall, ed. CAMBRIDGE
HISTORY OF JAPAN, Volume 4: EARLY MODERN JAPAN (1991:
Cambridge University Press), 706-769.

_____. THE LOVE SUICIDE AT AMIJIMA. 1953: Harvard University Press.
See introduction on pleasure quarters.

_____. "Bakufu versus Kabuki," *Harvard Journal of Asiatic Studies* 18 (1955),
326-356.

_____. "Sumptuary Regulation and Status in Early Tokugawa Japan," *Harvard
Journal of Asiatic Studies* 25 (1964-1965), 123-164.

Cecilia Segawa Seigle. YOSHIWARA: THE GLITTERING WORLD OF THE
JAPANESE COURTESAN. 1993: University of Hawaii Press.

Liza Crihfield. "Yoshiwara," KŌDANSHA ENCYCLOPEDIA OF JAPAN
8: 349-351.

Joseph DeBecker. THE NIGHTLESS CITY, OR THE HISTORY OF THE
YOSHIWARA YŪKWAKU. 1899; reprint edition, 1971: Tuttle.

Lawrence Rogers. "She Loves Me, She Loves Me Not: *Shinjū* and Shikidō
Ōkagami," *Monumenta Nipponica* 49.1 (1994), 31-60. Commentary on
and partial translation of a 17th-century guide to the Edo pleasure
quarters.

Andrew L. Markus. "The Carnival of Edo: *Misemono* Spectacles from
Contemporary Accounts," *Harvard Journal of Asiatic Studies* 45.2
(1985), 499-541.

_____. "*Shogakai*: Celebrity Banquets of the Late Edo Period," *Harvard
Journal of Asiatic Studies* 53.1 (1993), 135-167.

Donald Jenkins et al. THE FLOATING WORLD REVISITED. 1994:
University of Hawaii Press.

Richard Lane. IMAGES FROM THE FLOATING WORLD: THE JAPANESE PRINT. 1978: Putnam.

_____. MASTERS OF THE JAPANESE PRINT: THEIR WORLD AND THEIR WORK. 1962: Doubleday.

James Michener. THE FLOATING WORLD: THE STORY OF JAPANESE PRINTS. 1954: Random House.

Henry D. Smith II. "World without Walls: Kuwagata Keisai's Panoramic Vision of Japan," in Gail Lee Bernstein & Haruhiro Fukui, eds. JAPAN AND THE WORLD: ESSAYS ON JAPANESE HISTORY AND POLITICS IN HONOUR OF ISHIDA TAKESHI (1988: St. Martin's), 3-19.

Paul Varley & Isao Kumakura, eds. TEA IN JAPAN: ESSAYS ON THE HISTORY OF CHANOYU. 1989: University of Hawaii Press.

Earl Miner, Hiroko Odagiri & Robert E. Morrell. THE PRINCETON COMPANION OF CLASSICAL JAPANESE LITERATURE. 1985: Princeton University Press. Covers literature from earliest times to 1868.

Shūichi Katō. A HISTORY OF JAPANESE LITERATURE: THE YEARS OF ISOLATION. Don Sanderson, transl. 1979: Kōdansha International. Volume 2 of a 3-volume survey.

Sōkichi Tsuda. AN INQUIRY INTO THE JAPANESE MIND AS MIRRORED IN LITERATURE: THE FLOWERING PERIOD OF COMMON PEOPLE LITERATURE. 1988: Greenwood Press.

Donald Keene. WORLD WITHIN WALLS: JAPANESE LITERATURE OF THE PRE-MODERN ERA, 1600-1867. 1976: Holt, Rinehart & Winston.

_____. BUNRAKU: THE ART OF THE JAPANESE PUPPET THEATER. 1965: Kōdansha International.

_____. NŌ AND BUNRAKU: TWO FORMS OF JAPANESE THEATRE. 1990: Columbia University Press.

_____, transl. MAJOR PLAYS OF CHIKAMATSU. 1961: Kōdansha International.

_____, transl. CHŪSHINGURA. 1971: Columbia University Press.

_____. TRAVELERS OF A HUNDRED AGES: THE JAPANESE AS REVEALED THROUGH 1,000 YEARS OF DIARIES. 1989: Henry Holt.

Jane Marie Law. "Religious Authority and Ritual Puppetry: The Case of *Dōkumbō Denki*," *Monumenta Nipponica* 47.1 (1992), 77-97. On a central narrative in Awaji puppetry.

Stanleigh H. Jones, Jr., transl. YOSHITSUNE AND THE THOUSAND CHERRY TREES: A MASTERPIECE OF THE EIGHTEENTH-CENTURY JAPANESE PUPPET THEATER. 1993: Columbia University Press.

C. Andrew Gerstle. "The Concept of Tragedy in Japanese Drama," *Japan Review* 1 (1990), 49-72.

_____. CIRCLES OF FANTASY: CONVENTION IN THE PLAYS OF CHIKAMATSU. 1985: Council on East Asian Studies, Harvard University.

Jacqueline Mueller. "A Chronicle of Great Peace: Chikamatsu Monzaemon's *Goban Taiheiki*," *Harvard Journal of Asiatic Studies* 46.1 (1986), 221-267.

Steven Heine. "Tragedy and Salvation in the Floating World: Chikamatsu's Double Suicide Drama as Millenarian Discourse," *Journal of Asian Studies* 53.2 (1994), 367-393.

Masakatsu Gunji. KABUKI. 1983: Kōdansha International.

James R. Brandon, William P. Malm & Donald H. Shively. STUDIES IN KABUKI: ITS ACTING, MUSIC, AND HISTORICAL CONTEXT. 1977: University of Hawaii Press.

James R. Brandon, ed. CHŪSHINGURA: STUDIES IN KABUKI AND THE PUPPET THEATER. 1982: University of Hawaii Press.

_____, transl. KABUKI: FIVE CLASSIC PLAYS. 1975: Harvard University Press; 1992: University of Hawaii Press.

Barbara E. Thornbury. SUKEROKU'S DOUBLE IDENTITY: THE DRAMATIC STRUCTURE OF EDO KABUKI. 1982: Center for Japanese Studies, University of Michigan.

Charles J. Dunn, ed. & transl. THE ACTORS' ANALECTS *(YAKUSHA RONGO)*. 1969: Columbia University Press.

Samuel Leiter. KABUKI ENCYCLOPEDIA: AN ENGLISH-LANGUAGE ADAPTATION OF *KABUKI JITEN.* 1979: Greenwood.

Faubion Bowers. JAPANESE THEATRE. 1959: Hill & Wang.

Ury Eppstein. "The Stage Observed: Western Attitudes toward Japanese Theatre," *Monumenta Nipponica* 48.2 (1993), 147-166.

Masako Nakagawa Graham. "The Consort and the Warrior: *Yōhiki Monogatari,*" *Monumenta Nipponica* 45.1 (1990), 1-26. A translation of a *ko-jōruri* puppet play.

Howard Hibbett. THE FLOATING WORLD IN JAPANESE FICTION. 1959: Grove.

Saikaku Ihara (1642-1693). THE JAPANESE FAMILY STOREHOUSE. G. W. Sargent, transl. 1959: Cambridge University Press.

_____. THE LIFE OF AN AMOROUS WOMAN AND OTHER WRITINGS. Ivan Morris, transl. 1963: New Directions.

_____. FIVE WOMEN WHO LOVED LOVE. W. T. DeBary, transl. 1956: Tuttle.

_____. TALES OF JAPANESE JUSTICE. T. Kondō & A. Marks, transl. 1980: University of Hawaii Press.

_____. THIS SCHEMING WORLD. M. Takatsuka & D. C. Stubbs, transl. 1965: Tuttle.

_____. WORLDLY MENTAL CALCULATIONS. B. Befu, transl. 1976: University of California Press.

_____. THE LIFE OF AN AMOROUS MAN. K. Hamada, transl. 1964: Tuttle.

_____. COMRADE LOVES OF THE SAMURAI. E. Powys Mathers, transl. 1981: Tuttle.

_____. TALES OF SAMURAI HONOR. C. A. Callahan, transl. 1982: Monumenta Nipponica Monographs.

_____. THE GREAT MIRROR OF MALE LOVE. Paul Gordon Schalow, transl. 1990: Stanford University Press.

Christopher Drake. "The Collision of Traditions in Saikaku's Haikai," *Harvard Journal of Asiatic Studies* 52.1 (1992), 5-75.

_____. "Saikaku's Haikai Requiem: *A Thousand Haikai Alone in a Single Day*, The First Hundred Verses," *Harvard Journal of Asiatic Studies* 52.2 (1992), 481-588.

Paul Gordon Schalow. "The Invention of a Literary Tradition of Male Love: Kitamura Kigin's *Iwatsutsuji*," *Monumenta Nipponica* 48.1 (1993), 1-31.

Charles E. Fox. "Old Stories, New Mode: Ejima Kiseki's *Ukiyo Oyaji Katagi*," *Monumenta Nipponica* 43.1 (1988), 63-93.

Robert W. Leutner. SHIKITEI SANBA AND THE COMIC TRADITION IN EDO FICTION. 1985: Harvard-Yenching Institute Monograph Series.

J. Scott Miller. "The Hybrid Narrative of Kyōden's *Sharebon*," *Monumenta Nipponica* 43.2 (1988), 133-152.

Ikku Jippensha. *HIZAKURIGE*, OR SHANKS' MARE. Thomas Satchell, transl. The most famous comic novel of feudal Japan, written in 1802; reprinted 1960: Tuttle.

Andrew Lawrence Markus. THE WILLOW IN AUTUMN: RYŪTEI TANE-HIKO, 1783 1842. 1994: Council on East Asian Studies, Harvard University. Deals with the life and works of a popular Edo writer.

Harold Bolitho. "Travelers' Tales: Three Eighteenth-Century Travel Journals," *Harvard Journal of Asiatic Studies* 50.2 (1990), 485-504.

Richard Lane. "The Beginnings of the Modern Japanese Novel: *Kana-Zōshi*, 1600-1682," *Harvard Journal of Asiatic Studies* 20.3-4 (1957), 644-701.

Gen Itasaka. "Characteristics of the Literature of Edo," *The Japan Society Newsletter* 9.5 (1981-1982), 1-5.

Jack Rucinski. "A Japanese Burlesque: *Nise Monogatari*," *Monumenta Nipponica* 30.1 (1975), 1-18.

Haruko Iwasaki. "Portrait of a Daimyō: Comical Fiction by Matsudaira Sadanobu," *Monumenta Nipponica* 38.1 (1983), 1-48.

Nobuko Ishii. "*Sekkyō-bushi*," *Monumenta Nipponica* 44.3 (1989), 283-307.

Heinz Morioka & Miyoko Sasaki. RAKUGO: THE POPULAR NARRATIVE
ART OF JAPAN. 1990: Council on East Asian Studies, Harvard
University.

R. H. Blyth. EDO SATIRICAL VERSE ANTHOLOGIES. 1961: Hokuseidō.

_____. JAPANESE LIFE AND CHARACTER IN SENRYŪ. 1960:
Hokuseidō.

_____. ORIENTAL HUMOR. 1959: Hokuseidō.

_____. HAIKU. 4 volumes. 1950-1952: Hokuseidō.

Bashō. THE NARROW ROAD TO THE DEEP NORTH, AND OTHER
TRAVEL SKETCHES. Nobuyuki Yuasa, transl. 1966: Penguin. Five
travel sketches by the greatest haiku poet, Matsuo Bashō (1644-1694).

_____. A HAIKU JOURNEY: BASHŌ'S "THE NARROW ROAD TO THE
FAR NORTH" AND SELECTED HAIKU. Dorothy Britton, transl.
1974: Kōdansha International.

_____. NARROW ROAD TO THE INTERIOR. Sam Hamill, transl. 1991:
Shambala.

_____. BACK ROADS TO FAR TOWNS: BASHŌ'S TRAVEL JOURNAL.
Cid Corman & Susumu Kamaike, transl. 1986: White Pine Press.

_____. ON LOVE AND BARLEY: HAIKU. Lucien Stryk, transl. & ed. 1985:
University of Hawaii Press.

Makoto Ueda. BASHŌ AND HIS INTERPRETERS: SELECTED HOKKU
WITH COMMENTARY. 1991: Stanford University Press.

_____. MATSUO BASHŌ. 1983: Kōdansha International.

David L. Barnhill. "Bashō as Bat: Wayfaring and Antistructure in the Journals
of Matsuo Bashō," *Journal of Asian Studies* 49.2 (1990), 274-290.

_____. "The Journey Itself Home: The Religiosity of the Literary Works of
Matsuo Bashō (1644-1694)." 1986: Ph.D. dissertation in Religious
Studies, Stanford University.

Haruo Shirane. "Matsuo Bashō and the Poetics of Scent," *Harvard Journal of
Asiatic Studies* 52.1 (1992), 77-110.

Joan Hertzog O'Mara. "The Haiga Genre and the Art of Yosa Buson (1716-84)." 1989: Ph.D. dissertation in History of Art, University of Michigan.

Leon Zolbrod. "The Busy Year: Buson's Life and Work, 1777," *Transactions, Asiatic Society of Japan*, 4th series, 3 (1988), 53-81.

Issa Kobayashi. AUTUMN WIND: A SELECTION FROM THE POEMS OF ISSA. Lewis Mackenzie, transl. 1984: Kōdansha International.

Patrick McElligott. "The Life and Work of Kobayashi Issa." 1984: Ph.D. dissertation in Oriental and African Languages and Literatures, University of London.

Burton Watson, transl. RYŌKAN: ZEN MONK-POET OF JAPAN. 1992: Columbia University Press.

Frits Vos. "The Zen Priest Ryōkan: His Life and Poetry," *Japan Foundation Newsletter* 20.5-6 (1993), 1-9.

Akinari Ueda. *UGETSU MONOGATARI*: TALES OF MOONLIGHT AND RAIN. 1980: Hokuseidō. "Gothic" tales first published in 1776.

Dennis Washburn. "Ghostwriters and Literary Haunts: Subordinating Ethics to Art in *Ugetsu Monogatari*," *Monumenta Nipponica* 45.1 (1990), 39-74.

Constantine N. Vaporis. "Caveat Viator: Advice to Travelers in the Edo Period," *Monumenta Nipponica* 44.4 (1989), 461-483. A translation of Yasumi Roan's 1810 *Ryokō yōjinshū* ("Precautions for Travelers").

James L. McClain. "*Bonshōgatsu*: Festivals and State Power in Kanazawa," *Monumenta Nipponica* 47.2 (1992), 163-202.

Carolyn Wheelwright, ed. WORD IN FLOWER: THE VISUALIZATION OF CLASSICAL LITERATURE IN SEVENTEENTH-CENTURY JAPAN. 1989: Yale University Art Gallery.

Ronald P. Toby. "Carnival of the Aliens: Korean Embassies in Edo-Period Art and Popular Culture," *Monumenta Nipponica* 41.4 (1986), 415-456.

David Chibbett. THE HISTORY OF JAPANESE PRINTING AND BOOK ILLUSTRATION. 1977: Kōdansha International.

Kogorō Yoshida. TANROKUBON: RARE BOOKS OF SEVENTEENTH-CENTURY JAPAN. 1984: Kōdansha International & Harper & Row.

Winston Davis. "Pilgrimage and World Renewal: A Study of Folk Religion and
    Social Values in Tokugawa Japan," *History of Religion* 23.2 and 23.3
    (1983-84), 97-116, 197-221.

Anne Walthall. "Peripheries: Rural Culture in Tokugawa Japan," *Monumenta
    Nipponica* 39.4 (1984), 371-392.

_____. "Japanese *Gimin*: Peasant Martyrs in Popular Memory," *American
    Historical Review* 91.5 (1986), 1076-1102.

TOKUGAWA: WAYS OF THE WARRIOR
[See also pages 62-65]

Martin C. Collcutt. "Bushidō," KŌDANSHA ENCYCLOPEDIA OF JAPAN
    1: 221-223.

Shōichi Fukushima. "Bushidō in Tokugawa Japan: A Reassessment of the
    Warrior Ethos." 1984: Ph.D. dissertation in Physical Education,
    University of California at Berkeley.

William Scott Wilson, ed. IDEALS OF THE SAMURAI: WRITINGS OF
    JAPANESE WARRIORS. 1982: Ohara.

Daisetz T. Suzuki. ZEN AND JAPANESE CULTURE. 1959: Pantheon.
    See especially chapters 4 ("Zen and the Samurai"), and 5-6 ("Zen and
    Swordsmanship").

Inazō Nitobe. BUSHIDŌ: THE SOUL OF JAPAN. 1899: Putnam.

Donn F. Draeger & Gordon Warner. JAPANESE SWORDSMANSHIP:
    TECHNIQUE AND PRACTICE. 1982: Weatherhill.

John M. Rogers. "Arts of War in Times of Peace: Archery in *Honchō Bugei
    Shōden*," *Monumenta Nipponica* 45.3 (1990), 253-284. Includes a
    translation of the chapter on archery from a 1714 history of martial arts
    by Hinatsu Shirōzaemon Shigetaka.

_____. "Arts of War in Times of Peace: Swordsmanship in *Honchō Bugei
    Shōden*, Chapter 5," *Monumenta Nipponica* 45.4 (1990), 413-447.
    Includes a translation of Hinatsu's chapter on swordsmanship.

Donn F. Draeger & Robert W. Smith. COMPREHENSIVE ASIAN FIGHTING ARTS. 1980: Kōdansha International.

Donn F. Draeger. CLASSICAL BUJUTSU. 1973: Weatherhill.

_____. CLASSICAL BUDŌ. 1974: Weatherhill.

_____. NINJUTSU: THE ART OF INVISIBILITY. 1977: Lotus Press.

Oscar Ratti & Adele Westbrook. SECRETS OF THE SAMURAI: A SURVEY OF THE MARTIAL ARTS OF FEUDAL JAPAN. 1973: Tuttle.

John J. Donohue. THE FORGE OF THE SPIRIT: STRUCTURE, MOTION, AND MEANING IN THE JAPANESE MARTIAL TRADITION. 1991: Garland. An anthropological survey of Japan's martial arts tradition.

Joe Hyams. ZEN IN THE MARTIAL ARTS. 1979: Tarcher.

Bruce A. Haines. KARATE'S HISTORY AND TRADITIONS. 1968: Tuttle.

John Allyn. THE FORTY-SEVEN RŌNIN STORY. 1970: Tuttle.

Jack Seward. HARA-KIRI: JAPANESE RITUAL SUICIDE. 1968: Tuttle.

Musashi Miyamoto. A BOOK OF FIVE RINGS: THE CLASSIC GUIDE TO STRATEGY. Victor Harris, transl. 1974: Overlook. Written in 1645 by the most renowned swordsman of feudal Japan.

Tsunetomo Yamamoto. *HAGAKURE*: THE BOOK OF THE SAMURAI. William Scott Wilson, transl. 1979: Kōdansha International. A classic text written in 1716.

Kokichi Katsu. MUSUI'S STORY: THE AUTOBIOGRAPHY OF A TOKUGAWA SAMURAI. Teruko Craig, transl. 1988: University of Arizona Press.

Yūjirō Ōguchi. "The Reality Behind *Musui Dokugen*: The World of the *Hatamoto* and *Gokenin*," Gaynor Sekimori., transl., *Journal of Japanese Studies* 16.2 (1990), 289-308. See also Kate Wildman Nakai's "The Reality Behind *Musui Dokugen*: Introduction to the Article by Ōguchi Yūjirō" (pp. 285-287).

Noel Perrin. GIVING UP THE GUN: JAPAN'S REVERSION TO THE SWORD, 1543-1879. 1979: Godine.

Saikaku Ihara. COMRADE LOVES OF THE SAMURAI. E. Powys Mathers, transl. 1981: Tuttle.

_____. TALES OF SAMURAI HONOR. C. A. Callahan, transl. 1982: Monumenta Nipponica Monographs.

BAKUMATSU / RESTORATION

Edwin O. Reischauer & Albert M. Craig. JAPAN: TRADITION AND TRANSFORMATION (1989: Houghton Mifflin), chapter 4.

John W. Dower, ed. ORIGINS OF THE MODERN JAPANESE STATE: SELECTED WRITINGS OF E. H. NORMAN. 1975: Pantheon. Includes Norman's classic *Japan's Emergence As a Modern State* (1940) and *Feudal Background of Japanese Politics* (1944).

E. H. Norman. SOLDIER AND PEASANT IN JAPAN: THE ORIGINS OF CONSCRIPTION. 1965: Institute of Pacific Relations; reprint of articles originally published in *Pacific Affairs*, March and June 1943.

Albert Craig. CHŌSHŪ IN THE MEIJI RESTORATION, 1853-1868. 1961: Harvard University Press.

_____. "The Restoration Movement in Chōshū," *Journal of Asian Studies* 18.2 (1959), 187-198.

Marius Jansen. SAKAMOTO RYŌMA AND THE MEIJI RESTORATION. 1961: Princeton University Press.

_____ & Gilbert Rozman, eds. JAPAN IN TRANSITION: FROM TOKUGAWA TO MEIJI. 1986: Princeton University Press.

_____. "The Meiji Restoration," in Marius B. Jansen, ed. CAMBRIDGE HISTORY OF JAPAN, Volume 5: THE NINETEENTH CENTURY (1989: Cambridge University Press), 308-366.

Charles L. Yates. "Restoration and Rebellion in Satsuma: The Life of Saigō Takamori (1827-1877)." 1987: Ph.D. dissertation in East Asian Studies, Princeton University.

Thomas C. Smith. "The Discontented," *Journal of Asian Studies* 21.2 (1962), 215-219. Review of above monographs by Craig and Jansen.

_____. "Old Values and New Techniques in the Modernization of Japan," *Far Eastern Quarterly* 14.3 (1955); reprinted in John A. Harrison, ed. JAPAN (1972: University of Arizona Press), 1-9.

_____. "Japan's Aristocratic Revolution," *Yale Review* (1961), 370-383; reprinted in Jon Livingston et al., IMPERIAL JAPAN, 1800-1945 (1973: Pantheon), 91-101.

Michio Nagai & Miguel Urrutia, eds. MEIJI ISHIN: RESTORATION AND REVOLUTION. 1985: United Nations University Press.

George B. Sansom. "Forerunners of the Restoration Movement," in his THE WESTERN WORLD AND JAPAN (1965: Knopf), 248-274.

Masakazu Iwata. "Forces Behind the Restoration Movement," in his ŌKUBO TOSHIMICHI: THE BISMARK OF JAPAN (1964: University of California Press), 103-111.

Marlene Mayo. "Late Tokugawa and Early Meiji," in Arthur Tiedemann, ed. AN INTRODUCTION TO JAPANESE CIVILIZATION (1974: Heath), 131-180.

Tetsuo Najita. "Restorationism in Late Tokugawa," in his JAPAN (1974: University of Chicago Press), 43-68.

W. G. Beasley, ed. SELECT DOCUMENTS ON JAPANESE FOREIGN POLICY, 1853-1868. 1955: Oxford University Press.

_____. THE MEIJI RESTORATION. 1972: Stanford University Press.

_____. "Self-Strengthening and Restoration: Chinese and Japanese Responses to the West in the mid-Nineteenth Century," *Acta Asiatica* 34 (1974), 91-107.

_____. "Japanese Castaways and British Interpreters," *Monumenta Nipponica* 46.1 (1991), 91-103.

_____. "The Foreign Threat and the Opening of the Ports," in Marius B. Jansen, ed. CAMBRIDGE HISTORY OF JAPAN, Volume 5: THE NINE-TEENTH CENTURY (1989: Cambridge University Press), 259-307.

√

H. D. Harootunian. Review of Beasley's MEIJI RESTORATION in *Journal of Asian Studies* 33.4 (1974), 661-672.

_____. TOWARD RESTORATION: THE GROWTH OF POLITICAL CONSCIOUSNESS IN TOKUGAWA JAPAN. Revised edition. 1991: University of California Press.

Thomas M. Huber. THE REVOLUTIONARY ORIGINS OF MODERN JAPAN. 1981: Stanford University Press.

Conrad Totman. THE COLLAPSE OF THE TOKUGAWA BAKUFU, 1862-1868. 1980: University of California Press.

_____. "From *Sakoku* to *Kaikoku*: The Transformation of Foreign-Policy Attitudes, 1853-1868," *Monumenta Nipponica* 35.1 (1980), 1-19.

___√__. "Ethnicity in the Meiji Restoration: An Interpretive Essay," *Monumenta Nipponica* 37.3 (1982), 269-288.

Masahide Bitō. "*Bushi* and the Meiji Restoration," *Acta Asiatica* 49 (1985), 78-96.

James L. McClain. "Failed Expectations: Kaga Domain on the Eve of the Meiji Restoration," *Journal of Japanese Studies* 14.2 (1988), 403-447.

Robert G. Flershem & Yoshiko N. Flershem. "Kaga's Tardy Support of the Meiji Restoration: Background Reasons," *Transactions, Asiatic Society of Japan*, 4th series, 3 (1988), 83-130.

M. William Steele. "Edo in 1868: The View from Below," *Monumenta Nipponica* 45.2 (1990), 127-155. How commoners experienced the events of 1868.

Paul Akamatsu. MEIJI 1868: REVOLUTION AND COUNTERREVOLUTION IN JAPAN. 1972: Harper & Row.

Yoshio Sakata & John W. Hall. "The Motivation of Political Leadership in the Meiji Restoration," *Journal of Asian Studies* 16.1 (1956); reprinted in Harrison, JAPAN (1972: University of Arizona Press), 179-198.

John W. Hall. "The Meiji Restoration and its Meaning," in his JAPAN: FROM PREHISTORY TO MODERN TIMES (1970: Delacorte), 265-272.

George M. Wilson. PATRIOTS AND REDEEMERS IN JAPAN: MOTIVES IN THE MEIJI RESTORATION. 1992: University of Chicago Press.

√

Germaine Hoston. "Conceptualizing Bourgeois Revolution: The Prewar Japanese and the Meiji Restoration," *Comparative Studies in Society and History* 33.3 (1991), 539-581.

Jean-Pierre Lehmann. THE ROOTS OF MODERN JAPAN. 1982: St. Martin's.

Ncil Waters. JAPAN'S LOCAL PRAGMATISTS: THE TRANSITION FROM BAKUMATSU TO MEIJI IN THE KAWASAKI REGION. 1983: Council on East Asian Studies, Harvard University.

Peter Frost. THE BAKUMATSU CURRENCY CRISIS. 1970: Council on East Asian Studies, Harvard University.

Donald R. Bernard. THE LIFE AND TIMES OF JOHN MANJIRŌ. 1992: McGraw-Hill.

Masao Miyoshi. AS WE SAW THEM: THE FIRST JAPANESE EMBASSY TO THE UNITED STATES (1860). 1979: University of California Press; 1994: Kōdansha.

THE FIRST JAPANESE EMBASSY TO THE UNITED STATES OF AMERICA. 1920: America-Japan Society; reprinted 1977.

Lewis Bush. 77 SAMURAI: JAPAN'S FIRST EMBASSY TO AMERICA. 1968: Kōdansha International. Based on the book by Itsurō Hattori.

John McMaster. "Alcock and Harris: Foreign Diplomacy in Bakumatsu Japan," *Monumenta Nipponica* 22.4 (1967), 305-367.

Toshio Yokoyama. JAPAN IN THE VICTORIAN MIND: A STUDY OF STEREOTYPED IMAGES OF A NATION 1850-80. 1987: Macmillan.

D. J. M. Tate. THE MIKADO'S JAPAN: BEING GLIMPSES OF NINE-TEENTH CENTURY JAPAN FROM COMMODORE PERRY'S VISIT (1853) UNTIL THE PROMULGATION OF THE MEIJI CONSTITU-TION (1889) AS SEEN AND REPORTED BY THE ILLUSTRATED LONDON NEWS AND OTHER CONTEMPORARY SOURCES. 1990: J. Nicholson.

Shōzō Fujita. "Spirit of the Meiji Restoration," *Japan Interpreter* 6.1 (1970), 70-97.

Shunzō Sakamaki. JAPAN AND THE UNITED STATES, 1790-1853. 1973: Scholarly Resources reprint; originally a Columbia University Ph.D. dissertation, first published in *Transactions of the Asiatic Society of Japan*, 1939.

Hideo Ibe. JAPAN THRICE OPENED: AN ANALYSIS OF JAPAN-UNITED STATES RELATIONS. Lynne E. Riggs & Manabu Takechi, transl. 1992: Praeger.

Pat Barr. THE COMING OF THE BARBARIANS: A STORY OF WESTERN SETTLEMENT IN JAPAN 1953-1870. 1988: Penguin.

S. E. Morison. "OLD BRUIN": COMMODORE MATTHEW C. PERRY, 1794-1858. 1967: Little, Brown.

Arthur Walworth. BLACK SHIPS OFF JAPAN. 1946: Knopf.

Peter Booth Wiley. YANKEES IN THE LAND OF THE GODS: COMMODORE PERRY AND THE OPENING OF JAPAN. 1990: Viking.

Oliver Statler. SHIMODA STORY. 1969: Random House.

Meron Medzini. FRENCH POLICY IN JAPAN DURING THE CLOSING YEARS OF THE TOKUGAWA REGIME. 1971: Council on East Asian Studies, Harvard University.

Hazel J. Jones. LIVE MACHINES: HIRED FOREIGNERS AND MEIJI JAPAN. 1980: University of British Columbia Press.

_____. "Bakumatsu Foreign Employees," *Monumenta Nipponica* 29.3 (1974), 305-328.

Roy Seijun Hanashiro. "The Establishment of the Japanese Imperial Mint and the Role of Hired Foreigners: 1868-1875." 1988: Ph.D. dissertation in History, University of Hawaii.

Donald Roden. "In Search of the Real Horace Capron: An Historiographical Perspective on Japanese-American Relations," *Pacific Historical Review* 55.3 (1986), 549-575.

James L. Huffman. "Edward Howard House: In the Service of Meiji Japan," *Pacific Historical Review* 56.2 (1987), 231-258.

Erving E. Beauregard. "Samuel Magill Bryan: Creator of Japan's International Postal Service," *Journal of Asian History* 26.1 (1992).

R. Henry Brunton. SCHOOLMASTER TO AN EMPIRE: RICHARD HENRY BRUNTON IN MEIJI JAPAN, 1868-1876. Edward R. Beauchamp, ed. 1991: Greenwood Press.

Neil Pedlar. THE IMPORTED PIONEERS: WESTERNERS WHO HELPED BUILD MODERN JAPAN. 1990: Japan Library Ltd.

Ardath W. Burks, ed. THE MODERNIZERS: OVERSEAS STUDENTS, FOREIGN EMPLOYEES, AND MEIJI JAPAN. 1984: Westview.

Clark L. Beck & Ardath W. Burks. ASPECTS OF MEIJI MODERNIZATION: THE JAPAN HELPERS AND THE HELPED. 1983: Transaction.

CONFLICT & REBELLION IN TOKUGAWA & EARLY MEIJI

√

Tetsuo Najita & J. Victor Koschmann, eds. CONFLICT IN MODERN JAPANESE HISTORY: THE NEGLECTED TRADITION. 1982: Princeton University Press. See especially essays by Koschmann, Huber, Steele, Hashimoto, and Vlastos.

Hugh Borton. PEASANT UPRISINGS IN JAPAN OF THE TOKUGAWA PERIOD. 1968: Paragon reprint; originally published in *Transactions, Asiatic Society of Japan*, 1938.

Herbert P. Bix. PEASANT PROTEST IN JAPAN, 1590-1884. 1986: Yale University Press.

_____. "Miura Meisuke, or Peasant Rebellion Under the Banner of 'Distress'," *Bulletin of Concerned Asian Scholars* 10.2 (1978), 18-26.

Stephen Vlastos. PEASANT PROTESTS AND UPRISINGS IN TOKUGAWA JAPAN. 1986: University of California Press.

_____. "Opposition Movements in Early Meiji, 1868-1885," in Marius B. Jansen, ed. CAMBRIDGE HISTORY OF JAPAN, Volume 5: THE NINETEENTH CENTURY (1989: Cambridge University Press), 367-431.

Anne Walthall. SOCIAL PROTEST AND POPULAR CULTURE IN EIGH-
TEENTH-CENTURY JAPAN. 1986: University of Arizona Press.

_____. "Narratives of Peasant Uprisings in Japan," *Journal of Asian Studies*
42.3 (May 1983), 571-588.

_____. "Japanese *Gimin*: Peasant Martyrs in Popular Memory," *American
Historical Review* 91.5 (1986), 1076-1102.

William W. Kelly. DEFERENCE AND DEFIANCE IN NINETEENTH-
CENTURY JAPAN. 1985: Princeton University Press.

James W. White. THE DEMOGRAPHY OF SOCIOPOLITICAL CONFLICT
IN JAPAN, 1721-1846. 1992: Institute of East Asian Studies,
University of California, Berkeley, Center for Japanese Studies.

_____. "State Growth and Popular Protest in Tokugawa Japan," *Journal of
Japanese Studies* 14.1 (1988), 1-25.

_____. "Scholarly Discourse and Peasant Discontent: Four Studies of Popular
Contention in the Tokugawa Period," *Journal of Japanese Studies* 15.1
(1989), 159-175. Review of books by Bix, Kelly, Vlastos, and Walthall.

Roger Bowen. "Japanese Peasants: Moral? Rational? Revolutionary?
Duped?—A Review Article," *Journal of Asian Studies* 47.4 (1988),
821-832. Review of books by Bix, Vlastos, Walthall, and Smethurst
(see below).

W. Donald Burton. "Peasant Struggle in Japan, 1590-1760," *Journal of Peasant
Studies* 5.2 (1978), 135-171.

_____. "Review Essay: Rural and Urban Protest in Tokugawa Japan," *Bulletin
of Concerned Asian Scholars* 21.1 (1989), 53-66. Review of books by
Bix, Vlastos, and Walthall.

Conrad Totman. "Tokugawa Peasants: Win, Lose, or Draw?" *Monumenta
Nipponica* 41.4 (1986), 457-476. A basically pessimistic view of
Tokugawa peasant life, from an ecological perspective. Includes an
excellent bibliography.

Yoshio Yasumaru. "Rebellion and Peasant Consciousness in the Edo Period,"
in Andrew Turton & Shigeharu Tanabe, eds. HISTORY AND
PEASANT CONSCIOUSNESS IN SOUTHEAST ASIA (1984:
National Museum of Ethnology, Osaka), 401-420.

Constantine N. Vaporis. "Post Station and Assisting Villages: Corvée Labor and Peasant Contention," *Monumenta Nipponica* 41.4 (1986), 377-414.

Tetsuo Najita. "Ōshio Heihachirō (1793-1837)," in Albert Craig & Donald Shively, eds. PERSONALITY IN JAPANESE HISTORY (1970: University of California Press), 155-179.

J. Rahder. "Record of the Kurume Uprising," *Acta Orientalia* 14 (1936), 81-108.

✓

Yoshio Sugimoto. "Structural Sources of Popular Revolts and the Tōbaku Movement at the Time of the Meiji Restoration," *Journal of Asian Studies* 34.4 (1975), 875-889.

Patricia Sippel. "Popular Protest in Early Modern Japan: The Bushū Outburst," *Harvard Journal of Asiatic Studies* 37.2 (1977), 273-322.

Irwin Scheiner. "Benevolent Lords and Honorable Peasants: Rebellion and Peasant Consciousness in Tokugawa Japan," in T. Najita & I. Scheiner, eds. JAPANESE THOUGHT IN THE TOKUGAWA PERIOD, 1600-1868 (1978: University of Chicago Press), 39-62.

_____. "The Mindful Peasant: Sketches for a Study of Rebellion," *Journal of Asian Studies* 32.4 (1973), 579-591.

Winston Davis. "Pilgrimage and World Renewal: A Study of Folk Religion and Social Values in Tokugawa Japan," *History of Religion* 23.2 and 23.3 (1983-84), 97-116, 197-221.

Thomas M. Huber. THE REVOLUTIONARY ORIGINS OF MODERN JAPAN. 1981: Stanford University Press.

E. H. Norman. SOLDIER AND PEASANT IN JAPAN: THE ORIGINS OF CONSCRIPTION. Originally published in *Pacific Affairs* 16.1 and 16.2 (1943). Published separately in 1943, with reprint edition in 1965 by the Institute of Pacific Relations.

✓

James H. Buck. "The Satsuma Rebellion of 1877—From Kagoshima Through the Seige of Kumamoto Castle," *Monumenta Nipponica* 28.4 (1973), 427-446

Augustus H. Mounsey. THE SATSUMA REBELLION: AN EPISODE OF MODERN JAPANESE HISTORY. 1979 reprint of 1879 account of the great rebellion of 1877: University Publications of America.

Nobutake Ike. THE BEGINNINGS OF POLITICAL DEMOCRACY IN
    JAPAN. 1950: Johns Hopkins.

Roger W. Bowen. REBELLION AND DEMOCRACY IN MEIJI JAPAN:
    A STUDY OF COMMONERS IN THE POPULAR RIGHTS
    MOVEMENT. 1980: University of California Press.

_____. "Rice Roots Democracy and Popular Rebellion in Meiji Japan," *Journal
    of Peasant Studies* 6.1 (1978), 3-39

Richard J. Smethurst. AGRICULTURAL DEVELOPMENT AND TENANCY
    DISPUTES IN JAPAN, 1870-1940. 1986: Princeton University Press.
    See also the exchange between Smethurst and Nishida Yoshiaki in
    Journal of Japanese Studies 15.2 (1989), 389-437.

MEIJI: STATE & POLITICS

E. H. Norman. JAPAN'S EMERGENCE AS A MODERN STATE (1940) and
    FEUDAL BACKGROUND OF JAPANESE POLITICS (1944);
    reprinted in J. W. Dower, ed. ORIGINS OF THE MODERN
    JAPANESE STATE (1975: Pantheon).

_____. SOLDIER AND PEASANT IN JAPAN: THE ORIGINS OF
    CONSCRIPTION. Originally published in *Pacific Affairs* 16.1 and
    16.2 (1943). Published separately in 1943, with reprint edition in 1965
    by the Institute of Pacific Relations.

John W. Dower. "E. H. Norman, Japan, and the Uses of History." Introduction
    to ORIGINS (cited above), 3-101. A critique of "modernization theory"
    and the values of "value-free" scholarship.

Shigeki Tōyama. "The Appreciation of Norman's Historiography," *Japan
    Interpreter* 13.1 (1980), 1-14.

_____. "The Meiji Restoration and the Present Day," *Bulletin of Concerned
    Asian Scholars* 2.1 (1969), 10-14.

Edwin O. Reischauer & Albert M. Craig. JAPAN: TRADITION AND TRANS-
    FORMATION (1989: Houghton Mifflin), chapter 5.

Marius Jansen. "The Meiji State: 1868-1912," in James B. Crowley, ed. MODERN EAST ASIA: ESSAYS IN INTERPRETATION (1970: Harcourt Brace & World), 95-121.

_____. "Meiji History (1868-1912)," KŌDANSHA ENCYCLOPEDIA OF JAPAN 3: 192-197.

W. G. Beasley. "Meiji Political Institutions," in Marius B. Jansen, ed. CAMBRIDGE HISTORY OF JAPAN, Volume 5: THE NINETEENTH CENTURY (1989: Cambridge University Press), 618-673.

Michio Umegaki. AFTER THE RESTORATION: THE BEGINNING OF JAPAN'S MODERN STATE. 1988: New York University Press.

Marlene J. Mayo. "Late Tokugawa and Early Meiji Japan," in Arthur E. Tiedemann, ed. AN INTRODUCTION TO JAPANESE CIVILIZATION (1974: Heath), 131-180.

Roger F. Hackett. "The Era of Fulfillment, 1877-1911," in Tiedemann, AN INTRODUCTION TO JAPANESE CIVILIZATION (1974: Heath), 181-215.

Osamu Kuno. "The Meiji State, Minponshugi, and Ultranationalism," in J. Victor Koschmann, ed. AUTHORITY AND THE INDIVIDUAL IN JAPAN (1978: University of Tokyo Press), 60-80.

Joseph Pittau. "The Meiji Political System: Different Interpretations," in Joseph Roggendorf, ed. STUDIES IN JAPANESE CULTURE: TRADITION AND EXPERIMENT (1965: Monumenta Nipponica Monographs), 99-122.

Kenneth B. Pyle. "Meiji Conservatism," in Marius B. Jansen, ed. CAMBRIDGE HISTORY OF JAPAN, Volume 5: THE NINETEENTH CENTURY (1989: Cambridge University Press), 674-720.

Barrington Moore, Jr. SOCIAL ORIGINS OF DICTATORSHIP AND DEMOCRACY (1966: Beacon), chapter 5.

Ellen Kay Trimberger. REVOLUTION FROM ABOVE: MILITARY BUREAUCRATS AND DEVELOPMENT IN JAPAN, TURKEY, EGYPT, AND PERU. 1978: Transaction.

Takeshi Ishida. THE INTRODUCTION OF WESTERN POLITICAL CONCEPTS INTO JAPAN. Nissan Occasional Papers, No. 2. 1986: Nissan Institute of Japanese Studies, Oxford.

D. Eleanor Westney. IMITATION AND INNOVATION: THE TRANSFER OF
WESTERN ORGANIZATIONAL PATTERNS TO MEIJI JAPAN.
1987: Harvard University Press.

Donald Calman. THE NATURE AND ORGINS OF JAPANESE IMPERIAL-
ISM: A RE-INTERPRETATION OF THE GREAT CRISIS OF 1873.
1992: Routledge. See the important review by Herbert P. Bix in
Journal of Japanese Studies 20.2 (1994), 532-536, comparing this work
with Hilary Conroy's THE JAPANESE SEIZURE OF KOREA.

Robert Scalapino. DEMOCRACY AND THE PARTY MOVEMENT IN PRE-
WAR JAPAN: THE FAILURE OF THE FIRST ATTEMPT. 1953:
University of California Press.

Nobutake Ike. THE BEGINNINGS OF POLITICAL DEMOCRACY IN
JAPAN. 1950: Johns Hopkins.

Roger W. Bowen. REBELLION AND DEMOCRACY IN MEIJI JAPAN:
A STUDY OF COMMONERS IN THE POPULAR RIGHTS MOVE-
MENT. 1980: University of California Press.

Japan, House of Representatives, Parliamentary Museum. HISTORY OF
CONSTITUTIONALISM IN JAPAN: WITH NOTES AND RELATED
CHRONOLOGY. 1987.

George M. Beckmann. THE MAKING OF THE MEIJI CONSTITUTION:
THE OLIGARCHS AND THE CONSTITUTIONAL DEVELOPMENT
OF JAPAN, 1868-1891. 1957: University of Kansas Press.

George Akita. FOUNDATIONS OF CONSTITUTIONAL GOVERNMENT IN
MODERN JAPAN, 1868-1900. 1967: Harvard University Press.

Junji Banno. THE ESTABLISHMENT OF THE JAPANESE CONSTITUTION-
AL SYSTEM. J. A. A. Stockwin, transl. 1992: Routledge.

Hirobumi Itō. COMMENTARIES ON THE CONSTITUTION OF THE
EMPIRE OF JAPAN. Miyoji Itō, transl. 1931: Igirisu-hōritsu Gakkō.

Joseph Pittau. POLITICAL THOUGHT IN EARLY MEIJI JAPAN, 1868-1889.
1967: Harvard University Press.

Johannes Siemes. HERMAN ROESLER AND THE MAKING OF THE MEIJI
STATE. 1968: Monumenta Nipponica Monographs & Tuttle.

Ryōsuke Ishii, ed. JAPANESE LEGISLATION IN THE MEIJI ERA. 1958: Obunsha.

R. H. P. Mason. JAPAN'S FIRST GENERAL ELECTION: 1890. 1969: Cambridge University Press.

Andrew Fraser. NATIONAL ELECTION POLITICS IN TOKUSHIMA. 1972: Australian National University, Faculty of Asian Studies, Occasional Papers no. 14.

_____. A POLITICAL PROFILE OF TOKUSHIMA PREFECTURE. 1971: Australian National University, Faculty of Asian Studies, Occasional Papers no. 11.

Daniel B. Ramsdell. THE JAPANESE DIET: STABILITY AND CHANGE IN THE JAPANESE HOUSE OF REPRESENTATIVES, 1890-1990. 1992: University Press of America.

Taiichirō Mitani. "The Establishment of Party Cabinets, 1898-1932," Peter Duus, transl., in Peter Duus, ed. CAMBRIDGE HISTORY OF JAPAN, Volume 6: THE TWENTIETH CENTURY (1988: Cambridge University Press), 55-96.

Robert M. Spaulding. IMPERIAL JAPAN'S HIGHER CIVIL SERVICE EXAMINATIONS. 1967: Princeton University Press.

Stephen J. Anderson. "The Elitist Origins of the Japanese Welfare State Before 1945: Bureaucrats, Military Officers, Social Interests, and Politicians," *Transactions, Asiatic Society of Japan*, 4th series, 2 (1987), 59-77.

Sidney DeVere Brown. "Kido Takyoshi and the Young Emperor Meiji: A Subject as His Sovereign's Pedagogue, 1868-1877," *Transactions, Asiatic Society of Japan*, 4th series, 1 (1986), 1-21.

Albert M. Craig. "Kido Kōin and Ōkubo Toshimichi: A Psychohistorical Analysis," in Albert M. Craig & Donald H. Shively, eds. PERSON-ALITY IN JAPANESE HISTORY (1970: University of California Press), 264-308.

Masakazu Iwata. ŌKUBO TOSHIMICHI, THE BISMARK OF JAPAN. 1964: University of California Press.

Roger F. Hackett. YAMAGATA ARITOMO IN THE RISE OF MODERN JAPAN, 1838-1922. 1971: Harvard University Press.

Yoshitake Oka. FIVE POLITICAL LEADERS OF MODERN JAPAN. 1986: University of Tokyo Press. Includes essays on Itō Hirobumi and Ōkuma Shigenobu.

Joyce C. Lebra. ŌKUMA SHIGENOBU: STATESMAN OF MEIJI JAPAN. 1973: Australian National University Press.

_____. "Ōkuma Shigenobu and the 1881 Political Crisis," *Journal of Asian Studies* 16.4 (1959), 475-487.

Andrew Fraser. "The Expulsion of Ōkuma from the Government in 1881," *Journal of Asian Studies* 26.2 (1967), 213-236.

Haru Matsukata Reischauer. SAMURAI AND SILK: A JAPANESE AND AMERICAN HERITAGE. 1986: Belknap Press of Harvard University Press.

George E. Uyehara. THE POLITICAL DEVELOPMENT OF JAPAN, 1867-1909. 1910: Dutton.

Walter McLaren. POLITICAL HISTORY OF JAPAN DURING THE MEIJI ERA, 1867-1912. 1916: Russell.

Roger Hackett. "Political Modernization and the Meiji Genrō," in Robert E. Ward, ed. POLITICAL DEVELOPMENT IN MODERN JAPAN (1973: Princeton University Press), 65-97.

_____. "The Meiji Leaders and Modernization: The Case of Yamagata Aritomo," in Marius Jansen, ed. CHANGING JAPANESE ATTITUDES TOWARD MODERNIZATION (1965: Princeton University Press), 243-273.

John W. Hall. "A Monarch for Modern Japan," in Ward, POLITICAL DEVELOPMENT IN MODERN JAPAN (1973: Princeton University Press), 11-64.

Bernard Silberman. MINISTERS OF MODERNIZATION: ELITE MOBILITY IN THE MEIJI RESTORATION, 1868-1873. 1964: University of Arizona Press.

_____. "Bureaucratic Development and the Structure of Decision-Making in the Meiji Period," in John A. Harrison, ed. JAPAN (1973: University of Arizona Press), 69-82. Originally published in *Journal of Asian Studies*, 27.1 (1967).

Louis G. Perez. "Mutsu Munemitsu and the Diet Crisis of 1893," *Journal of Asian History* 25.1 (1991), 29-59.

David Wurfel, ed. MEIJI JAPAN'S CENTENNIAL: ASPECTS OF POLITI-CAL THOUGHT AND ACTION. 1968: University of Kansas Press.

Hidehiro Sonoda. "The Decline of the Japanese Warrior Class, 1840-1880," *Japan Review* 1 (1990), 73-111.

Harry D. Harootunian. "The Progress of Japan and the Samurai Class, 1868-1882," *Pacific Historical Review* 28 (1959), 255-266

_____. "The Economic Rehabilitation of the Samurai in the Early Meiji Period," *Journal of Asian Studies* 19.4 (1960), 434-444.

Masatoshi Sakeda & George Akita. "The Samurai Disestablished: Abei Iwane and His Stipend," *Monumenta Nipponica* 41.3 (1986), 299-330.

Neil L. Waters. "The Second Transition: Early to Mid-Meiji in Kanagawa Prefecture," *Journal of Asian Studies* 49.2 (1990), 305-322. The local "self-government" system established 1888-1890.

MEIJI: THOUGHT & CULTURE

Edwin O. Reischauer & Albert M. Craig. JAPAN: TRADITION AND TRANSFORMATION (1989: Houghton Mifflin), chapter 6.

George B. Sansom. "Early Meiji: Western Influences," in his THE WESTERN WORLD AND JAPAN (1965: Knopf), 378-442.

Sukehiro Hirakawa. "Japan's Turn to the West," Bob Tadashi Wakabayashi, transl., in Marius B. Jansen, ed. CAMBRIDGE HISTORY OF JAPAN, Volume 5: THE NINETEENTH CENTURY (1989: Cambridge University Press), 432-498.

Shigeki Tōyama. "Reforms of the Meiji Restoration and the Birth of Modern Intellectuals," *Acta Asiatica* 13 (1967), 55-99.

Michio Kitahara. "The Rise of Four Mottoes in Japan," *Journal of Asian History* 20.1 (1986), 54-64.

Kenneth B. Pyle. "Meiji Conservatism," in Marius B. Jansen, ed. CAMBRIDGE
    HISTORY OF JAPAN, Volume 5: THE NINETEENTH CENTURY
    (1989: Cambridge University Press), 674-720.

Osamu Kuno. "The Meiji State, Minponshugi, and Ultranationalism," in J. Victor
    Koschmann, ed. AUTHORITY AND THE INDIVIDUAL IN JAPAN
    (1978: University of Tokyo Press), 60-80.

Daikichi Irokawa. THE CULTURE OF THE MEIJI PERIOD. Marius Jansen,
    transl. & ed. 1985: Princeton University Press.

_____. "Freedom and the Concept of People's Rights," *Japan Quarterly* 14.2
    (1967), 175-183.

Carol Gluck. JAPAN'S MODERN MYTHS: IDEOLOGY IN THE LATE
    MEIJI PERIOD. 1985: Princeton University Press. See also the review
    by Atsuko Hirai entitled "The State and Ideology in Meiji Japan—
    A Review Article," in *Journal of Asian Studies* 46.1 (1987), 89-103.

Masaaki Kōsaka. JAPANESE THOUGHT IN THE MEIJI ERA. 1958.
    See series citation on page 149.

Marius Jansen, ed. CHANGING JAPANESE ATTITUDES TOWARD
    MODERNIZATION. 1965: Princeton University Press.

S. Cho & N. Runeby, eds. TRADITIONAL THOUGHT AND IDEOLOGICAL
    CHANGE: SWEDEN AND JAPAN IN THE AGE OF INDUSTRIAL-
    IZATION. 1988: Department of Japanese and Korean, University of
    Stockholm.

Gilbert Rozman. "Social Change," in Marius B. Jansen, ed. CAMBRIDGE
    HISTORY OF JAPAN, Volume 5: THE NINETEENTH CENTURY
    (1989: Cambridge University Press), 499-568.

James Edward Ketelaar. OF HERETICS AND MARTYRS IN MEIJI JAPAN:
    BUDDHISM AND ITS PERSECUTION. 1993: Princeton University
    Press.

Herbert Passin. SOCIETY AND EDUCATION IN JAPAN. 1965: Teachers
    College and East Asian Institute, Columbia University.

Carmen Blacker. THE JAPANESE ENLIGHTENMENT: A STUDY OF THE
    WRITINGS OF FUKUZAWA YUKICHI. 1964: Cambridge University
    Press.

Yukichi Fukuzawa. THE AUTOBIOGRAPHY OF YUKICHI FUKUZAWA. Eiichi Kiyooka, transl. 1966: Columbia University Press.

William R. Braisted, transl. & ed. *MEIROKU ZASSHI*: JOURNAL OF THE JAPANESE ENLIGHTENMENT 1976: Harvard University Press.

Albert Craig. "Fukuzawa Yukichi: The Political Foundations of Meiji Nationalism," in Robert E. Ward, ed. POLITICAL DEVELOPMENT IN MODERN JAPAN (1973: Princeton University Press), 99-148.

Earl Kinmonth. "Fukuzawa Reconsidered: *Gakumon no Susume* and Its Audience," *Journal of Asian Studies* 37.4 (1978), 677-696.

_____. "Nakamura Keiu and Samuel Smiles: a Victorian Confucian and a Confucian Victorian," *American Historical Review* 85.3 (1980), 535-556.

_____. THE SELF-MADE MAN IN MEIJI JAPANESE THOUGHT: FROM SAMURAI TO SALARY MAN. 1981: University of California Press.

Sarah Metzger-Court. "Economic Progress and Social Cohesion: 'Self-Help' and the Achieving of a Delicate Balance in Meiji Japan," *Japan Forum* 3.1 (1991), 11-21.

Ronald Loftus. "The Inversion of Progress: Taoka Reiun's *Hibunmeiron*," *Monumenta Nipponica* 40.2 (1985), 191-208.

Thomas Havens. NISHI AMANE AND MODERN JAPANESE THOUGHT. 1970: Princeton University Press.

Ivan Hall. MORI ARINORI. 1973: Harvard University Press.

Alan Grapard. "Japan's Ignored Cultural Revolution," *History of Religions* 23 (1984), 240-265.

Donald Shively, ed. TRADITION AND MODERNIZATION IN JAPANESE CULTURE. 1971: Princeton University Press. See especially Shively's essay "The Japanization of the Middle Meiji," 77-119.

_____. "Motoda Eifu: Confucian Lecturer to the Meiji Emperor," in David Nivison & Arthur Wright, eds. CONFUCIANISM IN ACTION (1959: Stanford University Press), 302-333.

Hilary Conroy, Sandra Davis & Wayne Patterson, eds. JAPAN IN TRANSI-
TION: THOUGHT AND ACTION IN THE MEIJI ERA, 1868-1912.
1985: Farleigh Dickinson University Press.

Michael C. Brownstein. "From *Kokugaku* to *Kokubungaku*: Canon-Formation
in the Meiji Period," *Harvard Journal of Asiatic Studies* 47.2 (1987),
435-460.

Warren W. Smith. CONFUCIANISM IN MODERN JAPAN: A STUDY OF
CONSERVATISM IN JAPANESE INTELLECTUAL HISTORY.
1959: Hokuseidō.

Germaine A. Hoston. THE STATE, IDENTITY, AND THE NATIONAL
QUESTION IN CHINA AND JAPAN. 1994: Princeton University
Press.

_____. "The State, Modernity, and the Fate of Liberalism in Prewar Japan,"
Journal of Asian Studies 51.2 (1992), 287-316.

Kenneth B. Pyle. THE NEW GENERATION IN MEIJI JAPAN: PROBLEMS
IN CULTURAL IDENTITY, 1885-1895. 1969: Stanford University
Press.

_____. "Advantages of Followership: German Economics and Japanese
Bureaucrats, 1890-1925," *Journal of Japanese Studies* 1.1 (1974),
127-164.

Chūhei Sugiyama & Hiroshi Mizuta, eds. ENLIGHTENMENT AND BEYOND:
POLITICAL ECONOMY COMES TO JAPAN. 1988: University of
Tokyo Press.

W. Dean Kinzley. "Japan's Discovery of Poverty: Changing Views of Poverty
and Social Welfare in the Nineteenth Century," *Journal of Asian History*
22.1 (1988), 1-24.

Eiji Yutani. "*Nihon no Kasō Shakai* of Gennosuke Yokoyama, Translated and
with an Introduction." 1985: Ph.D. dissertation in History, University
of California.

Peter Duus. "Whig History, Japanese Style: The Min'yusha Historians and the
Meiji Restoration," *Journal of Asian Studies* 33.3 (1974), 415-436.

Masao Maruyama. "Fukuzawa, Uchimura, and Okakura," *Developing Economies*
4.4 (1966), 594-611.

F. G. Notehelfer. "On Idealism and Realism in the Thought of Okakura Tenshin," *Journal of Japanese Studies* 16.2 (1990), 309-353.

_____. AMERICAN SAMURAI: CAPTAIN L. L. JANES AND JAPAN. 1984: Princeton University Press.

Irwin Scheiner. CHRISTIAN CONVERTS AND SOCIAL PROTEST IN MEIJI JAPAN. 1970: University of California Press.

Ray A. Moore, ed. CULTURE AND RELIGION IN JAPANESE-AMERICAN RELATIONS: ESSAYS ON UCHIMURA KANZŌ, 1861-1930. 1981: Center for Japanese Studies, University of Michigan.

Takeo Doi. "Uchimura Kanzō: Japanese Christianity in Comparative Perspective," in Albert Craig, ed. JAPAN: A COMPARATIVE VIEW (1979: Princeton University Press), 182-213.

Katsuichirō Kamei. "Uchimura Kanzō, Intolerant Believer," *Japan Interpreter* 10.1 (1975), 16-43.

Kanzō Uchimura. HOW I BECAME A CHRISTIAN: OUT OF MY DIARY, BY A "HEATHEN CONVERT." 1895: Keiseisha; reprinted 1968: Modern Literature House.

Helen Ballhatchet. "Confucianism and Christianity in Meiji Japan: The Case of Kozaki Hiromichi," *Journal of the Royal Asiatic Society* 1988, No. 2, 349-369.

John Caiger. "The Aims and Content of School Courses in Japanese History, 1872-1945," in Edmund R. Skrzypczak, ed. JAPAN'S MODERN CENTURY (1968: Tuttle), 51-82.

Donald T. Roden. SCHOOLDAYS IN IMPERIAL JAPAN: A STUDY IN THE CULTURE OF A STUDENT ELITE. 1980: University of California Press.

_____. "'Monasticism' and the Paradox of the Meiji Higher Schools," *Journal of Asian Studies* 37.3 (1978), 413-425.

Nanette Twine. "Standardizing Written Japanese: A Factor in Modernization," *Monumenta Nipponica* 43.4 (1988), 429-454.

John D. Pierson. TOKUTOMI SOHŌ, 1863-1957: A JOURNALIST FOR MODERN JAPAN. 1980: Princeton University Press.

James L. Huffman. POLITICS OF THE MEIJI PRESS: THE LIFE OF FUKUCHI GEN'ICHIRŌ. 1980: University of Hawaii Press.

Gregory Kent Ornatowski. "Press, Politics, and Profits: The *Asahi Shimbun* and the Prewar Japanese Newspaper." 1985: Ph.D. dissertation in History and East Asian Languages, Harvard University.

Janet A. Walker. THE JAPANESE NOVEL OF THE MEIJI PERIOD AND THE IDEAL OF INDIVIDUALISM. 1979: Princeton University Press.

Chia-ning Chang. "Theoretical Speculations and Literary Representations: Writers and Critics of Social Literature in the Meiji Inter-War Years (1895-1904)." 1985: Ph.D. dissertation in Asian Languages, Stanford University.

Richard J. Bowring. MORI ŌGAI AND THE MODERNIZATION OF JAPANESE CULTURE. 1979: Cambridge University Press.

Byron K. Marshall. "Professors and Politics: The Meiji Academic Elite," *Journal of Japanese Studies* 3.1 (1977), 71-97.

_____. ACADEMIC FREEDOM AND THE JAPANESE IMPERIAL UNIVERSITY, 1868-1939. 1992: University of California Press.

James R. Bartholomew. THE FORMATION OF SCIENCE IN JAPAN: BUILDING A RESEARCH TRADITION. 1989: Yale University Press.

_____. "Japanese Modernization and the Imperial Universities, 1876-1920," *Journal of Asian Studies* 37.2 (1978), 251-271.

_____. "Science, Bureaucracy, and Freedom in Meiji and Taishō Japan," in Tetsuo Najita & J. Victor Koschmann, eds. CONFLICT IN MODERN JAPANESE HISTORY (1982: Princeton University Press), 226-257.

Jay Rubin. INJURIOUS TO PUBLIC MORALS: WRITERS AND THE MEIJI STATE. 1984: University of Washington Press.

Stefan Tanaka. "Imaging History: Inscribing Belief in the Nation," *Journal of Asian Studies* 53.1 (1994), 24-44. Explores the relationship between art criticism and nationalism.

Donald Keene. "The Sino-Japanese War of 1894-95 and Japanese Culture," in his LANDSCAPES AND PORTRAITS: APPRECIATIONS OF JAPANESE CULTURE (1971: Kōdansha International), 259-299.

Edward Seidensticker. LOW CITY, HIGH CITY: TOKYO FROM EDO TO
THE EARTHQUAKE: HOW THE SHŌGUN'S ANCIENT CAPITAL
BECAME A GREAT MODERN CITY, 1867-1923. 1983: Knopf.

Robert Lyons Danly. IN THE SHADE OF SPRING LEAVES: THE LIFE AND
WRITINGS OF HIGUCHI ICHIYO, A WOMAN OF LETTERS IN
MEIJI JAPAN. 1981: Yale University Press.

Laurence Kominz. "Pilgrimage to Tolstoy: Tokutomi Roka's *Junrei Kikō*,"
Monumenta Nipponica 41.1 (1986), 51-101.

Ury Eppstein. "The Stage Observed: Western Attitudes toward Japanese
Theatre," *Monumenta Nipponica* 48.2 (1993), 147-166.

Ann Yonemura. YOKOHAMA: PRINTS FROM NINETEENTH-CENTURY
JAPAN. 1990: Smithsonian Institution Press. Some 150 woodblock
prints capturing Japan's "Westernization."

Julia Meech-Pekarik. THE WORLD OF THE MEIJI PRINT: IMPRESSIONS
OF A NEW CIVILIZATION. 1986: Weatherhill.

P. F. Kornicki. "Public Display and Changing Values: Early Meiji Exhibitions
and Their Precursors," *Monumenta Nipponica* 49.2 (1994), 167-196.

Centenary Cultural Council Series on JAPANESE CULTURE IN THE MEIJI
ERA. Edited by Kaikoku Hyakunen Kinen Bunka Jigyōkai, 1955-1958.
All volumes translated from the Japanese.

1. Yoshie Okazaki. JAPANESE LITERATURE IN THE MEIJI ERA.
2. Hideo Kishimoto. JAPANESE RELIGION IN THE MEIJI ERA.
3. Toyotaka Komiya. JAPANESE MUSIC AND DRAMA IN THE
    MEIJI ERA.
4. Kunio Yanagita. JAPANESE MANNERS AND CUSTOMS IN
    THE MEIJI ERA.
5. Keizō Shibusawa. JAPANESE LIFE AND CULTURE IN THE
    MEIJI ERA.
6. _____. JAPANESE SOCIETY IN THE MEIJI ERA.
7. Jintarō Fujii. OUTLINE OF JAPANESE HISTORY IN THE
    MEIJI ERA.
8. Naoteru Uyeno. JAPANESE ARTS AND CRAFTS IN THE
    MEIJI ERA.
9. Masaaki Kōsaka. JAPANESE THOUGHT IN THE MEIJI ERA.
10. Ryōsuke Ishii. JAPANESE LEGISLATION IN THE MEIJI ERA.

Centenary Cultural Council Series on A HISTORY OF JAPANESE-AMERICAN
CULTURAL RELATIONS, 1853-1926.

1. Keishi Ohara. JAPANESE TRADE AND INDUSTRY IN THE
   MEIJI-TAISHŌ ERA.
2. Ki Kimura. JAPANESE LITERATURE: MANNERS AND
   CUSTOMS IN THE MEIJI-TAISHŌ ERA
3. Hikomatsu Kamikawa. JAPANESE-AMERICAN DIPLOMATIC
   RELATIONS IN THE MEIJI-TAISHŌ ERA.

TOKUGAWA-MEIJI: FIRST-HAND MATERIALS

Michael Cooper, ed. THEY CAME TO JAPAN: AN ANTHOLOGY OF
EUROPEAN REPORTS ON JAPAN, 1543-1640. 1965: University of
California Press.

Richard Blaker. THE NEEDLE WATCHER: THE WILL ADAMS STORY,
BRITISH SAMURAI. 1973: Tuttle.

Richard Cocks. DIARY OF RICHARD COCKS, CAPE-MERCHANT IN THE
ENGLISH FACTORY IN JAPAN, 1615-1622. 2 volumes.
N. Murakami, ed. 1899: Sankosha.

Englebert Kaempfer. HISTORY OF JAPAN... 1690-1692. 3 volumes. J. G. S.
Schenchzer, transl. 1906: MacLehose. Kaempfer's manuscript is
included in *The History of Science and Technology, Series One:
The Papers of Sir Hans Slaone, 1663-1753, Parts 2 & 3* (forthcoming:
Adam Matthew Publications, microfilm).

C. P. Thunberg. TRAVELS IN EUROPE, AFRICA, AND ASIA. 4 volumes.
1795: Dandre.

V. M. Golovnin. MEMOIRS OF A CAPTIVITY IN JAPAN. 3 volumes. 1824;
reprinted in 1973: Henry Colburn.

Philipp Franz von Siebold. MANNERS AND CUSTOMS OF THE JAPANESE.
1930: Japan-Institut.

Illustrated London News. 1842-1975.

Gerard Siary. "The Image of Japan in European Travelogues from 1853 to 1905," *Transactions, Asiatic Society of Japan*, 4th series, 2 (1987), 155-170.

D. J. M. Tate. THE MIKADO'S JAPAN: BEING GLIMPSES OF NINETEENTH CENTURY JAPAN FROM COMMODORE PERRY'S VISIT (1853) UNTIL THE PROMULGATION OF THE MEIJI CONSTITUTION (1889) AS SEEN AND REPORTED BY THE ILLUSTRATED LONDON NEWS AND OTHER CONTEMPORARY SOURCES. 1990: J. Nicholson.

E. O. Reischauer, ed. JAPAN. 1974. Facsimile articles from *The New York Times* beginning in the 1850s.

Jean-Pierre Lehmann. THE IMAGE OF JAPAN FROM FEUDAL ISOLATION TO WORLD POWER, 1850-1905. 1978: Allen & Unwin.

Colin Holmes & A. H. Ion. "Bushidō and the Samurai: Images in British Public Opinion, 1894-1914," *Modern Asian Studies* 14.2 (1980), 309-329.

John Ashmead. THE IDEA OF JAPAN, 1853-1895: JAPAN AS DESCRIBED BY AMERICAN AND OTHER TRAVELLERS FROM THE WEST. 1987: Garland.

Ranald MacDonald. RANALD MACDONALD: THE NARRATIVE OF HIS EARLY LIFE ON THE COLUMBIA UNDER THE HUDSON'S BAY COMPANY'S REGIME, OF HIS EXPERIENCES IN THE PACIFIC WHALE FISHERY, AND OF HIS GREAT ADVENTURE TO JAPAN: WITH A SKETCH OF HIS LATER LIFE ON THE WESTERN FRONTIER, 1824-1894. William S. Lewis & Naojirō Murakami, eds. 1990: Oregon Historical Society Press.

Roger Pineau, ed. THE JAPANESE EXPEDITION 1852-1854. THE PERSONAL JOURNAL OF COMMODORE MATTHEW C. PERRY. 1969: Smithsonian Institution.

Francis L. Hawks, ed. NARRATIVE OF THE EXPEDITION OF AN AMERICAN SQUADRON... UNDER COMMODORE M. C. PERRY. 3 volumes. 1856: Nicholson.

Wilhelm Heine. WITH PERRY TO JAPAN: A MEMOIR. Frederic Trautmann, transl. 1990: University of Hawaii Press.

James Morrow. A SCIENTIST WITH PERRY IN JAPAN: THE JOURNAL OF DR. JAMES MORROW. Allan B. Cole, ed. 1947: University of North Carolina Press.

George Henry Preble. THE OPENING OF JAPAN: A DIARY OF DISCOV-
ERY IN THE FAR EAST, 1853-1856. 1962: Tuttle.

Townsend Harris. THE COMPLETE JOURNAL OF TOWNSEND HARRIS.
Revised edition. M. E. Cosenza, ed. 1959: Tuttle.

Henry C. J. Heusken. JAPAN JOURNAL, 1855-1861. Jeannette C. Van der
Corput & Robert C. Wilson, eds. 1964: Rutgers University Press.

L. Oliphant. NARRATIVE OF THE EARL OF ELGIN'S MISSION TO CHINA
AND JAPAN IN THE YEARS 1857, 1858, 1859. 2 volumes. 1860:
Blackwood.

Sir Rutherford Alcock. THE CAPITAL OF THE TYCOON: A NARRATIVE OF
THREE YEARS' RESIDENCE IN JAPAN. 2 volumes. 1863: Harper.

Sir Ernest M. Satow. A DIPLOMAT IN JAPAN. 1921: Seeley Service.

Francis Hall. JAPAN THROUGH AMERICAN EYES: THE JOURNAL OF
FRANCIS HALL, KANAGAWA AND YOKOHAMA, 1859-1866.
F. G. Notehelfer, ed. 1992: Princeton University Press.

Hugh Cortazzi. VICTORIANS IN JAPAN: IN AND AROUND THE TREATY
PORTS. 1987: Athlone.

William E. Griffis. THE MIKADO'S EMPIRE. 1876: Harper. 2 volumes;
see especially volume 2, "Personal Experiences, Observations, and
Studies in Japan."

_____. AN AMERICAN TEACHER IN EARLY MEIJI JAPAN. 1976:
University of Hawaii Press. Excerpts from the Griffis diary compiled by
Edward Beauchamp.

Richard Henry Brunton. BUILDING JAPAN, 1968-1876. William Elliot Griffis
& Hugh Cortazzi, eds. 1991: Japan Library. An account by a civil
engineer hired to build lighthouses, Yokohama's sewer system, etc.

_____. SCHOOLMASTER TO AN EMPIRE: RICHARD HENRY BRUNTON
IN MEIJI JAPAN, 1868-1876. Edward R. Beauchamp, ed. 1991:
Greenwood Press.

John R. Black. YOUNG JAPAN: YOKOHAMA AND YEDO. A NARRA-
TIVE OF THE SETTLEMENT AND THE CITY FROM THE
SIGNING OF THE TREATIES IN 1858 TO THE CLOSE OF THE
YEAR 1879. 2 volumes. 1969: Oxford University Press.

Edward S. Morse. JAPAN DAY BY DAY. 2 volumes. 1936: The Morse Society. Covers 1877-1883.

Thomas C. Mendenhall. AN AMERICAN SCIENTIST IN EARLY MEIJI JAPAN: THE AUTOBIOGRAPHICAL NOTES OF THOMAS C. MENDENHALL. Richard Rubinger, ed. 1989: University of Hawaii Press.

Erwin O. E. Von Baelz. AWAKENING JAPAN: THE DIARY OF A GERMAN DOCTOR. 1932: Viking.

Clara A. N. Whitney. CLARA'S DIARY: AN AMERICAN GIRL IN MEIJI JAPAN. M. William Steele & Tamiko Ichimata, eds. 1983: Kōdansha International.

Isabella L. Bird. UNBEATEN TRACKS IN JAPAN: AN ACCOUNT OF TRAVELS ON HORSEBACK IN THE INTERIOR INCLUDING VISITS TO THE ABORIGINES OF YEZO AND THE SHRINES OF NIKKO AND ISE. 2 volumes. 1881: Putnam; 1987: Beacon Press.

Rudyard Kipling. KIPLING'S JAPAN: COLLECTED WRITINGS. Hugh Cortazzi & George Webb, eds. 1988: Athlone.

Mary Crawford Fraser. A DIPLOMAT'S WIFE IN JAPAN: SKETCHES AT THE TURN OF THE CENTURY. Hugh Cortazzi, ed. 1984: Weatherhill.

Richard Gordon Smith. TRAVELS IN THE LAND OF THE GODS: 1898-1907: THE JAPAN DIARIES OF RICHARD GORDON SMITH. 1986: Prentice Hall.

P. Pratt. HISTORY OF JAPAN: COMPILED FROM THE RECORDS OF THE ENGLISH EAST INDIA COMPANY. M. Paske-Smith, ed. 1931: J. L. Thompson.

Sir Thomas S. Raffles. REPORT ON JAPAN TO THE SECRET COMMITTEE OF THE ENGLISH EAST INDIA COMPANY. 1929: J. L. Thompson.

Basil Hall Chamberlain. THINGS JAPANESE. BEING NOTES ON VARIOUS SUBJECTS CONNECTED WITH JAPAN FOR THE USE OF TRAVELLERS AND OTHERS. 6th edition. 1939: Kegan Paul.

Douglas Sladen. QUEER THINGS ABOUT JAPAN. 1904: Treherne.

Walter W. McLaren. A POLITICAL HISTORY OF JAPAN DURING THE MEIJI ERA, 1867-1912. 1916; reprinted 1965: Russell.

Lafcadio Hearn (1850-1904). See the numerous works by this most famous of the early interpreters of Japan to the West.

Pat Barr. THE DEER CRY PAVILION: A STORY OF WESTERNERS IN JAPAN, 1868-1905. 1968: Macmillan.

Harold S. Williams. FOREIGNERS IN MIKADOLAND. 1963: Tuttle.

_____. TALES OF FOREIGN SETTLEMENTS IN JAPAN. 1958: Tuttle.

_____. SHADES OF THE PAST; OR INDISCREET TALES OF JAPAN. 1959: Tuttle.

R. Tsunoda et al. SOURCES OF JAPANESE TRADITION. 1958: Columbia University Press.

David J. Lu. SOURCES OF JAPANESE HISTORY. 2 volumes. 1974: McGraw-Hill.

Shunsuke Kamei. "Japanese See America: A Century of Firsthand Impressions," *Japan Interpreter* 9.1 (1976), 6-35. Selections from seventeen individuals.

"Diary of an Official of the Bakufu," *Transactions, Asiatic Society of Japan*, 2nd series, 8 (1930), 98-119.

Ernest M. Satow, transl. *KINSE SHIRIAKU*: A HISTORY OF JAPAN [1853-1869]. 1873: Japan Mail.

W. G. Beasley, ed. SELECT DOCUMENTS ON JAPANESE FOREIGN POLICY, 1853-1868. 1955: Oxford University Press.

W. W. McLaren, ed. JAPANESE GOVERNMENT DOCUMENTS, *Transactions, Asiatic Society of Japan*, 1st series, 42 (1914).

Japan, Foreign Service. TREATIES AND CONVENTIONS BETWEEN THE EMPIRE OF JAPAN AND OTHER POWERS TOGETHER WITH UNIVERSAL CONVENTIONS, REGULATIONS AND COM-MUNICATIONS, SINCE MARCH 1854. Revised edition. 1884: Kokubunsha; 1987: Inter Documentation Co. (microfiche).

Centre for East Asian Cultural Studies (Tokyo). MEIJI JAPAN THROUGH
    CONTEMPORARY SOURCES. 3 volumes. 1970: Center for East
    Asian Cultural Studies.

Melissa Banta & Susan Taylor, eds. A TIMELY ENCOUNTER: NINE-
    TEENTH CENTURY PHOTOGRAPHS OF JAPAN: AN EXHIBI-
    TION OF PHOTOGRAPHS FROM THE COLLECTIONS OF THE
    PEABODY MUSEUM OF ARCHAEOLOGY AND ETHNOLOGY
    AND THE WELLESLEY COLLEGE MUSEUM. 1988: Peabody
    Museum Press.

The Far East, volumes 1-7 (1870-1875).

Takayoshi Kido. THE DIARY OF KIDO TAKAYOSHI. Sidney DeVere Brown
    & Akiko Hirota, transl. 1984-1986: University of Tokyo Press.
    Volume 1 covers 1868-1871; volume 2, 1871-1874; and volume 3,
    1874-1877.

William Braisted, transl. & ed. MEIROKU ZASSHI:, JOURNAL OF THE
    JAPANESE ENLIGHTENMENT. 1976: Harvard University Press.
    The major journal of the early reformers, 1874-1875.

Yukichi Fukuzawa (1835-1901). THE AUTOBIOGRAPHY OF FUKUZAWA
    YUKICHI. 1966: Hokuseidō.

_____. AN ENCOURAGEMENT OF LEARNING. David A. Dilworth &
    Umeyo Hirano, transl. 1969: Monumenta Nipponica Monographs.

_____. AN OUTLINE OF A THEORY OF CIVILIZATION. David A.
    Dilworth & G. Cameron Hurst III, transl. 1973: Monumenta Nipponica
    Monographs.

_____. THE SPEECHES OF FUKUZAWA: A TRANSLATION AND
    CRITICAL STUDY. Wayne H. Oxford, transl. 1973: Hokuseidō.

_____. FUKUZAWA YUKICHI ON EDUCATION. Eiichi Kiyooka &
    Kazuyoshi Nakayama, transl. 1985: University of Tokyo Press.

_____. FUKUZAWA YUKICHI ON JAPANESE WOMEN: SELECTED
    READINGS. Eiichi Kiyooka, transl. & ed. 1988: University of
    Tokyo Press.

Chōmin Nakae. A DISCOURSE ON GOVERNMENT: NAKAE CHŌMIN AND HIS *SANSUIJIN KEIRIN MONDŌ*. Margaret Dardess, transl. 1977: Program in East Asian Studies, Western Washington State College.

_____. A DISCOURSE BY THREE DRUNKARDS ON GOVERNMENT. Nobuko Tsukui, transl. 1984: Weatherhill.

Kakuzō Okakura THE IDEALS OF THE EAST. 1903: Dutton.

_____. THE AWAKENING OF JAPAN. 1905: Century.

_____. THE BOOK OF TEA: A JAPANESE HARMONY OF ART, CULTURE AND THE SIMPLE LIFE. 2nd edition. 1935: Angus & Robertson; 1989: Kōdansha International.

F. G. Notehelfer. "On Idealism and Realism in the Thought of Okakura Tenshin," *Journal of Japanese Studies* 16.2 (1990), 309-353.

Department of Education, Japan. OUTLINES OF THE MODERN EDUCATION IN JAPAN. 1893: Department of Education, Japan.

Alfred Stead, ed. JAPAN BY THE JAPANESE: SURVEY BY HIGHEST AUTHORITIES. 2 volumes. 1904: Heinemann.

F. Brinkley, ed. JAPAN: DESCRIBED AND ILLUSTRATED BY THE JAPANESE. 1897: Millet.

Shigenobu Ōkuma, comp. FIFTY YEARS OF NEW JAPAN. 2 volumes. 1909: Dutton. Articles by prominent Japanese leaders.

Sohō Tokutomi. THE FUTURE JAPAN. Vinh Sinh, transl. & ed.; Hiroaki Matsuzawa & Nicholas Wickenden, co-eds. 1989: University of Alberta Press.

Tōson Shimazaki. BEFORE THE DAWN. William E. Naff, transl. 1987: University of Hawaii Press. The novel that best captures the rapid changes of the Meiji period.

Inazō Nitobe. BUSHIDŌ: THE SOUL OF JAPAN. 10th edition. 1905: Putnam.

_____. THE JAPANESE NATION. ITS LAND, ITS PEOPLE, ITS LIFE. 1912: Putnam.

_____, et al. WESTERN INFLUENCES IN MODERN JAPAN. 1931: University of Chicago Press.

_____. THE WORKS OF INAZŌ NITOBE. 5 volumes. 1972: University of Tokyo Press.

Tōten Miyazaki. MY THIRTY-THREE YEARS' DREAM: THE AUTOBIOG-RAPHY OF MIYAZAKI TŌTEN. Shinkichi Etō & Marius B. Jansen, transl. 1984: Princeton University Press.

ECONOMIC DEVELOPMENT

"Economic History," THE KŌDANSHA ENCYCLOPEDIA OF JAPAN 2:146-165. Essays by William Hauser on the economy to 1867 (146-151), Kazuo Yamaguchi on the early modern economy to 1945 (151-154), Martin Bronfenbrenner on the 1945-1952 occupation period (154-158), and Hugh Patrick on the postwar and contemporary economy (158-165).

Edwin O. Reischauer & Albert M. Craig. JAPAN: TRADITION AND TRANSFORMATION (1989: Houghton Mifflin), chapters 5 and 6.

Yasusuke Murakami & Hugh T. Patrick, general eds. THE POLITICAL ECONOMY OF JAPAN. Stanford University Press. Volume 1: THE DOMESTIC TRANSFORMATION (Kōzō Yamamura & Yasukichi Yasuba, eds., 1987); Volume 2: THE CHANGING INTERNATIONAL CONTEXT (Daniel I. Okimoto & Takashi Inoguchi, eds., 1988); Volume 3: CULTURAL AND SOCIAL DYNAMICS (Shumpei Kumon & Henry Rosovsky, eds., 1992).

Ryōshin Minami. THE ECONOMIC DEVELOPMENT OF JAPAN: A QUAN-TITATIVE STUDY. Translated from 1981 Japanese edition by Ralph Thompson & Ryōshin Minami. 1986: St. Martin's.

Thomas C. Smith. NATIVE SOURCES OF JAPANESE INDUSTRIALIZA-TION, 1750-1920. 1988: University of California Press. Reviewed by Osamu Saitō in *Journal of Economic History* 49 (1989), 992-999.

Chūhei Sugiyama. THE ORIGINS OF ECONOMIC THOUGHT IN MODERN JAPAN. 1994: Routledge.

Tessa Morris-Suzuki. A HISTORY OF JAPANESE ECONOMIC THOUGHT. 1991: Routledge.

Mikio Sumiya & Kōji Taira, eds. AN OUTLINE OF JAPANESE ECONOMIC HISTORY, 1603-1940. 1979: University of Tokyo Press.

Germaine A. Hoston. MARXISM AND THE CRISIS OF DEVELOPMENT IN PREWAR JAPAN. 1986: Princeton University Press. Analyzes the debate among prewar Japanese intellectuals over analysis of Japan's capitalist development.

_____. THE STATE, IDENTITY, AND THE NATIONAL QUESTION IN CHINA AND JAPAN. 1994: Princeton University Press.

Takafusa Nakamura. ECONOMIC GROWTH IN PREWAR JAPAN. Robert A. Feldman, transl. 1983: Yale University Press.

_____. THE POSTWAR JAPANESE ECONOMY: ITS DEVELOPMENT AND STRUCTURE. 1981: University of Tokyo Press.

Kazushi Ohkawa & Henry Rosovsky. "A Century of Japanese Economic Growth," in William W. Lockwood, ed. THE STATE AND ECONOMIC ENTERPRISE IN JAPAN (1965: Princeton University Press), 47-92.

George Allen. A SHORT ECONOMIC HISTORY OF MODERN JAPAN. Revised edition. 1962: Macmillan.

William Lockwood. THE ECONOMIC DEVELOPMENT OF JAPAN: GROWTH AND STRUCTURAL CHANGE, 1868-1938. 1954. Expanded edition, 1968: Princeton University Press.

_____, ed. THE STATE AND ECONOMIC ENTERPRISE IN JAPAN. 1965: Princeton University Press.

Penelope Francks. JAPANESE ECONOMIC DEVELOPMENT: THEORY AND PRACTICE. 1992: Routledge.

W. J. Macpherson. THE ECONOMIC DEVELOPMENT OF JAPAN c. 1868-1941. 1987: Macmillan Education.

Kunio Yoshihara. JAPANESE ECONOMIC DEVELOPMENT: A SHORT INTRODUCTION. 1979: Oxford University Press.

Nazli Choucri, Robert C. North, & Susumu Yamakage. THE CHALLENGE OF JAPAN BEFORE WORLD WAR II AND AFTER: A STUDY OF NATIONAL GROWTH AND EXPANSION. 1992: Routledge.

Bank of Japan. HUNDRED YEAR STATISTICS OF THE JAPANESE ECONOMY. 1966: Nihon Ginkō.

Thelma Liesner. ONE HUNDRED YEARS OF ECONOMIC STATISTICS: UNITED KINGDOM, UNITED STATES OF AMERICA, AUSTRALIA, CANADA, FRANCE, GERMANY, ITALY, JAPAN, SWEDEN. 2nd edition. 1989: Economist Publications.

Kazushi Ohkawa, Miyohei Shinohara & Mataji Umemura, eds. LONG-TERM ECONOMIC STATISTICS OF JAPAN. 1965: Tōyō Keizaishi Shimposha. 14 volumes; the standard set of statistics.

_____, Miyohei Shinohara, with Larry Meissner. PATTERNS OF JAPANESE ECONOMIC DEVELOPMENT: A QUANTITATIVE APPRAISAL. 1979: Yale University Press. Synthesis of the preceding 14 volume series.

_____. LECTURES ON DEVELOPING ECONOMIES: JAPAN'S EXPERI-ENCE AND ITS RELEVANCE. 1989: University of Tokyo Press.

_____ & Lawrence Klein, eds. ECONOMIC GROWTH: THE JAPANESE EXPERIENCE SINCE THE MEIJI ERA (Proceedings of the 1st Conference). 1968: R. D. Irwin.

_____ & Yūjirō Hayami, eds. ECONOMIC GROWTH: THE JAPANESE EXPERIENCE SINCE THE MEIJI ERA (Proceedings of the 2nd Conference). 1973: Japan Economic Research Center (Tokyo).

_____ & Henry Rosovsky. JAPANESE ECONOMIC GROWTH: TREND ACCELERATION IN THE TWENTIETH CENTURY. 1973: Stanford University Press.

_____ & Henry Rosovsky. "Capital Formation in Japan," in THE INDUSTRIAL ECONOMIES—CAPITAL, LABOR & ENTERPRISE: THE UNITED STATES, JAPAN & RUSSIA, volume 7, part 2 of THE CAMBRIDGE ECONOMIC HISTORY OF EUROPE (1978: Cambridge University Press), 134-165.

_____. DIFFERENTIAL STRUCTURE AND AGRICULTURE: ESSAYS ON DUALISTIC GROWTH. 1972: Kinokuniya.

_____, Bruce F. Johnston & Hiromitsu Kaneda. AGRICULTURE AND ECONOMIC GROWTH: JAPAN'S EXPERIENCE. 1969: University of Tokyo Press.

_____ & Gustav Ranis, eds. JAPAN AND THE DEVELOPING COUNTRIES. 1985: Basil Blackwell. Lessons for developing countries from Japan's experience.

Erich Pauer. "The Years Economic Historians Lost: Japan, 1850-1890," *Japan Forum* 3.1 (1991), 1-9.

Penelope Francks. TECHNOLOGY AND AGRICULTURAL DEVELOPMENT IN PRE-WAR JAPAN. 1982: Yale University Press.

Chikashi Moriguchi. "Rice and Melons—Japanese Agriculture in the Shōwa Era," in Carol Gluck & Stephen R. Graubard, eds. SHŌWA: THE JAPAN OF HIROHITO (1992: Norton), 131-140.

Yūjirō Hayami. A CENTURY OF AGRICULTURAL GROWTH IN JAPAN: ITS RELEVANCE TO ASIAN DEVELOPMENT. 1975: University of Minnesota Press.

_____ & Saburō Yamada, eds. THE AGRICULTURAL DEVELOPMENT OF JAPAN: A CENTURY'S PERSPECTIVE. 1991: University of Tokyo Press.

Takekazu Ogura. AGRICULTURAL DEVELOPMENT IN MODERN JAPAN. Revised edition. 1968: Fuji.

James Nakamura. AGRICULTURAL PRODUCTION AND THE ECONOMIC DEVELOPMENT OF JAPAN, 1873-1922. 1966: Princeton University Press. See also Henry Rosovsky's review of this work under the title "Rumbles in the Ricefields: Professor Nakamura vs. the Official Statistics" in *Journal of Asian Studies* 27.2 (1968), 347-360.

_____. "Growth of Japanese Agriculture, 1875-1920," in William W. Lockwood, ed. THE STATE AND ECONOMIC ENTERPRISE IN JAPAN (1965: Princeton University Press), 249-324.

Linda Johnson. "Prosperity and Welfare: Agricultural Improvement in Meiji Japan," *Transactions, Asiatic Society of Japan*, 4th series, 5 (1990), 1-24.

Yukiko Kawahara. "Local Development in Japan: The Case of Shimane Prefecture from 1800-1930." 1990: Ph.D. dissertation in Oriental Studies, University of Arizona. On government encouragement of the silk industry.

Kären Esther Wigen. "Regional Inversions: The Spatial Contours of Economic Change in the Southern Japanese Alps, 1750-1920." 1990: Ph.D. dissertation in Geography, University of California.

David Luke Howell. "The Capitalist Transformation of the Hokkaidō Fishery, 1672-1935." 1989: Ph.D. dissertation in History, Princeton University.

Miyohei Shinohara. STRUCTURAL CHANGES IN JAPAN'S ECONOMIC DEVELOPMENT. 1970: Kinokuniya.

Shin'ya Sugiyama. JAPAN'S INDUSTRIALIZATION IN THE WORLD ECONOMY, 1859-1899: EXPORT TRADE AND OVERSEAS COMPETITION. 1988: Athlone.

Kaoru Sugihara. "Japan as an Engine of the Asian International Economy, c. 1880-1936," *Japan Forum* 2.1 (1990), 127-145.

Allen Kelley & Jeffrey Williamson. LESSONS FROM JAPANESE DEVELOP-MENT: AN ANALYTIC ECONOMIC HISTORY. 1974: University of Chicago Press.

Allen Kelley. "Writing History Backwards: Meiji Japan Revisited," *Journal of Economic History* 31.4 (1971), 729-776.

Henry Rosovsky. CAPITAL FORMATION IN JAPAN, 1868-1940. 1961: Free Press.

Kōichi Emi. GOVERNMENTAL FISCAL ACTIVITY AND ECONOMIC GROWTH IN JAPAN, 1868-1960. 1963: Kinokuniya.

Roy Seijun Hanashiro. "The Establishment of the Japanese Imperial Mint and the Role of Hired Foreigners: 1868-1875." 1988: Ph.D. dissertation in History, University of Hawaii.

T. F. M. Adams & Iwao Hoshii. A FINANCIAL HISTORY OF MODERN JAPAN. 1964: Research (Tokyo).

Raymond W. Goldsmith. FINANCIAL DEVELOPMENT OF JAPAN, 1868-1977. 1983: Yale University Press.

_____. THE FINANCIAL DEVELOPMENT OF INDIA, JAPAN, AND THE UNITED STATES. 1983: Yale University Press.

Shōichi Rōyama. "Money and the Japanese," in Carol Gluck & Stephen R. Graubard, eds. SHŌWA: THE JAPAN OF HIROHITO (1992: Norton), 177-190.

Kent E. Calder. "Linking Welfare and the Developmental State: Postal Savings in Japan," *Journal of Japanese Studies* 16.1 (1990), 31-59.

Fuji Bank, ed. BANKING IN MODERN JAPAN. 1961. A 245-page Special Issue of *Fuji Bank Bulletin* 11.4.

S. Broadbridge. INDUSTRIAL DUALISM IN JAPAN. 1967: Aldine.

Johzen Takeuchi. THE ROLE OF LABOUR-INTENSIVE SECTORS IN JAPANESE INDUSTRIALIZATION. 1991: United Nations University Press.

Martin Bronfenbrenner. "Some Lessons of Japan's Economic Development, 1853-1938," *Pacific Affairs* 34.1 (1961), 7-27.

Jun Ui, ed. INDUSTRIAL POLLUTION IN JAPAN. 1992: United Nations University Press.

David Howell. "Proto-Industrial Origins of Japanese Capitalism," *Journal of Asian Studies* 51.2 (1992), 269-286.

Susan B. Hanley. "A High Standard of Living in Nineteenth-Century Japan: Fact or Fantasy?" *Journal of Economic History* 43 (1983), 183-192. See also Yasukichi Yasuba, "Standard of Living in Japan Before Industrialization: From What Level Did Japan Begin?", *Journal of Economic History* 46.1 (1986), 217-224; and Susan B. Hanley, "Standard of Living in Nineteenth-Century Japan: Reply to Yasuba," *Journal of Economic History* 46.1 (1986), 225-226.

E. Sydney Crawcour. "Economic Change in the Nineteenth Century," in Marius B. Jansen, ed. CAMBRIDGE HISTORY OF JAPAN, Volume 5: THE NINETEENTH CENTURY (1989: Cambridge University Press), 569-617.

Thomas C. Smith. POLITICAL CHANGE AND INDUSTRIAL DEVELOP-MENT IN JAPAN: GOVERNMENTAL ENTERPRISE, 1868-1880. 1955: Stanford University Press.

Henry Rosovsky. "Japan's Transition to Modern Economic Growth, 1869-1885," in his INDUSTRIALIZATION IN TWO SYSTEMS. 1966: Wiley.

Shigeto Tsuru. "The Take-Off of Japan, 1868-1900," in his ESSAYS ON ECONOMIC DEVELOPMENT (1968: Kinokuniya), 105-122.

E. Sydney Crawcour. "Industrialization and Technological Change, 1885-1920," in Peter Duus, ed. CAMBRIDGE HISTORY OF JAPAN, Volume 6: THE TWENTIETH CENTURY (1988: Cambridge University Press), 385-450.

Yoshio Andō. "The Formation of Heavy Industry—One of the Processes of Industrialization in the Meiji Period," *Developing Economies* 3.4 (1965), 450-470.

Japan Business History Institute. JAPANESE YEARBOOK ON BUSINESS HISTORY. 1984- . See especially Tsunehiko Yui, "The Development of the Organizational Structure of Higher Management in Meiji Japan" (Vol. 1), "Development, Organization, and Business Strategy of Industrial Enterprises in Japan (1915-1935) (Vol. 5); Hiroshi Hazama, "Labor Management in Japan" (Vol. 2); Masaki Kobayashi, "Japan's Early Industrialization and the Transfer of Government Enterprises: Government and Business" (Vol. 2); and the yearly summaries of "The Works of Japanese Business Historians."

Mansel G. Blackford. THE RISE OF MODERN BUSINESS IN GREAT BRITAIN, THE UNITED STATES, AND JAPAN. 1988: University of North Carolina Press.

Johannes Hirschmeier. THE ORIGINS OF ENTREPRENEURSHIP IN MEIJI JAPAN. 1964: Harvard University Press.

_____ & Tsunehiko Yui. THE DEVELOPMENT OF JAPANESE BUSI-NESS, 1600-1980. 1981: Allen & Unwin.

Harvard Graduate School of Business Administration. *Business History Review* 46.1 (1970): "Special Issue: Japanese Entrepreneurship."

Haru Matsukata Reischauer. SAMURAI AND SILK: A JAPANESE AND AMERICAN HERITAGE. 1986: Belknap Press of Harvard University Press.

Eiichi Shibusawa. THE AUTOBIOGRAPHY OF SHIBUSAWA EIICHI: FROM PEASANT TO ENTREPRENEUR. Teruko Craig, transl. 1994: University of Tokyo Press.

Byron Marshall. CAPITALISM AND NATIONALISM IN PREWAR JAPAN: THE IDEOLOGY OF THE BUSINESS ELITE, 1868-1941. 1967: Stanford University Press.

Kōzō Yamamura. "A Re-examination of Entrepreneurship in Meiji Japan (1868-1912)," *Economic History Review* 21.1 (1968), 144-158.

_____. "Entrepreneurship, Ownership, and Management in Japan," in THE INDUSTRIAL ECONOMIES— CAPITAL, LABOR & ENTERPRISE: THE UNITED STATES, JAPAN & RUSSIA, volume 7, part 2 of THE CAMBRIDGE ECONOMIC HISTORY OF EUROPE (1978: Cambridge University Press), 134-165.

_____. "Success Illgotten? The Role of Meiji Militarism in Japan's Technical Progress," *Journal of Economic History* 37.1 (1977), 113-135.

_____. "The Japanese Economy, 1911-1930: Concentration, Conflicts, and Crises," in B. Silberman & H. Harootunian, eds. JAPAN IN CRISIS (1974: Princeton University Press), 299-328.

_____. "Then Came the Great Depression: Japan's Interwar Years," in Herman van der Wee, ed. THE GREAT DEPRESSION REVISITED (1972: Martinus Nijhoff), 182-211.

_____. "Zaibatsu, Prewar and Zaibatsu, Postwar," *Journal of Asian Studies* 23.4 (1964), 539-554.

_____. "Japan's Deus ex Machina: Western Technology in the 1920s," *Journal of Japanese Studies* 12.1 (1986), 65-94.

Kazuo Shibagaki. "The Early History of the Zaibatsu," *Developing Economies* 4.4 (1966), 535-566.

Hidemasa Morikawa. ZAIBATSU: THE RISE AND FALL OF FAMILY ENTERPRISE GROUPS IN JAPAN. 1992: University of Tokyo Press.

John G. Roberts. MITSUI: THREE CENTURIES OF JAPANESE BUSINESS. 1973: Weatherhill.

Oland B. Russell. THE HOUSE OF MITSUI. 1939: Little, Brown.

Huuc C. Maat. "Financial Development and Industrial Organisation in Japan, 1873-1899: The Case of Mitsui," *Japan Forum* 3.1 (1991), 23-35.

Seiichirō Yonekura. "The Japanese Iron and Steel Industry: Continuity and Discontinuity, 1850-1970. " 1990: Ph.D. dissertation in History and East Asian Languages, Harvard University.

Mark Fruin. KIKKŌMAN: COMPANY, CLAN, AND COMMUNITY. 1983: Harvard University Press.

William D. Wray. MANAGING INDUSTRIAL ENTERPRISE: CASES FROM JAPAN'S PREWAR EXPERIENCE. 1989: Council on East Asian Studies, Harvard University.

_____. MITSUBISHI AND THE N.Y.K., 1870-1914: BUSINESS STRATEGY IN THE JAPANESE SHIPPING INDUSTRY. 1984: Council on East Asian Studies, Harvard University.

Tsunehiko Yui & Keiichirō Nakagawa, eds. BUSINESS HISTORY OF SHIPPING: STRATEGY AND STRUCTURE. 1985: University of Tokyo Press.

Stephen John Ericson. "State and Private Enterprise: Railroad Development in Meiji Japan." 1985: Ph.D. dissertation in History, Harvard University.

Richard J. Samuels. THE BUSINESS OF THE JAPANESE STATE: ENERGY MARKETS IN COMPARATIVE AND HISTORICAL PERSPECTIVE. 1987: Cornell University Press.

_____. "RICH NATION, STRONG ARMY": NATIONAL SECURITY AND THE TECHNOLOGICAL TRANSFORMATION OF JAPAN. 1994: Cornell University Press.

Yoshikatsu Hayashi. "The Introduction of American Technology into the Japanese Electrical Industry: Another Aspect of Japanese-American Relations at the Turn of the Century." 1986: Ph.D. dissertation in History, University of California at Santa Barbara.

Barbara Molony. TECHNOLOGY AND INVESTMENT: THE PREWAR JAPANESE CHEMICAL INDUSTRY. 1990: Council on East Asian Studies, Harvard University.

Yukiko Fukasaku. TECHNOLOGY AND INDUSTRIAL DEVELOPMENT IN PREWAR JAPAN: THE MITSUBISHI NAGASAKI SHIPYARD, 1884-1934. 1992: Routledge.

Takeshi Hayashi. THE JAPANESE EXPERIENCE IN TECHNOLOGY: FROM TRANSFER TO SELF-RELIANCE. 1990: United Nations University Press.

Hirofumi Yamamoto, ed. TECHNOLOGICAL INNOVATION AND THE DEVELOPMENT OF TRANSPORTATION IN JAPAN. 1993: University of Tokyo Press.

Michael A. Barnhart. JAPAN PREPARES FOR TOTAL WAR: THE SEARCH FOR ECONOMIC SECURITY, 1919-1941. 1987: Cornell University Press.

Hugh T. Patrick. "The Economic Muddle of the 1920's," in James W. Morley, ed. DILEMMAS OF GROWTH IN PREWAR JAPAN (1971: Princeton University Press), 211-266.

Edward J. Lincoln. "The Shōwa Economic Experience," in Carol Gluck & Stephen R. Graubard, eds. SHŌWA: THE JAPAN OF HIROHITO (1992: Norton), 191-208.

Arthur E. Tiedemann. "Big Business and Politics in Prewar Japan," in Morley, DILEMMAS OF GROWTH IN PREWAR JAPAN (1971: Princeton University Press), 267-316.

William Miles Fletcher. THE JAPANESE BUSINESS COMMUNITY AND NATIONAL TRADE POLICY, 1920-1942. 1989: University of North Carolina Press.

Thomas Richard Schalow. "The Role of the Financial Panic of 1927 and Failure of the 15th Bank in the Economic Decline of the Japanese Aristocracy." 1989: Ph.D. dissertation in History, Princeton University.

Yukio Chō. "Exposing the Incompetence of the Bourgeoisie: The Financial Panic of 1927," *Japan Interpreter* 8.4 (1974), 492-501.

_____. "Keeping Step with the Military: The Beginning of the Automobile Age," *Japan Interpreter* 7.2 (1972), 168-178.

_____. "From the Shōwa Economic Crisis to Military Economy—with Special Reference to the Inoue and Takahashi Financial Policies," *Developing Economies* 5.4 (1967), 568-596.

Bai Gao. "Arisawa Hiromi and His Theory for a Managed Economy," *Journal of Japanese Studies* 20.1 (1994), 115-153. On an economic theorist who contributed greatly to policies for managing Japan's economy both before and after 1945.

Mitsuharu Itō. "Munitions Unlimited: The Controlled Economy," *Japan Interpreter* 7.3-4 (1972), 353-363.

Makoto Takahashi. "The Development of Wartime Economic Controls," *Developing Economies* 5.4 (1967), 648-665.

Richard Rice. "Economic Mobilization in Wartime Japan: Business, Bureaucracy, and Military in Conflict," *Journal of Asian Studies* 38.4 (1979), 689-706.

Takeshi Yuzawa & Masaru Udagawa, eds. FOREIGN BUSINESS IN JAPAN BEFORE WORLD WAR II: PROCEEDINGS OF THE FUJI CONFERENCE. 1990: University of Tokyo Press.

Akira Kudō & Terushi Hara, eds. INTERNATIONAL CARTELS IN BUSINESS HISTORY: THE INTERNATIONAL CONFERENCE ON BUSINESS HISTORY, 18. 1992: University of Tokyo Press. Focuses on manufactured goods in the interwar years.

Mira Wilkins. "American-Japanese Direct Foreign Investment Relationships, 1930-1952," *Business History Review* (1982), 497-518.

Mark Mason. AMERICAN MULTINATIONALS AND JAPAN: THE POLITICAL ECONOMY OF JAPANESE CAPITAL CONTROLS, 1899-1980. 1992: Council on East Asian Studies, Harvard University.

Kenneth L. Bauge. VOLUNTARY EXPORT RESTRICTION AS A FOREIGN COMMERCIAL POLICY WITH SPECIAL REFERENCE TO JAPANESE COTTON TEXTILES, 1930-1962. 1967: Garland.

Dorothy Borg & Shumpei Okamoto, eds. PEARL HARBOR AS HISTORY: JAPANESE-AMERICAN RELATIONS, 1931-1941. 1973: Columbia University Press. See especially articles by Katsurō Yamamura (on Finance Ministry) and Hideichirō Nakamura (on Japan Economic Federation).

Chalmers Johnson. MITI AND THE JAPANESE MIRACLE: THE GROWTH OF INDUSTRIAL POLICY, 1925-1975. 1982: Stanford University Press. Especially chapters 3-5 on pre-1945 economic bureaucracy.

Lonny Edward Carlile. "Zaikai and the Politics of Production in Japan, 1940-1962." 1989: Ph.D. dissertation in Political Science, University of California.

David Friedman. THE MISUNDERSTOOD MIRACLE: INDUSTRIAL
DEVELOPMENT AND POLITICAL CHANGE IN JAPAN. 1988:
Cornell University Press. A study of the machine tool industry since the
1930s, explaining how flexibility was Japanese manufacturers' greatest
competitive asset.

E. G. Shumpeter, ed. THE INDUSTRIALIZATION OF JAPAN AND
MANCHUKUO, 1930-1940. 1940: Macmillan.

Kate L. Mitchell. INDUSTRIALIZATION OF THE WESTERN PACIFIC.
1942: Institute of Pacific Relations.

Edwin W. Pauley. REPORT ON JAPANESE REPARATIONS TO THE
PRESIDENT OF THE UNITED STATES, NOVEMBER 1945 TO
APRIL 1946. Department of State Publication 3174, Far Eastern Series
25. The Pauley Report.

U.S. Department of State. REPORT OF THE MISSION ON JAPANESE
COMBINES, PART I, ANALYTICAL AND TECHNICAL DATA.
Department of State Publication 2628, Far Eastern Series 14. 1946.
The Edwards Report.

Jerome B. Cohen. THE JAPANESE ECONOMY IN WAR AND RECON-
STRUCTION. 1949: University of Minnesota Press.

T. A. Bisson. JAPAN'S WAR ECONOMY. 1945: Macmillan.

_____. ZAIBATSU DISSOLUTION IN JAPAN. 1954: University of
California Press.

Eleanor M. Hadley. ANTI-TRUST IN JAPAN. 1970: Princeton University
Press.

_____. "Zaibatsu" and "Zaibatsu Dissolution," KŌDANSHA ENCYCLOPEDIA
OF JAPAN 8: 361-366.

Mitsubishi Economic Research Institute, ed. MITSUI-MITSUBISHI-
SUMITOMO: PRESENT STATUS OF THE FORMER ZAIBATSU
ENTERPRISES. 1955: Mitsubishi Economic Research Institute.

Shannon Boyd-Bailey McCune. INTELLIGENCE ON THE ECONOMIC
COLLAPSE OF JAPAN IN 1945. 1989: University Press of America.

Keiichirō Nakagawa, ed. STRATEGY AND STRUCTURE OF BIG
BUSINESS. 1976: University of Tokyo Press.

_____, ed. SOCIAL ORDER AND ENTREPRENEURSHIP. 1977: University of Tokyo Press.

_____, ed. MARKETING AND FINANCE IN THE COURSE OF INDUSTRIALIZATION. 1978: University of Tokyo Press.

_____, ed. GOVERNMENT AND BUSINESS. 1980: University of Tokyo Press.

_____ & Tsunehiko Yui. SHIPPING BUSINESS IN THE 19TH AND 20TH CENTURIES. 1984: University of Tokyo Press.

LABOR & INDUSTRIAL RELATIONS

"Labor," THE KŌDANSHA ENCYCLOPEDIA OF JAPAN 4: 343-360. Essays on labor history by Solomon Levine, Robert Evans, Jr., and Ken Kurita.

Kōji Taira. "Economic Development, Labor Markets, and Industrial Relations in Japan, 1905-1955," in Peter Duus, ed. CAMBRIDGE HISTORY OF JAPAN, Volume 6: THE TWENTIETH CENTURY (1988: Cambridge University Press), 606-653.

Andrew Gordon. LABOR AND IMPERIAL DEMOCRACY IN PREWAR JAPAN. 1991: University of California Press.

_____. THE EVOLUTION OF LABOR RELATIONS IN JAPAN: HEAVY INDUSTRY, 1853-1955. 1985: Council on East Asian Studies, Harvard University.

Joe B. Moore. "The Japanese Worker," _Bulletin of Concerned Asian Scholars_ 6.3 (1974), 35-47. A critical evaluation of basic works in this field.

"Essays on 'The Japanese Employment System'," _Journal of Japanese Studies_ 4.2 (1978), 225-300. Includes Sydney Crawcour, "The Japanese Employment System" (225-245); Robert E. Cole, "The Late-Developer Hypothesis: An Evaluation of its Relevance for Japanese Employment Practices" (247-265); and W. Mark Fruin, "The Japanese Company Controversy: Ideology and Organization in a Historical Perspective" (267-300). See also Ronald Dore, "More About Late Development," _Journal of Japanese Studies_ 5.1 (1979), 137-151.

Hiroshi Hazama. "Labor Management in Japan," in Keiichirō Nakagawa & Hidemasa Morikawa, eds. JAPANESE YEARBOOK ON BUSINESS HISTORY, Volume 2. 1985: Japan Business History Institute.

Kazuo Ōkōchi, Bernard Karsh & Solomon B. Levine, eds. WORKERS AND EMPLOYERS IN JAPAN: THE JAPANESE EMPLOYMENT RELATIONS SYSTEM. 1974: Princeton University Press.

Mikio Sumiya. "The Emergence of Modern Japan" and "Contemporary Arrangements: An Overview," in Ōkōchi, Karsh & Levine, WORKERS AND EMPLOYERS IN JAPAN (1974: Princeton University Press), 15-48, 49-87.

_____. "The Japanese System of Industrial Relations," in Peter Doeringer, ed. INDUSTRIAL RELATIONS IN INTERNATIONAL PERSPECTIVE: ESSAYS ON RESEARCH AND POLICY (1981: Holmes & Meier), 287-323.

_____. "The Development of Japanese Labor Relations," *Developing Economies* 4.4 (1966), 499-515.

_____. SOCIAL IMPACT OF INDUSTRIALIZATION IN JAPAN. 1963: University of Tokyo Press.

Hugh Patrick, ed. JAPANESE INDUSTRIALIZATION AND ITS SOCIAL CONSEQUENCES. 1976: University of California Press. See especially the historically oriented articles by Hazama on life styles of industrial workers; Cole & Tominaga on changing occupational structure; Saxonhouse on women in cotton spinning; Chūbachi & Taira on poverty.

W. Dean Kinzley. "Japan's Discovery of Poverty: Changing Views of Poverty and Social Welfare in the Nineteenth Century," *Journal of Asian History* 22.1 (1988), 1-24.

Eiji Yutani. "*Nihon no Kasō Shakai* of Gennosuke Yokoyama, Translated and with an Introduction." 1985: Ph.D. dissertation in History, University of California.

Solomon Levine & Hisashi Kawada. HUMAN RESOURCES IN JAPANESE INDUSTRIAL DEVELOPMENT. 1980: Princeton University Press.

Kōji Taira. ECONOMIC DEVELOPMENT AND THE LABOR MARKET IN JAPAN. 1970: Columbia University Press.

_____. "Factory Labor and the Industrial Revolution in Japan," in THE INDUSTRIAL ECONOMIES—CAPITAL, LABOR & ENTERPRISE: THE UNITED STATES, JAPAN & RUSSIA, volume 7, part 2 of THE CAMBRIDGE ECONOMIC HISTORY OF EUROPE (1978: Cambridge University Press), 166-214.

Ron Napier. "The Transformation of the Japanese Labor Market, 1894-1937," in T. Najita & J. V. Koschmann, eds. CONFLICT IN MODERN JAPANESE HISTORY (1982: Princeton University Press), 342-365.

Ernest J. Notar. "Japan's Wartime Labor Policy: A Search for Method," *Journal of Asian Studies* 44.2 (1985), 311-328.

Sheldon Garon. THE STATE AND LABOR IN MODERN JAPAN. 1987: University of California Press.

Thomas O. Wilkenson. THE URBANIZATION OF JAPANESE LABOR, 1868-1955. 1966: University of Massachusetts Press.

Gary D. Allinson. JAPANESE URBANISM: INDUSTRY AND POLITICS IN KARIYA, 1872-1972. 1975: University of California Press.

Jeffrey Eldon Hanes. "Seki Hajime and the Making of Modern Osaka." 1988: Ph.D. dissertation in History, University of California. Traces one city official's fforts to improve industrial labor conditions in prewar Osaka.

Kazuo Ōkōchi. LABOR IN MODERN JAPAN. 1958: Science Council of Japan.

I. F. Ayusawa. A HISTORY OF LABOR IN MODERN JAPAN. 1966: University of Hawaii Press.

Taishirō Shirai & Haruo Shimada. "Japan," in John T. Dunlop & Walter Galenson, eds. LABOR IN THE TWENTIETH CENTURY (1978: Academic Press), 241-322.

Robert Scalapino. "Japan," in Walter Galenson, ed. LABOR AND ECONOMIC DEVELOPMENT (1959: Wiley), 75-145.

_____. THE EARLY JAPANESE LABOR MOVEMENT: LABOR AND POLITICS IN A DEVELOPING SOCIETY. 1984: University of California Press.

Anthony Woodiwiss. LAW, LABOUR AND SOCIETY IN JAPAN: FROM REPRESSION TO RELUCTANT RECOGNITION. 1991: Routledge.

Masanori Nakamura, ed. THE TRANSFORMATION OF FEMALE LABOUR
IN MODERN JAPAN. 1994: United Nations University Press.
Technology and female labor, from the late 19th century to the postwar
high-growth period.

Yasue Aoki Kidd. WOMEN WORKERS IN THE JAPANESE COTTON
MILLS: 1880-1920. *Cornell University East Asian Papers* 20 (1978).

Gail Lee Bernstein. "Women in the Silk-reeling Industry in Nineteenth-Century
Japan," in Gail Lee Bernstein & Haruhiro Fukui, eds. JAPAN AND
THE WORLD: ESSAYS ON JAPANESE HISTORY AND POLITICS
IN HONOUR OF ISHIDA TAKESHI (1988: St. Martin's), 54-77.

E. Patricia Tsurumi. "Female Textile Workers and the Failure of Early Trade
Unionism in Japan," *History Workshop* 18 (1984), 3-27.

_____. "Problem Consciousness and Modern Japanese History: Female Textile
Workers of Meiji and Taishō," *Bulletin of Concerned Asian Scholars*
18.4 (1986), 41-48.

_____. FACTORY GIRLS: WOMEN IN THE THREAD MILLS OF MEIJI
JAPAN. 1990: Princeton University Press.

Janet E. Hunter, ed. JAPANESE WOMEN WORKING. 1993: Routledge.
On 20th century working women.

_____. "Women's Labour Force Participation in Interwar Japan," *Japan Forum*
2.1 (1990), 105-125.

Thomas C. Smith. "The Right to Benevolence: Dignity and Japanese Workers,
1890-1920," *Comparative Studies in Society and History* 26.4 (1984),
587-613.

Stephen E. Marsland. THE BIRTH OF THE JAPANESE LABOR
MOVEMENT: TAKANO FUSATARŌ AND THE RŌDŌ KUMIAI
KISEIKAI. 1989: University of Hawaii Press.

Stephen S. Large. THE YŪAIKAI, 1912-1919: THE RISE OF LABOR IN
JAPAN. 1972: Monumenta Nipponica Monographs.

_____. "The Japanese Labor Movement, 1912-1919: Suzuki Bunji and the
Yūaikai," *Journal of Asian Studies* 29.3 (1970), 559-579.

F. G. Notehelfer. "Between Tradition and Modernity: Labor and the Ashio Copper Mine," *Monumenta Nipponica* 39.1 (1984), 11-24.

George O. Totten. "Japanese Industrial Relations at the Crossroads: The Great Noda Strike of 1927-1928," in B. Silberman & H. Harootunian, eds. JAPAN IN CRISIS (1974: Princeton University Press), 398-436.

Shūichi Harada. LABOR CONDITIONS IN JAPAN. 1928: Columbia University Press.

Robert E. Cole. JAPANESE BLUE COLLAR: THE CHANGING TRADITION. 1971: University of California Press.

Ronald P. Dore. BRITISH FACTORY—JAPANESE FACTORY: THE ORIGINS OF NATIONAL DIVERSITY IN EMPLOYMENT RELATIONS. 1973: University of California Press.

Michael Cusumano. THE JAPANESE AUTOMOBILE INDUSTRY: TECHNOLOGY AND MANAGEMENT AT NISSAN AND TOYOTA. 1985: Harvard University Press.

Solomon B. Levine. INDUSTRIAL RELATIONS IN POSTWAR JAPAN. 1958: University of Illinois Press.

James C. Abegglen. MANAGEMENT AND WORKER: THE JAPANESE SOLUTION. 1973: Sophia University & Kōdansha International. Revision of the author's THE JAPANESE FACTORY (1958).

Eitarō Kishimoto. "The Characteristics of Labor-Management Relations in Japan and Their Historical Formation," *Kyoto University Economic Review* 35.2 (1965), 33-55.

Tsunehiko Yui & Keiichirō Nakagawa, eds. JAPANESE MANAGEMENT IN HISTORICAL PERSPECTIVE. 1989: University of Tokyo Press.

Kenji Okuda. "Managerial Evolution in Japan," *Management Japan* 5.3 (1971), 13-19; 5.4 (1972), 15-23; 6.1 (1972), 28-35.

Masumi Tsuda. "Study of Japanese Management Development Practices," *Hitotsubashi Journal of Social Studies* 9.1 (1977), 1-12.

Osamu Mano. "Recent Research on the Japanese Personnel Management System in Japan: A Comparative Perspective," *Hokudai Economic Papers* 9 (1979-1980), 1-23.

John W. Bennet & I. Ishino. PATERNALISM IN THE JAPANESE ECONO-
    MY: ANTHROPOLOGICAL STUDIES OF OYABUN-KOBUN
    PATTERNS. 1963: University of Minnesota Press.

Michael Yoshino. JAPAN'S MANAGERIAL SYSTEM: TRADITION AND
    INNOVATION. 1968: Massachusetts Institute of Technology Press.

N. Noda. "How Japan Absorbed American Management Methods," in British
    Institute of Management, MODERN JAPANESE MANAGEMENT
    (1970: Publications Ltd., for British Institute of Management), 29-66.

Keiichirō Nakagawa, ed. LABOR AND MANAGEMENT. 1979: University of
    Tokyo Press.

LANDLORD, TENANT & THE RURAL SECTOR

Tadashi Fukutake. JAPANESE RURAL SOCIETY. R. P. Dore, transl. 1967:
    Cornell University Press. See the bibliographies to each chapter in
    this work.

Richard K. Beardsley, John W. Hall & Robert E. Ward. VILLAGE JAPAN.
    1959: University of Chicago Press.

Takeo Yazaki. SOCIAL CHANGE AND THE CITY IN JAPAN: FROM
    EARLIEST TIMES THROUGH THE INDUSTRIAL REVOLUTION.
    1968: Japan Publications.

Robert J. Smith. KURUSU: A JAPANESE VILLAGE, 1951-1975. 1978:
    Stanford University Press.

Chie Nakane. KINSHIP AND ECONOMIC ORGANIZATION IN RURAL
    JAPAN. 1967: Athlone.

John William Robertson-Scott. THE FOUNDATIONS OF JAPAN. 1922:
    Appleton.

John F. Embree. SUYE MURA, A JAPANESE VILLAGE. 1939: University of
    Chicago Press.

Donna Kay Keuck. "The Books and the Photographs of Suye Mura." 1990:
    Ph.D. dissertation in Sociology, Cornell University.

Shiroshi Nasu. ASPECTS OF JAPANESE AGRICULTURE. 1941: Institute of Pacific Relations.

Thomas C. Smith. THE AGRARIAN ORIGINS OF MODERN JAPAN. 1959: Stanford University Press.

_____. "The Japanese Village in the Seventeenth Century" (1952) and "The Land Tax in the Tokugawa Period" (1958), both reprinted in John W. Hall & Marius B. Jansen, eds. STUDIES IN THE INSTITUTIONAL HISTORY OF EARLY MODERN JAPAN (1968: Princeton University Press), 263-299.

_____. "Landlords and Rural Capitalists in the Modernization of Japan," *Journal of Economic History* 16.2 (1956), 165-181.

_____. "Landlords' Sons in the Business Elite," *Economic Development and Cultural Change* 9.1, part 2 (1960), 93-108.

Penelope Francks. "Peasantry, Proletariat, or Private Enterprise? The Japanese Farmer in the Industrialization Process," *Japan Forum* 2.1 (1990), 91-104.

M. William Steele. "From Custom to Right: The Politicization of the Village in Early Meiji Japan," *Modern Asian Studies* 23.4 (1989), 729-748.

William Chambliss. CHIARAIJIMA VILLAGE: LAND TENURE, TAXA-TION, AND LOCAL TRADE, 1811-1884. 1965: University of Arizona Press.

Hugh Borton. PEASANT UPRISINGS IN JAPAN OF THE TOKUGAWA PERIOD. 1968: Paragon. Reprint of study originally published in *Transactions, Asiatic Society of Japan*, 1938.

Takashi Nagatsuka. THE SOIL: A PORTRAIT OF RURAL LIFE IN MEIJI JAPAN. Anne Walthall, transl. 1989: Routledge.

E. H. Norman. SOLDIER AND PEASANT IN JAPAN: THE ORIGINS OF CONSCRIPTION. 1965: Institute of Pacific Relations. Reprint of two-part article orignally published in *Pacific Affairs*, March & June 1943.

_____. JAPAN'S EMERGENCE AS A MODERN STATE (1940: Institute of Pacific Relations), chapter 5. Reprinted in J. W. Dower, ed. ORIGINS OF THE MODERN JAPANESE STATE. 1979: Pantheon.

Irwin Scheiner. "The Mindful Peasant: Sketches for a Study of Rebellion," *Journal of Asian Studies* 32.4 (1973), 579-591.

Mikiso Hane. PEASANTS, REBELS, AND OUTCASTES: THE UNDERSIDE OF MODERN JAPAN. 1982: Pantheon.

Barrington Moore, Jr. SOCIAL ORIGINS OF DICTATORSHIP AND DEMOCRACY: LORD AND PEASANT IN THE MAKING OF THE MODERN WORLD. 1966: Beacon. See 228-313 on Japan.

Ronald P. Dore. LAND REFORM IN JAPAN. 1959: Oxford University Press. 1-125 on prewar.

_____. "Making Sense of History," *Archives Europiennes de Sociologie* 10.2 (1969), 295-305. Review of Barrington Moore.

_____ & Tsutomu Ōuchi. "Rural Origins of Japanese Fascism," in James Morley, ed. DILEMMAS OF GROWTH IN PREWAR JAPAN (1971: Princeton University Press), 181-209. Critique of Barrington Moore.

_____. "The Meiji Landlord: Good or Bad?", *Journal of Asian Studies* 18.3 (1959), 343-355.

_____. "Agricultural Improvement in Japan," *Economic Development and Cultural Change* 9.1 part 2 (1960), 69-92.

_____. "Land Reform and Japan's Economic Development," *Developing Economies* 3.4 (1965), 487-496.

_____. SHINOHATA: A PORTRAIT OF A JAPANESE VILLAGE. 1980: Pantheon.

Morris D. Morris. "The Problem of the Peasant Agriculturist in Meiji Japan, 1873-1885," *Far Eastern Quarterly* 15.3 (1956), 357-370.

Kunio Niwa. "The Reform of the Land Tax and the Government Programme for the Encouragement of Industry," *Developing Economies* 4.4 (1966), 567-593.

Penelope Francks. TECHNOLOGY AND AGRICULTURAL DEVELOPMENT IN PRE-WAR JAPAN. 1984: Yale University Press.

Richard J. Smethurst. AGRICULTURAL DEVELOPMENT AND TENANCY DISPUTES IN JAPAN, 1870-1940. 1986: Princeton University Press. See also the review by John Lie and response by Smethurst to Lie and to Herbert P. Bix (see article below) in *Bulletin of Concerned Asian Scholars* 19.3 (1987), 43-52; the exchange between Smethurst and Nishida Yoshiaki in *Journal of Japanese Studies* 15.2 (1989), 389-437; and Masanori Nakamura's "The Japanese Landlord System and Tenancy Disputes: A Response to Richard Smethurst's Criticisms" in *Bulletin of Concerned Asian Scholars* 20.1 (1988), 36-50.

Herbert P. Bix. "Class Conflict in Rural Japan: On Historical Methodology," *Bulletin of Concerned Asian Scholars* 19.3 (1987), 29-42. In part, a review of above books by Francks and Smethurst.

Ann Waswo. JAPANESE LANDLORDS: THE DECLINE OF A RURAL ELITE. 1977: University of California Press.

_____. "The Origins of Tenant Unrest," in B. Silberman& H. Harootunian, eds. JAPAN IN CRISIS (1974: Princeton University Press), 374-397.

_____. "The Transformation of Rural Society, 1900-1950," in Peter Duus, ed. CAMBRIDGE HISTORY OF JAPAN, Volume 6: THE TWENTIETH CENTURY (1988: Cambridge University Press), 541-605.

Kenneth Pyle. "The Technology of Japanese Nationalism: The Local Improvement Movement, 1900-1918," *Journal of Asian Studies* 33.1 (1973), 51-65.

Tsutomu Ōuchi. "Agricultural Depression and Japanese Villages," *Developing Economies* 5.4 (1967), 597-627.

Shōbei Shiota. "The Rice Riots and the Social Problem," *Developing Economies* 4.4 (1966), 516-534.

Shūzō Teruoka. "Japanese Capitalism and Its Agricultural Problems— Culminating in the Rice Riots," *Developing Economies* 4.4 (1966), 472-498.

Michael Lawrence Lewis. RIOTERS AND CITIZENS: MASS PROTEST IN IMPERIAL JAPAN. 1990: University of California Press.

George O. Totten. "Labor and Agrarian Disputes in Japan Following World War I," *Economic Development and Cultural Change* 9.1, part 2 (1960), 187-212.

Miriam S. Farley. "Japan's Unsolved Tenancy Problem," *Far Eastern Survey* 6.14 (1937), 153-159.

Galen M. Fisher. "The Landlord-Peasant Struggle in Japan," *Far Eastern Survey* 6.18 (1937), 201-206.

W. Ladejinsky. "Farm Tenancy and Japanese Agriculture," *Foreign Agriculture* (Bureau of Agricultural Economics, U.S. Department of Agriculture) 1.9 (1937), 425-446.

Seiyei Wakukawa. "The Japanese Farm-Tenancy System," in Douglas G. Haring, ed. JAPAN'S PROSPECT (1946: Harvard University Press), 115-173.

Thomas R. H. Havens. FARM AND NATION IN MODERN JAPAN: AGRARIAN NATIONALISM, 1870-1940. 1974: Princeton University Press.

_____. "Two Popular Views of Rural Self-Rule in Modern Japan," in Japan P. E. N. Club, ed. STUDIES ON JAPANESE CULTURE, volume 2 (1973: The Japan P. E. N. Club), 249-255.

Richard J. Smethurst. A SOCIAL BASIS FOR PREWAR JAPANESE MILITARISM: THE ARMY AND THE RURAL COMMUNITY. 1974: University of California Press.

_____. "The Creation of the Imperial Military Reserve Association in Japan," *Journal of Asian Studies* 30.4 (1971), 815-828.

Henry D. Smith II. Review of preceding two books by Havens and Smethurst, *Journal of Japanese Studies* 2.1 (1976), 131-147.

Daikichi Irokawa. "The Survival Struggle of the Japanese Community," *Japan Interpreter* 9.4 (1975), 466-494.

Tsutomu Takizawa. "Historical Background of Agricultural Land Reform in Japan," *Developing Economies* 10.3 (1972), 290-310.

Carol Gluck. "The People in History: Recent Trends in Japanese Historiography," *Journal of Asian Studies* 38.1 (1978), 25-50.

"TAISHŌ DEMOCRACY"

Peter Duus. "Taishō and Early Shōwa History (1912-1945)," KŌDANSHA ENCYCLOPEDIA OF JAPAN 3: 197-203.

Edwin O. Reischauer & Albert M. Craig. JAPAN: TRADITION AND TRANSFORMATION (1989: Houghton Mifflin), chapter 7.

R. Tsunoda et al. SOURCES OF JAPANESE TRADITION. 1958: Columbia University Press. See Chapter 26, "The High Tide of Prewar Liberalism," for basic documents.

Thorstein Veblen. "The Opportunity of Japan," 1915; reprinted in his ESSAYS IN OUR CHANGING ORDER (1934: Viking), 248-266.

John Dewey. CHARACTERS AND EVENTS, volume 1, 1929: Holt. Contains three pertinent essays: "Liberalism in Japan" (1919); "On the Two Sides of the Eastern Sea" (1919); and "Japan Revisited: Two Years Later" (1921).

Yūsuke Tsurumi. PRESENT DAY JAPAN. 1926: Columbia University Press.

A. Morgan Young. JAPAN IN RECENT TIMES, 1912-1926. 1929: Morrow.

_____. IMPERIAL JAPAN, 1926-1938. 1938: Morrow.

Shigeki Tōyama. "Politics, Economics, and the International Environment in the Meiji and Taishō Periods," *Developing Economies* 4.4 (1966), 419-446.

Arthur E. Tiedemann. "Taishō and Early Shōwa Japan," in his AN INTRODUC- TION TO JAPANESE CIVILIZATION (1974: Heath), 217-245.

Takayoshi Matsuo. "The Development of Democracy in Japan—Taishō Democracy, Its Flowering and Breakdown," *Developing Economies* 4.4 (1966), 612-637.

Kenneth Pyle. "Advantages of Followership: German Economics and Japanese Bureaucrats, 1890-1925," *Journal of Japanese Studies* 1.1 (1974), 127-164.

_____. "State and Society in the Interwar Years," *Journal of Japanese Studies* 3.2 (1977), 421-430. A review essay.

Robert Scalapino. DEMOCRACY AND THE PARTY MOVEMENT IN PRE-WAR JAPAN: THE FAILURE OF THE FIRST ATTEMPT. 1953: University of California Press.

George O. Totten, ed. DEMOCRACY IN PREWAR JAPAN: GROUNDWORK OR FACADE? 1965: Yale University Press.

Gino K. Piovesana. "Men and Social Ideas of the Early Taishō period," *Monumenta Nipponica* 19.1-2 (1964), 111-129.

Yoshitake Oka. FIVE POLITICAL LEADERS OF MODERN JAPAN. 1985: University of Tokyo Press. Contains essays on Hara Takashi, Inukai Tsuyoshi, and Saionji Kimmochi, as well as the Meiji leaders Itō Hirobumi and Ōkuma Shigenobu.

Lesley Connors. THE EMPEROR'S ADVISOR: SAIONJI KINMOCHI AND PRE-WAR JAPANESE POLITICS. 1987: Croom Helm.

Tetsuo Najita. HARA KEI IN THE POLITICS OF COMPROMISE, 1905-1915. 1967: Harvard University Press.

Peter Duus. PARTY RIVALRY AND POLITICAL CHANGE IN TAISHŌ JAPAN. 1968: Harvard University Press.

_____. "The Era of Party Rule: Japan, 1905-1932," in James B. Crowley, ed. MODERN EAST ASIA: ESSAYS IN INTERPRETATION (1970: Harcourt Brace & World), 180-206.

_____. "Liberal Intellectuals and Social Conflict in Taishō Japan," in T. Najita & J. V. Koschmann, eds. CONFLICT IN MODERN JAPANESE HISTORY (1982: Princeton University Press), 412-440.

_____. "Yoshino Sakuzō: The Christian as Political Critic," *Journal of Japanese Studies* 4.2 (1978), 301-326.

_____. "Nagai Ryūtarō and the 'White Peril', 1905-1944," *Journal of Asian Studies* 31.1 (1971), 41-48.

Taiichirō Mitani. "The Establishment of Party Cabinets, 1898-1932," Peter Duus, transl., in Peter Duus, ed. CAMBRIDGE HISTORY OF JAPAN, Volume 6: THE TWENTIETH CENTURY (1988: Cambridge University Press), 55-96.

Byron K. Marshall. ACADEMIC FREEDOM AND THE JAPANESE IMPERI-
AL UNIVERSITY, 1868-1939. 1992: University of California Press.

Andrew E. Barshay. STATE AND INTELLECTUAL IN IMPERIAL JAPAN:
THE PUBLIC MAN IN CRISIS. 1988: University of California Press.
Focuses on Nanbara Shigeru and Hasegawa Nyozekan.

J. Thomas Rimer, ed. CULTURE AND IDENTITY: JAPANESE INTELLEC-
TUALS DURING THE INTERWAR YEARS. 1990: Princeton
University Press.

Kevin M. Doak. DREAMS OF DIFFERENCE: THE JAPANESE ROMANTIC
SCHOOL AND THE CRISIS OF MODERNITY. 1994: University of
California Press.

Bernard S. Silberman & H. D. Harootunian, eds. JAPAN IN CRISIS: ESSAYS
ON TAISHŌ DEMOCRACY. 1974: Princeton University Press.
Fifteen contributions by leading scholars. Includes general interpretative
essays by the editors; case studies of Yoshino Sakuzō, Natsume Sōseki,
and Kawakami Hajime; essays on both leftwing and nationalist thought;
economic analyses; and a study of the bureaucracy after 1900.

J. Victor Koschmann, ed. AUTHORITY AND THE INDIVIDUAL IN JAPAN:
CITIZEN PROTEST IN HISTORICAL PERSPECTIVE. 1978:
University of Tokyo Press.

Tatsuo Arima. THE FAILURE OF FREEDOM: A PORTRAIT OF MODERN
JAPANESE INTELLECTUALS. 1969: Harvard University Press.
Includes essays on Uchimura Kanzō, Arishima Takeo, Akutagawa
Ryūnosuke, anarchists, literary "naturalists," proletarian writers, and the
"White Birch" group.

Stefan Tanaka. JAPAN'S ORIENT: RENDERING PASTS INTO HISTORY.
1993: University of California Press. On the scholarly construction of
"Orient" (Tōyō) and "China" (Shina) in modern Japan, particularly by
Shiratori Kurakichi. Reviewed by Kyu Hyun Kim in *Journal of Asian
Studies* 53.1 (1994), 233-234; and by Takashi Fujitani in *Journal of
Japanese Studies* 20.2 (1994), 547-551.

Frank O. Miller. MINOBE TATSUKICHI: INTERPRETER OF CONSTITU-
TIONALISM IN JAPAN. 1965: University of California Press.

Richard Minear. JAPANESE TRADITION AND WESTERN LAW:
EMPEROR, STATE, AND LAW IN THE THOUGHT OF HOZUMI
YATSUKA. 1970: Harvard University Press.

Roger F. Hackett. YAMAGATA ARITOMO IN THE RISE OF MODERN
JAPAN, 1838-1922. 1971: Harvard University Press.

Sharon Minichiello. RETREAT FROM REFORM: PATTERNS OF
POLITICAL BEHAVIOR IN INTERWAR JAPAN. 1984: University
of Hawaii Press. Focuses on Nagai Ryūtarō.

Germaine A. Hoston. THE STATE, IDENTITY, AND THE NATIONAL
QUESTION IN CHINA AND JAPAN. 1994: Princeton University
Press.

_____. "The State, Modernity, and the Fate of Liberalism in Prewar Japan,"
Journal of Asian Studies 51.2 (1992), 287-316.

Tōru Takemoto. FAILURE OF LIBERALISM IN JAPAN: SHIDEHARA
KIJŪRŌ'S ENCOUNTER WITH ANTI-LIBERALS. 1979: University
Press of America.

Sharon H. Nolte. LIBERALISM IN MODERN JAPAN: ISHIBASHI TANZAN
AND HIS TEACHERS, 1905-1960. 1987: University of California
Press.

Mary Louise Hanneman. "Hasegawa Nyozekan, Liberalism, and the Japanese
National Character: An Intellectual Biography." 1991: Ph.D. dissertation in History, University of Washington (Seattle).

John Del Vandenbrink. "State and Industrial Society in Modern Japan:
The Liberal Critique, 1916-1926." 1985: Ph.D. dissertation in History,
University of Chicago.

Shumpei Okamoto. "The Emperor and the Crowd: The Historical Significance
of the Hibiya Riot," in Najita & Koschmann, CONFLICT IN MODERN
JAPANESE HISTORY (1982: Princeton University Press), 258-275.

Arlo Ayres Brown. "The Great Tokyo Riot: The History and Historiography of
the Hibiya Incendiary Incident of 1905." 1986: Ph.D. dissertation in
East Asian Languages and Cultures, Columbia University.

Noel F. Busch. TWO MINUTES TO NOON. 1962: Simon & Schuster.
Concerns the great Kantō earthquake of 1923.

Donald T. Roden. SCHOOLDAYS IN IMPERIAL JAPAN: A STUDY IN THE
CULTURE OF A STUDENT ELITE. 1980: University of California
Press.

Masao Maruyama. "Patterns of Individuation and the Case of Japan: A Conceptual Scheme," in M. Jansen, ed. CHANGING JAPANESE ATTITUDES TOWARD MODERNIZATION (1965: Princeton University Press), 489-531.

Yutaka Arase. "Mass Communication Between the Two World Wars," *Developing Economies* 5.4 (1967), 748-766.

Gregory J. Kasza. "Democracy and the Founding of Japanese Public Radio," *Journal of Asian Stuides* 45.4 (1986), 745-767.

Akira Fujitake. "The Formation and Development of Mass Culture," *Developing Economies* 5.4 (1967), 767-782.

Harris I. Martin. "Popular Music and Social Change in Prewar Japan," *Japan Interpreter* 7.3-4 (1972), 332-352.

Brian Powell. "Japan's First Modern Theater: The Tsukiji Shōgekijō and Its Company, 1924-26," *Monumenta Nipponica* 30.1 (1975), 69-86.

Shūji Takashina. "Japan and the Avant-Garde," *Japan Foundation Newsletter* 14.1 (1986), 1-8.

Donald Richie. JAPANESE CINEMA: FILM STYLE AND NATIONAL CHARACTER. 1984: Anchor.

Joseph L. Anderson & Donald Richie. THE JAPANESE FILM: ART AND INDUSTRY. 1959; expanded edition, 1982: Princeton University Press.

Hidetoshi Katō. "Service-Industry Business Complexes—The Growth and Development of 'Terminal Culture'," *Japan Interpreter* 7.3-4 (1972), 376-382.

_____. "The Trend Toward Affirmation of War: Norakuro," *Japan Interpreter* 7.2 (1972), 179-186.

Linda Lou Sieg. "Political Change in Local Community: Electoral Politics in Hyōgo Prefecture, 1919-1928." 1983: Ph.D. dissertation in History, Temple University.

Shūichi Katō. "Taishō Democracy as the Pre-Stage for Japanese Militarism," in B. Silberman & H. Harootunian, eds. JAPAN IN CRISIS (1974: Princeton University Press), 217-236.

Seizaburō Shinobu. "From Party Politics to Military Dictatorship," *Developing Economies* 5.4 (1967), 666-684.

Marius B. Jansen. "From Hatoyama to Hatoyama," *Far Eastern Quarterly* 14.1 (1954), 65-79. Review of *Taishō Seiji Shi*, 4 volumes, by Shinobu Seizaburō.

Edward Seidensticker. LOW CITY, HIGH CITY: TOKYO FROM EDO TO THE EARTHQUAKE: HOW THE SHŌGUN'S ANCIENT CAPITAL BECAME A GREAT MODERN CITY, 1867-1923. 1983: Knopf.

_____. TOKYO RISING: THE CITY SINCE THE GREAT EARTHQUAKE. 1991: Harvard University Press.

Henry D. Smith II. "Tokyo as an Idea: An Exploration of Japanese Urban Thought Until 1945," *Journal of Japanese Studies* 4.1 (1978), 45-80.

James W. White. "Internal Migration in Prewar Japan," *Journal of Japanese Studies* 4.1 (1978), 81-124.

THE POLITICAL LEFT

R. Tsunoda et al. SOURCES OF JAPANESE TRADITION. 1958: Columbia University Press. See Chapter 28, "The Japanese Social Movement," for documents.

Roger W. Bowen. REBELLION AND DEMOCRACY IN MEIJI JAPAN: COMMONERS IN THE POPULAR RIGHTS MOVEMENT. 1980: University of California Press.

_____. "Rice Roots Democracy and Popular Rebellion in Meiji Japan," *Journal of Peasant Studies* 6.1 (1978), 1-39.

_____. "Political Protest in Prewar Japan: The Case of Fukushima Prefecture," *Bulletin of Concerned Asian Scholars* 16.2 (1984), 23-32.

Nobutake Ike. THE BEGINNINGS OF POLITICAL DEMOCRACY IN JAPAN. 1950: Johns Hopkins.

J. Thomas Rimer, ed. CULTURE AND IDENTITY: JAPANESE INTELLEC-TUALS DURING THE INTERWAR YEARS. 1990: Princeton University Press.

Masakazu Yamazaki. "The Intellectual Community of the Shōwa Era," in Carol Gluck & Stephen R. Graubard, eds. SHŌWA: THE JAPAN OF HIROHITO (1992: Norton), 245-264.

Peter Duus & Irwin Scheiner. "Socialism, Liberalism, and Marxism, 1901-1931," in Peter Duus, ed. CAMBRIDGE HISTORY OF JAPAN, Volume 6: THE TWENTIETH CENTURY (1988: Cambridge University Press), 654-710.

John Crump. THE ORIGINS OF SOCIALIST THOUGHT IN JAPAN. 1983: St. Martin's.

_____. HATTA SHŪZŌ AND PURE ANARCHISM IN INTERWAR JAPAN. 1993: St. Martin's.

_____. "Anarchist Opposition to Japanese Militarism, 1926-1937," *Japan Forum* 4.1 (1992), 73-79.

Stefano Bellieni. "Notes on the History of the Left-Wing Movement in Meiji Japan," Instituto Orientale di Napoli (1979).

Jon Halliday. "The Beginnings of the Left," in his A POLITICAL HISTORY OF JAPANESE CAPITALISM (1975: Pantheon), 62-81.

Hyman Kublin. ASIAN REVOLUTIONARY: THE LIFE OF SEN KATAYA-MA. 1964: Princeton University Press.

_____. "The Japanese Socialists and the Russo-Japanese War," *Journal of Modern History* 22.4 (1950), 322-339.

Isō Abe. "Socialism in Japan," in Shigenobu Ōkuma, comp. FIFTY YEARS OF NEW JAPAN (1910: Dutton), 494-512.

Marius B. Jansen. THE JAPANESE AND SUN YAT-SEN. 1954: Harvard University Press.

_____. "Ōi Kentarō's Radicalism and Chauvinism," *Far Eastern Quarterly* 11.3 (1952), 305-316.

F. G. Notehelfer. KŌTOKU SHŪSUI: PORTRAIT OF A JAPANESE RADICAL. 1971: Cambridge University Press.

Ira L. Flotkin. ANARCHISM IN JAPAN: A STUDY OF THE GREAT TREASON AFFAIR, 1910-1911. 1990: E. Mellen Press.

George Elison. "Kōtoku Shūsui: The Change in Thought," *Monumenta Nipponica* 22.3-4 (1967), 437-467. Accompanied by a translation of Kōtoku's 1910 "Discussion of Violent Revolution from a Jail Cell," 468-481.

J. Victor Koschmann, ed. AUTHORITY AND THE INDIVIDUAL IN JAPAN: CITIZEN PROTEST IN HISTORICAL PERSPECTIVE. 1977: University of Tokyo Press.

Kenneth Strong. OX AGAINST THE STORM: A BIOGRAPHY OF TANAKA SHŌZŌ—JAPAN'S CONSERVATIONIST PIONEER. 1978: University of British Columbia Press.

"Symposium: The Ashio Copper Mine Pollution Incident," *Journal of Japanese Studies* 1.2 (1975), 347-408. Articles by K. Pyle, F. Notehelfer, and A. Stone.

Irwin Scheiner. CHRISTIAN CONVERTS AND SOCIAL PROTEST IN MEIJI JAPAN. 1970: University of California Press.

Nobuya Bamba & John F. Howes, eds. PACIFISM IN JAPAN: THE CHRISTIAN AND SOCIALIST TRADITION. 1978: University of British Columbia Press. Includes essays on Kitamura Tōkoku, Kinoshita Naoe, Uchimura Kanzō, Kōtoku Shūsui, Abe Isoo, Kagawa Toyohiko, Yanaihara Tadao, and Tabata Shinobu.

George B. Bickle, Jr. THE NEW JERUSALEM: ASPECTS OF UTOPIANISM IN THE THOUGHT OF KAGAWA TOYOHIKO. 1976: University of Arizona Press.

Stephen S. Large. "Buddhism, Socialism, and Protest in Prewar Japan: The Career of Seno'o Giro," *Modern Asian Studies* 21.1 (1987), 153-171.

Gail Lee Bernstein. JAPANESE MARXIST: A PORTRAIT OF KAWAKAMI HAJIME, 1879-1946. 1976: Harvard University Press.

_____. "Kawakami Hajime: A Japanese Marxist in Search of the Way," in Bernard Silberman & H. Harootunian, eds. JAPAN IN CRISIS (1974: Princeton University Press), 86-109.

Atsuko Hirai. INDIVIDUALISM AND SOCIALISM: THE LIFE AND THOUGHT OF KAWAI EIJIRŌ (1891-1944). 1986: Council on East Asian Studies, Harvard University.

Henry D. Smith II. JAPAN'S FIRST STUDENT RADICALS. 1972: Harvard
University Press.

George O. Totten. THE SOCIAL DEMOCRATIC MOVEMENT IN PREWAR
JAPAN. 1966: Yale University Press.

_____. "Labor and Agrarian Disputes in Japan Following World War One,"
Economic Development and Cultural Change 9.1, part 2 (1960),
187-212.

_____. "Japanese Industrial Relations at the Crossroads: The Great Noda Strike
of 1927-1928," in Bernard Silberman & H. D. Harootunian, eds.
JAPAN IN CRISIS (1974: Princeton University Press), 398-436.

A. Morgan Young. THE SOCIALIST AND LABOR MOVEMENT IN JAPAN,
BY AN AMERICAN SOCIOLOGIST. 1921: Japan Chronicle.

Evelyn Colbert. THE LEFT WING IN JAPANESE POLITICS. 1952: Institute
of Pacific Relations.

Stephen S. Large. THE YŪAIKAI, 1912-19: THE RISE OF LABOR IN
JAPAN. 1972: Monumenta Nipponica Monographs.

_____. ORGANIZED WORKERS & SOCIALIST POLITICS IN INTERWAR
JAPAN. 1981: Cambridge University Press.

_____. "The Japanese Labor Movement, 1912-1919: Suzuki Bunji and the
Yūaikai," *Journal of Asian Studies* 29.3 (1970), 559-579.

_____. "Nishio Suehiro and the Japanese Social Democratic Movement,
1920-1940," *Journal of Asian Studies* 36.1 (1976), 37-56.

_____. "Revolutionary Worker: Watanabe Masanosuke and the Japanese
Communist Party," *Asian Profile* 3.4 (1975), 371-390.

_____. "The Romance of Revolution in Japanese Anarchism and Communism
During the Taishō Period," *Modern Asian Studies* 2.3 (1977), 441-467.

Peter Duus. "Ōyama Ikuo and the Search for Democracy," in James Morley, ed.
DILEMMAS OF GROWTH IN PREWAR JAPAN (1971: Princeton
University Press), 423-458.

Byron K. Marshall, ed. THE AUTOBIOGRAPHY OF ŌSUGI SAKAE. 1992:
University of California Press.

Thomas A. Stanley. ŌSUGI SAKAE, ANARCHIST IN TAISHŌ JAPAN: THE CREATIVITY OF THE EGO. 1982: Council on East Asian Studies, Harvard University.

Bradford Simcock. "The Anarcho-Syndicalist Thought and Activity of Ōsugi Sakae, 1885-1923," *Harvard University Papers on Japan* (1970), 31-54.

Tatsuo Arima. "The Anarchists: The Negation of Politics," in his THE FAILURE OF FREEDOM: A PORTRAIT OF MODERN JAPANESE INTELLECTUALS (1969: Harvard University Press), 51-69.

Miriam Silverberg. CHANGING SONG: THE MARXIST MANIFESTOS OF NAKANO SHIGEHARU. 1990: Princeton University Press.

Victor Garcia & Wat Tyler. MUSEIFUSHUGI: THE REVOLUTIONARY IDEA IN JAPAN. 1981: Cienfuegos.

George M. Beckmann & Genji Ōkubo. THE JAPANESE COMMUNIST PARTY, 1922-1945. 1969: Stanford University Press.

George Beckmann. "Japanese Adaptations of Marx-Leninism," *Asian Cultural Studies* 3 (1962), 103-114.

_____. "The Radical Left and the Failure of Communism," in James Morley, ed. DILEMMAS OF GROWTH IN PREWAR JAPAN (1971: Princeton University Press), 139-178.

Yoshitomo Takeuchi. "The Role of Marxism in Japan," *Developing Economies* 5.4 (1969), 927-947.

Germaine A. Hoston. THE STATE, IDENTITY, AND THE NATIONAL QUESTION IN CHINA AND JAPAN. 1994: Princeton University Press.

_____. MARXISM AND THE CRISIS OF DEVELOPMENT IN PREWAR JAPAN. 1986: Princeton University Press. Analyzes the debate among prewar Japanese intellectuals over analysis of Japan's capitalist development.

_____. "Conceptualizing Bourgeois Revolution: The Prewar Japanese and the Meiji Restoration," *Comparative Studies in Society and History* 33.3 (1991), 539-581.

_____. "Marxism and National Socialism in Taishō Japan: The Thought of Takabatake Motoyuki," *Journal of Asian Studies* 44.1 (1984), 43-64.

Joshua A. Fogel. "The Debates over the Asiatic Mode of Production in Soviet Russia, China, and Japan," *American Historical Review* 93.1 (1988), 56-79.

Yasukichi Yasuba. "Anatomy of the Debate on Japanese Capitalism," *Journal of Japanese Studies* 2.1 (1975), 63-82.

Robert Scalapino. THE JAPANESE COMMUNIST MOVEMENT, 1920-1966. 1967: University of California Press.

Central Committee, Communist Party of Japan. THE FIFTY YEARS OF THE COMMUNIST PARTY OF JAPAN. 1973: Central Committee, Communist Party of Japan (Nihon Kyōsantō).

A. Roger Swearingen & Paul Langer. RED FLAG IN JAPAN: INTERNATIONAL COMMUNISM IN ACTION, 1919-1951. 1952: Harvard University Press.

Paul Langer. COMMUNISM IN JAPAN: A CASE OF POLITICAL NATURALIZATION. 1972: Hoover Institution Press.

Hiroaki Matsuzawa. "'Theory' and 'Organization' in the Japan Communist Party," in J. Victor Koschmann, ed. AUTHORITY AND THE INDIVIDUAL IN JAPAN (1978: University of Tokyo Press), 108-127.

Patricia G. Steinhoff. TENKŌ: IDEOLOGY AND SOCIAL INTEGRATION IN PREWAR JAPAN. 1991: Garland.

_____. "Tenkō and Thought Control," in Gail Lee Bernstein & Haruhiro Fukui, eds. JAPAN AND THE WORLD: ESSAYS ON JAPANESE HISTORY AND POLITICS IN HONOUR OF ISHIDA TAKESHI (1988: St. Martin's), 78-94.

Kazuko Tsurumi. "Six Types of Change in Personality: Case Studies of Ideological Conversion in the 1930's," in her SOCIAL CHANGE AND THE INDIVIDUAL (1966: Princeton University Press), 29-79.

Ian Neary. "Tenkō of an Organization: The Suiheisha in the Late 1930's," *Proceedings of the British Association for Japanese Studies*, volume 2, part 2 (1977), 64-76.

Shigeharu Nakano. "The House in the Village," in Brett de Bary, transl. THREE WORKS BY NAKANO SHIGEHARU, *Cornell University East Asian Papers* 21 (1979), 21-73.

John H. Boyle. "The Role of the Radical Left Wing in the Japanese Suffrage Movement," *Studies on Asia* 6 (1965), 81-96.

Mikiso Hane, transl. & ed. REFLECTIONS ON THE WAY TO THE GALLOWS: REBEL WOMEN IN PREWAR JAPAN. 1988: University of California Press.

Bunsō Hashikawa. "Antiwar Values—the Resistance in Japan," *Japan Interpreter* 9.1 (1974), 86-97.

_____. "The 'Civil Society' Ideal and Wartime Resistance," in Koschmann, AUTHORITY AND THE INDIVIDUAL IN JAPAN (1978: University of Tokyo Press), 128-142.

Chalmers Johnson. AN INSTANCE OF TREASON: OZAKI HOTSUMI AND THE SORGE SPY RING. 1964: Stanford University Press.

F. W. Deakin & G. R. Storry. THE CASE OF RICHARD SORGE. 1966: Chatto & Windus.

G. T. Shea. LEFTWING LITERATURE IN JAPAN. 1964: University of Tokyo Press.

Yoshio Iwamoto. "Aspects of the Proletarian Literary Movement in Japan," in Silberman & Harootunian, JAPAN IN CRISIS (1974: Princeton University Press), 156-182.

Tatsuo Arima. "Proletarian Literature: The Tyranny of Politics," in his THE FAILURE OF FREEDOM (1969: Harvard University Press), 173-213.

Donald Keene. "Proletarian Literature of the 1920s" and "Tenkō Literature: The Writings of Ex-Communists," in his DAWN TO THE WEST: JAPANESE LITERATURE OF THE MODERN ERA (1984: Holt, Rinehart & Winston), 594-628 and 846-905.

Vlasta Hilska. "Japanese Proletarian Literature," in Vlasta Hilska & Zdenka Vasiljevova, PROBLEMS OF MODERN JAPANESE SOCIETY (1971: Universita Karlova), 11-52.

Naoe Kinoshita. PILLAR OF FIRE. 1972: Allen & Unwin. Translation by
Kenneth Strong of 1904 novel by one of the pioneers of socialism in
Japan.

Takiji Kobayashi. "THE FACTORY SHIP" AND "THE ABSENTEE LAND-
LORD". 1973: University of Washington Press. Translation by Frank
Motofuji of two works by the most famous proletarian writer.

NATIONALISM & THE EMPEROR SYSTEM

R. Tsunoda et al. SOURCES OF JAPANESE TRADITION. 1958: Columbia
University Press. See Chapter 27 for documents pertaining to "The Rise
of Revolutionary Nationalism."

Robert K. Hall. SHŪSHIN: THE ETHICS OF A DEFEATED NATION. 1949:
Teachers College, Columbia University. Includes extensive translations
from ethics textbooks of 1936-1940.

Japanese Ministry of Education. *KOKUTAI NO HONGI*: CARDINAL
PRINCIPLES OF THE NATIONAL ENTITY OF JAPAN. Translated
by John Gauntlett and edited by Robert K. Hall. 1949: Harvard
University Press. The consummate official explanation of the Japanese
national polity *(kokutai)*, originally published in 1937.

_____. "The Way of the Subject" *(Shinmin no Michi)*, reprinted in Otto
Tolischus, TOKYO RECORD (1943: Reynal & Hitchcock), 405-427.

Masao Maruyama. THOUGHT AND BEHAVIOR IN MODERN JAPANESE
POLITICS. 1963: Oxford University Press. Pioneer essays on
nationalism and fascism in modern Japan.

_____. Introduction to Ivan Morris, NATIONALISM AND THE RIGHT-
WING IN JAPAN: A STUDY OF POSTWAR TRENDS (1960:
Oxford University Press), xvii-xxvii.

Kazuko Tsurumi. SOCIAL CHANGE AND THE INDIVIDUAL: JAPAN
BEFORE AND AFTER DEFEAT IN WORLD WAR II. 1966:
Princeton University Press. Excellent essays on indoctrination and
"socialization for death."

Masanori Nakamura. "The Emperor System of the 1900's," *Bulletin of Concerned Asian Scholars* 16.2 (1984), 2-11.

_____. THE JAPANESE MONARCHY: AMBASSADOR JOSEPH GREW AND THE MAKING OF THE "SYMBOL EMPEROR SYSTEM," 1931-1991. Herbert Bix, Jonathan Baker-Bates, & Derek Bowen, transl. 1992: M. E. Sharpe.

Jirō Kamishima. "Mental Structure of the Emperor System," *Developing Economies* 5.4 (1967), 702-726.

Noboru Kojima. "Militarism and the Emperor System," *Japan Interpreter* 8.2 (1973), 219-227.

Michio Takeyama. "The Emperor System," *Journal of Social and Political Ideas in Japan* 2.2 (1964), 21-27.

Peter Nosco, ed. THE EMPEROR SYSTEM AND RELIGION IN JAPAN. *Japanese Journal of Religious Studies* 17.2-17.3 (1990). Special double issue.

Adrian C. Mayer. "Recent Succession Ceremonies of the Emperor of Japan," *Japan Review* 2 (1991), 35-61. Deals with Meiji, Taishō, and Shōwa.

Hiroaki Ōsawa. "Emperor versus Army Leaders: The 'Complications' Incident of 1886," *Acta Asiatica* 59 (1990), 1-17.

Osamu Terasaki. "How Radicals in the Popular Rights Movement Viewed the Emperor: A Brief Analysis," *Acta Asiatica* 59 (1990), 18-37.

Hiroshi Yasuda. "The Modern Emperor System as It Took Shape before and after the Sino-Japanese War of 1894-5," *Acta Asiatica* 59 (1990), 38-58.

Junji Banno. "Emperor, Cabinet, and Diet in Meiji Politics (1880-1913)," *Acta Asiatica* 59 (1990), 59-76.

Tomoko Masuda. "The Emperor's Right of Supreme Command as Exercised up to 1930: A Study Based Especially on the Takarabe & Kuratomi Diaries," *Acta Asiatica* 59 (1990), 77-100.

John W. Hall. "A Monarch for Modern Japan," in Robert E. Ward, ed. POLITICAL DEVELOPMENT IN MODERN JAPAN (1965: Princeton University Press), 11-64.

Byron K. Marshall. CAPITALISM AND NATIONALISM IN PREWAR
JAPAN: THE IDEOLOGY OF THE BUSINESS ELITE, 1868-1941.
1967: Stanford University Press.

Daniel C. Holtom. THE NATIONAL FAITH OF JAPAN: A STUDY IN
MODERN SHINTŌ. 1938: Dutton.

_____. MODERN JAPAN AND SHINTŌ NATIONALISM. Revised edition.
1947: University of Chicago Press.

Helen Hardacre. SHINTŌ AND THE STATE, 1868-1988. 1991: Princeton
University Press.

Nobushige Hozumi. ANCESTOR WORSHIP AND JAPANESE LAW.
6th edition. 1940: Maruzen.

John Paul Reed. KOKUTAI: A STUDY OF CERTAIN SACRED AND
SECULAR ASPECTS OF JAPANESE NATIONALISM. 1940:
University of Chicago Press.

Carol Gluck. JAPAN'S MODERN MYTHS: IDEOLOGY IN THE LATE
MEIJI PERIOD. 1985: Princeton University Press. See also the review
by Atsuko Hirai entitled "The State and Ideology in Meiji Japan—
A Review Article," in *Journal of Asian Studies* 46.1 (1987), 89-103.

Tetsuo Najita. JAPAN: THE INTELLECTUAL FOUNDATIONS OF
MODERN JAPANESE POLITICS. 1974; 1980: University of Chicago
Press.

_____. "Nakano Seigō and the Spirit of the Meiji Restoration," in James Morley,
ed. DILEMMAS OF GROWTH IN PREWAR JAPAN (1971:
Princeton University Press), 375-421.

_____ & H. D. Harootunian. "Japanese Revolt against the West: Political and
Cultural Criticism in the Twentieth Century," in Peter Duus, ed.
CAMBRIDGE HISTORY OF JAPAN, Volume 6: THE TWENTIETH
CENTURY (1988: Cambridge University Press), 711-774.

Leslie R. Oates. POPULIST NATIONALISM IN PREWAR JAPAN: A BIOG-
RAPHY OF NAKANO SEIGŌ. 1985: Allen & Unwin.

Delmer M. Brown. NATIONALISM IN JAPAN: AN INTRODUCTORY
HISTORICAL ANALYSIS. 1955: University of California Press.

James W. White, Michio Umegaki, & Thomas R. H. Havens, eds. THE
    AMBIVALENCE OF NATIONALISM: MODERN JAPAN
    BETWEEN EAST AND WEST. 1990: University Press of America.

Marlene Mayo, ed. THE EMERGENCE OF IMPERIAL JAPAN: SELF
    DEFENSE OR CALCULATED AGGRESSION? 1970: Heath.
    See especially essays by Yoshitake Oka and Sannosuke Matsumoto.

Kimitada Miwa. "The Rejection of Localism: An Origin of Ultranationalism in
    Japan," *Japan Interpreter* 9.1 (1974), 68-79.

Grant Goodman, ed. IMPERIAL JAPAN AND ASIA—A REASSESSMENT.
    1967: Occasional Papers of the East Asia Institute, Columbia
    University.

Wilbur M. Fridell. "Government Ethics Textbooks in Late Meiji Japan," *Journal
    of Asian Studies* 29.4 (1970), 823-834.

Harold J. Wray. "A Study in Contrasts: Japanese School Textbooks, 1903 and
    1941-1945," *Monumenta Nipponica* 27.1 (1973), 69-86.

Kenneth B. Pyle. "The Technology of Japanese Nationalism: The Local
    Improvement Movement, 1900-1918," *Journal of Asian Studies* 33.1
    (1973), 51-65.

Mikiso Hane. "Nationalism and the Decline of Liberalism in Meiji Japan,"
    Studies on Asia 4 (1963), 69-80.

Osamu Kuno. "The Meiji State, Minponshugi and Ultranationalism," in
    J. V. Koschmann, ed. AUTHORITY & THE INDIVIDUAL IN JAPAN
    (1978: University of Tokyo Press), 60-80.

Kimitada Miwa. "Fukuzawa Yukichi's 'Departure from Asia': A Prelude to the
    Sino-Japanese War," in Edmund Skrzypczak ed. JAPAN'S MODERN
    CENTURY (1968: Tuttle), 1-26.

Albert M. Craig. "Fukuzawa Yukichi: The Philosophical Foundations of Meiji
    Nationalism," in Robert Ward, ed. POLITICAL DEVELOPMENT IN
    MODERN JAPAN (1965: Princeton University Press), 99-148.

Symposium on Japanese Nationalism, *Journal of Asian Studies* 31.1 (1971).
    Kenneth Pyle, "Some Recent Approaches to Japanese Nationalism"
    (5-16); Tetsuo Najita, "Restorationism in the Political Thought of
    Yamagata Daini (1725-1767)" (17-30); Fred Notehelfer, "Kōtoku Shūsui
    & Nationalism" (31-40); Peter Duus, "Nagai Ryūtarō & the 'White Peril,'
    1905-1944" (41-48); Sannosuke Matsumoto, "The Significance of
    Nationalism in Modern Japanese Thought" (49-56); Harry Harootunian,
    "Nationalism as Intellectual History" (57-62).

Stefan Tanaka. "Imaging History: Inscribing Belief in the Nation," *Journal of
    Asian Studies* 53.1 (1994), 24-44. Explores the relationship between art
    criticism and nationalism.

Donald Keene. "The Sino-Japanese War of 1894-95 and Japanese Culture,"
    in his LANDSCAPES AND PORTRAITS: APPRECIATIONS OF
    JAPANESE CULTURE (1971: Kōdansha International), 259-299.

E. H. Norman. "The Gen'yōsha: A Study in the Origins of Japanese
    Imperialism," *Pacific Affairs* 17 (1944), 261-284.

Inazō Nitobe. BUSHIDŌ: THE SOUL OF JAPAN. 1899; reprinted 1969:
    Tuttle.

George Masaaki Oshiro. "Internationalist in Prewar Japan: Nitobe Inazō,
    1862-1933." 1987: Ph.D. dissertation in Asian Studies, University of
    British Columbia.

George M. Wilson. RADICAL NATIONALIST IN JAPAN: KITA IKKI,
    1883-1937. 1969: Harvard University Press.

Kōichi Nomura. "Kita Ikki," *Developing Economies* 4.2 (1966), 231-244.

Andrew E. Barshay. STATE AND INTELLECTUAL IN IMPERIAL JAPAN:
    THE PUBLIC MAN IN CRISIS. 1988: University of California Press.
    Focuses on Nanbara Shigeru and Hasegawa Nyozekan.

Thomas R. H. Havens. FARM AND NATION IN MODERN JAPAN:
    AGRARIAN NATIONALISM, 1870-1940. 1974: Princeton University
    Press.

Richard J. Smethurst. A SOCIAL BASIS FOR PREWAR JAPANESE
    MILITARISM: THE ARMY AND THE RURAL COMMUNITY.
    1974: University of California Press.

Henry D. Smith II. Review of preceding two books by Havens and Smethurst, *Journal of Japanese Studies* 2.1 (1976), 131-147.

Herbert P. Bix. "Rethinking 'Emperor-System Fascism': Ruptures and Continuities in Modern Japanese History," *Bulletin of Concerned Asian Scholars* 14.2 (1982), 2-19.

_____. "Emperor-System Fascism: A Study of the Shift Process in Japanese Politics," *Shakai Rōdō Kenkyū* 27.2 and 27.3-4 (1981), 1-14, 99-129.

_____. "The Shōwa Emperor's 'Monologue' and the Problem of War Responsibility," *Journal of Japanese Studies* 18.2 (1992), 295-363.

Ben-Ami Shillony. REVOLT IN JAPAN: THE YOUNG OFFICERS AND THE FEBRUARY 26, 1936 INCIDENT. 1972: Princeton University Press.

_____. POLITICS AND CULTURE IN WARTIME JAPAN. 1982: Oxford University Press.

George M. Wilson, ed. CRISIS POLITICS IN PREWAR JAPAN. 1970: Monumenta Nipponica Monographs.

Richard Storry. THE DOUBLE PATRIOTS: A STUDY OF JAPANESE NATIONALISM. 1957: Houghton Mifflin.

Donald Keene. "Japanese Literature and Politics in the 1930s," *Journal of Japanese Studies* 2.2 (1976), 225-248.

_____. "Japanese Writers and the Greater East Asia War," in his LAND-SCAPES AND PORTRAITS (1971: Kōdansha International), 300-321; article originally published in 1964.

_____. "The Barren Years: Japanese War Literature," *Monumenta Nipponica* 33.1 (1978), 67-112.

_____. "War Literature," in his DAWN TO THE WEST: JAPANESE LITERATURE OF THE MODERN ERA (1984: Holt, Rinehart & Winston), 906-961.

Louis Allen. "Japanese Literature of the Second World War," *Proceedings of the British Association for Japanese Studies*, volume 2, part 1 (1977), 117-152.

James B. Crowley. "A New Asian Order: Some Notes on Prewar Japanese
    Nationalism," in Bernard Silberman & H. Harootunian, eds. JAPAN IN
    CRISIS (1974: Princeton University Press), 270-298.

_____. "Intellectuals as Visionaries of the New Asian Order," in James Morley,
    ed. DILEMMAS OF GROWTH IN PREWAR JAPAN (1971: Princeton
    University Press), 319-373.

_____. "A New Deal for Japan and Asia: One Road to Pearl Harbor," in his
    MODERN EAST ASIA: ESSAYS IN INTERPRETATION (1970:
    Harcourt Brace & World), 235-264.

Ivan Morris. "If Only We Might Fall...," an essay on the kamikaze pilots in his
    THE NOBILITY OF FAILURE: TRAGIC HEROES IN THE
    HISTORY OF JAPAN (1975: Holt, Rinehart & Winston), 276-334.

Otto D. Tolischus, ed. THROUGH JAPANESE EYES. 1945: Reynal &
    Hitchcock. Quotations by Japanese ideologues.

Shinichi Fujii. TENNŌ SEIJI: DIRECT IMPERIAL RULE. 1944: Yūhikaku.

Joshua A. Fogel. POLITICS AND SINOLOGY: THE CASE OF NAITŌ
    KŌNAN (1866-1934). 1984: Council on East Asian Studies, Harvard
    University.

Stefan Tanaka. JAPAN'S ORIENT: RENDERING PASTS INTO HISTORY.
    1993: University of California Press. On the scholarly construction of
    "Orient" (Tōyō) and "China" (Shina) in modern Japan, particularly by
    Shiratori Kurakichi. Reveiwed by Kyu Hyun Kim in Journal of Asian
    Studies 53.1 (1994), 233-234; and by Takashi Fujitani in Journal of
    Japanese Studies 20.2 (1994), 547-551.

"FASCISM," MILITARISM & THE SHŌWA CRISIS

Edwin O. Reischauer & Albert M. Craig. JAPAN: TRADITION AND
    TRANSFORMATION (1989: Houghton Mifflin), chapter 7.

Shunsuke Tsurumi. AN INTELLECTUAL HISTORY OF WARTIME JAPAN,
    1931-1945. 1986: KPI.

Masao Maruyama. THOUGHT AND BEHAVIOR IN MODERN JAPANESE POLITICS. Ivan Morris, ed. 1963: Oxford University Press. Classic early postwar essays. See especially "The Ideology and Dynamics of Japanese Fascism" (1947).

Tetsuo Najita & J. Victor Koschmann, eds. CONFLICT IN MODERN JAPANESE HISTORY: THE NEGLECTED TRADITION. 1982: Princeton University Press.

Peter Duus & Daniel Okimoto. "Fascism and the History of Pre-War Japan: The Failure of a Concept," *Journal of Asian Studies* 39.1 (1979), 65-76.

Gordon M. Berger. "Changing Historiographical Perspectives on Early Shōwa Politics: 'The Second Approach'," *Journal of Asian Studies* 34.2 (1975), 473-484.

W. Miles Fletcher. "Intellectuals and Fascism in Early Shōwa Japan," *Journal of Asian Studies* 39.1 (1979), 39-63.

_____. THE SEARCH FOR A NEW ORDER: INTELLECTUALS AND FASCISM IN PREWAR JAPAN. 1982: University of North Carolina Press.

Germaine A. Hoston. THE STATE, IDENTITY, AND THE NATIONAL QUESTION IN CHINA AND JAPAN. 1994: Princeton University Press.

_____. "Marxism and Japanese Expansionism: Takahashi Kamekichi and the Theory of 'Petty Imperialism'," *Journal of Japanese Studies* 10.1 (1984), 1-30.

_____. "Marxism and National Socialism in Taishō Japan: The Thought of Takabatake Motoyuki," *Journal of Asian Studies* 44.1 (1984), 43-64.

Jon Halliday. A POLITICAL HISTORY OF JAPANESE CAPITALISM. 1975: Pantheon. See especially 133-140 on "The Question of Japanese 'Fascism'."

E. J. Hobsbawn. "Vulnerable Japan," *New York Review of Books* 22 (1975), 26-32.

George M. Wilson. "A New Look at the Problem of 'Japanese Fascism'," *Comparative Studies in Society and History* 10.4 (1968), 401-412.

Barrington Moore, Jr. SOCIAL ORIGINS OF DICTATORSHIP AND
    DEMOCRACY (1966: Beacon), 228-313.

Ronald Dore. "Making Sense of History," *Archives Europiennes de Sociologie*
    10.2 (1969), 295-305. Review of Barrington Moore's SOCIAL
    ORIGINS.

_____ & Tsutomu Ōuchi. "Rural Origins of Japanese Fascism," in James
    Morley, ed. DILEMMAS OF GROWTH IN PREWAR JAPAN (1971:
    Princeton University Press), 181-209. Critique of Barrington Moore.

Shūichi Katō. "Taishō Democracy As the Pre-Stage for Japanese Militarism,"
    in B. Silberman & H. Harootunian, eds. JAPAN IN CRISIS (1974:
    Princeton University Press), 217-236.

Seizaburō Shinobu. "From Party Politics to Military Dictatorship," *Developing
    Economies* 5.4 (1967), 666-684.

Sannosuke Matsumoto. "The Roots of Political Disillusionment: 'Public' and
    'Private' in Japan," in J. Victor Koschmann, ed. AUTHORITY AND
    THE INDIVIDUAL IN JAPAN (1978: Tokyo University Press), 31-51.

Herbert Bix. "Kawakami Hajime and the Organic Law of Japanese Fascism,"
    Japan Interpreter 12.1 (1978), 118-133.

_____. "Rethinking 'Emperor-System Fascism': Ruptures and Continuities in
    Modern Japanese History," *Bulletin of Concerned Asian Scholars* 14.2
    (1982), 2-19.

_____. "Emperor-System Fascism: A Study of the Shift Process in Japanese
    Politics," *Shakai Rōdō Kenkyū* 27.2 and 27.3-4 (1981), 1-14, 99-129.

Gavan McCormack. "Nineteen-Thirties Japan: Fascism?" *Bulletin of Concerned
    Asian Scholars* 14.2 (1982), 20-32.

Gregory Kasza. "Fascism From Below? A Comparative Perspective on the
    Japanese Right, 1931- 1936," *Journal of Contemporary History* 19.4
    (1984), 607-630.

Takeshi Ishida. "Elements of Tradition and 'Renovation' in Japan During the 'Era
    of Fascism'," *Social Science Abstracts* 17 (Shakai Kagaku Kenkyūjo,
    Tokyo University, 1976), 111-140.

Tetsunari Matsuzawa. JAPANESE FASCISM AND THE TENNŌ IMPERIAL
    STATE. 1984: Japanese Studies Centre, Monash University.

Jirō Kamishima. "Mental Structure of the Emperor System," *Developing
    Economies* 5.4 (1967), 702-726.

Noboru Kojima. "Militarism and the Emperor System," *Japan Interpreter* 8.2
    (1973), 219-227.

Shinichi Kitaoka. "Diplomacy and the Military in Shōwa Japan," in Carol Gluck
    & Stephen R. Graubard, eds. SHŌWA: THE JAPAN OF HIROHITO
    (1992: Norton), 155-176.

Chihiro Hosoya. "The Military and the Foreign Policy of Prewar Japan,"
    Hitotsubashi Journal of Law and Politics 7 (1974), 1-7.

Carol Gluck & Stephen R. Graubard, eds. SHŌWA: THE JAPAN OF HIRO-
    HITO. 1992: Norton. Originally published as v. 119, no. 3 (summer
    1990), of *Daedalus*.

Ivan Morris, ed. JAPAN 1931-1945: MILITARISM, FASCISM, JAPANISM?
    1963: Heath.

Paul Brooker. THE FACES OF FRATERNALISM: NAZI GERMANY,
    FASCIST ITALY, AND IMPERIAL JAPAN. 1991: Oxford University
    Press.

Heinz Lubasz, ed. FASCISM: THREE MAJOR REGIMES. 1973: Wiley.
    Excerpts from Richard Storry, Robert Scalapino, Masao Maruyama,
    Fairbank-Reischauer-Craig text, plus statements by Kita Ikki, Prince
    Konoe, and General Araki.

Y. M. Zhukov, ed. THE RISE AND FALL OF THE GUNBATSU: A STUDY
    IN MILITARY HISTORY. 1975: Progress. An orthodox Soviet
    analysis.

Meirion Harries. SOLDIERS OF THE SUN: THE RISE AND FALL OF THE
    IMPERIAL JAPANESE ARMY, 1868-1945. 1991: Random House.

Sakuzō Yoshino. "Fascism in Japan," *Contemporary Japan* 1.2 (1932), 185-197.

O. Tanin & E. Yohan. MILITARISM AND FASCISM IN JAPAN. 1934:
    International. Marxist analysis, with introduction by Karl Radek.

Emil Lederer. "Fascist Tendencies in Japan," *Pacific Affairs* 7 (1934), 373-385.

Toshio Shiratori. "Fascism versus Popular Front," *Contemporary Japan* 6.4 (1938), 581-589.

Otto Koellreutter. "National Socialism and Japan," *Contemporary Japan* 8.2 (1939), 194-202.

Victor A. Yakhontoff. "The Fascist Movement in Japan," *Science and Society* 3.1 (1939), 28-41.

Saburō Ienaga. THE PACIFIC WAR, 1931-1945. Frank Baldwin, transl. 1978: Pantheon.

Gordon M. Berger. PARTIES OUT OF POWER IN JAPAN, 1931-1941. 1977: Princeton University Press. See also review by M. Peattie in *Journal of Japanese Studies* 4.1 (1978), 198-208.

_____. "Imperial Rule Assistance Association," KŌDANSHA ENCYCLOPEDIA OF JAPAN 3: 280-281.

Richard J. Smethurst. A SOCIAL BASIS FOR PREWAR JAPANESE MILITARISM: THE ARMY AND THE RURAL COMMUNITY. 1974: University of California Press.

Patricia G. Steinhoff. "Tenkō and Thought Control," in Gail Lee Bernstein & Haruhiro Fukui, eds. JAPAN AND THE WORLD: ESSAYS ON JAPANESE HISTORY AND POLITICS IN HONOUR OF ISHIDA TAKESHI (1988: St. Martin's), 78-94.

Richard H. Mitchell. THOUGHT CONTROL IN PREWAR JAPAN. 1976: Cornell University Press. See also the critique of this study by Herbert Bix in *Japan Interpreter* 12.1 (1978), 118-133.

_____. "Japan's Peace Preservation Law of 1925, Its Origin and Significance," *Monumenta Nipponica* 28.3 (1973), 317-346.

_____. CENSORSHIP IN IMPERIAL JAPAN. 1984: Princeton University Press.

_____. JANUS-FACED JUSTICE: POLITICAL CRIMINALS IN IMPERIAL JAPAN. 1992: University of Hawaii Press.

Gregory James Kasza. THE STATE AND THE MASS MEDIA IN JAPAN, 1918-1945. 1988: University of California Press.

Roger Wayne Purdy. "The Ears and Voice of the Nation: The Dōmei News Agency and Japan's News Network, 1936-1945." 1987: Ph.D. dissertation in History, University of California (Santa Barbara).

Gregory Kent Ornatowski. "Press, Politics, and Profits: The *Asahi Shimbun* and the Prewar Japanese Newspaper." 1985: Ph.D. dissertation in History and East Asian Languages, Harvard University.

Elise K. Tipton. THE JAPANESE POLICE STATE: THE TOKKŌ IN INTERWAR JAPAN. 1990: University of Hawaii Press.

Richard Deacon. KEMPEITAI: A HISTORY OF THE JAPANESE SECRET SERVICE. 1983: Beaufort.

George M. Wilson. RADICAL NATIONALIST IN JAPAN: KITA IKKI, 1883-1937. 1969: Harvard University Press.

Sharon Minichiello. RETREAT FROM REFORM: PATTERNS OF POLITICAL BEHAVIOR IN INTERWAR JAPAN. 1984: University of Hawaii Press. Focuses on Nagai Ryūtarō.

Gordon M. Berger. "Politics and Mobilization in Japan, 1931-1945," in Peter Duus, ed. CAMBRIDGE HISTORY OF JAPAN, Volume 6: THE TWENTIETH CENTURY (1988: Cambridge University Press), 97-153.

Robert Scalapino. DEMOCRACY AND THE PARTY MOVEMENT IN PREWAR JAPAN: THE FAILURE OF THE FIRST ATTEMPT. 1953: University of California Press.

Hugh Borton. JAPAN SINCE 1931: ITS POLITICAL AND SOCIAL DEVELOPMENT. 1940: Institute of Pacific Relations.

James W. Morley, ed. DILEMMAS OF GROWTH IN PREWAR JAPAN. 1971: Princeton University Press.

George M. Wilson, ed. CRISIS POLITICS IN PREWAR JAPAN: INSTITU-TIONAL AND IDEOLOGICAL PROBLEMS OF THE 1930S. 1970: Monumenta Nipponica Monographs. Articles by Wilson on "renovation," Ben-Ami Shillony on military radicals, and Robert Spaulding on renovationist bureaucrats.

James B. Crowley. JAPAN'S QUEST FOR AUTONOMY: NATIONAL SECURITY AND FOREIGN POLICY, 1930-1938. 1966: Princeton University Press.

Mark R. Peattie. ISHIWARA KANJI AND JAPAN'S CONFRONTATION WITH THE WEST. 1975: Princeton University Press.

Saburō Shiroyama. WAR CRIMINAL: THE LIFE AND DEATH OF HIROTA KŌKI. 1974; transl. 1977: Kōdansha International.

Yoshitake Oka. KONOE FUMIMARO: A POLITICAL BIOGRAPHY. Shumpei Okamoto & Patricia Murray, transl. 1983: University of Tokyo Press.

Gordon M. Berger. "Japan's Young Prince: Konoe Fumimaro's Early Political Career, 1916-31," *Monumenta Nipponica* 29.4 (1974), 451-476.

Ben-Ami Shillony. REVOLT IN JAPAN: THE YOUNG OFFICERS AND THE FEBRUARY 26, 1936 INCIDENT. 1973: Princeton University Press

_____. "The February 26 Affair: Politics of a Military Insurrection," in George Wilson, ed. CRISIS POLITICS IN PREWAR JAPAN (1970: Monumenta Nipponica Monographs), 25-50.

_____. "Myth and Reality in Japan of the 1930s," in W. G. Beasley, ed. MODERN JAPAN: ASPECTS OF HISTORY, LITERATURE AND SOCIETY (1975: Allen & Unwin), 81-88.

_____. "Japanese Intellectuals During the Pacific War," *Proceedings of the British Association for Japanese Studiess*, volume 2, part 1 (1977), 90-99.

_____. POLITICS AND CULTURE IN WARTIME JAPAN. 1982: Oxford University Press.

_____. "Universities and Students in Wartime Japan," *Journal of Asian Studies* 45.4 (1986), 769-787.

Richard Rice. "Economic Mobilization in Wartime Japan: Business, Bureaucracy, and Military in Conflict," *Journal of Asian Studies* 38.4 (1979), 689-706.

Chalmers Johnson. MITI AND THE JAPANESE MIRACLE. 1982: Stanford
    University Press. See especially chapters on pre-1945 Ministry of
    Commerce and Industry & Munitions Ministry.

Ernest J. Notar. "Japan's Wartime Labor Policy: A Search for Method," *Journal
    of Asian Studies* 44.2 (1985), 311-328.

Zdenka Vasiljevova. "The Industrial Patriotic Movement: A Study on the
    Structure of Fascist Dictatorship in Wartime Japan," in Vlasta Hilska &
    Zdenka Vasiljevova, PROBLEMS OF MODERN JAPANESE
    SOCIETY (1971: Universita Karlova, Praha), 65-157.

Robert J. C. Butow. TŌJŌ AND THE COMING OF THE WAR. 1961:
    Princeton University Press.

David Anson Titus. PALACE AND POLITICS IN PREWAR JAPAN.
    1974: Columbia University Press.

David Bergamini. JAPAN'S IMPERIAL CONSPIRACY. 1971: Morrow.

Charles D. Sheldon. "Japan's Aggression and the Emperor, 1931-1941, from
    Contemporary Diaries," *Modern Asian Studies* 10.1 (1976), 1-40.

Kentarō Awaya. "Emperor Shōwa's Accountability for War," *Japan Quarterly*
    38.4 (1991), 386-398.

Herbert P. Bix. "The Shōwa Emperor's 'Monologue' and the Problem of War
    Responsibility," *Journal of Japanese Studies* 18.2 (1992), 295-363.

"Mountains Collapse: The Death of Hirohito," *Bulletin of Concerned Asian
    Scholars* 21.1 (1989), 50-52. Statement concerning Hirohito's war
    responsibility, signed by 17 scholars in the United States, Canada,
    Australia, New Zealand, and Japan.

John W. Dower. "Two Reflections on the Death of the Shōwa Emperor," post-
    script to his JAPAN IN WAR AND PEACE (1994: The New Press),
    337-354.

Shigeru Honjō. EMPEROR HIROHITO AND HIS CHIEF AIDE-DE-CAMP:
    THE HONJŌ DIARY, 1933-36. Mikiso Hane, transl. 1983: University
    of Tokyo Press.

Sei-ichi Imai. "Cabinet, Emperor and Senior Statesmen," in Dorothy Borg &
    Shumpei Okamoto, eds. PEARL HARBOR AS HISTORY (1973:
    Columbia University Press), 53-79.

Tessa Morris-Suzuki. SHŌWA: AN INSIDE HISTORY OF HIROHITO'S JAPAN. 1984: Athlone.

Mainichi Daily News. FIFTY YEARS OF LIGHT AND DARK: THE HIRO-HITO ERA. 1975: Mainichi Newspapers.

Paul Manning. HIROHITO: THE WAR YEARS. 1986: Dodd, Mead.

Jerrold M. Packard. SONS OF HEAVEN: A PORTRAIT OF THE JAPANESE MONARCHY. 1987: Scribner.

Edward Behr. HIROHITO: BEHIND THE MYTH. 1989: Villard Books.

Toshiaki Kawahara. HIROHITO AND HIS TIMES: A JAPANESE PERSPEC-TIVE. 1990: Kōdansha International.

Edwin Palmer Hoyt. HIROHITO: THE EMPEROR AND THE MAN. 1991: Praeger.

Stephen S. Large. EMPEROR HIROHITO AND SHŌWA JAPAN: A POLITI-CAL BIOGRAPHY. 1992: Routledge.

Thomas R. H. Havens. VALLEY OF DARKNESS: THE JAPANESE PEOPLE AND WORLD WAR TWO. 1978: Norton; 1986: University Press of America.

IMPERIALISM, COLONIALISM & WAR

[See also the "Japan Abroad" bibliography, pp. 249-345]

W. G. Beasley. JAPANESE IMPERIALISM, 1894-1945. 1987: Oxford University Press.

Edwin O. Reischauer & Albert M. Craig. JAPAN: TRADITION AND TRANSFORMATION (1989: Houghton Mifflin), chapter 7.

Paul H. Clyde & Burton F. Beers. THE FAR EAST: A HISTORY OF WESTERN IMPACTS AND EASTERN RESPONSES, 1830-1975. 6th edition. 1975; reprinted 1991: Waveland Press.

James W. Morley, ed. JAPAN'S FOREIGN POLICY, 1868-1941: A RESEARCH GUIDE. 1974: Columbia University Press.

Ian Nish. JAPANESE FOREIGN POLICY, 1869-1942. 1977: Routledge & Kegan Paul.

Sydney Giffard. JAPAN AMONG THE POWERS, 1890-1990. 1994: Yale University Press.

Robert Scalapino, ed. THE FOREIGN POLICY OF MODERN JAPAN. 1977: University of California Press.

Michael Blaker. JAPANESE INTERNATIONAL NEGOTIATING STYLE. 1977: Columbia University Press.

Kazuo Shibagaki. "The Logic of Japanese Imperialism," *Social Science Abstracts* 14 (Shakai Kagaku Kenkyūjo, Tokyo University, 1973), 70-87.

Ronald L. Tarnstrom. THE WARS OF JAPAN. 1992: Trogen Books.

Edwin Palmer Hoyt. JAPAN'S WAR: THE GREAT PACIFIC CONFLICT, 1853-1952. 1986: McGraw-Hill.

Richard Storry. JAPAN AND THE DECLINE OF THE WEST IN ASIA. 1979: Macmillan.

Frances V. Moulder. JAPAN, CHINA AND THE MODERN WORLD ECONOMY: TOWARD A REINTERPRETATION OF EAST ASIAN DEVELOPMENT, ca. 1600 to ca. 1918. 1977: Cambridge University Press.

Meirion Harries. SOLDIERS OF THE SUN: THE RISE AND FALL OF THE IMPERIAL JAPANESE ARMY, 1868-1945. 1991: Random House.

Donald Calman. THE NATURE AND ORGINS OF JAPANESE IMPERIALISM: A RE-INTERPRETATION OF THE GREAT CRISIS OF 1873. 1992: Routledge. See the important review by Herbert P. Bix in *Journal of Japanese Studies* 20.2 (1994), 532-536, comparing this work with Hilary Conroy's THE JAPANESE SEIZURE OF KOREA.

Theodore Failor Cook. "The Japanese Officer Corps: The Making of a Military Elite, 1872-1945." 1987: Ph.D. dissertation, Princeton University.

James B. Crowley. "Japan's Foreign Military Policies," in James W. Morley, ed. JAPAN'S FOREIGN POLICY (1974: Columbia University Press), 3-117.

Akira Iriye. "Japan's Drive to Great-Power Status," in Marius B. Jansen, ed. CAMBRIDGE HISTORY OF JAPAN, Volume 5: THE NINETEENTH CENTURY (1989: Cambridge University Press), 721-782.

_____. "The Historical Background," in his THE COLD WAR IN ASIA: A HISTORICAL INTRODUCTION (1974: Prentice-Hall), 8-46.

_____. PACIFIC ESTRANGEMENT: JAPANESE AND AMERICAN EXPANSION, 1897-1911. 1972: Harvard University Press.

Grant Goodman, ed. IMPERIAL JAPAN AND ASIA—A REASSESSMENT. 1967: Occasional Papers for the East Asia Institute, Columbia University.

Marius B. Jansen. "Modernization and Foreign Policy in Meiji Japan," in Robert Ward, ed. POLITICAL DEVELOPMENT IN MODERN JAPAN (1968: Princeton University Press), 149-188.

_____. "Japanese Views of China During the Meiji Period," in Albert Feuerwerker et al. APPROACHES TO MODERN CHINESE HISTORY (1967: University of California Press), 163-189.

_____. JAPAN AND CHINA: FROM WAR TO PEACE, 1894-1972. 1975: Rand McNally.

Joshua A. Fogel. POLITICS AND SINOLOGY: THE CASE OF NAITŌ KŌNAN. 1984: Council on East Asian Studies, Harvard University.

_____. THE CULTURAL DIMENSION OF SINO-JAPANESE RELATIONS: ESSAYS ON THE INTERACTIONS BETWEEN CHINA AND JAPAN IN THE NINETEENTH AND TWENTIETH CENTURIES. 1994: M. E. Sharpe.

Munemitsu Mutsu. KENKENROKU: A DIPLOMATIC RECORD OF THE SINO-JAPANESE WAR, 1894-1895. Gordon M. Berger, transl. 1982: Princeton University Press.

Peter Duus, Ramon H. Myers, & Mark R. Peattie, eds. THE JAPANESE INFORMAL EMPIRE IN CHINA, 1895-1937. 1989: Princeton University Press.

Ian Nish. THE ORIGINS OF THE RUSSO-JAPANESE WAR. 1985: Longman.

Shumpei Okamoto. THE JAPANESE OLIGARCHY AND THE RUSSO-JAPANESE WAR. 1971: Columbia University Press.

Richard Connaughton. THE WAR OF THE RISING SUN AND TUMBLING BEAR: A MILITARY HISTORY OF THE RUSSO-JAPANESE WAR OF 1904-1905. 1991: Routledge.

Chiharu Inaba. "Polish-Japanese Military Collaboration during the Russo-Japanese War," *Japan Forum* 4.2 (1992), 229-246.

F. Hilary Conroy. THE JAPANESE SEIZURE OF KOREA, 1868-1910: A STUDY OF REALISM AND IDEALISM IN INTERNATIONAL RELATIONS. 1960: University of Pennsylvania Press.

Andrew C. Nahm, ed. KOREA UNDER JAPANESE COLONIAL RULE: STUDIES OF THE POLICY AND TECHNIQUES OF JAPANESE COLONIALISM. 1973: Center for Korean Studies, Institute of International and Area Studies, Western Michigan University.

Stewart Lone & Gavan McCormack. KOREA SINCE 1850. 1993: Longman Cheshire.

Edwin H. Gragert. LANDOWNERSHIP UNDER COLONIAL RULE: KOREA'S JAPAN EXPERIENCE, 1900-1935. 1994: University of Hawaii Press.

Michael Weiner. RACE AND MIGRATION IN IMPERIAL JAPAN: THE LIMITS OF ASSIMILATION. 1994: Routledge. Focuses on colonial rule in Korea and Japanese treatment of Korean labor.

Mark R. Peattie. NAN'YŌ: THE RISE AND FALL OF THE JAPANESE IN MICRONESIA, 1885-1945. 1988: University of Hawaii Press.

Goh Abe. "An Ethnohistory of Palau under the Japanese Colonial Administration." 1986: Ph.D. dissertation in Anthropology, University of Kansas.

Ramon H. Myers & Mark R. Peattie, eds. THE JAPANESE COLONIAL EMPIRE 1895-1945. 1984: Princeton University Press.

Mark R. Peattie. "The Japanese Colonial Empire, 1895-1945," in Peter Duus, ed. CAMBRIDGE HISTORY OF JAPAN, Volume 6: THE TWENTIETH CENTURY (1988: Cambridge University Press), 217-270.

Ikuhiko Hata. "Colonial Expansion, 1905-1941," in Peter Duus, ed.
CAMBRIDGE HISTORY OF JAPAN, Volume 6: THE TWENTIETH
CENTURY (1988: Cambridge University Press), 271-314.

E. Patricia Tsurumi. JAPANESE COLONIAL EDUCATION IN TAIWAN,
1895-1945. 1977: Harvard University Press.

Ian Nish. THE ANGLO-JAPANESE ALLIANCE: THE DIPLOMACY OF
TWO ISLAND EMPIRES, 1894-1907. 1966: Athlone.

_____. ALLIANCE IN DECLINE: A STUDY IN ANGLO-JAPANESE
RELATIONS, 1908-1923. 1972: Athlone.

Roger Dingman. POWER IN THE PACIFIC: THE ORIGINS OF NAVAL
ARMS LIMITATION, 1914-1922. 1976: University of Chicago Press.

James Morley. THE JAPANESE THRUST INTO SIBERIA, 1918. 1957:
Columbia University Press.

Takashi Saitō. "Japan's Foreign Policy in the International Environment of the
Nineteen-Twenties," *Developing Economies* 5.4 (1967), 685-701.

Akira Iriye. AFTER IMPERIALISM: THE SEARCH FOR A NEW ORDER IN
THE FAR EAST, 1921-1931. 1965: Harvard University Press; 1990:
Imprint Publications.

_____. "The Failure of Economic Expansion: 1918-1931," in B. Silberman &
H. Harootunian, eds. JAPAN IN CRISIS (1974: Princeton University
Press), 237-269.

_____. "The Failure of Military Expansionism," in James Morley, ed. DILEM-
MAS OF GROWTH IN PREWAR JAPAN (1971: Princeton University
Press), 107-138.

Nobuya Bamba. JAPANESE DIPLOMACY IN A DILEMMA: NEW LIGHT
ON JAPAN'S CHINA POLICY, 1924-1929. 1972: University of
British Columbia Press.

Richard Storry. "The Road to War: 1931-1945," in Arthur E. Tiedemann, ed.
AN INTRODUCTION TO JAPANESE CIVILIZATION (1974: Heath),
247-276.

Sadako N. Ogata. DEFIANCE IN MANCHURIA: THE MAKING OF
JAPANESE FOREIGN POLICY, 1931-1932. 1964: University of
California Press.

Mark Peattie. ISHIWARA KANJI AND JAPAN'S CONFRONTATION WITH THE WEST. 1975: Princeton University Press.

Christopher Thorne. THE LIMITS OF FOREIGN POLICY: THE WEST, THE LEAGUE AND THE FAR EASTERN CRISIS OF 1931-1933. 1973: Oxford University Press.

Ian Hill Nish. JAPAN'S STRUGGLE WITH INTERNATIONALISM: JAPAN, CHINA, AND THE LEAGUE OF NATIONS, 1931-1933. 1993: K. Paul International.

Gordon Berger. "The Three-dimensional Empire: Japanese Attitudes and the New Order in Asia, 1937-1945," *Japan Interpreter* 12.3-4 (1979), 355-383.

James B. Crowley. JAPAN'S QUEST FOR AUTONOMY: NATIONAL SECURITY AND FOREIGN POLICY, 1930-1938. 1968: Princeton University Press.

_____. "A New Asian Order: Some Notes on Prewar Japanese Nationalism," in Silberman & Harootunian, JAPAN IN CRISIS (1974: Princeton University Press), 270-298.

_____. "Intellectuals as Visionaries of the New Asian Order," in Morley, DILEMMAS OF GROWTH IN PREWAR JAPAN (1971: Princeton University Press), 319-373.

_____. "A New Deal for Japan and Asia: One Road to Pearl Harbor," in Crowley, MODERN EAST ASIA: ESSAYS IN INTERPRETATION (1970: Harcourt Brace & World), 235-264.

James Morley, ed. JAPAN ERUPTS: THE LONDON NAVAL CONFERENCE & THE MANCHURIAN INCIDENT, 1928-1932. 1984: Columbia University Press. First in a projected 5-volume version of the 1962-1963 Japanese series *Taiheiyō Sensō e no Michi* (Road to the Pacific War).

_____. THE CHINA QUAGMIRE: JAPAN'S EXPANSION ON THE ASIAN CONTINENT, 1933-1941. 1983: Columbia University Press.

_____. DETERRENT DIPLOMACY: JAPAN, GERMANY, AND THE USSR, 1935-1940. 1976: Columbia University Press.

_____. THE FATEFUL CHOICE: JAPAN'S ADVANCE INTO SOUTHEAST ASIA, 1939-1941. 1980: Columbia University Press.

Stephen E. Pelz. RACE TO PEARL HARBOR: THE FAILURE OF THE SECOND LONDON NAVAL CONFERENCE AND THE ONSET OF WORLD WAR II. 1974: Harvard University Press.

Donald A. Jordan. CHINESE BOYCOTTS VERSUS JAPANESE BOMBS: THE FAILURE OF CHINA'S "REVOLUTIONARY DIPLOMACY," 1931-32. 1991: University of Michigan Press.

Parks M. Coble. FACING JAPAN: CHINESE POLITICS AND JAPANESE IMPERIALISM, 1931-1937. 1991: Council on East Asian Studies, Harvard University.

Youli Sun. CHINA AND THE ORIGINS OF THE PACIFIC WAR, 1931-1941. 1993: St. Martin's.

James C. Hsiung & Susan I. Levine, eds. CHINA'S BITTER VICTORY: THE WAR WITH JAPAN, 1937-1945. 1992: M. E. Sharpe.

Chang-tai Hung. WAR AND POPULAR CULTURE: RESISTANCE IN MODERN CHINA, 1937-1945. 1994: University of California Press.

Abraham Ben-Zvi. THE ILLUSION OF DETERRENCE: THE ROOSEVELT PRESIDENCY AND THE ORIGINS OF THE PACIFIC WAR. 1987: Westview Press.

Saburō Shiroyama. WAR CRIMINAL: THE LIFE AND DEATH OF HIROTA KŌKI. John Bester, transl. 1974: Kōdansha International.

Hiroyuki Agawa. THE RELUCTANT ADMIRAL: YAMAMOTO AND THE IMPERIAL NAVY. 1979: Kōdansha International.

Edwin P. Hoyt. THREE MILITARY LEADERS: HEIHACHIRŌ TŌGŌ, ISOROKU YAMAMOTO, TOMOYUKI YAMASHITA. 1994: Kōdansha International.

_____. YAMAMOTO: THE MAN WHO PLANNED PEARL HARBOR. 1990: McGraw-Hill.

_____. THE LAST KAMIKAZE: THE STORY OF ADMIRAL MATOME UGAKI. 1993: Praeger.

_____. WARLORD: TŌJŌ AGAINST THE WORLD. 1993: Scarborough House.

Robert J. C. Butow. TŌJŌ AND THE COMING OF THE WAR. 1961: Stanford University Press.

J. W. Dower. EMPIRE AND AFTERMATH: YOSHIDA SHIGERU AND THE JAPANESE EXPERIENCE, 1878-1954. 1979: Council on East Asian Studies, Harvard University.

F. C. Jones. JAPAN'S NEW ORDER IN EAST ASIA: ITS RISE AND FALL, 1937-45. 1954: Oxford University Press.

Richard Deacon. KEMPEITAI: A HISTORY OF THE JAPANESE SECRET SERVICE. 1983: Beaufort.

Nobutake Ike, transl. JAPAN'S DECISION FOR WAR: RECORDS OF THE 1941 POLICY CONFERENCES. 1967: Stanford University Press.

Louis Morton. "Japan's Decision for War," in K. R. Greenfield, ed. COMMAND DECISIONS (1959: Harcourt Brace), 63-87.

Valdo Ferretti. "Captain Fujii Shigeru and the Decision for War in 1941," *Japan Forum* 3.2 (1991), 221-230.

John McKechney, S. J. "The Pearl Harbor Controversy: A Debate Among Historians," *Monumenta Nipponica* 18.1-4 (1963), 45-88.

Dorothy Borg & Shumpei Okamoto, eds. PEARL HARBOR AS HISTORY: JAPANESE-AMERICAN RELATIONS, 1931-1941. 1973: Columbia University Press.

Gordon W. Prange. AT DAWN WE SLEPT: THE UNTOLD STORY OF PEARL HARBOR. 1981: Penguin.

_____, with Donald M. Goldstein Katherine V. Dillon. PEARL HARBOR: THE VERDICT OF HISTORY. 1985: McGraw-Hill.

_____, with Donald M. Goldstein & Katherine V. Dillon. GOD'S SAMURAI: LEAD PILOT AT PEARL HARBOR. 1990: Brassey's. A biography of naval aviator Fuchida Mitsuo.

Ikuhiko Hata. JAPANESE NAVAL ACES AND FIGHTER UNITS IN WORLD WAR II. 1989: Naval Institute Press.

H. P. Willmott. EMPIRES IN THE BALANCE: JAPANESE AND ALLIED
    PACIFIC STRATEGIES TO APRIL 1942. 1982: Naval Institute Press.

Saburō Ienaga. THE PACIFIC WAR, 1931-1945. Frank Baldwin, transl. 1978:
    Pantheon.

Takeshi Matsuda. "The Coming of the Pacific War: Japanese Perspectives,"
    Reviews in American History 14.4 (1986), 629-652.

Alvin D. Coox. "The Pacific War," in Peter Duus, ed. CAMBRIDGE HISTORY
    OF JAPAN, Volume 6: THE TWENTIETH CENTURY (1988:
    Cambridge University Press), 315-382.

John Costello. THE PACIFIC WAR, 1941-1945. 1982: Quill.

Ronald H. Spector. EAGLE AGAINST THE SUN: THE AMERICAN WAR
    WITH JAPAN. 1984: Free Press.

John Toland. THE RISING SUN: THE DECLINE AND FALL OF THE
    JAPANESE EMPIRE, 1936-1945. 1970: Random House.

L. J. Lind. THE MIDGET SUBMARINE ATTACK ON SYDNEY. 1990:
    Bellrope Press.

John J. Stephan. HAWAII UNDER THE RISING SUN: JAPAN'S PLANS FOR
    CONQUEST AFTER PEARL HARBOR. 1984: University of Hawaii
    Press.

P. Scott Corbett. QUIET PASSAGES: THE EXCHANGE OF CIVILIANS
    BETWEEN THE UNITED STATES AND JAPAN DURING THE
    SECOND WORLD WAR. 1987: Kent State University Press.

James J. Weingartner. "Trophies of War: U.S. Troops and the Mutilation of
    Japanese War Dead, 1941-1945," *Pacific Historical Review* 61.1 (1992),
    53-67.

Leon V. Sigal. FIGHTING TO A FINISH: THE POLITICS OF WAR TERMI-
    NATION IN THE UNITED STATES AND JAPAN, 1945. 1988:
    Cornell University Press.

Martin Schofield Quigley. PEACE WITHOUT HIROSHIMA: SECRET
    ACTION AT THE VATICAN IN THE SPRING OF 1945. 1991:
    Madison Books.

David Bergamini. JAPAN'S IMPERIAL CONSPIRACY. 1971: Morrow.

Joyce Lebra, ed. JAPAN'S GREATER EAST ASIA CO-PROSPERITY
    SPHERE IN WORLD WAR II: SELECTED READINGS AND
    DOCUMENTS. 1975: Oxford University Press.

_____. JAPANESE-TRAINED ARMIES IN SOUTHEAST ASIA: INDEPEN-
    DENCE AND VOLUNTEER FORCES IN WORLD WAR II. 1977:
    Columbia University Press.

_____. JUNGLE ALLIANCE: JAPAN AND THE INDIAN NATIONAL
    ARMY. 1971: Donald Moore.

"The War and Japan: Revisionist Views," Special Issue of *Japan Echo* 11
    (1984). Articles by Japanese writers.

Haywood S. Hansell. THE STRATEGIC AIR WAR AGAINST GERMANY
    AND JAPAN: A MEMOIR. 1986: Office of Air Force History, U.S.
    Air Force.

George Feifer. TENNŌZAN: THE BATTLE OF OKINAWA AND THE
    ATOMIC BOMB. 1992: Ticknor and Fields.

Akira Iriye. POWER AND CULTURE: THE JAPANESE-AMERICAN WAR,
    1941-1945. 1981: Harvard University Press.

John W. Dower. "Rethinking World War Two in Asia," *Reviews in American
    History* 12.2 (1984), 155-169. Review essay focusing on the scholar-
    ship of Akira Iriye.

_____. WAR WITHOUT MERCY: RACE AND POWER IN THE PACIFIC
    WAR. 1986: Pantheon.

_____. "Race, Language, and War in Two Cultures" and "Fear and Prejudice in
    U.S.-Japan Relations," in his JAPAN IN WAR AND PEACE (1994:
    The New Press), 257-338.

Haruko Taya Cook & Theodore F. Cook, eds. JAPAN AT WAR: AN ORAL
    HISTORY. 1992: The New Press.

SOCIETY, CULTURE & LAW

Irene Tauber. THE POPULATION OF JAPAN. 1958: Princeton University Press.

Tadashi Fukutake. THE JAPANESE SOCIAL STRUCTURE: ITS EVOLUTION IN THE MODERN CENTURY. Ronald Dore, transl. 2nd edition. 1989: University of Tokyo Press.

_____. JAPANESE SOCIETY TODAY. 1974: University of Tokyo Press.

_____. JAPANESE RURAL SOCIETY. 1967: Cornell University Press.

_____. MAN AND SOCIETY IN JAPAN. 1962: University of Tokyo Press.

H. Paul Varley. JAPANESE CULTURE: A SHORT HISTORY. 3rd edition. 1984: University of Hawaii Press.

J. Thomas Rimer. "High Culture in the Shōwa Period," in Carol Gluck & Stephen R. Graubard, eds. SHŌWA: THE JAPAN OF HIROHITO (1992: Norton), 265-278.

Takie Sugiyama Lebra. JAPANESE PATTERNS OF BEHAVIOR. 1976: University of Hawaii Press.

_____ & William P. Lebra, eds. JAPANESE CULTURE AND BEHAVIOR: SELECTED READINGS. 1974: University of Hawaii Press.

Robert J. Smith. JAPANESE SOCIETY: TRADITION, SELF AND THE SOCIAL ORDER. 1985: Cambridge University Press.

Chie Nakane. JAPANESE SOCIETY. 1970: University of California Press.

Jane M. Bachnik & Charles L. Quinn, Jr., eds. SITUATED MEANING: INSIDE AND OUTSIDE IN JAPANESE SELF, SOCIETY, AND LANGUAGE. 1994: Princeton University Press. Emphasizes the horizontal aspects of culture and society.

Takeshi Ishida. JAPANESE SOCIETY. 1972: University Press of America.

Ross Mouer & Yoshio Sugimoto. IMAGES OF JAPANESE SOCIETY: A STUDY IN THE STRUCTURE OF SOCIAL REALITY. 1986: KPI.

Hajime Nakamura. WAYS OF THINKING OF EASTERN PEOPLES: INDIA, CHINA, TIBET, JAPAN. 1964: University of Hawaii Press.

_____. A HISTORY OF THE DEVELOPMENT OF JAPANESE THOUGHT FROM 592 TO 1868. 1967: University of Tokyo.

Hiroshi Minami. PSYCHOLOGY OF THE JAPANESE PEOPLE. 1971: University of Toronto Press.

Takeo Doi. THE ANATOMY OF DEPENDENCE. 1973: Kōdansha International.

George A. DeVos. SOCIALIZATION FOR ACHIEVEMENT: ESSAYS ON THE CULTURAL PSYCHOLOGY OF THE JAPANESE. 1973: University of California Press.

Donald Roden. "Forays into Japanese Cultural Psychology," *Bulletin of Concerned Asian Scholars* 6.2 (1974), 27-32. Critique of DeVos.

Bradley M. Richardson. THE POLITICAL CULTURE OF JAPAN. 1974: University of California Press.

Motoko Tsuchida. " 'Public Opinion' Trends in Prewar Japan, 1918-1943: A Thematic Content Analysis of the *Asahi*, *Mainichi*, and *Yomiuri* Editorials and *Chūō Kōron* 'Kantōgen'." 1987: Ph.D. dissertation in Political Science, University of Missouri (Columbia).

Arthur E. Tiedemann, ed. AN INTRODUCTION TO JAPANESE CIVILIZA-TION. 1974: Heath. Includes survey essays on society (Kōya Azumi), religion (Wm. Theodore DeBary), law (Dan Fenno Henderson), literature (Donald Keene), and art (Hugo Munsterberg).

John W. Hall & Richard Beardsley, eds. TWELVE DOORS TO JAPAN. 1965: McGraw-Hill. Includes survey essays from various disciplinary perspectives.

R. K. Beardsley, J. W. Hall & R. E. Ward. VILLAGE JAPAN. 1959: University of Chicago Press.

Kurt Steiner. LOCAL GOVERNMENT IN JAPAN. 1965: Stanford University Press.

Carl Mosk. PATRIARCHY AND FERTILITY: JAPAN AND SWEDEN, 1880-1960. 1983: Academic Press.

Shigeru Itō. "An Analysis of Mortality in Meiji Cities," *Japan Forum* 5.1 (1993), 37-51.

William Donald Johnston. "Disease, Medicine, and the State: A Social History of Tuberculosis in Japan, 1850-1950." 1987: Ph.D. dissertation in History and East Asian Languages, Harvard University.

Edwina Palmer & Geoffrey W. Rice. "Divine Wind versus Devil Wind: Popular Responses to Pandemic Influenza in Japan, 1918-1919," *Japan Forum* 4.2 (1992), 317-328.

_____. "Pandemic Influenza in Japan, 1918-19: Mortality Patterns and Official Responses," *Journal of Japanese Studies* 19.2 (1993), 389-420.

William W. Kelly. "Regional Japan: The Price of Prosperity and the Benefits of Dependency," in Carol Gluck & Stephen R. Graubard, eds. SHŌWA: THE JAPAN OF HIROHITO (1992: Norton), 209-227.

Mariko Asano Tamanoi. "Songs as Weapons: The Culture and History of *Komori* (Nursemaids) in Modern Japan," *Journal of Asian Studies* 50.4 (1991), 793-817.

Edward Seidensticker. TOKYO RISING: THE CITY SINCE THE GREAT EARTHQUAKE. 1991: Harvard University Press.

John Embree. SUYE MURA. 1939: University of Chicago Press. The only prewar anthropological study in English based on field work in Japan.

Robert J. Smith & Ella Lury Wiswell. THE WOMEN OF SUYE MURA. 1982: University of Chicago Press. Based on fieldwork conducted in the 1930s in conjunction with the preceding project.

Donna Kay Keuck. "The Books and the Photographs of Suye Mura." 1990: Ph.D. dissertation in Sociology, Cornell University.

Kunio Yanagita. ABOUT OUR ANCESTORS: THE JAPANESE FAMILY SYSTEM. 1970: Japan Society for the Promotion of Science; 1988: Greenwood Press. Translation by Fanny Hagin Mayer & Yasuyo Ishiwara of essays by Japan's most eminent ethnologist.

J. Victor Koschmann, Keibo Ōiwa & Shinji Yamashita, eds. INTERNATIONAL PERSPECTIVES ON YANAGITA KUNIO AND JAPANESE FOLK-LORE STUDIES. 1985: China-Japan Program, Cornell University.

Kazuko Tsurumi. "Yanagita Kunio's Work as a Model of Endogenous Development," *Japan Quarterly* 22.3 (1975), 223-238.

Minoru Kawada. THE ORIGIN OF ETHNOGRAPHY IN JAPAN: YANAGITA KUNIO AND HIS TIMES. 1992: Kegan Paul International.

Ronald Morse. "Personalities and Issues in Yanagita Kunio Studies," *Japan Quarterly* 22.3 (1975), 239-254.

_____. "Yanagita Kunio and the Folklore Movement: The Search for Japan's National Character and Distinctiveness." 1974: Ph.D. dissertation in History, Princeton University.

_____, transl. LEGENDS OF TŌNO. 1975: Japan Foundation. An important transcription of local legends from Iwate prefecture by Yanagita.

Nyozekan Hasegawa. THE JAPANESE CHARACTER: A CULTURAL PROFILE. 1965: Kōdansha International.

Kurt Singer. MIRROR, SWORD AND JEWEL: THE GEOMETRY OF JAPANESE LIFE. 1981: Kōdansha International.

Ruth F. Benedict. THE CHRYSANTHEMUM AND THE SWORD. 1946: Houghton Mifflin. A famous study based on World War Two research on the Japanese "national character."

Lafcadio Hearn. JAPAN: AN ATTEMPT AT INTERPRETATION. 1913: Macmillan.

Carl Dawson. LAFCADIO HEARN AND THE VISION OF JAPAN. 1992: Johns Hopkins University Press.

Miriam Silverberg. "Constructing the Japanese Ethnography of Modernity," *Journal of Asian Studies* 51.1 (1992), 30-54. On the ethnographic study of urban culture in the 1920s and 1930s.

Carol Gluck. "The People in History: Recent Trends in Japanese Historiography," *Journal of Asian Studies* 38.1 (1978), 25-50.

Takeo Yazaki. SOCIAL CHANGE AND THE CITY IN JAPAN: FROM EARLIEST TIMES THROUGH THE INDUSTRIAL REVOLUTION. 1968: Japan Publications.

Mikiso Hane. PEASANTS, REBELS, AND OUTCASTES: THE UNDERSIDE OF MODERN JAPAN. 1982: Pantheon.

Hugh Patrick ed. JAPANESE INDUSTRIALIZATION AND ITS SOCIAL CONSEQUENCES. 1976: University of California Press.

Gary D. Allinson. JAPANESE URBANISM: INDUSTRY AND POLITICS IN KARIYA, 1872-1972. 1975: University of California Press.

Tetsuo Najita & J. Victor Koschmann, eds. CONFLICT IN MODERN JAPAN: THE NEGLECTED TRADITION. 1982: Princeton University Press.

J. Victor Koschmann, ed. AUTHORITY AND THE INDIVIDUAL IN JAPAN. 1978: University of Tokyo Press.

Kazuko Tsurumi. SOCIAL CHANGE AND THE INDIVIDUAL: JAPAN BEFORE AND AFTER DEFEAT IN WORLD WAR TWO. 1970: Princeton University Press.

Robert Bellah. "Values and Social Change in Modern Japan," *Asian Cultural Studies* 3 (International Christian University, 1962), 13-56.

_____. BEYOND BELIEF: ESSAYS ON RELIGION IN A POST-TRADITIONAL WORLD. 1970: Harper & Row. Includes revised version of preceding article.

_____. "Japan's Cultural Identity: Some Reflections on the Work of Watsuji Tetsurō," *Journal of Asian Studies* 24.4 (1965), 573-594.

Masao Miyoshi & H. D. Harootunian, eds. JAPAN IN THE WORLD. 1993: Duke University Press. A wide-ranging collection of postmodernist-flavored essays, situating Japan's recent relations with the world in historical and cultural context.

Marius B. Jansen, ed. CHANGING JAPANESE ATTITUDES TOWARD MODERNIZATION. 1965: Princeton University Press.

Ronald Dore, ed. ASPECTS OF SOCIAL CHANGE IN MODERN JAPAN. 1967: Princeton University Press.

Donald Shively, ed. TRADITION AND MODERNIZATION IN JAPANESE CULTURE. 1971: Princeton University Press.

Ezra F. Vogel, ed. MODERN JAPANESE ORGANIZATION AND DECISION-MAKING. 1975: University of California Press.

Albert M. Craig, ed. JAPAN: A COMPARATIVE VIEW. 1979: Princeton University Press.

Takeo Kuwabara. JAPAN AND WESTERN CIVILIZATION: ESSAYS ON COMPARATIVE CULTURE. Hidetoshi Katō, ed. 1984: University of Tokyo Press.

Tetsuo Najita & H. D. Harootunian. "Japanese Revolt against the West: Political and Cultural Criticism in the Twentieth Century," in Peter Duus, ed. CAMBRIDGE HISTORY OF JAPAN, Volume 6: THE TWENTIETH CENTURY (1988: Cambridge University Press), 711-774.

Irwin Scheiner, ed. MODERN JAPAN: AN INTERPRETIVE ANTHOLOGY. 1974: Macmillan.

Carol Gluck & Stephen R. Graubard, eds. SHŌWA: THE JAPAN OF HIRO-HITO. 1992: Norton. Originally published as v. 119, no. 3 (summer 1990), of *Daedalus*.

Donald Keene. LANDSCAPES AND PORTRAITS: AN APPRECIATION OF JAPANESE CULTURE. 1971: Kōdansha International.

W. G. Beasley, ed. MODERN JAPAN: ASPECTS OF HISTORY, LITERA-TURE AND SOCIETY. 1976: University of California Press.

George K. Yamamoto & Tsuyoshi Ishida, eds. SELECTED READINGS ON MODERN JAPANESE SOCIETY. 1971: McCutchan.

Yasushi Kuyama & Nobuo Kobayashi, eds. MODERNIZATION AND TRADITION IN JAPAN. 1969: International Institute for Japan Studies (Nishinomiya).

Robert J. Smith & Richard K. Beardsley, eds. JAPANESE CULTURE; ITS DEVELOPMENT AND CHARACTERISTICS. 1962: Aldine.

Bernard Silberman, ed. JAPANESE CHARACTER AND CULTURE. 1962: University of Arizona Press.

_____. "*Ringisei* —Traditional Values or Organizational Imperatives in the Japanese Upper Civil Service, 1868-1945," *Journal of Asian Studies* 32.2 (1973), 251-264.

_____ & H. Harootunian, eds. MODERN JAPANESE LEADERSHIP: TRANSITION AND CHANGE. 1966: Princeton University Press.

Joseph Roggendorf, ed. STUDIES IN JAPANESE CULTURE. 1965: Monumenta Nipponica Monographs.

Charles G. Cleaver. JAPANESE AND AMERICANS: CULTURAL PARALLELS AND PARADOXES. 1976: University of Minnesota Press.

Lewis Austin, ed. JAPAN—THE PARADOX OF PROGRESS. 1976: Yale University Press.

P. G. O'Neill, ed. TRADITION AND MODERN JAPAN. 1982: University of British Columbia Press.

Ivan Morris. THE NOBILITY OF FAILURE: TRAGIC HEROES IN THE HISTORY OF JAPAN. 1975: Holt, Rinehart & Winston.

Robert J. Lifton et al. SIX LIVES, SIX DEATHS: PORTRAITS FROM MODERN JAPAN. 1979: Yale University Press.

Agnes N. Keith. BEFORE THE BLOSSOMS FALL: LIFE AND DEATH IN JAPAN. 1975: Little, Brown.

Stuart Picken. DEATH AND THE JAPANESE. 1985: Athlone.

William R. LaFleur. LIQUID LIFE: ABORTION AND BUDDHISM IN JAPAN. 1992: Princeton University Press.

Kathleen Sue Uno. "Day Care and Family Life in Industrializing Japan, 1868-1926." 1987: Ph.D. dissertation in History, University of California.

David W. Plath. LONG ENGAGEMENTS: MATURITY IN MODERN JAPAN. 1980: Stanford University Press.

Albert Craig & Donald Shively, eds. PERSONALITY IN JAPANESE HISTORY. 1970: University of California Press.

Frank Gibney. FIVE GENTLEMEN OF JAPAN: THE PROTRAIT OF A NATION'S CHARACTER. 1953: Farrar, Straus & Young.

Joseph L. Anderson & Donald Richie. THE JAPANESE FILM: ART AND INDUSTRY. Expanded edition. 1984: Princeton University Press.

Donald Richie. THE JAPANESE MOVIE. 1982: Kōdansha International.

_____. OZU: HIS LIFE AND FILMS. 1974: University of California Press.

_____. THE FILMS OF AKIRA KUROSAWA. Revised edition. 1984: University of California Press.

Stephen Prince. THE WARRIOR'S CAMERA: THE CINEMA OF AKIRA KUROSAWA. 1991: Princeton University Press.

Noel Burch. TO THE DISTANT OBSERVER: FORM AND MEANING IN THE JAPANESE CINEMA. 1979: University of California Press.

Audie Bock. JAPANESE FILM DIRECTORS. 1978: Kōdansha International.

Tadao Satō. CURRENTS IN JAPANESE CINEMA. Gregory Barrett, transl. 1982: Kōdansha International.

Hiroyasu Fujioka. "The Search for 'Japanese Architecture' in Modern Ages," *Japan Foundation Newsletter* 15.3 (1987), 1-9.

Carl Steenstrup. A HISTORY OF LAW IN JAPAN UNTIL 1868. 1991: E. J. Brill.

Arthur von Mehren, ed. LAW IN JAPAN: THE LEGAL ORDER IN A CHANGING SOCIETY. 1963: Harvard University Press.

Dan Fenno Henderson. CONCILIATION AND JAPANESE LAW, TOKUGAWA AND MODERN. 2 volumes. 1965: University of Washington Press.

Frank K. Upham. LAW AND SOCIAL CHANGE IN POSTWAR JAPAN. 1987: Harvard University Press.

John Owen Haley. AUTHORITY WITHOUT POWER: LAW AND THE JAPANESE PARADOX. 1991: Oxford University Press.

Hiroshi Itoh. THE JAPANESE SUPREME COURT: CONSTITUTIONAL POLICIES. 1990: Markus Wiener.

Richard H. Mitchell. JANUS-FACED JUSTICE: POLITICAL CRIMINALS IN IMPERIAL JAPAN. 1992: University of Hawaii Press.

Rex Coleman & John Owen Haley, comp. AN INDEX TO JAPANESE LAW: A BIBLIOGRAPHY OF WESTERN LANGUAGE MATERIALS, 1867-1973. 1975: Japanese American Society for Legal Studies, University of Tokyo. Special issue of *Law in Japan: An Annual*.

Minoru Shikita & Shin'ichi Tsuchiya, eds. CRIME AND CRIMINAL POLICY IN JAPAN: ANALYSIS AND EVALUATION OF THE SHŌWA ERA, 1926-1988. 1992: Springer-Verlag.

EDUCATION & SCIENCE

[See also pp. 119-120]

Herbert Passin. SOCIETY AND EDUCATION IN JAPAN. 1965: Teachers College, Columbia University.

Government of Japan, Ministry of Education, ed. JAPAN'S MODERN EDUCATIONAL SYSTEM: A HISTORY OF THE FIRST HUNDRED YEARS. 1980: Ministry of Education.

Tokiomi Kaigo. JAPANESE EDUCATION: ITS PAST AND PRESENT. 1968: Kokusai Bunka Shinkōkai.

Richard Rubinger & Edward R. Beauchamp, eds. EDUCATION IN JAPAN: A SOURCE BOOK. 1989: Garland.

Teruhisa Horio. EDUCATIONAL THOUGHT AND IDEOLOGY IN MODERN JAPAN: STATE AUTHORITY AND INTELLECTUAL FREEDOM. Steven Platzer, ed. & transl. 1988: University of Tokyo Press.

Michio Nagai. "Westernization and Japanization: The Early Meiji Transformation of Education," in Donald Shively, ed. TRADITION & MODERNIZATION IN JAPANESE CULTURE (1971: Princeton University Press), 35-76.

_____. HIGHER EDUCATION IN JAPAN: ITS TAKE-OFF AND CRASH. 1971: University of Tokyo Press.

Ivan Hall. MORI ARINORI. 1973: Harvard University Press.

Matsutarō Ishikawa. "The Meiji Restoration and Educational Reforms," Rolf W. Giebel, transl., *Acta Asiatica* 54 (1988), 24-47.

R. Henry Brunton. SCHOOLMASTER TO AN EMPIRE: RICHARD HENRY
    BRUNTON IN MEIJI JAPAN, 1868-1876. Edward R. Beauchamp, ed.
    1991: Greenwood Press.

Benjamin C. Duke, comp. & ed. TEN GREAT EDUCATORS OF MODERN
    JAPAN: A JAPANESE PERSPECTIVE. 1989: University of Tokyo
    Press.

Ann M. Harrington. "Women and Higher Education in the Japanese Empire
    (1895-1945)," *Journal of Asian History* 21.2 (1987), 169-186.

Barbara Rose. TSUDA UMEKO AND WOMEN'S EDUCATION IN JAPAN.
    1992: Yale University Press.

Umeko Tsuda. THE ATTIC LETTERS: UME TSUDA'S CORRESPONDENCE
    TO HER AMERICAN MOTHER. Yoshiko Furuki, ed. 1991:
    Weatherhill.

Yoshiko Furuki. THE WHITE PLUM: A BIOGRAPHY OF UME TSUDA,
    PIONEER IN THE HIGHER EDUCATION OF JAPANESE WOMEN.
    1991: Weatherhill.

Christine Chapman. "The Meiji Letters of Tsuda Ume, Pioneer Educator of
    Women," *Japan Quarterly* 34.3 (1987), 263-270.

F. G. Notehelfer. "In Search of the Cultivated Mind: Changing Images of
    Education and the Educated in Meiji Japan," *Journal of Japanese
    Studies* 20.1 (1994), 257-262. Reviews above books by Brunton, Duke,
    Rose, Tsuda, and Furuki.

Akiko Kuno. UNEXPECTED DESTINATIONS: THE POIGNANT STORY
    OF JAPAN'S FIRST VASSAR GRADUATE. Kirsten McIvor, transl.
    1993: Kōdansha International. On the life of Ōyama Sutematsu
    (1851-1919).

Mark Elwood Lincicome. "Educational Discourse and the Dimensions of Reform
    in Meiji Japan." 1985: Ph.D. dissertation in Far Eastern Languages and
    Civilizations, University of Chicago.

E. P. Tsurumi. "Meiji Primary School Language and Ethics Textbooks: Old
    Values for a New Society?", *Modern Asian Studies* 8.2 (1974), 247-261.

John Caiger. "The Aims and Content of School Courses in Japanese History,
    1872-1945," in Edmund R. Skrzypczak, ed. JAPAN'S MODERN
    CENTURY (1968: Tuttle), 51-82.

Harold J. Wray. "A Study in Contrasts: Japanese School Textbooks of 1903 and 1941-5," *Monumenta Nipponica* 28.1 (1973), 69-86.

Nanette Twine. LANGUAGE AND THE MODERN STATE: THE REFORM OF MODERN WRITTEN JAPANESE. 1991: Routledge.

Earl H. Kinmonth. THE SELF-MADE MAN IN MEIJI JAPANESE THOUGHT: FROM SAMURAI TO SALARY MAN. 1981: University of California Press.

Donald T. Roden. SCHOOLDAYS IN IMPERIAL JAPAN: A STUDY IN THE CULTURE OF A STUDENT ELITE. 1980: University of California Press.

_____. "'Monasticism' and the Paradox of the Meiji Higher Schools," *Journal of Asian Studies* 37.3 (1978), 413-425.

_____. "Baseball and the Quest for National Dignity in Meiji Japan," *American Historical Review* 85.3 (1980), 511-534.

Tsuneo Satō. "Mathematics Education in Japan during the Meiji Period (1868-1912)." 1989: Ed.D. dissertation in Mathematics Education, Columbia University.

Ury Eppstein. "Musical Instruction in Meiji Education: A Study of Adaptation and Assimilation," *Monumenta Nipponica* 40.1 (1985), 1-37.

_____. "School Songs Before and After the War: From 'Children Tank Soldiers' to 'Everyone a Good Child'," *Monumenta Nipponica* 42.4 (1987), 431-447.

Byron K. Marshall. "Professors and Politics: The Meiji Academic Elite," *Journal of Japanese Studies* 3.1 (1977), 71-97.

_____. "Growth and Conflict in Japanese Higher Education, 1905-1930," in Tetsuo Najita & J. Victor Koschmann, eds. CONFLICT IN MODERN JAPANESE HISTORY (1982: Princeton University Press), 276-294.

_____. ACADEMIC FREEDOM AND THE JAPANESE IMPERIAL UNIVERSITY, 1868-1939. 1992: University of California Press.

Toshiaki Ōkubo. "The Birth of the Modern University in Japan," *Journal of World History* 10.4 (1967), 763-779.

James R. Bartholomew. "Japanese Modernization and the Imperial Universities, 1876-1920," *Journal of Asian Studies* 37.2 (1978), 251-271.

Chūhei Sugiyama & Hiroshi Mizuta, eds. ENLIGHTENMENT AND BEYOND: POLITICAL ECONOMY COMES TO JAPAN. 1988: University of Tokyo Press.

Ikuo Amano. "Educational Reforms in Modern Japan before and during World War II: Centering on the Discussions regarding the School System," Rolf W. Giebel, transl., *Acta Asiatica* 54 (1988), 48-74.

_____. EDUCATION AND EXAMINATION IN MODERN JAPAN. William K. Cummings & Fumiko Cummings, transl. 1990: University of Tokyo Press.

Thomas P. Rohlen. JAPAN'S HIGH SCHOOLS. 1983: University of California Press.

Tatsuo Kasama. "A Century of School Excursions," *Japan Quarterly* 34.3 (1987), 287-290.

Edward R. Beauchamp & James M. Vardaman, Jr., eds. JAPANESE EDUCATION SINCE 1945: A DOCUMENTARY STUDY. 1993: M.E. Sharpe.

Gary H. Tsuchimochi. EDUCATION REFORM IN POSTWAR JAPAN: THE 1946 U.S. EDUCATION MISSION. 1993: University of Tokyo Press.

Shigeru Nakayama, David L. Swain & Eri Yagi, eds. SCIENCE AND SOCIETY IN MODERN JAPAN: SELECTED HISTORICAL SOURCES. 1974: University of Tokyo Press & Massachusetts Institute of Technology Press.

Shigeru Nakayama. ACADEMIC AND SCIENTIFIC TRADITIONS IN CHINA, JAPAN, AND THE WEST. 1984: University of Tokyo Press.

James R. Bartholomew. THE FORMATION OF SCIENCE IN JAPAN: BUILDING A RESEARCH TRADITION. 1989: Yale University Press.

_____. "Japanese Culture and the Problem of Modern Science," in Arnold Thackray & Everett Mendelsohn, eds. SCIENCE AND VALUES (1975: Humanities Press), 109-155.

_____. "Science, Bureaucracy, and Freedom in Meiji and Taishō Japan," in Najita & Koschmann, CONFLICT IN MODERN JAPANESE HISTORY (1982: Princeton University Press), 226-257.

Kōzō Yamamura. "Japan's Deus ex Machina: Western Technology in the 1920s," *Journal of Japanese Studies* 12.1 (1986), 65-94.

John W. Dower. "'NI' and 'F': Japan's Wartime Atomic Bomb Research," in his JAPAN IN WAR AND PEACE (1994: The New Press), 55-100.

PHILOSOPHY & RELIGION

Gino Piovesana. RECENT JAPANESE PHILOSOPHICAL THOUGHT, 1862-1962: A SURVEY. 1968: Enderle.

_____. CONTEMPORARY JAPANESE PHILOSOPHICAL THOUGHT. 1969: St. John's University Press.

Kitarō Nishida. AN INQUIRY INTO THE GOOD. Masao Abe & Christopher Ives, transl. 1990: Yale University Press. Also published as A STUDY OF GOOD (1960: Japanese National Commission for UNESCO).

_____. LAST WRITINGS: NOTHINGNESS AND THE RELIGIOUS WORLDVIEW. David A. Dilworth, transl. 1987: University of Hawaii Press. Also translated as "The Logic of *Topos* and the Religious Worldview" by Michiko Yusa in *The Eastern Buddhist* 19.2 (1986), 1-29; 20.1 (1987), 81-119.

_____. ART AND MORALITY. 1973: East-West Center Press.

_____. FUNDAMENTAL PROBLEMS OF PHILOSOPHY. 1970: Sophia University Press.

_____. INTELLIGIBILITY AND THE PHILOSOPHY OF NOTHINGNESS. 1966: East-West Center Press.

Keiji Nishitani. NISHIDA KITARŌ. Seisaku Yamamoto & James W. Heisig, transl. 1991: University of California Press. A study of the founder of the Kyoto School.

Valdo Humbert Viglielmo. "Nishida Kitarō: The Early Years," in Donald
     Shively, ed. TRADITION & MODERNIZATION IN JAPANESE
     CULTURE (1971: Princeton University Press), 507-562.

Steve Odin. "An Explanation of Beauty: Nishida Kitarō's *Bi no Setsumei*,"
     Monumenta Nipponica 42.2 (1987), 211-217.

Michiko Yusa. "Nishida and the Question of Nationalism," *Monumenta
     Nipponica* 46.2 (1991), 203-209.

Pierre Lavelle. "The Political Thought of Nishida Kitarō," *Monumenta
     Nipponica* 49.2 (1994), 139-165.

Atsuko Hirai. "Anglo-American Influences on Nishida Kitarō," in Gail Lee
     Bernstein & Haruhiro Fukui, eds. JAPAN AND THE WORLD:
     ESSAYS ON JAPANESE HISTORY AND POLITICS IN HONOUR
     OF ISHIDA TAKESHI (1988: St. Martin's), 20-41.

James W. Heisig. "The Religious Philosophy of the Kyoto School," *Japanese
     Journal of Religious Studies* 17.1 (1990), 51-82.

Peter Nosco, ed. THE EMPEROR SYSTEM AND RELIGION IN JAPAN.
     Japanese Journal of Religious Studies 17.2-17.3 (1990). Special double
     issue.

Meera Viswanathan. "An Investigation into Essence: Kuki Shūzō's *'Iki' no
     Kōzō*," *Transactions, Asiatic Society of Japan*, 4th series, 4 (1989), 1-22.

Winston Bradley Davis. TOWARD MODERNITY: A DEVELOPMENTAL
     TYPOLOGY OF POPULAR RELIGIOUS AFFILIATIONS IN JAPAN.
     1977: *Cornell University East Asia Papers*.

_____. JAPANESE RELIGION AND SOCIETY: PARADIGMS OF STRUC-
     TURE AND CHANGE. 1992: State University of New York Press.

Mark R. Mullins, Susumu Shimazono, & Paul L. Swanson, eds. RELIGION
     AND SOCIETY IN MODERN JAPAN: SELECTED READINGS.
     1993: Asian Humanities Press.

Joseph M. Kitagawa. RELIGION IN JAPANESE HISTORY. 1990: Columbia
     University Press.

_____. ON UNDERSTANDING JAPANESE RELIGION. 1987: Princeton
     University Press. A collection of essays.

Ian Reader, Esben Andreason, & Finn Stefansson. JAPANESE RELIGIONS: PAST AND PRESENT. 1993: University of Hawaii Press.

H. Byron Earhart. JAPANESE RELIGION: UNITY AND DIVERSITY. 3rd edition. 1982: Wadsworth.

_____, ed. RELIGION IN THE JAPANESE EXPERIENCE: SOURCES & INTERPRETATIONS. 1974: Duxbury.

_____, ed. THE NEW RELIGIONS OF JAPAN: A BIBLIOGRAPHY OF WESTERN LANGUAGE MATERIALS. 1983: Center for Japanese Studies, University of Michigan.

Shigeyoshi Murakami. JAPANESE RELIGION IN THE MODERN CENTURY. H. Byron Earhart, transl. 1980: University of Tokyo Press.

Edward Norbeck. RELIGION AND SOCIETY IN MODERN JAPAN: CONTINUITY AND CHANGE. 1970: Rice University Press.

William R. LaFleur. LIQUID LIFE: ABORTION AND BUDDHISM IN JAPAN. 1992: Princeton University Press.

George A. DeVos & Takao Sofue, eds. RELIGION AND THE FAMILY IN EAST ASIA. 1986: University of California Press.

Kiyomi Morioka & William H. Newell, eds. THE SOCIOLOGY OF JAPANESE RELIGION. 1968: Brill.

Daniel C. Holtom. THE NATIONAL FAITH OF JAPAN: A STUDY IN MODERN SHINTŌ. 1938: Dutton.

_____. MODERN JAPAN AND SHINTŌ NATIONALISM. 1943; revised edition, 1947: University of Chicago Press.

Helen Hardacre. SHINTŌ AND THE STATE, 1868-1988. 1991: Princeton University Press.

_____. "Creating State Shintō: The Great Promulgation Campaign and the New Religions," *Journal of Japanese Studies* 12.1 (1986), 29-63.

James Edward Ketelaar. OF HERETICS AND MARTYRS IN MEIJI JAPAN: BUDDHISM AND ITS PERSECUTION. 1993: Princeton University Press.

Minor L. & Ann T. Rogers. "The Honganji: Guardian of the State (1868-1945)," *Japanese Journal of Religious Studies* 17.1 (1990), 3-28.

Stephen S. Large. "Buddhism, Socialism, and Protest in Prewar Japan: The Career of Seno'o Giro," *Modern Asian Studies* 21.1 (1987), 153-171.

Koremaru Sakamoto. "Religion and State in the Early Meiji Period (1868-1912)," *Acta Asiatica* 51 (1987), 42-61.

Sheldon M. Garon. "State and Religion in Imperial Japan, 1912-1945," *Journal of Japanese Studies* 12.2 (1986), 273-302.

Haruo Sakurai. "Tradition and Change in Local Community Shrines," *Acta Asiatica* 51 (1987), 62-76. On the government-enforced merger of shrines in the late Meiji period.

Ichirō Hori, ed. JAPANESE RELIGION. 1972: Kōdansha International.

_____. FOLK RELIGION IN JAPAN: CONTINUITY AND CHANGE. 1968: University of Tokyo Press & University of Chicago Press.

Shanti Devi. "Hospitality for the Gods: Popular Religion in Edo, Japan, an Example." 1985: Ph.D. dissertation in History, University of Hawaii.

Makoto Hayashi & Kazuo Yoshihara, eds. "Folk Religion and Religious Organizations in Asia," *Japanese Journal of Religious Studies* 15.2-15.3 (1988). Special double issue.

Tokutarō Sakurai. "The Major Features and Characteristics of Japanese Folk Belief," in Morioka and Newell, THE SOCIOLOGY OF JAPANESE RELIGION (1968: Brill), 13-24.

Robert J. Smith. ANCESTOR WORSHIP IN CONTEMPORARY JAPAN. 1974: Stanford University Press.

David Plath. "Where the Family of God Is the Family: The Role of the Dead in Japanese Households," *American Anthropologist* 66.2 (1964), 300-317.

Emily Groszos Ooms. WOMEN AND MILLENARIAN PROTEST IN MEIJI JAPAN: THE CASE OF DEGUCHI NAO AND ŌMOTOKYŌ. 1993: Cornell University Press.

Carmen Blacker. THE CATALPA BOW: A STUDY OF SHAMANISTIC PRACTICES IN JAPAN. 1975: Allen & Unwin.

Winston Bradley Davis. DOJO: MAGIC AND EXORCISM IN MODERN JAPAN. 1980: Stanford University Press.

Royall Tyler & Paul L. Swanson, eds. "Shugendō and Mountain Religion in Japan," *Japanese Journal of Religious Studies* 16.2-16.3 (1989). Special double issue.

Royall Tyler. "Kōfukuji and the Mountains of Yamato," *Japan Review* 1 (1990), 153-223.

H. Byron Earhart. A RELIGIOUS STUDY OF THE MT. HAGURO SECT OF SHUGENDŌ: AN EXAMPLE OF JAPANESE MOUNTAIN RELIGION. 1970: Monumenta Nipponica Monographs.

Anne-Marie Bouchy. "The Cult of Mount Atago and the Atago Confraternities," *Journal of Asian Studies* 46.2 (1987), 279-303.

Kenneth A. Marcure. "The *Danka* System," *Monumenta Nipponica* 40.1 (1985), 39-67. On affailiation of families with temples.

Mary Ann Harrington. JAPAN'S HIDDEN CHRISTIANS. 1993: Loyola University Press.

J. L. Breen. "Shintōists in Restoration Japan (1868-1872): Towards a Reassessment," *Modern Asian Studies* 24.3 (1990), 579-602.

John Breen. "Shintō and Christianity: The Dynamics of the Encounter in Bakumatsu Japan," *Transactions, Asiatic Society of Japan*, 4th series, 6 (1991), 49-60.

Helen Ballhatchet. "Confucianism and Christianity in Meiji Japan: The Case of Kozaki Hiromichi," *Journal of the Royal Asiatic Society* 1988, No. 2, 349-369.

Notto R. Thelle. BUDDHISM AND CHRISTIANITY IN JAPAN: FROM CONFLICT TO DIALOGUE, 1854-1899. 1987: University of Hawaii Press.

David Reid. NEW WINE: THE CULTURAL SHAPING OF JAPANESE CHRISTIANITY. 1991: Asian Humanities Press.

Kiyoko Takeda. "Japanese Christianity: Between Orthodoxy and Heterodoxy," in J. V. Koschmann, ed. AUTHORITY AND THE INDIVIDUAL IN JAPAN (1978: University of Tokyo Press), 82-107.

Christal Whelan. "Religion Concealed: The Kakure Kirishitan on Narushima," *Monumenta Nipponica* 47.3 (1992), 369-387.

Aasulv Lande. MEIJI PROTESTANTISM IN HISTORY AND HISTORIO-GRAPHY: A COMPARATIVE STUDY OF JAPANESE AND WESTERN INTERPRETATION OF EARLY PROTESTANTISM IN JAPAN. 1989: P. Lang.

Leith Morton. "Arishima Takeo and Christianity," in Harold Bolitho & Alan Rix, eds. A NORTHERN PROSPECT: AUSTRALIAN PAPERS ON JAPAN (1981: Japanese Studies Association of Australia), 67-82.

Irwin Scheiner. CHRISTIAN CONVERTS AND SOCIAL PROTEST IN MEIJI JAPAN. 1970: University of California Press.

Nobuya Bamba & John F. Howes, eds. PACIFISM IN JAPAN: THE CHRISTIAN AND SOCIALIST TRADITION. 1978: University of British Columbia Press.

George B. Bickle, Jr. THE NEW JERUSALEM: ASPECTS OF UTOPIANISM IN THE THOUGHT OF KAGAWA TOYOHIKO. 1976: University of Arizona Press.

Richard E. Durfee, Jr. "Portrait of an Unknowingly Ordinary Man: Endō Shūsaku, Christianity, and Japanese Historical Consciousness," *Japanese Journal of Religious Studies* 16.1 (1989), 41-62.

WOMEN

*Hesung Chun Koh et al., comp. KOREAN AND JAPANESE WOMEN: AN ANALYTIC BIBLIOGRAPHIC GUIDE. 1982: Greenwood.

*Kristina Ruth Huber. WOMEN IN JAPANESE SOCIETY: AN ANNO-TATED BIBLIOGRAPHY OF SELECTED ENGLISH MATERIALS. Bibliographies and Indexes in Women's Studies, Number 16. 1992: Greenwood Press.

Historical Studies

Chieko Irie Mulhern, ed. HEROIC WITH GRACE: LEGENDARY WOMEN OF JAPAN. 1991: M. E. Sharpe.

Gail Lee Bernstein, ed. RECREATING JAPANESE WOMEN, 1600-1945. 1991: University of California Press.

Joyce Ackroyd. "Women in Feudal Japan," *Transactions, Asiatic Society of Japan* (1959), 31-68.

Kikue Yamakawa. WOMEN OF THE MITO DOMAIN: RECOLLECTIONS OF SAMURAI FAMILY LIFE. Kate Wildman Nakai, transl. 1992: University of Tokyo Press. A translation of Yamakawa's 1943 *Buke no josei.*

Susan J. Pharr. "Japan: Historical and Contemporary Perspectives," in Janet Giele & Audrey Smock, eds. WOMEN: ROLE AND STATUS IN EIGHT COUNTRIES (1977: Wiley), 219-255.

Ronald P. Loftus. "Japanese Women in History and Society," *Journal of Ethnic Studies* 8.3 (1980), 109-122.

Junko Oguri & Nancy Andrew. "Women in Japanese Religion," KŌDANSHA ENCYCLOPEDIA OF JAPAN 8: 256-257.

Nancy Andrew. "History of Women in Japan," KŌDANSHA ENCYCLOPEDIA OF JAPAN 8: 257-260.

Joyce C. Lebra. "Women and Modernization," KŌDANSHA ENCYCLOPEDIA OF JAPAN 8: 260-261.

Susan J. Pharr. "Women in Contemporary Japan," KŌDANSHA ENCYCLOPEDIA OF JAPAN 8: 261-263.

Takashi Koyama. THE CHANGING SOCIAL POSITION OF WOMEN IN JAPAN. 1961: UNESCO (Paris).

Mary Beard. THE FORCE OF WOMEN IN JAPANESE HISTORY. 1953: Public Affairs.

Chiyoko Higuchi. HER PLACE IN THE SUN: WOMEN WHO SHAPED JAPAN. 1973: The East.

Mikiso Hane. PEASANTS, REBELS, AND OUTCASTES: THE UNDERSIDE OF MODERN JAPAN. 1982: Pantheon. See especially chapters on rural women (78-101), and poverty and prostitution (206-225) in Japan prior to 1945.

Yukichi Fukuzawa. FUKUZAWA YUKICHI ON JAPANESE WOMEN: SELECTED READINGS. Eiichi Kiyooka, transl. & ed. 1988: University of Tokyo Press.

Emily Groszos Ooms. WOMEN AND MILLENARIAN PROTEST IN MEIJI JAPAN: THE CASE OF DEGUCHI NAO AND ŌMOTOKYŌ. 1993: Cornell University Press.

Sheldon Garon. "The World's Oldest Debate? Prostitution and the State in Imperial Japan, 1900-1945," *American Historical Review* 98.3 (1993), 710-732.

T. Yamazaki. "Sandakan No. 8 Brothel," *Bulletin of Concerned Asian Scholars* 7.4 (1975), 52-60.

Bill Mihalopoulos. "The Making of Prostitutes: The *Karayuki-san*," *Bulletin of Concerned Asian Scholars* 25.1 (1993), 41-56.

James Francis Warren. AH KU AND KARAYUKI-SAN: PROSTITUTION IN SINGAPORE, 1870-1940. 1993: Oxford University Press.

Edwin McClellan. WOMAN IN THE CRESTED KIMONO: THE LIFE OF SHIBUE IO AND HER FAMILY DRAWN FROM MORI ŌGAI'S *SHIBUE CHŪSAI*. 1985: Yale University Press.

Alice Mabel Bacon. JAPANESE GIRLS AND WOMEN. 1902: Houghton Mifflin.

Sidney L. Gulick. WORKING WOMEN OF JAPAN. 1915: Missionary Education Movement of the United States and Canada.

Masanori Nakamura, ed. THE TRANSFORMATION OF FEMALE LABOUR IN MODERN JAPAN. 1994: United Nations University Press. Technology and female labor, from the late 19th century to the postwar high-growth period.

Yasue Aoki Kidd. WOMEN WORKERS IN THE JAPANESE COTTON MILLS, 1880-1920. 1978: *Cornell University East Asia Papers*, 20.

Gail Lee Bernstein. "Women in the Silk-reeling Industry in Nineteenth-Century Japan," in Gail Lee Bernstein & Haruhiro Fukui, cds. JAPAN AND THE WORLD: ESSAYS ON JAPANESE HISTORY AND POLITICS IN HONOUR OF ISHIDA TAKESHI (1988: St. Martin's), 54-77.

E. Patricia Tsurumi. "Female Textile Workers and the Failure of Early Trade Unionism in Japan," *History Workshop* 18 (1984), 3-27.

_____. "Problem Consciousness and Modern Japanese History: Female Textile Workers of Meiji and Taishō," *Bulletin of Concerned Asian Scholars* 18.4 (1986), 41-48.

_____. FACTORY GIRLS: WOMEN IN THE THREAD MILLS OF MEIJI JAPAN. 1990: Princeton University Press.

Sharlie Ushioda. "Women and War in Meiji Japan: The Case of Fukuda Hideko," *Peace and Change* 14.3 (1977), 9-12.

Janet E. Hunter, ed. JAPANESE WOMEN WORKING. 1993: Routledge. On 20th century women.

_____. "Women's Labour Force Participation in Interwar Japan," *Japan Forum* 2.1 (1990), 105-125.

Sheldon Garon. "Women's Groups and the Japanese State: Contending Approaches to Political Integration, 1890-1945," *Journal of Japanese Studies* 19.1 (1993), 5-41.

Sharon L. Sievers. FLOWERS IN SALT: THE BEGINNINGS OF FEMINIST CONSCIOUSNESS IN MODERN JAPAN. 1983: Stanford University Press. Covers 1868 to early 20th century.

Ann M. Harrington. "Women and Higher Education in the Japanese Empire (1895-1945)," *Journal of Asian History* 21.2 (1987), 169-186.

Barbara Rose. TSUDA UMEKO AND WOMEN'S EDUCATION IN JAPAN. 1992: Yale University Press.

Umeko Tsuda. THE ATTIC LETTERS: UME TSUDA'S CORRESPONDENCE TO HER AMERICAN MOTHER. Yoshiko Furuki, ed. 1991: Weatherhill.

Yoshiko Furuki. THE WHITE PLUM: A BIOGRAPHY OF UME TSUDA, PIONEER IN THE HIGHER EDUCATION OF JAPANESE WOMEN. 1991: Weatherhill.

Christine Chapman. "The Meiji Letters of Tsuda Ume, Pioneer Educator of Women," *Japan Quarterly* 34.3 (1987), 263-270.

Akiko Kuno. UNEXPECTED DESTINATIONS: THE POIGNANT STORY OF JAPAN'S FIRST VASSAR GRADUATE. Kirsten McIvor, transl. 1993: Kōdansha International. On the life of Ōyama Sutematsu (1851-1919).

Janice Bridges Bardsley. "Writing for the New Woman of Taishō Japan: Hiratsuka Raichō and the *Seitō* Journal, 1911-1916." 1989: Ph.D. dissertation in East Asian Languages and Cultures, UCLA.

Nancy Andrew. "The Seitōsha: An Early Japanese Women's Organization, 1911-1916," *Harvard University Papers on Japan* (1972), 45-69.

Ken Miyamoto. "Itō Noe and the Bluestockings," *Japan Interpreter* 10.2 (Autumn 1975), 190-203.

Tomoko Yamazaki. THE STORY OF YAMADA WAKA: FROM PROSTI-TUTE TO FEMINIST PIONEER. Ann Kostant & Wakako Hironaka, transl. 1985: Kōdansha International.

Dee Ann Vavich. "The Japanese Woman's Movement: Ichikawa Fusae, a Pioneer in Woman's Suffrage," *Monumenta Nipponica* 22.3-4 (1967), 402-436.

Patricia Murray. "Ichikawa Fusae and the Lonely Red Carpet," *Japan Interpreter* 10.2 (1975), 171-181.

Malia Sedgewick Johnson. "Margaret Sanger and the Birth Control Movement in Japan, 1921-1955." 1987: Ed.D. dissertation in Educational Foundations, University of Hawaii.

Chieko Mulhern. "Japan's First Newspaperwoman: Hani Motoko," *Japan Interpreter* 7.3-4 (1979), 310-329.

Motoko Hani. "Stories of My Life," *Japan Interpreter* 7.3-4 (1979), 310-354. Translation with introductory essay.

Akiko Tokuza. "Oku Mumeo and the Movements to Alter the Status of Women in Japan from the Taishō Period to the Present." 1988: Ph.D. dissertation in Speech, University of Michigan.

Robert J. Smith & Ella Lury Wiswell. THE WOMEN OF SUYE MURA.
1982: University of Chicago Press. Based on fieldwork in the 1930s.

Donna Kay Keuck. "The Books and the Photographs of Suye Mura." 1990:
Ph.D. dissertation in Sociology, Cornell University.

Robert J. Smith. "Japanese Village Women: Suye-mura, 1935-1936," *Journal of
Japanese Studies* 7.2 (1981), 259-284.

Sharon Nolte. "Women in a Prewar Japanese Village: Suye Mura Revisited,"
Journal of Peasant Studies 7.2 (1981), 259-284.

Kazuko Tsurumi. SOCIAL CHANGE AND THE INDIVIDUAL: JAPAN
BEFORE AND AFTER DEFEAT IN WORLD WAR II. 1970:
Princeton University Press. Chapters 7 & 8 on women.

T. Havens. "Women and War in Japan, 1937-45," *American Historical Review*
80.4 (1975), 913-934.

Janet Hunter. "An Absence of Change: Women in the Japanese Labour Force,
1937-1945," in T. G. Fraser & Peter Lowe, eds. CONFLICT AND
AMITY IN EAST ASIA: ESSAYS IN HONOUR OF IAN NISH
(1992: Macmillan), 59-76.

Chizuko Ueno. "The Genesis of the Urban Housewife," *Japan Quarterly* 34.2
(1987), 130-142.

First-Hand Accounts

Ekiken (Ekken) Kaibara. "THE WAY OF CONTENTMENT" AND "GREATER
LEARNING FOR WOMEN." 1913; reprint edition, 1979: University
Publications of America. Translations of two famous essays by a
Neo-Confucian scholar who lived from 1630 to 1714.

MEIROKU ZASSHI, JOURNAL OF THE JAPANESE ENLIGHTENMENT.
William R. Braisted, transl. 1976: Harvard University Press. This
famous intellectual journal of the 1870s contains various articles on
women.

Ai Hoshino. "The Education of Women," in Inazō Nitobe, ed. WESTERN
INFLUENCE IN MODERN JAPAN (1931: University of Chicago
Press), 215-230. The author was president of Tsuda College.

Fumiko Kaneko. THE PRISON MEMOIRS OF KANEKO FUMIKO. Jean Inglis, transl. 1991: M. E. Sharpe.

Contemporary Japan, volumes 1 to 10 (1932-1941). This semi-official Japanese publication contains numerous articles on women by Japanese authors.

Shidzue Ishimoto. FACING TWO WAYS: THE STORY OF MY LIFE. 1935: Farrar & Rinehart. See the 1984 edition, with introduction and afterword by Barbara Molony. Baroness Ishimoto was a pioneer in the Japanese women's movement.

Etsu Sugimoto. A DAUGHTER OF THE SAMURAI. 1928: Doubleday.

_____. A DAUGHTER OF THE NARIKIN. 1932: Doubleday.

_____. A DAUGHTER OF THE NOHFU. 1938: Hurst & Blackett.

Mikiso Hane, transl. & ed. REFLECTIONS ON THE WAY TO THE GALLOWS: REBEL WOMEN IN PREWAR JAPAN. 1988: University of California Press.

Yōko Matsuoka. DAUGHTER OF THE PACIFIC. 1952: Harper.

Women's Division of Sōka Gakkai, comp. WOMEN AGAINST WAR: PERSONAL ACCOUNTS OF FORTY JAPANESE WOMEN. Richard L. Gage, transl. 1986: Kōdansha International.

Sumie Mishima. MY NARROW ISLE: THE STORY OF A MODERN WOMAN IN JAPAN. 1941: John Day.

_____. THE BROADER WAY: A WOMAN'S LIFE IN THE NEW JAPAN. 1953: John Day.

Chiyono Sugimoto Kiyooka. BUT THE SHIPS ARE SAILING, SAILING. 1959: Hokuseidō. On life in Occupied Japan.

Nobuko Albery. BALLOON TOP. 1978: Pantheon. On growing up in Occupied Japan.

Laurence Caillet. THE HOUSE OF YAMAZAKI: THE LIFE OF IKUE YAMAZAKI. Megan Backus, transl. 1994: Kōdansha International.

Yasushi Inoue. CHRONICLES OF MY MOTHER. 1982: Kōdansha International. Recollections of a famous novelist.

James Trager. LETTERS FROM SACHIKO: A JAPANESE WOMAN'S VIEW
OF LIFE IN THE LAND OF THE ECONOMIC MIRACLE. 1982:
Atheneum.

Tetsuko Kuroyanagi. TOTTO-CHAN: THE LITTLE GIRL AT THE
WINDOW. Dorothy Britton, transl. 1982: Kōdansha International.
Autobiography of one of Japan's most famous television personalities.

Haruko Taya Cook & Theodore F. Cook, eds. JAPAN AT WAR: AN ORAL
HISTORY. 1992: The New Press. Includes numerous recollections by
Japanese women.

Literature By & About Women

Claire Zebroski Mamola. JAPANESE WOMEN WRITERS IN ENGLISH
TRANSLATION: AN ANNOTATED BIBLIOGRAPHY. 2 vols.
1989, 1992: Garland.

Kenneth Rexroth & Ikuko Atsumi. THE BURNING HEART: WOMEN POETS
OF JAPAN. 1977: Seabury.

Robert Lyons Danly. IN THE SHADE OF SPRING LEAVES: THE LIFE AND
WRITINGS OF HIGUCHI ICHIYO, A WOMAN OF LETTERS IN
MEIJI JAPAN. 1981: Yale University Press; 1993: Norton. Includes
nine stories.

Rebecca L. Copeland. "Mother Obsession and Womb Imagery in Japanese
Literature," *Transactions, Asiatic Society of Japan*, 4th series, 3 (1988),
131-150.

Paul McCarthy. "Images of Woman as Mother in Tanizaki's Fiction,"
Transactions, Asiatic Society of Japan, 4th series, 1 (1986), 23-44.

Akiko Yosano. TANGLED HAIR: SELECTED TANKA FROM *MIDAREGA-
MI*. Sanford Goldstein & Seishi Shinoda, transl. 1987: Tuttle. Poems
originally published in 1901.

Phyllis Hyland Larson. "Yosano Akiko: The Early Years." 1985: Ph.D. dissertation in Japanese, University of Minnesota.

Yukiko Tanaka, ed. TO LIVE AND TO WRITE: SELECTIONS BY
JAPANESE WOMEN WRITERS, 1913-1938. 1987: Seal Press.

Chiyo Uno. CONFESSIONS OF LOVE. Phyllis Birnbaum, transl. 1989: University of Hawaii Press.

Rebecca L. Copeland. THE SOUND OF THE WIND: THE LIFE AND WORKS OF UNO CHIYO. 1992: University of Hawaii Press.

_____. "Uno Chiyo: Not Just 'A Writer of Illicit Love'," *Japan Quarterly* 35.2 (1988), 176-182.

Takeo Arishima. A CERTAIN WOMAN. Kenneth Strong, transl. 1978: Columbia University Press.

Sawako Ariyoshi. THE DOCTOR'S WIFE. Wakako Hironaka & Ann Siller Kostant, transl. 1978: Kōdansha International.

_____. THE RIVER KI. Mildred Tahara, transl. 1980: Kōdansha International.

Fumiko Enchi. THE WAITING YEARS. John Bester, transl. 1976: Kōdansha International.

See also the treatment of women in fiction by Mori Ōgai (especially WILD GEESE), Nagai Kafū (especially GEISHA IN RIVALRY), Natsume Sōseki, Kawabata Yasunari, and Tanizaki Jun'ichirō (especially THE MAKIOKA SISTERS).

Noriko Mizuta Lippit & Kyōko Iriye Selden, transl. & ed. JAPANESE WOMEN WRITERS: TWENTIETH CENTURY SHORT FICTION. 1991: M. E. Sharpe.

Noriko Mizuta Lippit & Kyōko Iriye Selden,transl. STORIES BY CONTEM-PORARY JAPANESE WOMEN WRITERS. 1982: M. E. Sharpe.

Yukiko Tanaka, ed. TO LIVE AND TO WRITE: SELECTIONS BY JAPANESE WOMEN WRITERS 1913-1938. 1987: Seal Press.

_____ & Elizabeth Hanson, transl. THIS KIND OF WOMAN: TEN STORIES BY JAPANESE WOMEN WRITERS, 1960-1976. 1982: Stanford University Press.

Phyllis Birnbaum, transl. RABBITS, CRABS, ETC: STORIES BY JAPANESE WOMEN. 1982: University of Hawaii Press.

Yūko Tsushima. CHILD OF FORTUNE. G. Harcourt, transl. 1983: Kōdansha International.

Victoria V. Vernon. DAUGHTERS OF THE MOON: WISH, WILL, AND SOCIAL CONSTRAINT IN FICTION BY MODERN JAPANESE WOMEN. 1988: Institute of East Asian Studies, University of California.

Chieko Ariga. "Dephallicizing Women in *Ryūkyō shinshi*: A Critique of Gender Ideology in Japanese Literature," *Journal of Asian Studies* 51.3 (1992), 565-586.

Makoto Ueda, ed. THE MOTHER OF DREAMS AND OTHER SHORT STORIES: PORTRAYALS OF WOMEN IN MODERN JAPANESE FICTION. 1986: Kōdansha International.

Women in Contemporary Japan

Takie Sugiyama Lebra. JAPANESE WOMEN: CONSTRAINT AND FULFILLMENT. 1984: University of Hawaii Press.

Sumiko Iwao. THE JAPANESE WOMAN: TRADITIONAL IMAGE AND CHANGING REALITY. 1992: Free Press.

Joyce Lebra, Joy Paulson & Elizabeth Powers, eds. WOMEN IN CHANGING JAPAN. 1976: Stanford University Press.

Dorothy Robins-Mowry. THE HIDDEN SUN: WOMEN OF MODERN JAPAN. 1983: Westview.

Alice H. Cook & Hiroko Hayashi. WORKING WOMEN IN JAPAN. 1980: Cornell University Press.

Gail Lee Bernstein. HARUKO'S WORLD: A JAPANESE FARM WOMAN AND HER COMMUNITY. 1983: Stanford University Press.

Anne E. Imamura. URBAN JAPANESE HOUSEWIVES: AT HOME AND IN THE COMMUNITY. 1987: University of Hawaii Press.

Susan J. Pharr. POLITICAL WOMEN IN JAPAN: THE SEARCH FOR A PLACE IN POLITICAL LIFE. 1981: University of California Press.

_____. "The Politics of Women's Rights," in Robert E. Ward & Yoshikazu Sakamoto, eds., DEMOCRATIZING JAPAN: THE ALLIED OCCUPATION (1987: University of Hawaii Press), 221-252.

Michael Berger. "Japanese Women—Old Images and New Realities," *Japan Interpreter* 11.1 (1976), 56-67.

Takie Sugiyama Lebra. "Sex Equality for Japanese Women," *Japan Interpreter* 10.3-4 (1976), 284-295.

Liza Crihfield Dalby. GEISHA. 1983: University of California Press.

Mary C. Brinton. WOMEN AND THE ECONOMIC MIRACLE: GENDER AND WORK IN POSTWAR JAPAN. 1993: University of California Press.

Yuriko Saisho. WOMEN EXECUTIVES IN JAPAN. 1981: Yuri International.

Samuel Coleman. FAMILY PLANNING IN JAPANESE SOCIETY: TRADITIONAL BIRTH CONTROL IN A MODERN URBAN CULTURE. 1984: Princeton University Press.

Keiko Kiguchi. "Japanese Women in Transition," *Japan Quarterly* 29 (1982), 311-318.

MINORITY GROUPS: OUTCASTES, KOREANS, & AINU

George DeVos. JAPAN'S MINORITIES: BURAKUMIN, KOREANS, AINU AND OKINAWANS. 1983: Minority Rights Group.

_____ & Hiroshi Wagatsuma. JAPAN'S INVISIBLE RACE: CASTE IN CULTURE AND PERSONALITY. 1966: University of California Press.

Keiji Nagahara. "The Medieval Origins of the *Eta-Hinin*," *Journal of Japanese Studies* 5.2 (1979), 385-403.

Shigeaki Ninomiya. "An Inquiry Concerning the Origin, Development, and Present Situation of the Eta in Relation to the History of Social Classes in Japan," *Transactions, Asiatic Society of Japan*, 2nd series, 10 (1933), 46-154.

Mikiso Hane. PEASANTS, REBELS, AND OUTCASTES: THE UNDERSIDE OF MODERN JAPAN. 1982: Pantheon.

William Lyman Brooks. "Outcaste Society in Early Modern Japan." 1976: Ph.D. dissertation in History, Columbia University.

Ian Neary. POLITICAL PROTEST AND SOCIAL CONTROL IN PRE-WAR JAPAN: THE ORIGINS OF BURAKU LIBERATION. 1989: Humanities Press International.

_____. "Tenkō of an Organization: The Suiheisha in the Late 1930s," *Proceedings of the British Association for Japanese Studies*, volume 2, part 2 (1977), 64-76.

Roger I. Yoshino. THE INVISIBLE VISIBLE MINORITY: JAPAN'S BURAKUMIN. 1977: Buraku Kaihō Kenkyūsho.

John D. Donoghue. PARIAH PERSISTENCE IN CHANGING JAPAN. 1977: University Press of America.

Tōson Shimazaki. THE BROKEN COMMANDMENT. Kenneth Strong, transl. 1974: University of Tokyo Press.

Buraku Kaihō Kenkyūjo (Buraku Liberation League). LONG-SUFFERING BROTHERS & SISTERS, UNITE! 1981: Liberation Publishing House.

Frank K. Upham. LAW AND SOCIAL CHANGE IN POSTWAR JAPAN. 1987: Harvard University Press. Includes treatment of law and *burakumin*.

Edward W. Wagner. THE KOREAN MINORITY IN JAPAN. 1951: Institute of Pacific Relations.

Richard H. Mitchell. THE KOREAN MINORITY IN JAPAN. 1967: University of California Press.

Changsoo Lee & George DeVos, eds. KOREANS IN JAPAN: ETHNIC CONFLICT & ACCOMMODATION. 1981: University of California Press.

Michael Weiner. THE ORIGINS OF THE KOREAN COMMUNITY IN JAPAN, 1910-1923. 1989: Humanities Press International.

_____. RACE AND MIGRATION IN IMPERIAL JAPAN: THE LIMITS OF ASSIMILATION. 1994: Routledge. On colonial rule in Korea and Japanese treatment of Korean labor.

Kurt W. Tong. "Korea's Forgotten Atomic Bomb Victims," *Bulletin of Concerned Asian Scholars* 23.1 (1991), 31-37. Includes bibliography.

Shigeru Kayano. OUR LAND WAS A FOREST: AN AINU MEMOIR. Transl. by Kyōko Selden, with Lili Selden. 1994: Westview.

Josef Kreiner, ed. EUROPEAN STUDIES ON AINU LANGUAGE AND CULTURE. 1993: Iudicium Verlag.

LITERATURE

* International House of Japan Library, comp. MODERN JAPANESE LITERA-TURE IN TRANSLATION: A BIBLIOGRAPHY. 1979: Kōdansha International. Includes 1,500 authors from 1868-1978.

John Lewell. MODERN JAPANESE NOVELISTS: A BIOGRAPHICAL DICTIONARY. 1993: Kōdansha International.

Donald Keene. JAPANESE LITERATURE: AN INTRODUCTION FOR WESTERN READERS. 1953: Grove.

_____. WORLD WITHIN WALLS: JAPANESE LITERATURE OF THE PRE-MODERN ERA, 1600-1867. 1976: Grove.

_____. DAWN TO THE WEST: JAPANESE LITERATURE OF THE MODERN ERA. 2 volumes. 1984: Holt, Rinehart & Winston.

_____, ed. ANTHOLOGY OF JAPANESE LITERATURE: FROM THE EAR-LIEST ERA TO THE MID-NINETEENTH CENTURY. 1955: Grove.

_____, ed. MODERN JAPANESE LITERATURE: AN ANTHOLOGY. 1956: Grove.

_____. THE PLEASURES OF JAPANESE LITERATURE. 1988: Columbia University Press.

Aileen Gatten & Anthony Hood Chambers, eds. NEW LEAVES: STUDIES AND TRANSLATIONS OF JAPANESE LITERATURE IN HONOR OF EDWARD SEIDENSTICKER. 1993: University of Michigan Press.

J. Thomas Rimer. A READER'S GUIDE TO JAPANESE LITERATURE: FROM THE EIGHTH CENTURY TO THE PRESENT. 1988: Kōdansha International.

Shūichi Katō. A HISTORY OF JAPANESE LITERATURE: THE YEARS OF ISOLATION (volume 2) and THE MODERN YEARS (volume 3). Don Sanderson, transl. 1979: Kōdansha International.

Kōjin Karatani. ORIGINS OF MODERN JAPANESE LITERATURE. Brett de Bary, transl. 1993: Duke University Press.

Masao Miyoshi. ACCOMPLICES OF SILENCE: THE MODERN JAPANESE NOVEL. 1974: University of California Press.

Shōichi Sakae. "The Autobiography in Japan," Teruko Craig, transl., *Journal of Japanese Studies* 11.2 (1985), 357-368.

Edward Fowler. THE RHETORIC OF CONFESSION: SHISHŌSETSU IN EARLY TWENTIETH-CENTURY JAPANESE FICTION. 1988: University of California Press.

James A. Fujii. COMPLICIT FICTIONS: THE SUBJECT IN THE MODERN JAPANESE PROSE NARRATIVE. 1993: University of California Press.

P. A. Herbert. "The Novel and the Japanese Psyche," in Harold Bolitho & Alan Rix, eds. A NORTHERN PROSPECT: AUSTRALIAN PAPERS ON JAPAN (1981: Japanese Studies Association of Australia), 83-94.

Makoto Ueda. MODERN JAPANESE WRITERS AND THE NATURE OF LITERATURE. 1976: Stanford University Press.

_____. MODERN JAPANESE POETS AND THE NATURE OF LITERATURE. 1983: Stanford University Press.

J. Thomas Rimer. MODERN JAPANESE FICTION AND ITS TRADITIONS: AN INTRODUCTION. 1978: Princeton University Press.

_____. PILGRIMAGES: ASPECTS OF JAPANESE LITERATURE AND
CULTURE. 1988: University of Hawaii Press.

_____ & Robert E. Morrell. GUIDE TO JAPANESE POETRY. 1975:
G. K. Hall.

Earl Jackson, Jr. "The Heresy of Meaning: Japanese Symbolist Poetry," *Harvard
Journal of Asiatic Studies* 51.2 (1991), 561-598.

Lucy Beth Lower. "Poetry and Poetics: From Modern to Contemporary in
Japanese Poetry." 1987: Ph.D. dissertation, Harvard University.

Noriko Mizuta Lippit. REALITY AND FICTION IN MODERN JAPANESE
LITERATURE. 1980: M. E. Sharpe.

Hisaaki Yamanouchi. THE SEARCH FOR AUTHENTICITY IN MODERN
JAPANESE LITERATURE. 1978: Cambridge University Press.

David Pollack. READING AGAINST CULTURE: IDEOLOGY AND
NARRATIVE IN THE JAPANESE NOVEL. 1992: Cornell University
Press.

Kevin M. Doak. DREAMS OF DIFFERENCE: THE JAPANESE ROMANTIC
SCHOOL AND THE CRISIS OF MODERNITY. 1994: University of
California Press.

Arthur G. Kimball. CRISIS IN IDENTITY AND CONTEMPORARY JAPAN-
ESE NOVELS. 1972: Tuttle.

Irena Powell. WRITERS AND SOCIETY IN MODERN JAPAN. 1983:
Kōdansha International.

Victoria V. Vernon. DAUGHTERS OF THE MOON: WISH, WILL, AND
SOCIAL CONSTRAINT IN FICTION BY MODERN JAPANESE
WOMEN. 1988: Institute of East Asian Studies, University of
California.

Tōson Shimazaki. BEFORE THE DAWN. William E. Naff, transl. 1987:
University of Hawaii Press. The novel that best captures the rapid
changes of the Meiji period.

Nanette Twine. LANGUAGE AND THE MODERN STATE: THE REFORM
OF MODERN WRITTEN JAPANESE. 1991: Routledge.

John Lewell. MODERN JAPANESE NOVELISTS: A BIOGRAPHICAL
DICTIONARY. 1993: Kōdansha International.

See in particular translations of works by the following authors (names are
given in Japanese order):

Ihara Saikaku	1642-1693
Chikamatsu Monzaemon	1653-1724
Futabatei Shimei	1864-1910
Mori Ōgai	1862-1922
Natsume Sōseki	1867-1916
Higuchi Ichiyo	1872-1896
Tayama Katai	1871-1930
Shimazaki Tōson	1872-1943
Arishima Takeo	1878-1923
Nagai Kafū	1879-1959
Ishikawa Takuboku	1886-1912
Akutagawa Ryūnosuke	1892-1927
Shiga Naoya	1883-1971
Tanizaki Jun'ichirō	1886-1965
Kawabata Yasunari	1899-1972
Dazai Osamu	1909-1948

JAPAN ABROAD: FOREIGN RELATIONS, TIONS, EMPIRE, & WAR FROM THE RESTORATION TO 1945

Japan Abroad: Foreign Relations, Empire, & War From the Restoration to 1945

OVERVIEWS

[See also pp. 205-214]

Paul H. Clyde & Burton F. Beers. THE FAR EAST: A HISTORY OF WESTERN IMPACTS AND EASTERN RESPONSES, 1830-1975. 6th edition. 1975; reprinted 1991: Waveland Press.

James Morley, ed. JAPAN'S FOREIGN POLICY, 1868-1941. 1974: Columbia University Press.

Ian Nish. JAPANESE FOREIGN POLICY, 1869-1942. 1976: Routledge & Kegan Paul.

_____. "European Images of Japan: Some Thoughts on Modern European-Japanese Relations," *Japan Foundation Newsletter* 20.3 (1992), 1-5.

Meirion Harries. SOLDIERS OF THE SUN: THE RISE AND FALL OF THE IMPERIAL JAPANESE ARMY, 1868-1945. 1991: Random House.

W. G. Beasley. JAPANESE IMPERIALISM, 1894-1945. 1987: Oxford University Press.

Sydney Giffard. JAPAN AMONG THE POWERS, 1890-1990. 1994: Yale University Press.

Michael Montgomery. IMPERIALIST JAPAN: THE YEN TO DOMINATE. 1987: Helm.

Ramon H. Myers & Mark R. Peattie, eds. THE JAPANESE COLONIAL EMPIRE, 1895-1945. 1984: Princeton University Press.

Peter Duus, Ramon H. Myers, & Mark R. Peattie, eds. THE JAPANESE INFORMAL EMPIRE IN CHINA, 1895-1937. 1989: Princeton University Press.

Mark R. Peattie. NAN'YŌ: THE RISE AND FALL OF THE JAPANESE IN MICRONESIA, 1885-1945. 1988: University of Hawaii Press.

Richard Storry. JAPAN AND THE DECLINE OF THE WEST IN ASIA, 1894-1942. 1979: St. Martin's.

James B. Crowley, ed. MODERN EAST ASIA: ESSAYS IN INTERPRETATION. 1970: Harcourt Brace & World.

_____. "Historical Prologue to the 1930's," in his JAPAN'S QUEST FOR AUTONOMY: NATIONAL SECURITY AND FOREIGN POLICY, 1930-1938 (1968: Princeton University Press), 3-34.

_____. "Japan's Military Foreign Policies," in James Morley, ed. JAPAN'S FOREIGN POLICY (1974: Princeton University Press), 3-117.

Ikuhiko Hata. "Imperial Japanese Armed Forces," KŌDANSHA ENCYCLOPEDIA OF JAPAN 1: 86-88.

_____. "Colonial Expansion, 1905-1941," in Peter Duus, ed. CAMBRIDGE HISTORY OF JAPAN, Volume 6: THE TWENTIETH CENTURY (1988: Cambridge University Press), 271-314.

Shinji Kondō. JAPANESE MILITARY HISTORY. 1983: Garland.

Morinosuke Kajima. THE EMERGENCE OF JAPAN AS A WORLD POWER 1895-1925. 1968: Tuttle.

_____. A BRIEF DIPLOMATIC HISTORY OF MODERN JAPAN. 1965: Tuttle.

J. K. Fairbank, E. O. Reischauer & Albert Craig. EAST ASIA: THE MODERN TRANSFORMATION. 1965: Houghton Mifflin.

Chitoshi Yanaga. JAPAN SINCE PERRY. 1949: McGraw-Hill.

Hugh Borton. JAPAN'S MODERN CENTURY: FROM PERRY TO 1970. 2nd edition. 1970: Ronald.

W. G. Beasley. THE RISE OF MODERN JAPAN. 1990: St. Martin's.

Kenneth Pyle. THE MAKING OF MODERN JAPAN. 1978: Heath.

Peter Duus. THE RISE OF MODERN JAPAN. 1976: Houghton Mifflin.

Mikiso Hane. MODERN JAPAN: A HISTORICAL SURVEY. 2nd edition. 1992: Westview Press.

Janet Hunter. THE EMERGENCE OF MODERN JAPAN: AN INTRODUCTORY HISTORY SINCE 1853. 1989: Longman.

John Hunter Boyle. MODERN JAPAN: THE AMERICAN NEXUS. 1993: Harcourt Brace Jovanovich.

Marius B. Jansen. JAPAN AND CHINA: FROM WAR TO PEACE, 1894-1972. 1975: Rand McNally.

_____. "The Opening of Japan," *Japan Review* 2 (1991), 191-202. A broad look, beginning with the Bakumatsu period and including cultural issues.

Peter Lowe & Herman Moeshart, eds. WESTERN INTERACTIONS WITH JAPAN: EXPANSION, THE ARMED FORCES & READJUSTMENT, 1859-1956. 1990: Japan Library.

Ernest R. May & James C. Thomson, Jr., eds. AMERICAN-EAST ASIAN RELATIONS: A SURVEY. 1972: Harvard University Press.

Akira Iriye. ACROSS THE PACIFIC: AN INNER HISTORY OF AMERI-CAN-EAST ASIAN RELATIONS. 1967: Harcourt Brace & World.

_____. CHINA AND JAPAN IN THE GLOBAL SETTING. 1992: Harvard University Press.

_____. "Imperialism in East Asia," in Crowley, MODERN EAST ASIA: ESSAYS IN INTERPRETATION (1970: Harcourt Brace & World), 122-150.

_____. "The Legacy of Modern Japanese Diplomacy," *Journal of Social and Political Ideas in Japan* 3.2 (1965), 25-32. A survey of 1895-1945, originally published in *Chūō Kōron*.

Herbert Bix. "Imagistic Historiography and the Reinterpretation of Japanese Imperialism," *Bulletin of Concerned Asian Scholars* 7.3 (1975), 51-68.

Kazuo Shibagaki. "The Logic of Japanese Imperialism," *Social Science Abstracts* 14 (Shakai Kagaku Kenkyūjo, Tokyo University, 1973), 70-87.

Kimihide Mushakōji. "From Fear of Dependence to Fear of Independence— A Scenario of the Japanese International Learning Process," *Japan Annual of International Affairs* 3 (1963-1964), 68-86.

Seizaburō Satō. "Japan's World Order," in Irwin Scheiner, ed. MODERN JAPAN: AN INTERPRETIVE ANTHOLOGY (1974: Macmillan), 9-17.

_____. "The Foundations of Modern Japanese Foreign Policy," in Robert Scalapino, ed. THE FOREIGN POLICY OF MODERN JAPAN (1977: University of California Press), 367-389.

Hilary Conroy. "Lessons from Japanese Imperialism," *Monumenta Nipponica* 21.3-4 (1966), 333-345.

Hyman Kublin. "The Evolution of Japanese Colonialism," *Comparative Studies in Science and History* 2 (1959), 67-84.

Hosea B. Morse & Harley F. MacNair. FAR EASTERN INTERNATIONAL RELATIONS. 2nd edition. 1955: Houghton Mifflin.

Harley F. MacNair & Donald F. Lach. MODERN FAR EASTERN INTERNA-TIONAL RELATIONS. 2nd edition. 1955: Van Nostrand.

Sterling Tatsuji Takeuchi. WAR AND DIPLOMACY IN THE JAPANESE EMPIRE. 1935: University of Chicago Press. Covers 1890-1933.

Payson J. Treat. THE FAR EAST: A POLITICAL AND DIPLOMATIC HISTORY. Revised edition. 1935: Stanford University Press.

Robert Scalapino, ed. THE FOREIGN POLICY OF MODERN JAPAN. 1977: University of California Press.

_____. "The Foreign Policy of Modern Japan," in Roy C. Macridis, ed. FOREIGN POLICY IN WORLD POLITICS. 2nd edition (1962: Prentice-Hall), 270-313.

Michael Blaker. JAPANESE INTERNATIONAL NEGOTIATING STYLE. 1977: Columbia University Press.

T. G. Fraser & Peter Lowe, eds. CONFLICT AND AMITY IN EAST ASIA: ESSAYS IN HONOUR OF IAN NISH. 1992: Macmillan.

Jitsuo Tsuchiyama. "Alliance in Japanese Foreign Policy: Theory and Practice." 1984: Ph.D. dissertation in Government and Politics, University of Maryland.

Umut Arik. A CENTURY OF TURKISH-JAPANESE RELATIONS: TOWARDS A SPECIAL PARTNERSHIP. 1989: DEIK.

R. van Gulik, et al., eds. IN THE WAKE OF THE LIEFDE: CULTURAL RELATIONS BETWEEN THE NETHERLANDS AND JAPAN, SINCE 1600. 1986: De Bataafsche Leeuw.

P. A. Narasimha Murthy. INDIA AND JAPAN: DIMENSIONS OF THEIR RELATIONS: HISTORICAL AND POLITICAL. 1986: ABC Pub. House.

Stefan Tanaka. JAPAN'S ORIENT: RENDERING PASTS INTO HISTORY. 1993: University of California Press. On the scholarly construction of "Orient" (*Tōyō*) and "China" (*Shina*) in modern Japan, particularly by Shiratori Kurakichi. Reveiwed by Kyu Hyun Kim in *Journal of Asian Studies* 53.1 (1994), 233-234; and by Takashi Fujitani in *Journal of Japanese Studies* 20.2 (1994), 547-551.

BASIC CASE STUDIES FOR 1868-1945

James B. Crowley. "Japan's Military Foreign Policies," in James Morley, ed. JAPAN'S FOREIGN POLICY (1974: Columbia University Press), 3-117.

Seiji G. Hishida. THE INTERNATIONAL POSITION OF JAPAN AS A GREAT POWER. 1905: Columbia University Press; 1986: Inter Documentation Co. (microfiche).

Bert Edstrom. JAPAN'S FIGHT FOR GREAT POWER STATUS IN THE MEIJI PERIOD. 1989: University of Stockholm, Center for Pacific Studies.

Marius B. Jansen. "Modernization and Foreign Policy in Meiji Japan," in Robert E. Ward, ed. POLITICAL DEVELOPMENT IN MODERN JAPAN (1968: Princeton University Press), 149-188.

_____. THE JAPANESE AND SUN YAT-SEN. 1954: Harvard University Press.

Hilary Conroy. THE JAPANESE SEIZURE OF KOREA, 1868-1910. 1960: University of Pennsylvania Press.

Donald Calman. THE NATURE AND ORGINS OF JAPANESE IMPERIAL-ISM: A REINTERPRETATION OF THE GREAT CRISIS OF 1873. 1992: Routledge.

Shumpei Okamoto. THE JAPANESE OLIGARCHY AND THE RUSSO-JAPANESE WAR. 1970: Columbia University Press.

Akira Iriye. PACIFIC ESTRANGEMENT: JAPANESE AND AMERICAN EXPANSION, 1897-1911. 1972: Harvard University Press.

Ian Nish. THE ANGLO-JAPANESE ALLIANCE: THE DIPLOMACY OF
TWO ISLAND EMPIRES, 1894-1907. 1966; 2nd edition, 1985:
Athlone.

_____. ALLIANCE IN DECLINE: A STUDY IN ANGLO-JAPANESE
RELATIONS, 1908-1923. 1972: Athlone.

Shigeki Tōyama. "Politics, Economics, and the International Environment in the
Meiji and Taishō Periods," *Developing Economies* 4.4 (1966), 419-446.

James W. Morley. THE JAPANESE THRUST INTO SIBERIA, 1918. 1957:
Columbia University Press.

Roger Dingman. POWER IN THE PACIFIC: THE ORIGINS OF NAVAL
ARMS LIMITATION, 1914-1922. 1976: University of Chicago Press.

Akira Iriye. "Japanese Imperialism and Aggression: Reconsiderations" and
"Japan's Foreign Policies Between World Wars—Sources and Interpretations," in Esmonde M. Robertson, ed. THE ORIGINS OF THE
SECOND WORLD WAR: HISTORICAL INTERPRETATIONS
(1971: Macmillan), 243-271. Reprinted from *Journal of Asian Studies*,
volumes 23 (1963) and 26 (1967).

_____. AFTER IMPERIALISM: THE SEARCH FOR A NEW ORDER IN
THE FAR EAST, 1921-1931. 1965: Harvard University Press; 1990:
Imprint Publications.

_____. THE ORIGINS OF THE SECOND WORLD WAR IN ASIA AND THE
PACIFIC. 1987: Longman.

Takashi Saitō. "Japan's Foreign Policy in the International Environment of the
Nineteen-Twenties," *Developing Economies* 5.4 (1967), 685-701.

Richard Dean Burns & Edward M. Bennett, eds. DIPLOMATS IN CRISIS:
UNITED STATES-CHINESE-JAPANESE RELATIONS, 1919-1941.
1974: ABC Clio.

Roger Daniels. THE POLITICS OF PREJUDICE: THE ANTI-JAPANESE
MOVEMENT IN CALIFORNIA AND THE STRUGGLE FOR
JAPANESE EXCLUSION. 1968: Atheneum.

Kiyoshi Ōshima. "The World Economic Crisis and Japan's Foreign Economic
Policy," *Developing Economies* 5.4 (1967), 628-647.

William Miles Fletcher. THE JAPANESE BUSINESS COMMUNITY AND NATIONAL TRADE POLICY, 1920-1942. 1989: University of North Carolina Press.

Kenneth L. Bauge. VOLUNTARY EXPORT RESTRICTION AS A FOREIGN COMMERCIAL POLICY WITH SPECIAL REFERENCE TO JAPANESE COTTON TEXTILES, 1930-1962. 1967: Garland.

James B. Crowley. JAPAN'S QUEST FOR AUTONOMY: NATIONAL SECURITY AND FOREIGN POLICY, 1930-1938. 1968: Princeton University Press.

_____. "A New Deal for Japan and Asia: One Road to Pearl Harbor," in his MODERN EAST ASIA: ESSAYS IN INTERPRETATION (1970: Harcourt Brace & World), 235-264.

Sadako N. Ogata. DEFIANCE IN MANCHURIA: THE MAKING OF JAPANESE FOREIGN POLICY, 1931-1932. 1964: University of California Press.

Mark R. Peattie. ISHIWARA KANJI AND JAPAN'S CONFRONTATION WITH THE WEST. 1975: Princeton University Press.

Christopher Thorne. THE LIMITS OF FOREIGN POLICY: THE WEST, THE LEAGUE, AND THE FAR EASTERN CRISIS OF 1931-1933. 1973: Capricorn.

Dorothy Borg. THE UNITED STATES AND THE FAR EASTERN CRISIS OF 1933-1938: FROM THE MANCHURIAN INCIDENT THROUGH THE INITIAL STAGE OF THE UNDECLARED SINO-JAPANESE WAR. 1964: Harvard University Press.

Paul Hibbert Clyde. JAPAN'S PACIFIC MANDATE. 1935: Macmillan; 1986: Inter Documentation Co. (microfiche).

Stephen E. Pelz. RACE TO PEARL HARBOR: THE FAILURE OF THE SECOND LONDON NAVAL CONFERENCE AND THE ONSET OF WORLD WAR II. 1974: Harvard University Press.

Saburō Ienaga. THE PACIFIC WAR, 1931-1945. Frank Baldwin, transl. 1978: Pantheon.

Dorothy Borg & Shumpei Okamoto, eds. PEARL HARBOR AS HISTORY: JAPANESE-AMERICAN RELATIONS, 1931-1941. 1973: Columbia University Press.

James W. Morley, ed. DETERRENT DIPLOMACY: JAPAN, GERMANY, AND THE USSR, 1935-1940. 1976: Columbia University Press.

Gerhard Krebs. "Japanese-Spanish Relations, 1936-1945," *Transactions, Asiatic Society of Japan*, 4th series, 3 (1988), 21-52.

Joshua Fogel. POLITICS AND SINOLOGY: THE CASE OF NAITŌ KŌNAN. 1984: Council on East Asian Studies, Harvard University.

_____. THE CULTURAL DIMENSION OF SINO-JAPANESE RELATIONS: ESSAYS ON THE INTERACTIONS BETWEEN CHINA AND JAPAN IN THE NINETEENTH AND TWENTIETH CENTURIES. 1994: M. E. Sharpe.

Peter Duus, Ramon H. Myers, & Mark R. Peattie, eds. THE JAPANESE INFORMAL EMPIRE IN CHINA, 1895-1937. 1989: Princeton University Press.

John H. Boyle. CHINA AND JAPAN AT WAR, 1937-1945: THE POLITICS OF COLLABORATION. 1972: Stanford University Press.

Youli Sun. CHINA AND THE ORIGINS OF THE PACIFIC WAR, 1931-1941. 1993: St. Martin's.

James C. Hsiung & Susan I. Levine, eds. CHINA'S BITTER VICTORY: THE WAR WITH JAPAN, 1937-1945. 1992: M. E. Sharpe.

Chang-tai Hung. WAR AND POPULAR CULTURE: RESISTANCE IN MODERN CHINA, 1937-1945. 1994: University of California Press.

Robert J. C. Butow. TŌJŌ AND THE COMING OF THE WAR. 1961: Stanford University Press.

James W. Morley, ed. THE FATEFUL CHOICE: JAPAN'S ADVANCE INTO SOUTHEAST ASIA, 1939-1941. 1980: Columbia University Press.

Paul W. Schroeder. THE AXIS ALLIANCE AND JAPANESE-AMERICAN RELATIONS, 1941. 1958: Cornell University Press.

Nobutake Ike, transl. & ed. JAPAN'S DECISION FOR WAR: RECORDS OF THE 1941 POLICY CONFERENCES. 1967: Stanford University Press.

F. C. Jones. JAPAN'S NEW ORDER IN EAST ASIA: ITS RISE AND FALL, 1937-45. 1954: Oxford University Press.

Willard H. Elsbree. JAPAN'S ROLE IN SOUTHEAST ASIAN NATIONALIST MOVEMENTS, 1940-45. 1953: Harvard University Press.

Joyce C. Lebra. JAPANESE-TRAINED ARMIES IN SOUTHEAST ASIA: INDEPENDENCE AND VOLUNTEER FORCES IN WORLD WAR II. 1977: Columbia University Press.

_____, ed. JAPAN'S GREATER EAST ASIA CO-PROSPERITY SPHERE IN WORLD WAR II: SELECTED READINGS AND DOCUMENTS. 1975: Oxford University Press.

Alfred W. McCoy, ed. SOUTHEAST ASIA UNDER JAPANESE RULE. 1980: Yale University Southeast Asia Studies, Monograph Series 22.

E. Bruce Reynolds. THAILAND AND JAPAN'S SOUTHERN ADVANCE, 1940-1945. 1994: St. Martin's.

David Bergamini. JAPAN'S IMPERIAL CONSPIRACY. 1971: Morrow.

Charles D. Sheldon. "Japanese Agression and the Emperor, 1931-1941, from Contemporary Diaries," *Modern Asian Studies* 10.1 (1976), 1-40.

Herbert P. Bix. "The Shōwa Emperor's 'Monologue' and the Problem of War Responsibility," *Journal of Japanese Studies* 18.2 (1992), 295-363.

John Toland. THE RISING SUN: THE DECLINE AND FALL OF THE JAPANESE EMPIRE, 1936-1945. 1970: Random House.

John Costello. THE PACIFIC WAR, 1941-1945. 1981: Quill.

Ronald H. Spector. EAGLE AGAINST THE SUN: THE AMERICAN WAR WITH JAPAN. 1985: Free Press.

John W. Dower. EMPIRE AND AFTERMATH: YOSHIDA SHIGERU AND THE JAPANESE EXPERIENCE, 1878-1954. 1979: Council on East Asian Studies, Harvard University.

_____. WAR WITHOUT MERCY: RACE AND POWER IN THE PACIFIC WAR. 1986: Pantheon.

Christopher Thorne. ALLIES OF A KIND: THE UNITED STATES, BRITAIN, AND THE WAR AGAINST JAPAN, 1941-1945. 1979: Oxford University Press.

_____. THE ISSUE OF WAR: STATES, SOCIETIES, AND THE FAR
EASTERN CONFLICT OF 1941-1945. 1985: Hamilton.

Haruko Taya Cook & Theodore F. Cook, eds. JAPAN AT WAR: AN ORAL
HISTORY. 1992: The New Press.

MEIJI POLICY

Frances V. Moulder. JAPAN, CHINA AND THE MODERN WORLD
ECONOMY: TOWARD A REINTERPRETATION OF EAST ASIAN
DEVELOPMENT ca. 1600 TO ca. 1918. 1977: Cambridge University
Press.

W. G. Beasley. SELECT DOCUMENTS ON JAPANESE FOREIGN POLICY,
1853-1868. 1955: Oxford University Press.

Japan, Foreign Service. TREATIES AND CONVENTIONS BETWEEN THE
EMPIRE OF JAPAN AND OTHER POWERS TOGETHER WITH
UNIVERSAL CONVENTIONS, REGULATIONS AND COMMUNI-
CATIONS, SINCE MARCH 1854. Revised edition. 1884:
Kokubunsha; 1987: Inter Documentation Co. (microfiche).

G. B. Sansom. THE WESTERN WORLD AND JAPAN: A STUDY IN THE
INTERACTION OF EUROPEAN AND ASIATIC CULTURES. 1950:
Knopf.

Shigeki Tōyama. "Politics, Economics, and the International Environment in the
Meiji and Taishō Periods," *Developing Economies* 4.4 (1966), 419-446.

Marius B. Jansen. "Modernization and Foreign Policy in Meiji Japan," in Robert
E. Ward, ed. POLITICAL DEVELOPMENT IN MODERN JAPAN
(1968: Princeton University Press), 149-188.

_____. "The Ideological and Political Context of Meiji Expansionism" and
"Personalities and Precedents," chapters 1 and 2 in his THE JAPANESE
AND SUN YAT-SEN (1954: Harvard University Press), 13-58.

_____. "Japanese Imperialism: Late Meiji Perspectives," in Ramon H. Myers &
Mark Peattie, eds. THE JAPANESE COLONIAL EMPIRE, 1895-1945
(1984: Princeton University Press), 61-79.

Akira Iriye. "Japan's Drive to Great-Power Status," in Marius B. Jansen, ed. CAMBRIDGE HISTORY OF JAPAN, Volume 5: THE NINETEENTH CENTURY (1989: Cambridge University Press), 721-782.

Marlene Mayo, ed. THE EMERGENCE OF IMPERIAL JAPAN: SELF DEFENSE OR CALCULATED AGGRESSION? 1970: Heath.

_____. "Rationality in the Meiji Restoration: The Iwakura Mission," in Bernard S. Silberman & H. D. Harootunian, eds. MODERN JAPANESE LEADERSHIP: TRANSITION AND CHANGE (1966: University of Arizona Press), 323-370.

Hazel J. Jones. LIVE MACHINES: HIRED FOREIGNERS AND MEIJI JAPAN. 1980: University of British Columbia Press.

Neil Pedlar. THE IMPORTED PIONEERS: WESTERNERS WHO HELPED BUILD MODERN JAPAN. 1990: Japan Library Ltd.

F. C. Jones. EXTRATERRITORIALITY IN JAPAN AND THE DIPLOMATIC RELATIONS RESULTING IN ITS ABOLITION, 1853-1899. 1931: Yale University Press.

Jerry Dusenbury. "Revision of Unequal Treaties," KŌDANSHA ENCYCLO-PEDIA OF JAPAN 8: 148-149.

Louis Gabriel Perez. "Mutsu Munemitsu and the Revision of the 'Unequal Treaties'." 1986: Ph.D. dissertation in History, University of Michigan.

Zengo Ōhira. "Japan's Reception of the Law of Nations," _Annals of the Hitotsubashi Academy_ 4 (1953), 55-66.

Immanuel C. Y. Hsu. CHINA'S ENTRANCE INTO THE FAMILY OF NATIONS: THE DIPLOMATIC PHASE, 1858-1880. 1960: Harvard University Press. See 121-131 on Japan's use of the Chinese translation of Wheaton.

Shin'ya Murase. "The Most-Favored Nation Treatment in Japan's Treaty Practice During the Period 1854- 1905," _American Journal of International Law_ 70 (1976), 273-297.

James B. Crowley. "From Closed Door to Empire: The Foundation of the Meiji Military Establishment," in Silberman & Harootunian, MODERN JAPANESE LEADERSHIP (1966: University of Arizona Press), 261-285.

_____. "Japan's Military Foreign Policies," in J. W. Morley, ed. JAPAN'S FOREIGN POLICY (1974: Princeton University Press), 3-117.

E. Herbert Norman. SOLDIER AND PEASANT IN JAPAN: THE ORIGINS OF CONSCRIPTION. 1943: Institute of Pacific Relations.

Ernst L. Presseisen. BEFORE AGGRESSION: EUROPEANS PREPARE THE JAPANESE ARMY. 1965: University of Arizona Press.

Shingo Fukushima. "The Building of a National Army," *Developing Economies* 3.4 (1965), 516-539.

Hyman Kublin. "The 'Modern' Army of Early Meiji Japan," *Far Eastern Quarterly* 9.1 (1949), 20-41.

Roger F. Hackett. YAMAGATA ARITOMO IN THE RISE OF MODERN JAPAN, 1838-1922. 1971: Harvard University Press.

Alfred Stead, ed. JAPAN BY THE JAPANESE. 2 volumes. 1905: Heinemann. Includes an essay by Yamagata on the Army.

Shigenobu Ōkuma, ed. FIFTY YEARS OF THE NEW JAPAN. 2 volumes. 1909: Dutton.

Hilary Conroy. THE JAPANESE SEIZURE OF KOREA, 1868-1910. 1960: University of Pennsylvania Press.

_____. "Government vs. Patriot: The Background of Japan's Asiatic Expansion," *Pacific Historical Review* 20.1 (1951), 31-42.

Donald Calman. THE NATURE AND ORGINS OF JAPANESE IMPERIAL-ISM: A REINTERPRETATION OF THE GREAT CRISIS OF 1873. 1992: Routledge.

Key-Hiuk Kim. THE LAST PHASE OF THE EAST ASIAN WORLD ORDER: KOREA, JAPAN, AND THE CHINESE EMPIRE, 1860-1882. 1979: University of California Press.

George A. Lensen. BALANCE OF INTRIGUE: INTERNATIONAL RIVALRY IN KOREA AND MANCHURIA, 1884-1899. 1982: University of Hawaii Press.

Peter Duus. "Economic Dimensions of Meiji Imperialism: The Case of Korea, 1895-1910," in Myers & Peattie, THE JAPANESE COLONIAL EMPIRE, 1895-1945 (1984: Princeton University Press), 128-171.

William L. Langer. THE DIPLOMACY OF IMPERIALISM, 1890-1902. 2nd edition. 1951: Knopf.

Kimitada Miwa. "Fukuzawa Yukichi's 'Departure from Asia': A Prelude to the Sino-Japanese War," in Edmund R. Skrzypczak, ed. JAPAN'S MODERN CENTURY (1968: Sophia University & Tuttle), 1-26.

E. Herbert Norman. "The Gen'yōsha: A Study in the Origins of Japanese Imperialism," *Pacific Affairs* 17 (1944), 261-284.

Munemitsu Mutsu. KENKENROKU: A DIPLOMATIC RECORD OF THE SINO-JAPANESE WAR, 1894-1895. Gordon M. Berger, ed. & transl. 1984: Princeton University Press.

Jeffrey Dorwart. THE PIGTAIL WAR: AMERICAN INVOLVEMENT IN THE SINO-JAPANESE WAR, 1894-1895. 1975: University of Massachusetts Press.

Frank W. Ikle. "The Triple Intervention: Japan's Lesson in the Diplomacy of Imperialism," *Monumenta Nipponica* 22.1-2 (1967), 122-130.

Akira Iriye. PACIFIC ESTRANGEMENT: JAPANESE AND AMERICAN EXPANSION, 1879-1911. 1972: Harvard University Press.

Ian Nish. THE ANGLO-JAPANESE ALLIANCE: THE DIPLOMACY OF TWO ISLAND EMPIRES, 1894-1907. 2nd edition. 1985: Athlone.

Hilary Conroy. THE JAPANESE FRONTIER IN HAWAII, 1868-1898. 1953: University of California Press.

T. A. Bailey. "Japan's Protest Against the Annexation of Hawaii," *Journal of Modern History* 3.1 (1931), 46-61.

Josefa M. Saniel. JAPAN AND THE PHILIPPINES, 1868-1898. 1963: University of the Philippines Press.

E. Thadeus Flood. "The Shishi Interlude in Old Siam: An Aspect of the Meiji Impact in Old Siam," in David Wurfel, ed. MEIJI JAPAN'S CENTENNIAL: ASPECTS OF POLITICAL THOUGHT AND ACTION (1971: University of Kansas Press), 78-105.

Paul A. Varg. "The Foreign Policy of Japan and the Boxer Revolt," *Pacific Historical Review* 14.3 (1946), 279-285.

Ian Nish. "Japan's Indecision During the Boxer Disturbances," *Journal of Asian Studies* 20.4 (1961), 449-462.

_____. THE ORIGINS OF THE RUSSO-JAPANESE WAR. 1985: Longman.

Shumpei Okamoto. THE JAPANESE OLIGARCHY AND THE RUSSO-JAPANESE WAR. 1970: Columbia University Press.

Robert B. Valliant. "The Selling of Japan: Japanese Manipulation of Western Opinion, 1900-05," *Monumenta Nipponica* 29.4 (1974), 415-438.

Denis & Peggy Warner. THE TIDE AT SUNRISE: A HISTORY OF THE RUSSO-JAPANESE WAR 1904-1905. 1974: Charterhouse.

Richard Connaughton. THE WAR OF THE RISING SUN AND TUMBLING BEAR: A MILITARY HISTORY OF THE RUSSO-JAPANESE WAR OF 1904-1905. 1991: Routledge.

Chiharu Inaba. "Polish-Japanese Military Collaboration during the Russo-Japanese War," *Japan Forum* 4.2 (1992), 229-246.

Georges Blond. ADMIRAL TŌGŌ. Edward Hyams, transl. 1960: Macmillan.

Edwin A. Falk. TŌGŌ AND THE RISE OF JAPANESE SEA POWER. 1936: Green.

Jean-Pierre Lehmann. THE IMAGE OF JAPAN: A CHANGING SOCIETY, 1850-1905. 1978: Allen & Unwin.

Setsuko Ono. "A Western Image of Japan: What Did the West See Through The Eyes of Loti and Hearn?" 1972: Ph.D. dissertation in Political Science, University of Geneva.

WORLD WAR ONE & THE INTERWAR CRISIS

Richard Dean Burns & Edward M. Bennett, eds. DIPLOMATS IN CRISIS: UNITED STATES-CHINESE-JAPANESE RELATIONS, 1919-1941. 1974: ABC Clio.

Alvin D. Coox & Hilary Conroy, eds. CHINA AND JAPAN: A SEARCH FOR BALANCE SINCE WORLD WAR I. 1978: ABC Clio.

Gordon A. Craig & Felix Greene, eds. THE DIPLOMATS, 1919-1939. 1953: Princeton University Press.

Edward Mallett Carr. THE TWENTY YEARS' CRISIS, 1919-1939: AN INTRODUCTION TO THE STUDY OF INTERNATIONAL RELATIONS. 1939; reprinted 1964: Harper Torchbooks.

Japan & the Great War

Paul H. Clyde & Burton F. Beers. THE FAR EAST: A HISTORY OF WESTERN IMPACTS AND EASTERN RESPONSES, 1830-1975. 6th edition. 1975; reprinted 1991: Waveland Press. Chapters 21 and 22 cover World War One and its legacy in Asia.

Frederick F. Czupryna. "World War I," KŌDANSHA ENCYCLOPEDIA OF JAPAN 8: 270-271.

Kimitada Miwa. "Japanese Opinions on Woodrow Wilson in War and Peace," *Monumenta Nipponica* 22.3-4 (1967), 368-389.

Noriko Kawamura. "Odd Associates in World War I: Japanese-American Relations, 1914-1918." 1989: Ph.D. dissertation in History, University of Washington.

Charles N. Spinks. "Japan's Entrance into the World War," *Pacific Historical Review* 5.4 (1936), 297-311.

V. H. Rothwell. "The British Government and Japanese Military Assistance, 1914-1918," *History* 56 (1971), 35-45.

Carnegie Endowment for International Peace, Division of Intercourse and Education. THE IMPERIAL JAPANESE MISSION, 1917: A RECORD OF THE RECEPTION THROUGHOUT THE UNITED STATES OF THE SPECIAL MISSION HEADED BY VISCOUNT ISHII, TOGETHER WITH THE EXCHANGE OF NOTES EMBODY- ING THE ROOT-TAKAHIRA UNDERSTANDING OF 1908 AND THE LANSING-ISHII AGREEMENT OF 1917. 1918: Carnegie Endowment for International Peace.

[For materials concerning the 21 Demands and the Paris Peace Conference, see entries under "China Relations to 1931" on page 278.]

Steve Rabson. "Shimazaki Tōson on War," *Monumenta Nipponica* 46.4 (1991), 453-481.

The Siberian Intervention

James W. Morley. THE JAPANESE THRUST INTO SIBERIA, 1918. 1957: Columbia University Press.

Chihiro Hosoya. "Origin of the Siberian Intervention, 1917-1918," *Annals of the Hitotsubashi Academy* 9.1 (1958), 91-108.

_____. "Japanese Documents on the Siberian Intervention," *Hitotsubashi Journal of Law and Politics* 1 (1960), 30-53.

The Special Delegation of the Far Eastern Republic to the United States of America. JAPANESE INTERVENTION IN THE RUSSIAN FAR EAST. 1922: The Special Delegation of the Far Eastern Republic to the United States of America.

Henry Baerlein. THE MARCH OF THE SEVENTY THOUSAND. 1926: Parsons.

William S. Graves. AMERICA'S SIBERIAN ADVENTURE, 1918-1920. 1931: Cape & Smith.

G. Stewart. THE WHITE ARMIES OF RUSSIA: A CHRONICLE OF COUNTER-REVOLUTION AND ALLIED INTERVENTION. 1933: Macmillan.

John A. White. THE SIBERIAN INTERVENTION. 1950: Princeton University Press.

Betty M. Unterberger. AMERICA'S SIBERIAN EXPEDITION, 1918-1920. 1956: Duke University Press.

George Kennan. SOVIET-AMERICAN RELATIONS, 1917-1920: THE DECISION TO INTERVENE. 1958: Princeton University Press.

Richard R. Ullman. ANGLO-SOVIET RELATIONS 1917-1921: INTERVENTION AND THE WAR. 1961: Princeton University Press.

Christopher Lasch. "American Intervention in Siberia: A Reinterpretation," *Political Science Quarterly* 77 (1962), 205-223.

William Appleman Williams. "American Intervention in Russia: 1917-20,"
    in David Horowitz, ed. CONTAINMENT AND REVOLUTION
    (1967: Beacon), 26-75.

The Washington Conference & Washington System

Takashi Saitō. "Japan's Foreign Policy in the International Environment of the
    Nineteen-Twenties," *Developing Economies* 5.4 (1967), 685-701.

Roger Dingman. "Washington Conference" and "Washington Naval Treaty of
    1922," KŌDANSHA ENCYCLOPEDIA OF JAPAN 8: 234-235.

_____. POWER IN THE PACIFIC: THE ORIGINS OF NAVAL ARMS
    LIMITATION, 1914-1922. 1976: University of Chicago Press.

Sadao Asada. "Japan's 'Special Interests' and the Washington Conference,
    1921-1922," *American Historical Review* 67.1 (1961), 62-70.

William Appleman Williams. "China and Japan: A Challenge and a Choice of
    the Nineteen Twenties," *Pacific Historical Review* 26.3 (1957),
    259-279.

Yamato Ichihashi. THE WASHINGTON CONFERENCE AND AFTER.
    1928: Stanford University Press.

J. Chal Vinson. "The Annulment of the Lansing-Ishii Agreement," *Pacific
    Historical Review* 27.1 (1958), 57-69.

Harold & Margaret Sprout. TOWARD A NEW ORDER OF SEA POWER:
    AMERICAN NAVAL POLICY AND THE WORLD SCENE, 1918-
    1922. 1946: Princeton University Press.

Akira Iriye. AFTER IMPERIALISM: THE SEARCH FOR A NEW ORDER IN
    THE FAR EAST, 1921-1931. 1965: Harvard University Press; 1990:
    Imprint Publications.

_____. "The Failure of Economic Expansion: 1918-1931," in B. Silberman &
    H. Harootunian, eds. JAPAN IN CRISIS (1974: Princeton University
    Press), 237-269.

_____. "Japanese Imperialism and Aggression: Reconsiderations" and "Japan's
    Foreign Policies Between World Wars—Sources and Interpretations,"
    in Esmonde M. Robertson, ed. THE ORIGINS OF THE SECOND
    WORLD WAR: HISTORICAL INTERPRETATIONS (1971:
    Macmillan), 243-271.

_____. THE ORIGINS OF THE SECOND WORLD WAR IN ASIA AND THE PACIFIC. 1987: Longman.

Christopher George Longden Hall. "Britain, America, and the Search for Comprehensive Naval Limitation, 1927-1936." 1982: Ph.D. dissertation in Social Studies, Oxford University.

Roger Daniels. THE POLITICS OF PREJUDICE: THE ANTI-JAPANESE MOVEMENT IN CALIFORNIA AND THE STRUGGLE FOR JAPANESE EXCLUSION. 1962: University of California Press.

TAIWAN (FORMOSA)

Ramon H. Myers & Mark R. Peattie, eds. THE JAPANESE COLONIAL EMPIRE, 1895-1945. 1984: Princeton University Press. See especially essays by Chen on police and law (213-274), Tsurumi on education (275-311), Ho on colonial development (347-398), Mizoguchi and Yamamoto on capital development (399-419), and Myers and Yamada on agricultural development (420-452).

E. Patricia Tsurumi. JAPANESE COLONIAL EDUCATION IN TAIWAN, 1895-1945. 1977: Harvard University Press.

_____. "Education and Assimilation in Taiwan under Japanese Rule, 1895-1945," *Modern Asian Studies* 13.4 (1979), 617-641.

_____. "Mental Captivity and Resistance: Lessons from Taiwanese Anti-Colonialism," *Bulletin of Concerned Asian Scholars* 12.2 (1980), 2-13.

Harry J. Lamley. "Taiwan," KŌDANSHA ENCYCLOPEDIA OF JAPAN 7: 306-309.

George H. Kerr. FORMOSA: LICENSED REVOLUTION AND THE HOME RULE MOVEMENT, 1895-1945. 1974: University of Hawaii Press.

Andrew J. Grajdanzev. FORMOSA TODAY. 1942: Institute of Pacific Relations.

Masakazu Iwata. ŌKUBO TOSHIMICHI, THE BISMARK OF JAPAN (1964: University of California Press), 184-225 on the 1874 Formosan expedition.

Leonard Gordon. "Japan's Interest in Taiwan, 1872-1895," *Orient West* 9.1 (1964), 49-59.

_____. "Japan's Abortive Colonial Venture in Taiwan, 1874," *Journal of Modern History* 37.2 (1965), 171-185.

F. Q. Quo. "British Diplomacy and the Cession of Formosa, 1894-95," *Modern Asian Studies* 2.2 (1968), 141-154.

Chang Han-yu & Ramon Myers. "Japanese Colonial Development Policy in Taiwan, 1895-1906: A Case of Bureaucratic Entrepreneurship," *Journal of Asian Studies* 22.4 (1963), 433-449.

Ramon Myers & Adrienne Ching. "Agricultural Development in Taiwan Under Japanese Colonial Rule," *Journal of Asian Studies* 23.4 (1964), 555-570.

Edward I-te Chen. "Japanese Colonialism in Korea and Formosa: A Comparison of the Systems of Political Control," *Harvard Journal of Asiatic Studies* 30 (1970), 126-158.

Ching-chih Chen. "Impact of Japanese Colonial Rule on Taiwanese Elites," *Journal of Asian History* 22.1 (1988), 25-51.

Yosaburō Takekoshi. JAPANESE RULE IN FORMOSA. 1907: Longmans, Green.

KOREA

"Korea and Japan," KŌDANSHA ENCYCLOPEDIA OF JAPAN 4: 276-287. Especially essays by Benjamin Hazard (relations to 1875), Young Ick Lew (1876-1910), and Setsuko Miyata (1910-1945).

Donald Calman. THE NATURE AND ORIGINS OF JAPANESE IMPERIAL-ISM: A REINTERPRETATION OF THE GREAT CRISIS OF 1873. 1992: Routledge.

George DeVos & Changsoo Lee. "The Colonial Experience, 1910-1945," in DeVos & Lee, KOREANS IN JAPAN: ETHNIC CONFLICT AND ACCOMODATION (1980: University of California Press), 31-57.

Ramon H. Myers & Mark R. Peattie, eds. THE JAPANESE COLONIAL
    EMPIRE, 1895-1945. 1984: Princeton University Press. See especially
    essays by Duus on Meiji economic imperatives (128-171), Tsurumi on
    education (275-311), Robinson on publication curbs (312-343), Ho on
    colonial development (347-398), Mizoguchi & Yamamoto on capital
    formation (399-419), and Cumings on the colonial legacy (478-496).

Hilary Conroy. THE JAPANESE SEIZURE OF KOREA, 1868-1910.
    1960: University of Pennsylvania Press.

_____. "Chōsen Mondai: The Korean Problem in Meiji Japan," *Proceedings of
    the American Philosophical Association* 100 (1956), 443-454.

George Totten et al. "Japanese Imperialism & Aggression: Reconsiderations,"
    Journal of Asian Studies 22.4 (1963), 469-473. Concerning controversy
    provoked by Conroy's SEIZURE (above).

C. I. Eugene Kim & Han-kyo Kim. KOREA AND THE POLITICS OF
    IMPERIALISM, 1876-1910. 1967: University of California Press.

Vipan Chandra. IMPERIALISM, RESISTANCE, AND REFORM IN LATE
    NINETEENTH-CENTURY KOREA: ENLIGHTENMENT AND THE
    INDEPENDENCE CLUB. 1988: Institute of East Asian Studies,
    Center for Korean Studies, University of California.

Chin-sok Chong. THE KOREAN PROBLEM IN ANGLO-JAPANESE
    RELATIONS, 1904-1910: ERNEST THOMAS BETHELL AND HIS
    NEWSPAPERS: THE DAIHAN MAEIL SINBO AND THE KOREA
    DAILY NEWS. 1987: NANAM Publications.

Fred Harvey Harrington. GOD, MAMMON AND THE JAPANESE:
    DR. HORACE N. ALLEN AND K0REAN-AMERICAN RELATIONS,
    1884-1905. 1944: University of Wisconsin Press.

Woonsang Choi. THE FALL OF THE HERMIT KINGDOM. 1967: Oceana.

Stewart Lone. "The Japanese Annexation of Korea 1910: The Failure of East
    Asian Co-Prosperity," *Modern Asian Studies* 25.1 (1991), 143-173.

David Brudnoy. "Japan's Experiment in Korea," *Monumenta Nipponica* 25.1-2
    (1970), 155-195.

Lawrence H. Battistini. "The Korean Problem in the Nineteenth Century,"
    Monumenta Nipponica 8.1-2 (1952), 47-66.

Andrew C. Nahm, ed. KOREA UNDER JAPANESE COLONIAL RULE: STUDIES OF THE POLICY AND TECHNIQUES OF JAPANESE COLONIALISM. 1973: Center for Korean Studies, Western Michigan University.

_____. JAPANESE PENETRATION OF KOREA. 1959: Center for Korean Studies, Western Michigan University.

Edwin H. Gragert. LANDOWNERSHIP UNDER COLONIAL RULE: KOREA'S JAPAN EXPERIENCE, 1900-1935. 1994: University of Hawaii Press.

Michael Weiner. RACE AND MIGRATION IN IMPERIAL JAPAN: THE LIMITS OF ASSIMILATION. 1994: Routledge. Focuses on colonial rule in Korea and Japanese treatment of Korean labor.

C. I. Eugene Kim & Doretha E. Mortimore, eds. KOREA'S RESPONSE TO JAPAN: THE COLONIAL PERIOD, 1910-1945. 1974: Center for Korean Studies, Western Michigan University.

Michael Edson Washington. CULTURAL NATIONALISM IN COLONIAL KOREA, 1920-1925. 1988: University of Washington Press.

Edward I-te Chen. "Japanese Colonialism in Korea and Formosa: A Comparison of Systems of Political Control," *Harvard Journal of Asiatic Studies* 30 (1970), 126-158.

Mitsuhiko Kimura. "Financial Aspects of Korea's Economic Growth under Japanese Rule," *Modern Asian Studies* 20.4 (1986), 793-820.

_____. "Standards of Living in Colonial Korea: Did the Masses Become Worse Off or Better Off Under Japanese Rule," *Journal of Economic History* 53.3 (1993), 629-652.

Dennis McNamara. "The Keishō and the Korean Business Elite," *Journal of Asian Studies* 48.2 (1989), 310-323. On the Seoul Chamber of Commerce and Industry in colonial Korea.

Andrew Grajdanzev. MODERN KOREA. 1944: John Day.

Takashi Hatada. A HISTORY OF KOREA. 1969: ABC Clio.

Woo-Keun Han. THE HISTORY OF KOREA. 1971: University of Hawaii Press.

Ki-Baik Lee. A NEW HISTORY OF KOREA. 1983: Harvard University Press.

Stewart Lone & Gavan McCormack. KOREA SINCE 1850. 1993: Longman Cheshire.

Chong-sik Lee. THE POLITICS OF KOREAN NATIONALISM. 1965: University of California Press.

G. Trumbull Ladd. IN KOREA WITH MARQUIS ITŌ. 1908: Charles Scribner's sons.

_____. "The Annexation of Korea: An Essay in 'Benevolent Assimilation'," Yale Review 1.4 (1912), 639-656.

Japan Chronicle. THE KOREAN CONSPIRACY TRIAL: FULL REPORT OF THE PROCEEDINGS IN APPEAL BY THE SPECIAL CORRESPONDENT OF THE "JAPAN CHRONICLE." 1913: Japan Chronicle.

_____. THE INDEPENDENCE MOVEMENT IN KOREA: A RECORD OF SOME OF THE EVENTS OF THE SPRING OF 1919: Japan Chronicle.

Dae-yeol Ku. KOREA UNDER COLONIALISM: THE MARCH FIRST MOVEMENT AND ANGLO-JAPANESE RELATIONS. 1985: Royal Asiatic Society, Seoul.

Kyu Ho Youm. "Japanese Press Policy in Colonial Korea," Journal of Asian History 26.2 (1992), 140-159.

Edwin W. Pauley. REPORT ON JAPANESE ASSETS IN SOVIET-OCCUPIED KOREA TO THE PRESIDENT OF THE UNITED STATES, JUNE 1946. 1946: Government Publications Office.

Shōbei Shiota. "A 'Ravaged' People: The Koreans in World War II," Japan Interpreter 7.1 (1971), 43-53.

Wayne C. McWilliams. HOMEWARD BOUND, REPATRIATION OF JAPANESE FROM KOREA AFTER WORLD WAR II. 1988: Asian Research Service.

Sung-hwa Cheong. THE POLITICS OF ANTI-JAPANESE SENTIMENT IN KOREA: JAPANESE-SOUTH KOREAN RELATIONS UNDER AMERICAN OCCUPATION, 1945-1952. 1991: Greenwood Press.

CHINA RELATIONS TO 1931

Peter Duus, Ramon H. Myers, & Mark R. Peattie, eds. THE JAPANESE
INFORMAL EMPIRE IN CHINA, 1895-1937. 1989: Princeton
University Press.

Joshua Fogel. THE CULTURAL DIMENSION OF SINO-JAPANESE
RELATIONS: ESSAYS ON THE INTERACTIONS BETWEEN
CHINA AND JAPAN IN THE NINETEENTH AND TWENTIETH
CENTURIES. 1994: M. E. Sharpe.

Martin Collcutt. "China and Japan to 1911," KŌDANSHA ENCYCLOPEDIA
OF JAPAN 1: 280-287.

Katsumi Usui. "China and Japan after 1912," KŌDANSHA ENCYCLOPEDIA
OF JAPAN 1: 287-291.

Shinkichi Etō. "Japan's Policies Toward China," in J. W. Morley, ed. JAPAN'S
FOREIGN POLICY (1974: Columbia University Press), 236-264.

Marius B. Jansen. "Japanese Views of China During the Meiji Period," in Albert
Feuerwerker, et al. APPROACHES TO MODERN CHINESE
HISTORY (1967: University of California Press), 163-189.

_____. THE JAPANESE AND SUN YAT-SEN. 1954: Harvard University
Press.

_____. JAPAN AND CHINA: FROM WAR TO PEACE, 1894-1972. 1975:
Rand McNally.

Joseph D. Lowe. SINO-JAPANESE RELATIONS SINCE 1894. 1992: Lowe.

Tam Yue-him, ed. HONG KONG AND JAPAN: GROWING CULTURAL
AND ECONOMIC INTERACTIONS, 1845-1987. 1988: Japan Society
of Hong Kong.

Akira Iriye, ed. THE CHINESE AND THE JAPANESE: ESSAYS IN POLITI-
CAL AND CULTURAL INTERACTIONS. 1980: Princeton
University Press.

_____. CHINA AND JAPAN IN THE GLOBAL SETTING. 1992: Harvard
University Press.

_____. "The Ideology of Japanese Imperialism: Imperial Japan and China," in Grant Goodman, ed. IMPERIAL JAPAN AND ASIA: A REASSESSMENT (1967: Occasional Papers of the East Asia Institute, Columbia University), 32-45.

Stefan Tanaka. JAPAN'S ORIENT: RENDERING PASTS INTO HISTORY. 1993: University of California Press. On the scholarly construction of "Orient" (*Tōyō*) and "China" (*Shina*) in modern Japan, particularly by Shiratori Kurakichi. Reveiwed by Kyu Hyun Kim in *Journal of Asian Studies* 53.1 (1994), 233-234; and by Takashi Fujitani in *Journal of Japanese Studies* 20.2 (1994), 547-551.

Immanuel C. Y. Hsu. THE RISE OF MODERN CHINA. 1970: Oxford University Press.

Joshua A. Fogel. "Japanese Literary Travelers in Prewar China," *Harvard Journal of Asiatic Studies* 49.2 (1989), 575-602.

Hyman Kublin. "The Attitude of China During the Liu-Ch'iu Controversy, 1871-1881," *Pacific Historical Review* 18.2 (1949), 213-231.

T. F. Tsiang. "Sino-Japanese Diplomatic Relations, 1870-1894," *Chinese Social and Political Science Review* 14 (1933), 3-107.

Payson J. Treat. "The Cause of the Sino-Japanese War, 1894," *Pacific Historical Review* 8.2 (1939), 149-158.

Robert T. Pollard. "Dynamics of Japanese Imperialism," *Pacific Historical Review* 8.1 (1939), 5-35.

Akira Iriye. "Sino-Japanese War of 1894-1895," KŌDANSHA ENCYCLOPEDIA OF JAPAN 7: 197-198.

Munemitsu Mutsu. KENKENROKU: A DIPLOMATIC RECORD OF THE SINO-JAPANESE WAR, 1894-1895. Gordon M. Berger, transl. 1982: Princeton University Press.

Donald Keene. "The Sino-Japanese War of 1894-95 and Japanese Culture," in his LANDSCAPES AND PORTRAITS: APPRECIATIONS OF JAPANESE CULTURE (1971: Kōdansha International), 259-299.

Steve Rabson. "Shimazaki Tōson on War," *Monumenta Nipponica* 46.4 (1991), 453-481.

Shumpei Okamoto. IMPRESSIONS OF THE FRONT: WOODCUTS OF THE SINO-JAPANESE WAR. 1982: Philadelphia Museum of Art.

Yoshiaki Yamada & F. Warrington Eastlake. HEROIC JAPAN: A HISTORY OF THE WAR BETWEEN CHINA AND JAPAN. 1897; reprinted 1979: University Publications of America.

Jeffrey Dorwart. THE PIGTAIL WAR: AMERICAN INVOLVEMENT IN THE SINO-JAPANESE WAR, 1894-95. 1975: University of Massachusetts Press.

Keiichi Asada & Giichi Ono. EXPENDITURES OF THE SINO-JAPANESE WAR. 1922: Oxford University Press.

Chester C. Tan. THE BOXER CATASTROPHE. 1955: Columbia University Press.

George Alexander Lensen. BALANCE OF INTRIGUE: INTERNATIONAL RIVALRY IN KOREA AND MANCHURIA, 1884-1899. 1982: University of Hawaii Press.

Michael M. Hunt. FRONTIER DEFENSE AND THE OPEN DOOR: MANCHURIA IN CHINESE-AMERICAN RELATIONS, 1895-1911. 1973: Yale University Press.

_____. THE MAKING OF A SPECIAL RELATIONSHIP: THE UNITED STATES AND CHINA TO 1914. 1983: Columbia University Press.

Douglas R. Reynolds. CHINA, 1898-1912: THE XINZHENG REVOLUTION AND JAPAN. 1993: Council on East Asian Studies, Harvard University Press.

_____. "A Golden Decade Forgotten: Japan-China Relations, 1898-1907," *Transactions, Asiatic Society of Japan*, 4th series, 2 (1987), 93-153.

Paula Harrell. SOWING THE SEEDS OF CHANGE: CHINESE STUDENTS, JAPANESE TEACHERS, 1895-1905. 1992: Stanford University Press. Concerns Chinese students in Japan in the decade after the Sino-Japanese War.

Masaru Ikei. "Japan's Response to the Chinese Revolution of 1911," *Journal of Asian Studies* 25.2 (1966), 213-227.

Ernest P. Young. THE PRESIDENCY OF YUAN SHIH-K'AI. 1976: University of Michigan Press.

_____. "Twenty-One Demands," KŌDANSHA ENCYCLOPEDIA OF JAPAN 8: 120-121.

Kwan-hwa Yim. "Yuan Shih-kai and the Japanese," *Journal of Asian Studies* 24.1 (1964), 63-73.

Paul S. Dull. "Count Katō Kōmei and the Twenty-One Demands," *Pacific Historical Review* 19.2 (1950), 151-161.

Marius B. Jansen. "Yawata, Hanyehping, and the Twenty-One Demands," *Pacific Historical Review* 23.1 (1954), 31-48.

Arthur S. Link. WILSON: THE STRUGGLE FOR NEUTRALITY 1914-1915. 1960: Princeton University Press.

Harley F. MacNair & Donald F. Lach. MODERN FAR EASTERN INTERNATIONAL RELATIONS. 2nd edition. 1955: Van Nostrand.

Thomas E. La Fargue. CHINA AND THE WORLD WAR. 1937: Stanford University Press.

Madeline Chi. CHINA DIPLOMACY 1914-1918. 1970: Council on East Asian Studies, Harvard University.

Frank C. Langdon. "Japan's Failure to Establish Friendly Relations with China in 1917-1918," *Pacific Historical Review* 26.3 (1957), 245-258.

Westel Woodbury Willoughby. CHINA AT THE CONFERENCE: A REPORT. 1922: Johns Hopkins.

Russell H. Fifield. "Japanese Policy Toward the Shantung Question at the Paris Peace Conference," *Journal of Modern History* 23.3 (1951), 265-272.

_____. WOODROW WILSON AND THE FAR EAST: THE DIPLOMACY OF THE SHANTUNG QUESTION. 1952: Crowell.

_____. "Secretary Hughes and the Shantung Question," *Pacific Historical Review* 23.4 (1954), 373-385.

F. S. Cocks. THE SECRET TREATIES AND UNDERSTANDINGS. 2nd edition. 1931: Union of Democratic Control.

Alvin D. Coox & Hilary Conroy, eds. CHINA AND JAPAN: A SEARCH FOR BALANCE SINCE WORLD WAR I. 1978: ABC Clio. Includes essays concerning the Shantung intervention, Paris peace conference, bicultural relations, anti-Japanese activities in Manchuria, the war of 1937-1945, and post-1945 Sino-Japanese relations.

Richard Dean Burns & Edward M. Bennett, eds. DIPLOMATS IN CRISIS: UNITED STATES-CHINESE-JAPANESE RELATIONS, 1919-1941. 1974: ABC Clio.

Akira Iriye. AFTER IMPERIALISM: THE SEARCH FOR A NEW ORDER IN THE FAR EAST, 1921-1931. 1965: Harvard University Press; 1990: Imprint Publications.

Nobuya Bamba. JAPANESE DIPLOMACY IN A DILEMMA: NEW LIGHT ON JAPAN'S CHINA POLICY, 1924-1929. 1973: University of British Columbia Press.

William F. Morton. TANAKA GIICHI AND JAPAN'S CHINA POLICY. 1980: St. Martin's.

Gavan McCormack. CHANG TSO-LIN IN NORTHEAST CHINA, 1911-1928: CHINA, JAPAN, AND THE MANCHURIAN IDEA. 1977: University of California Press.

John W. Young. "The Hara Cabinet and Chang Tso-lin, 1920-1," *Monumenta Nipponica* 27.2 (1972), 125-142.

Paul S. Dull. "The Assassination of Chang Tso-lin," *Far Eastern Quarterly* 11.4 (1952), 453-463.

Akira Iriye. "Chang Hsueh-liang and the Japanese," *Journal of Asian Studies* 20.1 (1960), 33-43

Paul H. Clyde. INTERNATIONAL RIVALRIES IN MANCHURIA, 1689-1922. 1928: Ohio State University Press.

Carl Walter Young. INTERNATIONAL RELATIONS OF MANCHURIA. 1929: University of Chicago Press.

Sadako N. Ogata. "Expansion and Protection of Japan's Interests in Manchuria," in her DEFIANCE IN MANCHURIA (1964: University of California Press), 3-19, covering the period prior to 1931.

Herbert P. Bix. "Japanese Imperialism and the Manchurian Economy, 1900-31,"
　　The China Quarterly 51 (1972), 425-443.

Ralph William Huenemann. THE DRAGON AND THE IRON HORSE:
　　THE ECONOMICS OF RAILROADS IN CHINA, 1876-1937. 1983:
　　Harvard University Press.

Takeo Itō. LIFE ALONG THE SOUTH MANCHURIAN RAILWAY:
　　THE MEMOIRS OF ITŌ TAKEO. Transl. Joshua A. Fogel. 1989:
　　M. E. Sharpe.

RUSSIA & THE U.S.S.R

George Alexander Lensen. "Russia and Japan," KŌDANSHA ENCYCLOPEDIA
　　OF JAPAN 6: 340-344.

Chihiro Hosoya. "Japan's Policies Toward Russia," in J. W. Morley, ed.
　　JAPAN'S FOREIGN POLICY (1974: Columbia University Press),
　　340-406.

Donald W. Treadgold. "Russia and the Far East," in Ivo J. Lederer, ed.
　　RUSSIAN FOREIGN POLICY: ESSAYS IN HISTORICAL
　　PERSPECTIVE (1966: Yale University Press), 531-574.

George Alexander Lensen. THE RUSSIAN PUSH TOWARD JAPAN:
　　RUSSO-JAPANESE RELATIONS, 1697-1875. 1959: Princeton
　　University Press.

_____. KOREA AND MANCHURIA BETWEEN RUSSIA AND JAPAN,
　　1895-1904. 1966: Diplomatic Press. A reprint, with introduction,
　　of the diary of Sir Ernest Satow.

_____. RUSSIAN EASTWARD EXPANSION. 1964: Prentice-Hall.

John A. Harrison. JAPAN'S NORTHERN FRONTIER: A PRELIMINARY
　　STUDY IN COLONIZATION AND EXPANSION, WITH SPECIAL
　　REFERENCE TO THE RELATIONS OF JAPAN AND RUSSIA.
　　1953: University of Florida Press.

D. J. Dallin. THE RISE OF RUSSIA IN ASIA. 1949: Yale University Press.

Andrew Malozemoff. RUSSIAN FAR EASTERN POLICY, 1881-1905,
WITH SPECIAL EMPHASIS ON THE CAUSES OF THE RUSSO-
JAPANESE WAR. 1958: University of California Press.

B. A. Romanov. RUSSIA IN MANCHURIA, 1892-1906. 1952: University of
Michigan Press.

Theodore H. Von Laue. SERGEI WITTE AND THE INDUSTRIALIZATION
OF RUSSIA. 1963: Columbia University Press.

A. Yarmolinsky, ed. THE MEMOIRS OF COUNT WITTE. 1921: Doubleday,
Page.

Sidney Harcave, transl. & ed. THE MEMOIRS OF COUNT WITTE. 1990:
M. E. Sharpe.

Edward H. Zabriskie. AMERICAN-RUSSIAN RIVALRY IN THE FAR EAST:
A STUDY IN DIPLOMACY AND POWER POLITICS, 1895-1914.
1946: University of Pennsylvania Press.

Peter Yong-Shik Shin. "The Ōtsu Incident: Japan's Hidden History of the
Attempted Assassination of Future Emperor Nicholas II of Russia in the
Town of Ōtsu, Japan, May 11, 1891 and Its Implications for Historical
Analysis." 1989: Ph.D. dissertation in History, University of
Pennsylvania.

Ian Nish. THE ORIGINS OF THE RUSSO-JAPANESE WAR. 1985:
Longman.

Shumpei Okamoto. "Russo-Japanese War," KŌDANSHA ENCYCLOPEDIA OF
JAPAN 6: 345-347.

_____. THE JAPANESE OLIGARCHY AND THE RUSSO-JAPANESE WAR.
1970: Columbia University Press.

Denis & Peggy Warner. THE TIDE AT SUNRISE: A HISTORY OF THE
RUSSO-JAPANESE WAR, 1904-1905. 1974: Charterhouse.

D. Walder. THE SHORT VICTORIOUS WAR: THE RUSSO-JAPANESE
CONFLICT, 1904-1905. 1974: Harper & Row.

Frederic William Unger. THE AUTHENTIC HISTORY OF THE WAR
BETWEEN RUSSIA AND JAPAN. 1905: World Bible House.

Richard Hough. THE FLEET THAT HAD TO DIE. 1960: Ballentine.

Richard Connaughton. THE WAR OF THE RISING SUN AND TUMBLING
    BEAR: A MILITARY HISTORY OF THE RUSSO-JAPANESE WAR
    OF 1904-1905. 1991: Routledge.

Edwin P. Hoyt. THREE MILITARY LEADERS: HEIHACHIRŌ TŌGŌ,
    ISOROKU YAMAMOTO, TOMOYUKI YAMASHITA. 1994:
    Kōdansha International.

Steve Rabson. "Shimazaki Tōson on War," *Monumenta Nipponica* 46.4 (1991),
    453-481.

Tadayoshi Sakurai. HUMAN BULLETS: A SOLDIER'S STORY OF PORT
    ARTHUR. 1907: Houghton Mifflin.

Yō Sasaki. "The International Environment at the Time of the Sino-Japanese
    War (1894-1895): Anglo-Russian Far Eastern Policy and the Beginning
    of the Sino-Japanese War," *Memoirs of the Research Department of the
    Tōyō Bunko* 42 (1984), 1-74.

Kan'ichi Asakawa. THE RUSSO-JAPANESE CONFLICT: ITS CAUSES AND
    ISSUES. 1904: Houghton Mifflin.

John A. White. THE DIPLOMACY OF THE RUSSO-JAPANESE WAR. 1964:
    Princeton University Press.

Eugene P. Trani. THE TREATY OF PORTSMOUTH: AN ADVENTURE IN
    AMERICAN DIPLOMACY. 1969: University of Kentucky Press.

Raymond A. Esthus. DOUBLE EAGLE AND RISING SUN: THE RUSSIANS
    AND JAPANESE AT PORTSMOUTH IN 1905. 1988: Duke
    University Press.

Michael Futrell. "Colonel Akashi and Japanese Contacts with Russian
    Revolutionaries in 1904-5," *St. Anthony's Papers* (1967), 7-22.

Hyman Kublin. "The Japanese Socialists and the Russo-Japanese War," *Journal
    of Modern History* 22.4 (1950), 322-339.

Ernest Batson Price. THE RUSSO-JAPANESE TREATIES OF 1907-1916
    CONCERNING MANCHURIA AND MONGOLIA. 1933: Johns
    Hopkins.

Peter S. H. Tang. RUSSIAN AND SOVIET POLICY IN MANCHURIA AND OUTER MONGOLIA, 1911-1931. 1959: Duke University Press.

James W. Morley. THE JAPANESE THRUST INTO SIBERIA, 1918. 1957: Columbia University Press.

Adam B. Ulam. EXPANSION AND COEXISTENCE: THE HISTORY OF SOVIET FOREIGN POLICY, 1917-67. 1968: Praeger.

David J. Dallin. SOVIET RUSSIA AND THE FAR EAST. 1948: Yale University Press.

B. Nicolaevsky. "Russia, Japan, and the Pan-Asiatic Movement to 1925," *Far Eastern Quarterly* 8.3 (1949), 259-295.

Xenia Joukoff Eudin & Robert C. North. SOVIET RUSSIA AND THE EAST, 1920-1927. 1957: Stanford University Press.

George Alexander Lensen. JAPANESE RECOGNITION OF THE U.S.S.R.: SOVIET-JAPANESE RELATIONS, 1921-1930. 1970: Monumenta Nipponica Monographs.

_____. THE DAMNED INHERITANCE: THE SOVIET UNION AND THE MANCHURIAN CRISIS, 1924-1935. 1974: Diplomatic Press.

Ikuhiko Hata. REALITY AND ILLUSION: THE HIDDEN CRISIS BETWEEN JAPAN AND THE USSR, 1932-1934. 1967: Occasional Papers of the East Asia Institute, Columbia University.

James W. Morley, ed. DETERRENT DIPLOMACY: JAPAN, GERMANY, AND THE USSR, 1935-1940. 1976: Columbia University Press. Includes Tokushirō Ōhata on "The Anti-Comintern Pact, 1935-1939" (1-111) and Ikuhiko Hata on "The Japanese-Soviet Confrontation, 1935-1939" (113-178).

Max Beloff. THE FOREIGN POLICY OF SOVIET RUSSIA, 1929-1941. 2 volumes. 1953: Oxford University Press.

Harriet L. Moore. SOVIET FAR EASTERN DIPLOMACY, 1931-1945. 1945: Princeton University Press.

Victor A. Yakhontoff. RUSSIA AND THE SOVIET UNION IN THE FAR EAST. 1932: Allen & Unwin.

G. Safarov. THE FAR EAST ABLAZE. 1933: Worker's Library.

Larry W. Moses. "Soviet-Japanese Confrontation in Outer Mongolia: The Battle of Nomonhan-Khalkin Gol," *Journal of Asian History* 1.1 (1967), 64-85.

Katsu H. Young. "The Nomonhan Incident: Imperial Japan and the Soviet Union," *Monumenta Nipponica* 22.1-2 (1967), 82-102.

Alvin D. Coox. THE ANATOMY OF A SMALL WAR: THE SOVIET-JAPANESE STRUGGLE FOR CHANGKUFENG/ KHANSAN, 1938. 1977: Greenwood.

_____. NOMONHAN: JAPAN AGAINST RUSSIA, 1939. 2 volumes. 1985: Stanford University Press.

John J. Stephan. THE RUSSIAN FASCISTS: TRAGEDY AND FARCE IN EXILE, 1925-1945. 1978: Harper & Row.

Leonid L. Kutakov. JAPANESE FOREIGN POLICY ON THE EVE OF THE PACIFIC WAR: A SOVIET VIEW. 1972: Diplomatic Press.

Jonathan Haslam. THE SOVIET UNION AND THE THREAT FROM THE EAST, 1933-41: MOSCOW, TOKYO, AND THE PRELUDE TO THE PACIFIC WAR. 1992: University of Pittsburgh Press.

George Alexander Lensen. THE STRANGE NEUTRALITY: SOVIET-JAPANESE RELATIONS DURING THE SECOND WORLD WAR, 1941-1945. 1972: Diplomatic Press.

Diane Shaver Clemens. YALTA. 1970: Oxford University Press.

Raymond L. Garthoff. "The Soviet Manchurian Campaigns, August 1945," *Military Affairs* 34 (1970), 312-335.

Boris N. Stavinsky. "The Soviet Occupation of the Kurile Islands and the Plans for the Capture of Northern Hokkaidō," *Japan Forum* 5.1 (1993), 95-114.

U.S. Department of Defense. THE ENTRY OF THE SOVIET UNION INTO THE WAR AGAINST JAPAN: MILITARY PLANS, 1941-1945. 1955: Government Publications Office.

GREAT BRITAIN

Ian Nish. "Japan's Policies Toward Britain," in J. W. Morley, ed. JAPAN'S FOREIGN POLICY (1974: Columbia University Press), 184-235.

_____. "United Kingdom and Japan," KŌDANSHA ENCYCLOPEDIA OF JAPAN 8: 150-153.

_____. "Anglo-Japanese Alliance," KŌDANSHA ENCYCLOPEDIA OF JAPAN 1: 56-57.

William G. Beasley. GREAT BRITAIN AND THE OPENING OF JAPAN, 1834-1858. 1951: Luzac.

Toshio Yokoyama. JAPAN IN THE VICTORIAN MIND: A STUDY OF STEREOTYPED IMAGES OF A NATION 1850-80. 1987: Macmillan.

Grace Fox. BRITAIN AND JAPAN, 1858-1883. 1969: Clarendon.

Hugh Cortazzi & Gordon Daniels, eds. BRITAIN AND JAPAN, 1859-1991: THEMES AND PERSONALITIES. 1991: Routledge.

Olive Checkland. BRITAIN'S ENCOUNTER WITH MEIJI JAPAN, 1868-1912. 1989: Macmillan.

Marie Conte-Helm. JAPAN AND THE NORTH EAST OF ENGLAND: FROM 1862 TO THE PRESENT DAY. 1989: Athlone.

Ian Nish. THE ANGLO-JAPANESE ALLIANCE: THE DIPLOMACY OF TWO ISLAND EMPIRES, 1894-1907. 1966; 2nd edition, 1985: Athlone.

_____. ALLIANCE IN DECLINE: A STUDY IN ANGLO-JAPANESE RELATIONS, 1908-23. 1972: Athlone.

_____. "Japan and the Ending of the Anglo-Japanese Alliance," in K. Bourne & D. C. Watt, eds. STUDIES IN INTERNATIONAL HISTORY (1967: Longman's), 369-384.

_____, ed. ANGLO-JAPANESE ALIENATION, 1919-1952. 1982: Cambridge University Press.

Chin-sok Chong. THE KOREAN PROBLEM IN ANGLO-JAPANESE RELATIONS, 1904-1910: ERNEST THOMAS BETHELL AND HIS NEWSPAPERS: THE DAIHAN MAEIL SINBO AND THE KOREA DAILY NEWS. 1987: NANAM Publications.

John C. Perry. "Great Britain and the Emergence of Japan as a Naval Power," *Monumenta Nipponica* 21.3-4 (1966), 305-321.

Peter Lowe. GREAT BRITAIN AND JAPAN, 1911-1915. 1969: Macmillan.

Malcom D. Kennedy. THE ESTRANGEMENT OF GREAT BRITAIN AND JAPAN, 1917-35. 1969: University of California Press.

Dae-yeol Ku. KOREA UNDER COLONIALISM: THE MARCH FIRST MOVEMENT AND ANGLO-JAPANESE RELATIONS. 1985: Royal Asiatic Society, Seoul.

William Roger Louis. BRITISH STRATEGY IN THE FAR EAST, 1919-1939. 1971: Clarendon.

Irving S. Friedman. BRITISH RELATIONS WITH CHINA, 1931-1939. 1940: Institute of Pacific Relations.

Ann Trotter. BRITAIN AND EAST ASIA, 1933-1937. 1975: Cambridge University Press.

Stephen Lyon Endicott. DIPLOMACY AND ENTERPRISE: BRITISH CHINA POLICY, 1933-1937. 1975: University of British Columbia Press.

Bradford A. Lee. BRITAIN AND THE SINO-JAPANESE WAR, 1937-1939: A STUDY IN THE DILEMMAS OF BRITISH DECLINE. 1973: Stanford University Press.

R. John Pritchard. "Far Eastern Influences upon British Strategy towards the Great Powers, 1937-1939." 1979: Ph.D. dissertation, University of London.

Nicolas R. Clifford. RETREAT FROM CHINA: BRITISH POLICY IN THE FAR EAST, 1937-1941. 1967: University of Washington Press.

John W. Dower. EMPIRE AND AFTERMATH: YOSHIDA SHIGERU AND THE JAPANESE EXPERIENCE, 1878-1954 (1979: Council on East Asian Studies, Harvard University), 123-212.

Peter Lowe. GREAT BRITAIN AND THE ORIGINS OF THE PACIFIC WAR.
1977: Clarendon.

Christopher Thorne. ALLIES OF A KIND: THE UNITED STATES, BRITAIN,
AND THE WAR AGAINST JAPAN, 1941-1945. 1978: Oxford
University Press.

William Roger Louis. IMPERIALISM AT BAY, 1941-1945: THE UNITED
STATES AND THE DECOLONIALIZATION OF THE BRITISH
EMPIRE. 1977: Clarendon.

S. Woodburn Kirby, et al. THE WAR AGAINST JAPAN. 4 volumes.
1959: Her Majesty's Stationery Office.

E. L. Woodward & Rohan Butler, eds. DOCUMENTS ON BRITISH FOREIGN
POLICY, 1919-1939. 9 volumes. 1949-1955: Her Majesty's Stationery
Office.

Sir Ernest Satow. A DIPLOMAT IN JAPAN. 1921: Seeley Service.

Major General F. S. G. Piggott. BROKEN THREAD: AN AUTOBIOGRA-
PHY. 1950: Gale & Polden. Piggott served as military attache in Japan
before the outbreak of war.

Robert Craigie. BEHIND THE JAPANESE MASK. 1946: Hutchinson. Craigie
was the British ambassador to Japan from 1937 to 1942.

U.S. RELATIONS TO 1931

General Texts

John Hunter Boyle. MODERN JAPAN: THE AMERICAN NEXUS. 1993:
Harcourt Brace Jovanovich.

Ernest R. May & James C. Thomson, Jr., eds. AMERICAN-EAST ASIAN
RELATIONS: A SURVEY. 1972: Harvard University Press.
A collection of 17 essays organized by strict chronology and covering
the period 1794 to the 1960s.

Akira Iriye. "United States and Japan," KŌDANSHA ENCYCLOPEDIA OF
JAPAN 8: 154-160.

_____. "Japan's Policies Toward the United States," in J. W. Morley, ed. JAPAN'S FOREIGN POLICY (1974: Columbia University Press), 407-459.

_____. ACROSS THE PACIFIC—AN INNER HISTORY OF AMERICAN-EAST ASIAN RELATIONS. 1967: Harcourt Brace & World.

_____, ed. MUTUAL IMAGES: ESSAYS IN AMERICAN-JAPANESE RELATIONS. 1975: Harvard University Press.

_____. "Western Perceptions and Asian Realities," in Joe C. Dixon, ed. THE AMERICAN MILITARY AND THE FAR EAST (a 1980 U.S. Air Force symposium: Office of Air Force History), 9-19.

_____. THE ORIGINS OF THE SECOND WORLD WAR IN ASIA AND THE PACIFIC. 1987: Longman.

Shunsuke Kamei. "Japanese See America: A Century of Firsthand Impressions," *Japan Interpreter* 11.1 (1976), 6-35.

William L. Neumann. AMERICA ENCOUNTERS JAPAN: FROM PERRY TO MACARTHUR. 1963: Johns Hopkins.

Charles E. Neu. THE TROUBLED ENCOUNTER: THE UNITED STATES AND JAPAN. 1975: Wiley.

Edwin O. Reischauer. THE UNITED STATES AND JAPAN. 3rd edition. 1965: Harvard University Press.

John K. Emmerson. THE EAGLE AND THE RISING SUN: AMERICA AND JAPAN IN THE TWENTIETH CENTURY. 1988: Addison-Wesley.

Ralph E. Schaffer, ed. TOWARD PEARL HARBOR: THE DIPLOMATIC EXCHANGE BETWEEN JAPAN AND THE UNITED STATES, 1899-1941. 1991: Markus Wiener.

George Kennan. AMERICAN DIPLOMACY, 1900-1950. 1951: University of Chicago Press.

James C. Thomson, Jr., Peter W. Stanley & John C. Perry. SENTIMENTAL IMPERIALISTS: THE AMERICAN EXPERIENCE IN EAST ASIA. 1981: Harper & Row.

Robert A. Hart. THE ECCENTRIC TRADITION: AMERICAN DIPLOMACY IN THE FAR EAST. 1976: Charles Scribner's Sons.

Young Hum Kim. AMERICAN FRONTIER ACTIVITIES IN ASIA: U.S.-ASIAN RELATIONS IN THE TWENTIETH CENTURY. 1981: Nelson-Hall.

A. Whitney Griswold. THE FAR EASTERN POLICY OF THE UNITED STATES. 1938: Yale University Press.

Eleanor Tupper & George E. McReynolds. JAPAN IN AMERICAN PUBLIC OPINION. 1937: Macmillan.

Edwin Palmer Hoyt. JAPAN'S WAR: THE GREAT PACIFIC CONFLICT, 1853-1952. 1986: McGraw-Hill.

Case Studies

Hikomatsu Kamikawa. JAPANESE-AMERICAN RELATIONS IN THE MEIJI-TAISHŌ ERA. 1958: Obunsha.

Robert A. Rosenstone. MIRROR IN THE SHRINE: AMERICAN ENCOUN-TERS WITH MEIJI JAPAN. 1988: Harvard University Press.

Tyler Dennett. AMERICANS IN EASTERN ASIA: A CRITICAL STUDY OF UNITED STATES POLICY IN THE FAR EAST IN THE NINETEENTH CENTURY. 1922: Macmillan.

Robert S. Schwantes. "America and Japan," in May & Thomson, AMERICAN-EAST ASIAN RELATIONS (1972: Harvard University Press), 97-128. Focus on 19th century.

Erving E. Beauregard. "John A. Bingham, First American Minister Plenipotentiary to Japan (1873-1885)," *Journal of Asian History* 22.2 (1988), 101-130.

Haru Matsukata Reischauer. SAMURAI AND SILK: A JAPANESE AND AMERICAN HERITAGE. 1986: Belknap Press of Harvard University Press.

Mitziko Sawada. "Culprits and Gentlemen: Meiji Japan's Restrictions of Emigrants to the United States, 1891-1909," *Pacific Historical Review* 60.3 (1991), 339-359.

Akira Iriye. PACIFIC ESTRANGEMENT: JAPANESE AND AMERICAN EXPANSION, 1897-1911. 1972: Harvard University Press.

Mark Mason. AMERICAN MULTINATIONALS AND JAPAN: THE POLITICAL ECONOMY OF JAPANESE CAPITAL CONTROLS, 1899-1980. 1992: Council on East Asian Studies, Harvard University.

Yoshikatsu Hayashi. "The Introduction of American Technology into the Japanese Electrical Industry: Another Aspect of Japanese-American Relations at the Turn of the Century." 1986: Ph.D. dissertation in History, University of California at Santa Barbara.

Raymond A. Esthus. THEODORE ROOSEVELT AND JAPAN. 1966: University of Washington Press.

_____. DOUBLE EAGLE AND RISING SUN: THE RUSSIANS AND JAPANESE AT PORTSMOUTH IN 1905. 1988: Duke University Press.

Charles E. Neu. AN UNCERTAIN FRIENDSHIP: THEODORE ROOSEVELT AND JAPAN, 1906-1909. 1967: Harvard University Press.

Howard K. Beale. THEODORE ROOSEVELT AND THE RISE OF AMERICA TO WORLD POWER. 1956: Johns Hopkins.

T. A. Bailey. THEODORE ROOSEVELT AND THE JAPANESE-AMERICAN CRISIS. 1934: Stanford University Press.

_____. "The Root-Takahira Agreement of 1908," *Pacific Historical Review* 9 (1940), 19-35.

Charles Vevier. THE UNITED STATES AND CHINA, 1906-1913. 1955: University of British Columbia Press.

Noriko Kawamura. "Odd Associates in World War I: Japanese-American Relations, 1914-1918." 1989: Ph.D. dissertation in History, University of Washington.

Roy Watson Curry. WOODROW WILSON AND FAR EASTERN POLICY, 1913-1921. 1957: Bookman Associates.

Tien-yi Li. WOODROW WILSON'S CHINA POLICY, 1913-1917. 1969: Octagon.

Edward H. Buehrig. WOODROW WILSON AND THE BALANCE OF POWER. 1955: Indiana University Press.

Arthur S. Link. WILSON: THE STRUGGLE FOR NEUTRALITY, 1914-1915. 1960: Princeton University Press.

Arno Mayer. POLITICS AND DIPLOMACY OF PEACEMAKING: CONTAINMENT AND COUNTERREVOLUTION AT VERSAILLES, 1918-1919. 1967: Knopf.

Burton F. Beers. "Robert Lansing's Proposed Bargain with Japan," *Pacific Historical Review* 26.4 (1957), 391-400.

_____. VAIN ENDEAVOR: ROBERT LANSING'S ATTEMPT TO END THE AMERICAN-JAPANESE RIVALRY. 1962: Duke University Press.

Russell H. Fifield. WOODROW WILSON AND THE FAR EAST: THE DIPLOMACY OF THE SHANTUNG QUESTION. 1952: Crowell.

William Reynolds Braisted. THE UNITED STATES NAVY IN THE PACIFIC, 1897-1909. 1958: University of Texas Press.

_____. THE UNITED STATES NAVY IN THE PACIFIC, 1909-1922. 1971: University of California Press.

O. J. Clinard. JAPAN'S INFLUENCE ON AMERICAN NAVAL POWER, 1897-1917. 1947: Princeton University Press.

Harold & Margaret Sprout. THE RISE OF AMERICAN NAVAL POWER, 1776-1918. 1946: Princeton University Press.

_____. TOWARD A NEW ORDER OF SEA POWER: AMERICAN NAVAL POLICY AND THE WORLD SCENE, 1918-1922. 1946: Princeton University Press.

J. Chalmers Vinson. THE PARCHMENT PEACE: THE UNITED STATES SENATE AND THE WASHINGTON CONFERENCE, 1921-1922. 1955: University of Georgia Press.

Thomas H. Buckley. THE UNITED STATES AND THE WASHINGTON CONFERENCE, 1921-1922. 1970: University of Tennessee Press.

Herbert Yardley. THE AMERICAN BLACK CHAMBER. 1931: Blue Ribbon Books.

Roger Dingman. "American Policy and Strategy in East Asia, 1898-1950:
     The Creation of a Commitment," in Joe C. Dixon, ed. THE AMERI-
     CAN MILITARY AND THE FAR EAST (1980: a U.S. Air Force
     Symposium: Office of Air Force History), 20-45.

_____. "1917-1922," in May & Thomson, AMERICAN-EAST ASIAN
     RELATIONS (1972: Harvard University Press), 190-218.

_____. POWER IN THE PACIFIC: THE ORIGINS OF NAVAL ARMS
     LIMITATION, 1914-1922. 1976: University of Chicago Press.

Gerald Wheeler. PRELUDE TO PEARL HARBOR: THE UNITED STATES
     NAVY AND THE FAR EAST, 1921-1931. 1963: University of
     Missouri Press.

_____. "Isolated Japan: Anglo-American Diplomatic Cooperation, 1927-1936,"
     Pacific Historical Review 30.2 (1961), 165-178.

Akira Iriye. "1922-1931," in May & Thomson, AMERICAN-EAST ASIAN
     RELATIONS (1972: Harvard University Press), 221-242.

William A. Williams. "China and Japan: A Challenge and a Choice of the
     1920s," *Pacific Historical Review* 26.3 (1957), 259-279.

Roger Daniels. THE POLITICS OF PREJUDICE: THE ANTI-JAPANESE
     MOVEMENT IN CALIFORNIA AND THE STRUGGLE FOR
     JAPANESE EXCLUSION. 1968: University of California Press.

Warren I. Cohen. EAST ASIAN ART AND AMERICAN CULTURE:
     A STUDY IN INTERNATIONAL RELATIONS. 1992: Columbia
     University Press.

GERMANY

Erich Pauer. "Germany and Japan," KŌDANSHA ENCYCLOPEDIA OF
     JAPAN 3: 26-28.

Frank W. Ikle. "Japan's Policies Toward Germany," in J. W. Morley, ed.
     JAPAN'S FOREIGN POLICY (1974: Columbia University Press),
     265-339.

Minge C. Bee. "The Origins of German Far Eastern Policy," *Chinese Social and Political Science Review* 21 (1937), 65-97.

Kurt Bloch. GERMAN INTERESTS AND POLICIES IN THE FAR EAST. 1939: Institute of Pacific Relations.

John P. Fox. GERMANY AND THE FAR EASTERN CRISIS, 1931-1938: A STUDY IN DIPLOMACY AND IDEOLOGY. 1982: Oxford University Press.

John Huizenga. "Yōsuke Matsuoka and the Japanese-German Alliance," in Gordon A. Craig & Felix Gilbert, eds. THE DIPLOMATS, 1919-1939 (1953: Princeton University Press), 615-648.

J. W. Morley, ed. DETERRENT DIPLOMACY: JAPAN, GERMANY AND THE U.S.S.R., 1935-1940. 1976: Columbia University Press. Includes Tokushirō Ōhata, "The Anti-Comintern Pact, 1935-1939" (1-111) and Chihiro Hosoya, "The Tripartite Pact, 1939-1940" (179-257).

Frank W. Ikle. GERMAN-JAPANESE RELATIONS, 1936-1940: A STUDY OF TOTALITARIAN DIPLOMACY. 1956: Bookman Associates.

Carl Boyd. THE EXTRAORDINARY ENVOY: GENERAL HIROSHI ŌSHIMA AND DIPLOMACY IN THE THIRD REICH, 1934-1939. 1980: University Press of America.

_____. HITLER'S JAPANESE CONFIDANT: GENERAL ŌSHIMA HIROSHI AND MAGIC INTELLIGENCE, 1941-1945. 1993: University of Kansas.

James T. C. Liu. "German Mediation in the Sino-Japanese War, 1937-38," *Far Eastern Quarterly* 8.2 (1949), 157-17.1

Ernst L. Presseisen. GERMANY AND JAPAN: A STUDY IN TOTALITARIAN DIPLOMACY, 1933-1941. 1958: Martinus Nijhoff.

Johanna Menzel Meskill. HITLER AND JAPAN: THE HOLLOW ALLIANCE. 1966: Atherton.

Paul W. Schroeder. THE AXIS ALLIANCE AND JAPANESE-AMERICAN RELATIONS, 1941. 1958: Cornell University Press.

Milan Hauner. INDIA IN AXIS STRATEGY: GERMANY, JAPAN, AND INDIAN NATIONALISTS IN THE SECOND WORLD WAR. 1981: Klett-Cotta.

H. L. Trefousse. "Germany and Pearl Harbor," *Far Eastern Quarterly* 11.1 (1951), 35-50.

THE MANCHURIAN INCIDENT & AFTERMATH

[See also the numerous official publications concerning Manchuria and Manchukuo cited in the "Primary Materials" bibliography, especially pages 355-360.]

The Manchurian Incident

Mark R. Peattie. "Manchurian Incident," KŌDANSHA ENCYCLOPEDIA OF JAPAN 5: 97-99.

Takehiko Yoshihashi. "Manchukuo," KŌDANSHA ENCYCLOPEDIA OF JAPAN 5: 96-97.

James W. Morley, ed. JAPAN ERUPTS: THE LONDON NAVAL CONFERENCE AND THE MANCHURIAN INCIDENT, 1928-1932. 1984: Columbia University Press.

Sadako N. Ogata. DEFIANCE IN MANCHURIA: THE MAKING OF JAPANESE FOREIGN POLICY, 1931-1932. 1964: University of California Press.

Takehiko Yoshihashi. CONSPIRACY AT MUKDEN: THE RISE OF THE JAPANESE MILITARY. 1963: Yale University Press.

Sara R. Smith. THE MANCHURIAN CRISIS, 1931-1932. 1948: Columbia University Press.

Sandra Wilson. PRO-WESTERN INTELLECTUALS AND THE MANCHURIAN CRISIS OF 1931-33. Nissan Occasional Papers, No. 3. 1987: Nissan Institute of Japanese Studies, Oxford.

_____. "The Manchurian Crisis and Moderate Japanese Intellectuals: The Japan Council of the Institute of Pacific Relations," *Modern Asian Studies* 26.3 (1992), 507-544.

Christopher Thorne. THE LIMITS OF FOREIGN POLICY: THE WEST, THE LEAGUE, AND THE FAR EASTERN CRISIS OF 1931-1933. 1973: Capricorn.

Ian Hill Nish. JAPAN'S STRUGGLE WITH INTERNATIONALISM: JAPAN, CHINA, AND THE LEAGUE OF NATIONS, 1931-1933. 1993: K. Paul International.

Robert H. Ferrell. AMERICAN DIPLOMACY IN THE GREAT DEPRESSION: HOOVER-STIMSON FOREIGN POLICY, 1929-1933. 1957: Yale University Press.

Justus D. Doenecke. THE DIPLOMACY OF FRUSTRATION: THE MANCHURIAN CRISIS OF 1931-1933 AS REVEALED IN THE PAPERS OF STANLEY K. HORNBECK. 1981: Hoover Institution Press.

Armin Rappaport. HENRY L. STIMSON AND JAPAN, 1931-1933. 1963: University of Chicago Press.

Richard N. Current. SECRETARY STIMSON, A STUDY IN STATECRAFT. 1954: Rutgers University Press.

Elting E. Morison. TURMOIL AND TRADITION: A STUDY OF THE LIFE AND TIMES OF HENRY L. STIMSON. 1960: Houghton Mifflin.

Henry L. Stimson. THE FAR EASTERN CRISIS: RECOLLECTIONS AND OBSERVATIONS. 1936: Harper.

George Alexander Lensen. "Japan and Manchuria: Ambassador Forbes's Appraisal of American Policy Toward Japan in 1931-32," *Monumenta Nipponica* 23.1-2 (1968), 66-89.

Owen Lattimore. MANCHURIA: CRADLE OF CONFLICT. Revised edition. 1935: Macmillan.

John R. Stewart. MANCHURIA SINCE 1931. 1936: Institute of Pacific Relations.

F. C. Jones. MANCHURIA SINCE 1931. 1949: Royal Institute of International Affairs.

Louise Conrad Young. "Mobilizing for Empire: Japan and Manchukuo, 1931-1945." 1993: Ph.D. dissertation, Columbia University.

Irving I. Kramer. "Japan in Manchuria." Four articles in *Contemporary Japan:* volume 22 (1953), 584-611; 23 (1954), 75-100; 25 (1958), 224-237 and 299-417.

Takeo Itō. LIFE ALONG THE SOUTH MANCHURIAN RAILWAY:
THE MEMOIRS OF ITŌ TAKEO. Transl. Joshua A. Fogel. 1989:
M. E. Sharpe.

Chong-sik Lee. REVOLUTIONARY STRUGGLE IN MANCHURIA:
CHINESE COMMUNISM AND SOVIET INTEREST, 1922-1945.
1983: University of California Press.

_____. COUNTERINSURGENCY IN MANCHURIA: THE JAPANESE
EXPERIENCE. 1967: RAND Corporation Memorandum
RM-5012-ARPA.

Aisin Gioro Pu-Yi. FROM EMPEROR TO CITIZEN. 2 volumes. 1964-1965:
Peking Foreign Language Press.

E. B. Schumpeter, ed. THE INDUSTRIALIZATION OF JAPAN AND
MANCHUKUO, 1930-1940. 1940: Macmillan.

Basic Treaty Issues

John van Antwerp MacMurray. TREATIES AND AGREEMENTS WITH AND
CONCERNING CHINA, 1894-1919. 2 volumes. 1921: Oxford
University Press.

Carnegie Endowment for International Peace, Division of International Law.
MANCHURIA: TREATIES AND AGREEMENTS. 1921: Carnegie
Endowment for International Peace.

Shu-hsi Hsu. CHINA AND HER POLITICAL ENTITY: A STUDY OF
CHINA'S FOREIGN RELATIONS WITH REFERENCE TO KOREA,
MANCHURIA, AND MONGOLIA. 1926: Oxford University Press.

W. W. Willoughby. FOREIGN RIGHTS AND INTERESTS IN CHINA.
2 volumes. Revised edition. 1927: Johns Hopkins.

Carl Walter Young. THE INTERNATIONAL RELATIONS OF MANCHURIA:
A DIGEST AND ANALYSIS OF TREATIES, AGREEMENTS, AND
NEGOTIATIONS CONCERNING THE THREE EASTERN
PROVINCES OF CHINA. 1929: University of Chicago Press.

_____. JAPAN'S JURISDICTION AND INTERNATIONAL LEGAL
POSITION IN MANCHURIA. 3 volumes. 1931: Johns Hopkins.

1. THE INTERNATIONAL LEGAL STATUS OF THE KWANTUNG
LEASED TERRITORY.
2. JAPAN'S SPECIAL POSITION IN MANCHURIA: ITS ASSER
TION, LEGAL INTERPRETATION AND PRESENT MEANING.
3. JAPANESE JURISDICTION IN THE SOUTH MANCHURIAN
RAILWAY AREAS.

Thomas A. Bisson. BASIC TREATY ISSUES IN MANCHURIA BETWEEN
JAPAN AND CHINA. 1931: Foreign Policy Association.

Han-tao Wu. JAPAN'S ACTS OF TREATY VIOLATION AND ENCROACH-
MENT UPON THE SOVEREIGN RIGHTS OF CHINA IN THE
NORTHEASTERN PROVINCES. 1932: The Northeastern Affairs
Research Institute.

Mo Shen. JAPAN IN MANCHURIA: AN ANALYTIC STUDY OF TREATIES
AND DOCUMENTS. 1960: University of the Philippines Press.

W. W. Willoughby. THE SINO-JAPANESE CONTROVERSY AND THE
LEAGUE OF NATIONS. 1935: Johns Hopkins.

Royal Institute of International Affairs. SURVEY OF INTERNATIONAL
AFFAIRS. See especially the volumes for 1931 and 1937: Royal
Institute of International Affairs.

THE ROAD TO WAR, 1931-1941

[In addition to the references cited below, see also the detailed textbook
treatment in Marius Jansen, JAPAN AND CHINA (1975: Rand
McNally), 354-408; Hugh Borton, JAPAN'S MODERN CENTURY
(1970: Ronald), 367-428; Edwin O. Reischauer & Albert M. Craig,
JAPAN: TRADITION AND TRANSFORMATION (1989: Houghton
Mifflin), 245-267; and Mikiso Hane, MODERN JAPAN (1992:
Westview Press), 273-309.]

Pre (and Post) 1937

Dorothy Borg & Shumpei Okamoto, eds. PEARL HARBOR AS HISTORY:
JAPANESE-AMERICAN RELATIONS, 1931-1941. 1973: Columbia
University Press.

Ralph E. Schaffer, ed. TOWARD PEARL HARBOR: THE DIPLOMATIC EXCHANGE BETWEEN JAPAN AND THE UNITED STATES, 1899-1941. 1991: Markus Wiener.

Saburō Ienaga. THE PACIFIC WAR, 1931-1945. Frank Baldwin, transl. 1978: Pantheon.

James B. Crowley. JAPAN'S QUEST FOR AUTONOMY: NATIONAL SECURITY AND FOREIGN POLICY, 1930-38. 1966: Princeton University Press.

_____. "Japan's Foreign Military Policies," in James W. Morley, ed. JAPAN'S FOREIGN POLICY (1974: Columbia University Press), 54-103 for 1931 and after.

Yale C. Maxon. CONTROL OF JAPANESE FOREIGN POLICY: A STUDY OF CIVIL-MILITARY RIVALRY, 1930-1945. 1957: University of California Press.

James W. Morley, ed. JAPAN'S ROAD TO THE PACIFIC WAR series (adapted from the Japanese series *Taiheiyō Sensō e no Michi*). Columbia University Press:

1. JAPAN ERUPTS: THE LONDON NAVAL CONFERENCE AND THE MANCHURIAN INCIDENT, 1928-1932. 1984.
2. THE CHINA QUAGMIRE: JAPAN'S EXPANSION ON THE ASIAN CONTINENT, 1933-1941. 1983.
3. DETERRENT DIPLOMACY: JAPAN, GERMANY, AND THE U.S.S.R., 1935-1940. 1976.
4. THE FATEFUL CHOICE: JAPAN'S ADVANCE INTO SOUTH EAST ASIA, 1939-1941. 1980.

Gordon M. Berger. PARTIES OUT OF POWER IN JAPAN, 1931-1941. 1976: Princeton University Press.

Richard Storry. "The Road to War: 1931-1945," in Arthur E. Tiedemann, ed. AN INTRODUCTION TO JAPANESE CIVILIZATION (1974: Heath), 247-276.

Waldo H. Heinrichs, Jr. "1931-1937," in Ernest May & James Thomson, eds. AMERICAN-EAST ASIAN RELATIONS (1972: Harvard University Press), 243-259.

Gerald E. Wheeler. "The Road to War: The United States and Japan, 1931-1941." *Forum Series* pamphlet, 1963.

John K. Emmerson. THE EAGLE AND THE RISING SUN: AMERICA AND JAPAN IN THE TWENTIETH CENTURY. 1988: Addison-Wesley.

Akira Iriye. "Japanese Imperialism and Aggression: Reconsiderations" and "Japan's Foreign Policies Between World Wars—Sources and Interpretations," in Esmonde M. Robertson, ed. THE ORIGINS OF THE SECOND WORLD WAR: HISTORICAL INTERPRETATIONS (1971: Macmillan), 243-271.

_____. "The Failure of Military Expansionism," in James W. Morley, ed. DILEMMAS OF GROWTH IN PREWAR JAPAN (1971: Princeton University Press), 107-138.

_____. "The Historical Background," in his THE COLD WAR IN ASIA: A HISTORICAL INTRODUCTION (1974: Prentice-Hall), 8-46.

_____. THE ORIGINS OF THE SECOND WORLD WAR IN ASIA AND THE PACIFIC. 1987: Longman.

Henry P. Frei. JAPAN'S SOUTHWARD ADVANCE AND AUSTRALIA: FROM THE SIXTEENTH CENTURY TO WORLD WAR II. 1991: University of Hawaii Press.

Dorothy Borg. THE UNITED STATES AND THE FAR EASTERN CRISIS OF 1933-1938: FROM THE MANCHURIAN INCIDENT THROUGH THE INITIAL STAGES OF THE UNDECLARED SINO-JAPANESE WAR. 1964: Harvard University Press.

William L. Neumann. "Ambiguity and Ambivalence in Ideas of National Security in Asia," in Alexander DeConde, ed. ISOLATION AND SECURITY (1957: Duke University Press), 133-158.

Samuel E. Morison. THE RISING SUN IN THE PACIFIC, 1931-APRIL 1942. Volume 3 of Morison's HISTORY OF THE UNITED STATES NAVAL OPERATIONS IN WORLD WAR II. 1947; revised edition, 1953: Little, Brown.

Stephen E. Pelz. RACE TO PEARL HARBOR: THE FAILURE OF THE SECOND LONDON NAVAL CONFERENCE AND THE ONSET OF WORLD WAR II. 1974: Harvard University Press.

Kumao Harada. THE SAIONJI-HARADA MEMOIRS, 1931-40: COMPLETE
    TRANSLATION INTO ENGLISH. Available in 3 mircrofilm reels
    from University Publications of America.

Lesley Connors. THE EMPEROR'S ADVISOR: SAIONJI KINMOCHI AND
    PRE-WAR JAPANESE POLITICS. 1987: Croom Helm.

Kōichi Kido. THE DIARY OF MARQUIS KIDO, 1931-45: SELECTED
    TRANSLATIONS INTO ENGLISH. 1984: University Publications of
    America.

Shigeru Honjō. EMPEROR HIROHITO AND HIS CHIEF AIDE-DE-CAMP:
    THE HONJŌ DIARY, 1933-36. Mikiso Hane, transl. 1983: University
    of Tokyo Press.

Mark R. Peattie. ISHIWARA KANJI AND JAPAN'S CONFRONTATION
    WITH THE WEST. 1975: Princeton University Press.

Hiroyuki Agawa. THE RELUCTANT ADMIRAL: YAMAMOTO AND THE
    IMPERIAL NAVY. 1979: Kōdansha International.

Edwin Palmer Hoyt. YAMAMOTO: THE MAN WHO PLANNED PEARL
    HARBOR. 1990: McGraw-Hill.

Saburō Shiroyama. WAR CRIMINAL: THE LIFE AND DEATH OF HIROTA
    KŌKI. John Bester, transl. 1974: Kōdansha International.

Dan Kurzman. KISHI AND JAPAN: THE SEARCH FOR THE SUN. 1960:
    Ivan Obolensky.

Richard Dean Burns & Edward M. Bennett, eds. DIPLOMATS IN CRISIS:
    UNITED STATES-CHINESE-JAPANESE RELATIONS, 1919-1941.
    1974: ABC Clio.

Arthur Waldron, ed. HOW THE PEACE WAS LOST: THE 1935 MEMORAN-
    DUM "DEVELOPMENTS AFFECTING AMERICAN POLICY IN
    THE FAR EAST," PREPARED FOR THE STATE DEPARTMENT BY
    JOHN VAN ANTWERP MACMURRAY. 1991: Hoover Institution
    Press.

Waldo H. Heinrichs, Jr. AMERICAN AMBASSADOR: JOSEPH C. GREW
    AND THE DEVELOPMENT OF THE UNITED STATES DIPLO-
    MATIC TRADITION. 1966: Little, Brown.

Masanori Nakamura. THE JAPANESE MONARCHY: AMBASSADOR JOSEPH GREW AND THE MAKING OF THE "SYMBOL EMPEROR SYSTEM," 1931-1991. Herbert Bix, Jonathan Baker-Bates, & Derek Bowen, transl. 1992: M. E. Sharpe.

Joseph C. Grew. TEN YEARS IN JAPAN: A CONTEMPORARY RECORD DRAWN FROM THE DIARIES AND PRIVATE AND OFFICIAL PAPERS OF JOSEPH C. GREW, UNITED STATES AMBASSADOR TO JAPAN, 1932-1942. 1944: Simon & Schuster.

_____. TURBULENT ERA: A DIPLOMATIC RECORD OF FORTY YEARS, 1904-1945. 2 volumes. 1952: Houghton Mifflin.

Russell D. Buhite. NELSON T. JOHNSON AND AMERICAN POLICY TOWARD CHINA, 1925-1941. 1968: Michigan State University Press.

Warren I. Cohen. THE CHINESE CONNECTION: ROGER S. GREENE, THOMAS W. LAMONT, GEORGE E. SOKOLSKY AND AMERI-CAN-EAST ASIAN RELATIONS. 1978: Columbia University Press.

Irvine H. Anderson, Jr. STANDARD VACUUM OIL COMPANY AND UNITED STATES EAST ASIAN POLICY, 1933-1941. 1975: Princeton University Press.

Sandra C. Taylor. ADVOCATE OF UNDERSTANDING: SIDNEY GULICK AND THE SEARCH FOR PEACE WITH JAPAN. 1985: Kent State University Press.

Daniel B. Ramsdell. "Asia Askew: U.S. Best-Sellers on Asia, 1931-1980," *Bulletin of Concerned Asian Scholars* 15.4 (1983), 2-25.

1937-1941

Louis Morton. "War Plan ORANGE: Evolution of a Strategy," *World Politics* 11 (1959), 221-250.

_____. "Japan's Decision for War," in K. R. Greenfield, ed. COMMAND DECISIONS (1959: Harcourt Brace), 63-87.

Shinichi Kitaoka. "Diplomacy and the Military in Shōwa Japan," in Carol Gluck & Stephen R. Graubard, eds. SHŌWA: THE JAPAN OF HIROHITO (1992: Norton), 155-176.

Chihiro Hosoya. "The Military and the Foreign Policy of Prewar Japan,"
    Hitotsubashi Journal of Law and Politics 7 (1974), 1-7.

_____. "Japan's Decision for War in 1941," *Hitotsubashi Journal of Law and
    Politics* 5 (1967), 10-19.

_____. "Miscalculations in Deterrent Policy: Japanese-U.S. Relations,
    1938-1941," *Hitotsubashi Journal of Law and Politics* 6 (1968), 29-47.

_____. "Twenty-Five Years After Pearl Harbor: A New Look at Japan's
    Decision for War," in Grant K. Goodman, ed. IMPERIAL JAPAN AND
    ASIA (1967: Occasional Papers of the East Asia Institute, Columbia
    University), 52-63.

H. P. Willmott. EMPIRES IN THE BALANCE: JAPANESE AND ALLIED
    STRATEGIES TO APRIL 1942. 1982: Naval Institute.

Robert J. C. Butow. TŌJŌ AND THE COMING OF THE WAR. 1961:
    Princeton University Press.

_____. "The Hull-Nomura Conversations: A Fundamental Misconception,"
    American Historical Review 65.4 (1960), 822-836.

_____. "Backdoor Diplomacy in the Pacific: The Proposal for a Konoye-
    Roosevelt Meeting, 1941," *Journal of American History* 59.1 (1972),
    48-72.

_____. THE JOHN DOE ASSOCIATES: BACKDOOR DIPLOMACY FOR
    PEACE, 1941. 1974: Stanford University Press.

_____. "Marching off to War on the Wrong Foot: The Final Note Tokyo Did
    Not Send to Washington," *Pacific Historical Review* 63.1 (1994), 67-79.

Herbert Feis. THE ROAD TO PEARL HARBOR: THE COMING OF THE
    WAR BETWEEN THE UNITED STATES AND JAPAN. 1950:
    Princeton University Press.

David J. Lu. FROM THE MARCO POLO BRIDGE TO PEARL HARBOR:
    JAPAN'S ENTRY INTO WORLD WAR II. 1961: Public Affairs.

John Toland. THE RISING SUN: THE DECLINE AND FALL OF THE
    JAPANESE EMPIRE, 1936-1945. 1970: Random House.

David Bergamini. JAPAN'S IMPERIAL CONSPIRACY. 1971: Morrow.

Charles D. Sheldon. "Japanese Aggression and the Emperor, 1931-1941, from Contemporary Diaries," *Modern Asian Studies* 10.1 (1976), 1-40.

_____. "Scapegoat or Instigator of Japanese Aggression? Inoue Kiyoshi's Case Against the Emperor," *Modern Asian Studies* 12.1 (1978), 1-35.

William L. Langer & S. E. Gleason. THE WORLD CRISIS AND AMERICAN FOREIGN POLICY. 1952-1953: Harper.

   Volume 1: THE CHALLENGE TO ISOLATION, 1937-1940. 1952.
   Volume 2: THE UNDECLARED WAR, 1940-1941. 1953.

James H. Herzog. CLOSING THE OPEN DOOR: AMERICAN-JAPANESE DIPLOMATIC NEGOTIATIONS, 1936-1941. 1973: Naval Institute.

Jonathan Utley. GOING TO WAR WITH JAPAN, 1937-1941. 1985: University of Tennessee Press.

Donald J. Friedman. THE ROAD FROM ISOLATION: THE CAMPAIGN OF THE AMERICAN COMMITTEE FOR NON-PARTICIPATION IN JAPANESE AGGRESSION, 1938-1941. 1968: Council on East Asian Studies, Harvard University.

Immanuel Hsu. "Kurusu's Mission to the United States and the Abortive Modus Vivendi," *Journal of Modern History* 24.3 (1952), 301-307.

Richard N. Current. "How Stimson Meant to 'Maneuver' the Japanese," *Mississippi Valley Historical Review* 60 (1953), 67-74.

Ladislas Farago. THE BROKEN SEAL: THE STORY OF 'OPERATION MAGIC' AND THE PEARL HARBOR DISASTER. 1967: Random House.

Paul W. Schroeder. THE AXIS ALLIANCE AND JAPANESE-AMERICAN RELATIONS, 1941. 1958: Cornell University Press.

Nobutake Ike, transl. JAPAN'S DECISION FOR WAR: RECORDS OF THE 1941 POLICY CONFERENCES. 1967: Stanford University Press.

Valdo Ferretti. "Captain Fujii Shigeru and the Decision for War in 1941," *Japan Forum* 3.2 (1991), 221-230.

Abraham Ben-Zvi. THE ILLUSION OF DETERRENCE: THE ROOSEVELT PRESIDENCY AND THE ORIGINS OF THE PACIFIC WAR. 1987: Westview Press.

U.S. Department of State. PEACE AND WAR: UNITED STATES FOREIGN
    POLICY, 1931-1941. 1943: Government Printing Office. See
    especially the narrative summation on 1-151.

_____. FOREIGN RELATIONS OF THE UNITED STATES: JAPAN,
    1931-1941. 2 volumes. 1943: Government Printing Office. See
    especially the "Account of Informal Conversations Between the
    Government of the United States and the Government of Japan, 1941"
    in volume 2, 325-386.

U.S. Department of the Army (Historical Section, G-2, GHQ, FEC), "Politico-
    Military Evolution Toward War," in REPORTS OF GENERAL
    MACARTHUR (1966: Government Printing Office), volume 2,
    part 1: 30-43.

U.S. Congress, Joint Committee on the Pearl Harbor Attack. REPORT (1946).
    See especially 1: 1-49 and 289-444 on the diplomatic background prior
    to Pearl Harbor.

U.S. Department of Defense. THE "MAGIC" BACKGROUND OF PEARL
    HARBOR. 5 volumes. 1978: Department of Defense.

The Pearl Harbor Controversy

Hector C. Bywater. THE GREAT PACIFIC WAR. 1991: St. Martin's.
    The classic 1925 "prediction" of Japan's Pacific War strategy, originally
    subtitled "A History of the American-Japanese Campaign of 1931-33."

William H. Honan. VISIONS OF INFAMY: THE UNTOLD STORY OF HOW
    JOURNALIST HECTOR C. BYWATER DEVISED THE PLANS
    THAT LED TO PEARL HARBOR. 1991: St. Martin's.

John Costello. "Pearl Harbor—Warning or Decision?", in his THE PACIFIC
    WAR, 1941-1945 (1982: Quill), 617-659.

Martin V. Melosi. THE SHADOW OF PEARL HARBOR: POLITICAL
    CONTROVERSY OVER THE SURPRISE ATTACK, 1941-1946.
    1977: Texas A & M University Press.

_____. "National Security Misused: The Aftermath of Pearl Harbor," *Prologue*
    9.2 (1977), 75-90.

Louis Morton. "1937-1941," in May & Thomson, AMERICAN-EAST ASIAN
    RELATIONS (1972: Harvard University Press), 260-290.

Hilary Conroy & Harry Wray, eds. PEARL HARBOR REEXAMINED: PRO-
LOGUE TO THE PACIFIC WAR. 1990: University of Hawaii Press.

John McKechney, S. J. "The Pearl Harbor Controversy: A Debate Among
Historians," *Monumenta Nipponica* 18.1-4 (1963), 45-88.

Robert H. Ferrell. "Pearl Harbor and the Revisionists," *The Historian* 17 (1955),
reprinted in Esmonde M. Robertson, ed. THE ORIGINS OF THE
SECOND WORLD WAR (1971: Macmillan), 272-292.

Joseph Grew. "Pearl Harbor: From the Perspective of Ten Years," chapter 34 in
his TURBULENT ERA, volume 2 (1952: Houghton Mifflin),
1244-1375.

George M. Waller, ed. PEARL HARBOR: ROOSEVELT AND THE COMING
OF THE WAR. 3rd edition. 1976: Heath.

Michael Slackman. TARGET: PEARL HARBOR. 1990: University of Hawaii
Press.

Thomas Breslin. "Mystifying the Past: Establishment Historians and the Origins
of the Pacific War," *Bulletin of Concerned Asian Scholars* 8.4 (1976),
18-36.

Robert Dallek. FRANKLIN ROOSEVELT AND AMERICAN FOREIGN
POLICY, 1932-1945. 1979: Oxford University Press.

Roberta Wohlstetter. PEARL HARBOR: WARNING AND DECISION.
1962: Stanford University Press.

Richard Collier. THE ROAD TO PEARL HARBOR: 1941. 1981: Atheneum.

Gordon W. Prange. AT DAWN WE SLEPT: THE UNTOLD STORY OF
PEARL HARBOR. 1981: Penguin.

_____, with Donald M. Goldstein & Katherine V. Dillon. PEARL HARBOR:
THE VERDICT OF HISTORY. 1985: McGraw-Hill.

_____, with Donald M. Goldstein & Katherine V. Dillon. GOD'S SAMURAI:
LEAD PILOT AT PEARL HARBOR. 1990: Brassey's. A biography
of naval aviator Fuchida Mitsuo.

Edwin T. Layton, with Roger Pineau & John Costello. "AND I WAS THERE":
PEARL HARBOR AND MIDWAY— BREAKING THE SECRETS.
1985: Morrow.

John Toland. INFAMY: PEARL HARBOR AND ITS AFTERMATH. 1982: Doubleday.

David Kahn. "Did FDR Invite the Pearl Harbor Attack?", *New York Review of Books* (May 27, 1982), 36-40. Review of Prange and Toland.

John Costello. "Remember Pearl Harbor," *U.S. Naval Academy Proceedings* (1983), 53-62. Review of Prange and Toland.

Ronald H. Spector. "Someone Had Blundered, but Who?", *New York Times Book Review*, December 5, 1985, 9-10. Review of Prange's PEARL HARBOR and Layton's "AND I WAS THERE."

James R. Leutze. BARGAINING FOR SUPREMACY: ANGLO-AMERICAN NAVAL COLLABORATION, 1937-1941. 1977: University of North Carolina Press.

Arthur Marder. OLD FRIENDS, NEW ENEMIES: THE ROYAL NAVY AND THE IMPERIAL JAPANESE NAVY— STRATEGIC ILLUSIONS, 1936-1941. 1981: Oxford University Press.

Edwin Palmer Hoyt. YAMAMOTO: THE MAN WHO PLANNED PEARL HARBOR. 1990: McGraw-Hill.

Ikuhiko Hata. JAPANESE NAVAL ACES AND FIGHTER UNITS IN WORLD WAR II. 1989: Naval Institute Press.

Jeffrey M. Dorwart. CONFLICT OF DUTY: THE U.S. NAVY'S INTELLI-GENCE DILEMMA, 1919-1945. 1983: Naval Institute.

Harry E. Barnes, ed. PERPETUAL WAR FOR PERPETUAL PEACE: A CRITICAL EXAMINATION OF THE FOREIGN POLICY OF FRANKLIN DELANO ROOSEVELT AND ITS AFTERMATH. 1953: Caxton.

_____. PEARL HARBOR AFTER A QUARTER OF A CENTURY. 1972: Arno.

William Neumann. "How American Policy Toward Japan Contributed to War in the Pacific," in Harry E. Barnes, ed. PERPETUAL WAR FOR PERPETUAL PEACE (1953: Caxton), 231-268.

Noam Chomsky. "The Revolutionary Pacifism of A. J. Muste: On the Backgrounds of the Pacific War," in his AMERICAN POWER AND THE NEW MANDARINS (1969: Pantheon), 159-220.

Bruce M. Russett. NO CLEAR AND PRESENT DANGER: A SKEPTICAL
VIEW OF THE UNITED STATES ENTRY INTO WORLD WAR II.
1972: Harper & Row.

Thurston Clarke. PEARL HARBOR GHOSTS: A JOURNEY TO HAWAII,
THEN AND NOW. 1991: William Morrow.

The Japanese & the Jews

David Kranzler. JAPANESE, NAZIS AND JEWS: THE JEWISH REFUGEE
COMMUNITY OF SHANGHAI, 1938-1945. 1975: Paragon.

_____. "Japanese Policy Toward the Jews, 1938-1941," *Japan Interpreter* 11.4
(1977), 493-527.

Marvin Tokayer & May Swartz. THE FUGU PLAN: THE UNTOLD STORY
OF THE JAPANESE AND THE JEWS DURING WORLD WAR II.
1979: Paddington.

Herman Dicker. WANDERERS AND SETTLERS IN THE FAR EAST:
A CENTURY OF JEWISH LIFE IN CHINA AND JAPAN. 1962:
Twayne.

Ben-Ami Shillony. THE JEWS & THE JAPANESE: THE SUCCESSFUL
OUTSIDERS. 1992: C. E. Tuttle.

Pamela Shatzkes. "Kōbe: A Japanese Haven for Jewish Refugees, 1940-1941,"
Japan Forum 3.2 (1991), 257-273.

"JAPAN'S CASE"

Masamichi Rōyama. FOREIGN POLICY OF JAPAN, 1914-1939. 1941: Japan
Council, Institute of Pacific Relations ("Far Eastern Conflict" Series 7).

Kiyoshi K. Kawakami. AMERICAN-JAPANESE RELATIONS: AN INSIDE
VIEW OF JAPAN'S POLICIES AND PURPOSES. 1912: Fleming H.
Revell.

_____. JAPAN IN WORLD POLITICS. 1917: Macmillan.

_____. JAPAN AND WORLD PEACE. 1919: Macmillan.

_____. WHAT JAPAN THINKS. 1921: Macmillan.

_____. JAPAN SPEAKS ON THE SINO-JAPANESE CRISIS. 1932: Macmillan.

_____. MANCHUKUO: CHILD OF CONFLICT. 1933: Macmillan.

_____. JAPAN IN CHINA: HER MOTIVES AND AIMS. 1938: Macmillan.

Yūsuke Tsurumi. PRESENT-DAY JAPAN. 1926: Columbia University Press.

_____. "Japan in the Modern World," *Foreign Affairs* 9.2 (1931), 254-265.

Yōsuke Matsuoka. "Japan's Interests in Manchuria," *Asiatic Review* 27 (1931), 510-519.

League of Nations. DOCUMENT A: THE PRESENT CONDITION OF CHINA, WITH REFERENCE TO CIRCUMSTANCES AFFECTING INTERNATIONAL RELATIONS AND GOOD UNDERSTANDING BETWEEN NATIONS UPON WHICH PEACE DEPENDS. 1932: League of Nations.

_____. DOCUMENT B: RELATIONS OF JAPAN WITH MANCHURIA AND MONGOLIA. 1932: League of Nations.

_____. V. K. Wellington Koo. MEMORANDA PRESENTED TO THE LYTTON COMMISSION. 2 volumes. 1932-33: League of Nations.

_____. The Lytton Commission. REPORT OF THE COMMISSION OF INQUIRY. 1932: League of Nations.

Japanese Association in China, comp. PRESENTING JAPAN'S SIDE OF THE CASE. 1931: Japanese Association in China.

Chih Meng. CHINA SPEAKS: ON THE CONFLICT BETWEEN CHINA AND JAPAN. 1932: Kennikat.

Yasaka Takagi. "World Peace Machinery and the Asia Monroe Doctrine," *Pacific Affairs* 5 (1932), 941-953.

George H. Blakeslee. "The Japanese Monroe Doctrine," *Foreign Affairs* 11.4 (1933), 671-681.

Kikujirō Ishii. "The Permanent Basis of Japanese Foreign Policy," *Foreign Affairs* 11.2 (1933), 220-229.

_____. DIPLOMATIC COMMENTARIES. William R. Langdon, transl. & ed. 1936: Johns Hopkins.

W. Watkin Davies. "Japan and Western Example," *The Fortnightly* (June 1935), 718-727.

Hiroshi Saitō. JAPAN'S POLICIES AND PURPOSES: SELECTIONS FROM RECENT ADDRESSES AND WRITINGS. 1935: Jones.

George Bronson Rhea. THE CASE FOR MANCHUKUO. 1935: Appleton-Century.

W. W. Willoughby. THE SINO-JAPANESE CONTROVERSY AND THE LEAGUE OF NATIONS. 1935: Johns Hopkins.

Jinji G. Kasai. THE UNITED STATES AND JAPAN IN THE PACIFIC: AMERICAN NAVAL MANEUVERS AND JAPAN'S PACIFIC POLICY. 1935; reprinted 1970: Arno.

Tōta Ishimaru. JAPAN MUST FIGHT BRITAIN. G. V. Rayment, transl. 1936: Telegraph.

Ginjiro Fujihara. THE SPIRIT OF JAPANESE INDUSTRY. 1936: Hokuseidō.

Herbert Max Bratter. "The Cases for Japan and China," *Asia* 37 (November 1937).

Foreign Affairs Association of Japan. WHY JAPAN HAD TO FIGHT IN SHANGHAI. 1937: Foreign Affairs Association of Japan.

_____. THE SINO-JAPANESE CONFLICT AND FINANCIAL RESOURCES: A SYMPOSIUM. 1937: Foreign Affairs Association of Japan.

_____. THE SINO-JAPANESE CONFLICT: A SHORT SURVEY. 1937: Foreign Affairs Association of Japan.

Kiyoshi Miki. "The China Affair and Japanese Thought," *Contemporary Japan* 6 (1938), 601-610.

Tatsuo Kawai. THE GOAL OF JAPANESE EXPANSION. 1938: Hokuseidō.

Royal Institute of International Affairs. SURVEY OF INTERNATIONAL
 AFFAIRS. Annual volumes include primary documents from various
 governments: Oxford University Press.

Royal Institute of International Affairs, Information Department. CHINA AND
 JAPAN. 3rd edition. 1941: Oxford University Press.

Charles R. Shepherd. THE CASE AGAINST JAPAN. 1939: Jarrolds.

W. W. Willoughby. JAPAN'S CASE EXAMINED. 1940: Johns Hopkins.

Seiji G. Hishida. JAPAN AMONG THE GREAT POWERS: A SURVEY OF
 HER INTERNATIONAL RELATIONS. 1940: Longmans, Green.

Kiyoshi Miki & Karoku Hosokawa. INTRODUCTORY STUDIES ON THE
 SINO-JAPANESE CONFLICT. 1941: Japan Council, Institute of
 Pacific Relations.

Sir Frederick Whyte. JAPAN'S PURPOSE IN ASIA. 1941: Royal Institute of
 International Affairs.

Greater East Asia War Inquiry Commission. THE AMERICAN-BRITISH
 CHALLENGE DIRECTED AGAINST JAPAN. 1943: Mainichi
 Shimbunsha. Japanese war-crimes charges against the Anglo-
 Americans.

IDEOLOGIES OF EMPIRE

[See also pages 191-205 on "Nationalism & the Emperor System" and
 "'Fascism,' Militarism & the Shōwa Crisis." Also the "Japan at War"
 citations on pages 323-328.]

Byron K. Marshall. CAPITALISM AND NATIONALISM IN PREWAR
 JAPAN: THE IDEOLOGY OF THE BUSINESS ELITE, 1868-1941.
 1967: Stanford University Press.

Marlene Mayo, ed. THE EMERGENCE OF IMPERIAL JAPAN:
 SELF-DEFENSE OR CALCULATED AGGRESSION? 1970: Heath.
 See especially the essays by Yoshitake Oka, Sannosuke Matsumoto, and
 Shōichi Fujii.

G. B. Sansom. THE WESTERN WORLD AND JAPAN: A STUDY IN THE
 INTERACTION OF EUROPEAN AND ASIATIC CULTURES. 1950:
 Knopf.

Kimitada Miwa. "Fukuzawa Yukichi's 'Departure from Asia': A Prelude to the Sino-Japanese War," in Edmund Skrzypczak ed. JAPAN'S MODERN CENTURY (1968: Monumenta Nipponica), 1-26.

Albert M. Craig. "Fukuzawa Yukichi: The Philosophical Foundations of Meiji Nationalism," in Robert Ward, ed. POLITICAL DEVELOPMENT IN MODERN JAPAN (1968: Princeton University Press), 99-148.

Marius B. Jansen. "Ōi Kentarō's Radicalism and Chauvinism," *Far Eastern Quarterly* 11.3 (1952), 305-316.

_____. THE JAPANESE AND SUN YAT-SEN. 1954: Harvard University Press.

E. Herbert Norman. "The Gen'yōsha: A Study in the Origins of Japanese Imperialism," *Pacific Affairs* 17.3 (1944), 261-284.

Kazuo Shibagaki. "The Logic of Japanese Imperialism," *Social Science Abstracts* 14 (Shakai Kagaku Kenkyūjo, Tokyo University, 1973), 70-87.

Masanori Nakamura. "The Emperor System of the 1900s," *Bulletin of Concerned Asian Scholars* 16.2 (1984), 2-11.

Donald Keene. "The Sino-Japanese War of 1894-95 and Japanese Culture," in his LANDSCAPES AND PORTRAITS: APPRECIATIONS OF JAPANESE CULTURE (1971: Kōdansha International), 259-299.

Mark R. Peattie. "Japanese Attitudes Toward Colonialism, 1895-1945," in Ramon Myers & Mark Peattie, eds. THE JAPANESE COLONIAL EMPIRE (1984: Princeton University Press), 80-127.

Shinkichi Etō. "Asianism and Duality of Japanese Colonialism, 1879-1945," in L. Blusse, H. L. Wesseling & G. D. Winius, eds. HISTORY AND UNDERDEVELOPMENT (1980: Centre for the History of European Expansion, Leiden), 114-126.

O. Tanin & E. Yohan. MILITARISM AND FASCISM IN JAPAN. 1934: Lawrence & Wishart. Translated from the Russian, with an introduction by Karl Radek.

_____. WHEN JAPAN GOES TO WAR. 1936: Lawrence & Wishart.

Masao Maruyama. THOUGHT AND BEHAVIOR IN MODERN JAPANESE POLITICS. 1963: Oxford University Press.

Shunsuke Tsurumi. AN INTELLECTUAL HISTORY OF WARTIME JAPAN,
    1931-1945. 1986: KPI.

Kazuko Tsurumi. SOCIAL CHANGE AND THE INDIVIDUAL: JAPAN
    BEFORE AND AFTER DEFEAT IN WORLD WAR II. 1966:
    Princeton University Press. Excellent essays on indoctrination and
    "socialization for death."

Toshio Iritani. GROUP PSYCHOLOGY OF THE JAPANESE IN WARTIME.
    1991: KPI.

Saburō Ienaga. THE PACIFIC WAR, 1931-1945. Frank Baldwin, transl. 1978:
    Pantheon.

Joyce Lebra, ed. JAPAN'S GREATER EAST ASIA CO-PROSPERITY
    SPHERE IN WORLD WAR II: SELECTED READINGS AND
    DOCUMENTS. 1975: Oxford University Press.

Richard Storry. THE DOUBLE PATRIOTS: A STUDY OF JAPANESE
    NATIONALISM. 1957: Houghton Mifflin.

Grant Goodman, ed. IMPERIAL JAPAN AND ASIA. 1967: Occasional Papers
    of the East Asia Institute, Columbia University. Includes Akira Iriye's
    "The Ideology of Japanese Imperialism" (32-45) and George Wilson's
    "Reflections on Japanese Imperialist Ideology" (46-51).

Hilary Conroy. "Japanese Nationalism and Expansionism," *American Historical
    Review* 60 (1955), 818-829.

T. R. H. Havens. "Nationalism," KŌDANSHA ENCYCLOPEDIA OF JAPAN
    5: 342-343.

George M. Wilson. "Ultranationalism," KŌDANSHA ENCYCLOPEDIA OF
    JAPAN 8: 145-146.

Gordon Berger. "The Three-dimensional Empire: Japanese Attitudes and the
    New Order in Asia, 1937-1945," *Japan Interpreter* 12.3-4 (1979),
    355-383.

_____. "New Order Movement (Shin Taisei Undō)," KŌDANSHA
    ENCYCLOPEDIA OF JAPAN 5: 365-366.

James B. Crowley. "A New Deal for Japan and Asia: One Road to Pearl
    Harbor," in his MODERN EAST ASIA (1970: Harcourt Brace &
    World), 235-264.

————. "A New Asian Order: Some Notes on Prewar Japanese Nationalism," in B. Silberman & H. Harootunian, eds. JAPAN IN CRISIS (1974: Princeton University Press), 270-298.

————. "Intellectuals as Visionaries of the New Asian Order," in James W. Morley, ed. DILEMMAS OF GROWTH IN PREWAR JAPAN (1972: Princeton University Press), 319-373.

Louis M. Allen. "Fujiwara and Suzuki: Patterns of Asian Liberation," in William H. Newell, ed. JAPAN IN ASIA (1981: Singapore University Press), 83-103.

William Miles Fletcher. "Intellectuals and Fascism in Early Shōwa Japan," *Journal of Asian Studies* 39.1 (1979), 39-63.

————. THE SEARCH FOR A NEW ORDER: INTELLECTUALS AND FASCISM IN PREWAR JAPAN. 1982: University of North Carolina Press.

Mark R. Peattie. ISHIWARA KANJI AND JAPAN'S CONFRONTATION WITH THE WEST. 1975: Princeton University Press.

L. R. Oates. "Two Leading Japanese Pan-Asianists: Tōyama Mitsuru and Ishiwara Kanji," in Harold Bolitho & Alan Rix, eds. A NORTHERN PROSPECT: AUSTRALIAN PAPERS ON JAPAN (1981: Japanese Studies Association of Australia), 28-33.

Katsumi Usui. "Pursuing an Illusion: The New Order in East Asia," *Japan Interpreter* 6.3 (1970), 326-337.

Tōru Yano. "Southern Expansion Doctrine," KŌDANSHA ENCYCLOPEDIA OF JAPAN 7: 236-237.

Jaya Deva. JAPAN'S KAMPF. 1942: Left Book Club.

Otto D. Tolischus, ed. THROUGH JAPANESE EYES. 1945: Reynal & Hitchcock.

Chalmers A. Johnson. AN INSTANCE OF TREASON: OZAKI HOZUMI AND THE SORGE SPY RING. 1964: Stanford University Press.

F. W. Deakin & G. R. Storry. THE CASE OF RICHARD SORGE. 1966: Chatto & Windus.

Gordon Prange, with Donald M. Goldstein & Katherine Dillon. TARGET TOKYO: THE STORY OF THE SORGE SPY RING. 1984: McGraw-Hill.

Japanese Ministry of Education. *KOKUTAI NO HONGI*: CARDINAL PRINCIPLES OF THE NATIONAL ENTITY OF JAPAN. Translated by John O. Gauntlett and edited by Robert K. Hall. 1949: Harvard University Press. The basic expression of government orthodoxy, first issued in 1937.

_____. THE WAY OF THE SUBJECT (*Shinmin no Michi*), 1941; in Otto Tolischus, TOKYO RECORD (1943: Reynal & Hitchcock), 405-427.

John Paul Reed. KOKUTAI: A STUDY OF CERTAIN SACRED AND SECULAR ASPECTS OF JAPANESE NATIONALISM. 1940: University of Chicago Press.

Robert K. Hall. SHŪSHIN: THE ETHICS OF A DEFEATED NATION. 1949: Columbia University Press.

Ury Eppstein. "School Songs Before and After the War: From 'Children Tank Soldiers' to 'Everyone a Good Child'," *Monumenta Nipponica* 42.4 (1987), 431-447.

D. C. Holtom. THE NATIONAL FAITH OF JAPAN: A STUDY IN MODERN SHINTŌ. 1938: Dutton.

_____. MODERN JAPAN AND SHINTŌ NATIONALISM. 1943; revised edition, 1947: University of Chicago Press.

John W. Dower. WAR WITHOUT MERCY: RACE AND POWER IN THE PACIFIC WAR. 1986: Pantheon.

_____. "Race, Language, and War in Two Cultures," in his JAPAN IN WAR AND PEACE (1994: The New Press), 257-285.

ECONOMICS OF EMPIRE

[See also the general "Economic Development" section on pages 157-169, as well as the citations to primary materials within pages 347-372.]

Overviews

Takafusa Nakamura. ECONOMIC GROWTH IN PREWAR JAPAN. 1982: University of Tokyo Press.

William Lockwood. THE ECONOMIC DEVELOPMENT OF JAPAN: GROWTH AND STRUCTURAL CHANGE, 1868-1938. 1954: Princeton University Press.

Frances V. Moulder. JAPAN, CHINA AND THE MODERN WORLD ECONOMY: TOWARD A REINTERPRETATION OF EAST ASIAN DEVELOPMENT, ca. 1600 TO ca. 1918. 1977: Cambridge University Press.

Nazli Choucri, Robert C. North, & Susumu Yamakage. THE CHALLENGE OF JAPAN BEFORE WORLD WAR II AND AFTER: A STUDY OF NATIONAL GROWTH AND EXPANSION. 1992: Routledge.

Byron K. Marshall. CAPITALISM AND NATIONALISM IN PREWAR JAPAN: THE IDEOLOGY OF THE BUSINESS ELITE, 1868-1941. 1967: Stanford University Press.

Jon Halliday. A POLITICAL HISTORY OF JAPANESE CAPITALISM. 1975: Pantheon.

Shigeki Tōyama. "Politics, Economics, and the International Environment in the Meiji and Taishō Periods," *Developing Economies* 4 (1966), 419-426.

Shōichi Fujii. "Capitalism, International Politics, and the Emperor System," in Marlene Mayo, ed. THE EMERGENCE OF IMPERIAL JAPAN (1970: Heath), 75-82.

Kenneth E. Boulding & Alan H. Gleason. "War As an Investment: The Strange Case of Japan," *Peace Research Society (International) Papers* 3 (1965), reprinted in Kenneth E. Boulding & Tapan Mukerjee, eds. ECONOMIC IMPERIALISM: A BOOK OF READINGS (1972: University of Michigan Press), 240-261.

Yoshio Andō. "The Formation of Heavy Industry—One of the Processes of Industrialization in the Meiji Period," *Developing Economies* 3 (1965), 450-470.

Kōzō Yamamura. "Success Illgotten? The Role of Meiji Militarism in Japan's Technical Progress," *Journal of Economic History* 37.1 (1977), 113-135.

Hugh Borton. "The Economic Basis of the New Empire, 1890-1915," chapter 14 in his JAPAN'S MODERN CENTURY (1970: Ronald).

_____. "War and the Rise of Industrialization in Japan," in Jesse D. Clarkson & Thomas C. Cochran, eds. WAR AS A SOCIAL INSTITUTION (1941: Columbia University Press), 224-234.

Hilary Conroy. "A Rebuttal to Economic Determinism," in Marlene Mayo, ed. THE EMERGENCE OF IMPERIAL JAPAN (1970: Heath), 83-87.

Arthur E. Tiedemann. "Japan's Economic Foreign Policies, 1868-1893," in J. W. Morley, ed. JAPAN'S FOREIGN POLICY, 1868-1941 (1974: Columbia University Press), 118-152.

William D. Wray. MITSUBISHI AND THE N.Y.K., 1870-1914: BUSINESS STRATEGY IN THE JAPANESE SHIPPING INDUSTRY. 1984: Council on East Asian Studies, Harvard University.

Yukiko Fukasaku. TECHNOLOGY AND INDUSTRIAL DEVELOPMENT IN PRE-WAR JAPAN: THE MITSUBISHI NAGASAKI SHIPYARD, 1884-1934. 1992: Routledge.

John G. Roberts. MITSUI: THREE CENTURIES OF JAPANESE BUSINESS. 1973: Weatherhill.

G. Best. "Financing a Foreign War: Jacob Schiff and Japan, 1904-1905," *American Jewish Historical Quarterly* 62 (1972), 313-324.

Ushisaburō Kobayashi. WAR AND ARMAMENT LOANS OF JAPAN. 1922: Oxford University Press.

_____. WAR AND ARMAMENT TAXES OF JAPAN. 1922: Oxford University Press.

Michael A. Barnhart. JAPAN PREPARES FOR TOTAL WAR: THE SEARCH FOR ECONOMIC SECURITY, 1919-1941. 1987: Cornell University Press.

Giichi Ono. WAR AND ARMAMENT EXPENDITURES OF JAPAN. 1922: Oxford University Press.

Earl Kinmonth. "The Impact of Military Procurements on the Old Middle Classes in Japan, 1931-1941," *Japan Forum* 4.2 (1992), 247-265.

The Formal Empire

Ikuhiko Hata. "Colonial Expansion, 1905-1941," in Peter Duus, ed. CAMBRIDGE HISTORY OF JAPAN, Volume 6: THE TWENTIETH CENTURY (1988: Cambridge University Press), 271-314.

Ramon H. Myers & Mark R. Peattie, eds. THE JAPANESE COLONIAL EMPIRE, 1895-1945. 1984: Princeton University Press. See especially Peter Duus on "Economic Dimensions of Meiji Imperialism: The Case of Korea, 1895-1910" (128-171), and essays by Samuel Pao-San Ho, Toshiyuki Mizoguchi & Yūzō Yamamoto, and Ramon Myers & Saburō Yamada pertaining to "The Economic Dynamics of Empire," especially involving Korea and Taiwan (347-452).

James I. Nakamura. "Incentives, Productivity Gaps, and Agricultural Growth Rates in Prewar Japan, Taiwan and Korea," in B. Silberman & H. Harootunian, eds. JAPAN IN CRISIS (1974: Princeton University Press), 329-373.

Dennis McNamara. "The Keishō and the Korean Business Elite," *Journal of Asian Studies* 48.2 (1989), 310-323. On the Seoul Chamber of Commerce and Industry in colonial Korea.

Akira Iriye. "The Failure of Economic Expansion, 1918-1931," in Silberman & Harootunian, JAPAN IN CRISIS (1974: Princeton University Press), 237-269.

Arthur E. Tiedemann. "Big Business and Politics in Prewar Japan," in J. W. Morley, ed. DILEMMAS OF GROWTH IN PREWAR JAPAN (1971: Princeton University Press), 267-316.

Kiyoshi Ōshima. "The World Economic Crisis and Japan's Foreign Economic Policy," *Developing Economies* 5.4 (1967), 628-647.

Tsutomu Ōuchi. "Agricultural Depression and Japanese Villages," *Developing Economies* 4.4 (1967), 597-627.

Kōzō Yamamura. "Then Came the Great Depression: Japan's Interwar Years," in Herman van der Wee, ed. THE GREAT DEPRESSION REVISITED (1972: Martinus Nijhoff), 182-211.

_____. "The Japanese Economy, 1911-1930: Concentration, Conflicts, and Crises," in Silberman & Harootunian, JAPAN IN CRISIS (1974: Princeton University Press), 299-328.

Shigeto Tsuru. "Japan's Economy Under the Strain of the China Incident," in his ESSAYS ON JAPANESE ECONOMY (1958: Institute of Pacific Relations), 154-236.

Yukio Chō. "From the Shōwa Economic Crisis to Military Economy—with Special Reference to the Inoue and Takahashi Financial Policies," *Developing Economies* 5.4 (1967), 568-596.

_____. "Exposing the Incompetence of the Bourgeoisie: The Financial Panic of 1927," *Japan Interpreter* 8.4 (1974), 492-501.

_____. "Keeping Step With the Military: The Beginning of the Automobile Age," *Japan Interpreter* 7.2 (1972), 168-178.

Mitsuharu Itō. "Munitions Unlimited: The Controlled Economy," *Japan Interpreter* 7.3-4 (1972), 353-363.

Makoto Takahashi. "The Development of Wartime Economic Controls," *Developing Economies* 5.4 (1967), 648-665.

H. T. Oshima. "Japan's Economic Structure," *Pacific Affairs* 15 (1942), 261-279.

Richard Rice. "Economic Mobilization in Wartime Japan: Business, Bureaucracy, and Military in Conflict," *Journal of Asian Studies* 38.4 (1979), 689-706.

Ernest Notar. "Japan's Wartime Labor Policy: A Search for Method," *Journal of Asian Studies* 44.2 (1985), 311-328.

Jerome B. Cohen. JAPAN'S ECONOMY IN WAR AND RECONSTRUCTION. 1949: University of Minnesota Press.

T. A. Bisson. JAPAN'S WAR ECONOMY. 1945: Institute of Pacific Relations.

_____. ZAIBATSU DISSOLUTION IN JAPAN. 1954: University of California Press.

Eleanor M. Hadley. ANTI-TRUST IN JAPAN. 1970: Princeton University Press.

Mitsubishi Economic Research Institute. MITSUI-MITSUBISHI-SUMITOMO: PRESENT STATUS OF THE FORMER ZAIBATSU ENTERPRISES. 1955: Mitsubishi Economic Research Institute.

Kōzō Yamamura. "Zaibatsu, Prewar and Zaibatsu, Postwar," *Journal of Asian Studies* 23.4 (1964), 539-554.

Edwin W. Pauley. REPORT ON JAPANESE REPARATIONS TO THE PRESIDENT OF THE UNITED STATES, NOVEMBER 1945 TO APRIL 1946. Department of State Publication 3174, Far Eastern Series 25. The Pauley Report. See also separate Pauley reports on JAPANESE ASSETS IN MANCHURIA and JAPANESE ASSETS IN SOVIET-OCCUPIED KOREA.

U.S. Department of State. REPORT OF THE MISSION ON JAPANESE COMBINES, PART I, ANALYTICAL AND TECHNICAL DATA. Department of State Publication 2628, Far Eastern Series 14, 1946. The Edwards Report.

Frederick Thayer Merrill. JAPAN AND THE OPIUM MENACE. 1942: Institute of Pacific Relations.

Chalmers Johnson. MITI AND THE JAPANESE MIRACLE: THE GROWTH OF INDUSTRIAL POLICY, 1925-1975. 1982: Stanford University Press.

China & the Pacific

Stephen C. Thomas. FOREIGN INTERVENTION AND CHINA'S INDUSTRIAL DEVELOPMENT, 1870-1911. 1984: Westview.

Ping-shu Kao. FOREIGN LOANS TO CHINA. 1946: Sino-International Economic Research Center.

Charles F. Remer. FOREIGN INVESTMENTS IN CHINA. 1933: Macmillan.

_____. A STUDY OF CHINESE BOYCOTTS. 1935: Johns Hopkins.

Donald A. Jordan. CHINESE BOYCOTTS VERSUS JAPANESE BOMBS: THE FAILURE OF CHINA'S "REVOLUTIONARY DIPLOMACY," 1931-32. 1991: University of Michigan Press.

Emily Honig. SISTERS AND STRANGERS: WOMEN IN THE SHANGHAI
    COTTON MILLS, 1919-1949. 1986: Stanford University Press.

Ralph William Huenemann. THE DRAGON AND THE IRON HORSE:
    ECONOMICS OF RAILROADS IN CHINA, 1876-1937. 1983:
    Harvard University Press.

Kia-ngau Chang. CHINA'S STRUGGLE FOR RAILROAD DEVELOPMENT.
    1943: John Day.

Norton S. Ginsburg. "Manchurian Railway Development," *Far Eastern
    Quarterly* 8.4 (1949), 398-411.

H. L. Kingman. EFFECTS OF CHINESE NATIONALISM UPON
    MANCHURIAN RAILWAY DEVELOPMENTS, 1925-1931. 1932:
    University of California Press.

John Young. "South Manchurian Railway," KŌDANSHA ENCYCLOPEDIA OF
    JAPAN 7: 237-238.

Herbert Bix. "Japanese Imperialism and the Manchurian Economy, 1900-31,"
    China Quarterly 52 (1972), 425-443.

Kungtu C. Sun. THE ECONOMIC DEVELOPMENT OF MANCHURIA IN
    THE FIRST HALF OF THE TWENTIETH CENTURY. 1968:
    Council on East Asian Studies, Harvard University.

E. B. Schumpeter, ed. THE INDUSTRIALIZATION OF JAPAN AND
    MANCHUKUO, 1930-1940. 1940: Macmillan.

W. I. Ladejinsky. "Manchurian Agriculture Under Japanese Control," *Foreign
    Agriculture* 5 (1941), 309-340.

G. C. Allen. JAPAN, THE HUNGRY GUEST. 1938: Allen & Unwin.

_____. JAPANESE INDUSTRY: ITS RECENT DEVELOPMENT AND
    PRESENT CONDITION. 1940: Institute of Pacific Relations.

_____ & A. C. Donnithorne. WESTERN ENTERPRISE IN FAR EASTERN
    ECONOMIC DEVELOPMENT: CHINA AND JAPAN. 1954:
    Allen & Unwin.

C. D. Cowan, ed. THE ECONOMIC DEVELOPMENT OF CHINA AND
    JAPAN: STUDIES IN ECONOMIC HISTORY AND POLITICAL
    ECONOMY. 1964: Praeger.

Francis E. Hyde. FAR EASTERN TRADE, 1860-1914. 1973: Harper & Row.

John E. Orchard. JAPAN'S ECONOMIC POSITION: THE PROGRESS OF INDUSTRIALIZATION. 1930: McGraw-Hill.

E. F. Penrose. FOOD SUPPLY AND RAW MATERIALS IN JAPAN. 1930: University of Chicago Press.

Harold G. Moulton. JAPAN, AN ECONOMIC AND FINANCIAL APPRAISAL. 1931: Brookings Institution.

Albert E. Hindmarsh. THE BASIS OF JAPAN'S FOREIGN POLICY. 1936: Harvard University Press.

O. Tanin & E. Yohan. WHEN JAPAN GOES TO WAR. 1936: Lawrence & Wishart.

Freda Utley. JAPAN'S FEET OF CLAY. 1937: Norton.

G. E. Hubbard. EASTERN INDUSTRIALIZATION AND ITS EFFECTS ON THE WEST, WITH SPECIAL REFERENCE TO GREAT BRITIAN AND JAPAN. 2nd edition. 1938: Royal Institute of International Affairs.

William L. Holland & Kate Mitchell, eds. PROBLEMS OF THE PACIFIC, 1936: PROCEEDINGS OF THE SIXTH CONFERENCE OF THE INSTITUTE OF PACIFIC RELATIONS (AUGUST 15-29, 1936). 1937: University of Chicago Press.

_____. PROBLEMS OF THE PACIFIC, 1939. PROCEEDINGS OF THE STUDY MEETING OF THE INSTITUTE OF PACIFIC RELATIONS (NOVEMBER 18-DECEMBER 2, 1939). 1940: Institute of Pacific Relations.

Royal Institute of International Affairs. CHINA AND JAPAN. See the economic sections in the 1939 and 1941 editions of this publication (102-130 and 127-151 respectively).

Kate L. Mitchell. JAPAN'S INDUSTRIAL STRENGTH: AN INQUIRY INTO THE INDUSTRIALIZATION OF THE WESTERN PACIFIC. 1942: Knopf.

F. Sternberg. "Japan's Economic Imperialism," *Social Research* 13 (1945), 328-349.

Mark R. Peattie. NAN'YŌ: THE RISE AND FALL OF THE JAPANESE IN
MICRONESIA, 1885-1945. 1988: University of Hawaii Press.

Cooperation, Depression, Embargo

Dorothy Borg & Shumpei Okamoto, eds. PEARL HARBOR AS HISTORY:
JAPANESE-AMERICAN RELATIONS, 1931-1941. 1973: Columbia
University Press. On the Japanese side, see essays by Katsurō
Yamamura on the Finance Ministry; Yukio Chō on U.S. capital export
to Manchuria; and Hideichirō Nakamura on the Japan Economic
Frederation. On the U.S. side, see Lloyd Gardner on the Commerce and
Treasury Departments and Mira Wilkins on U.S. business.

Akira Kudō & Terushi Hara, eds. INTERNATIONAL CARTELS IN
BUSINESS HISTORY: THE INTERNATIONAL CONFERENCE ON
BUSINESS HISTORY, 18. 1992: University of Tokyo Press. Focuses
on manufactured goods in the interwar years.

Lloyd Gardner. ECONOMIC ASPECTS OF NEW DEAL DIPLOMACY.
1964: University of Wisconsin Press.

Michael J. Hogan. INFORMAL ENTENTE: THE PRIVATE STRUCTURE
OF COOPERATION IN ANGLO-AMERICAN ECONOMIC DIPLO-
MACY, 1918-1928. 1977: University of Missouri Press.

Joan Hoff Wilson. AMERICAN BUSINESS & FOREIGN POLICY 1920-1933.
1971: University of Kentucky Press.

Charles P. Kindleberger. THE WORLD IN DEPRESSION 1929-1939. 1973:
University of California Press.

Ronald Dore & Radha Sinha, with Mari Sako, eds. JAPAN AND WORLD
DEPRESSION, THEN AND NOW: ESSAYS IN MEMORY OF
E. F. PENROSE. 1987: St. Martin's.

Takafusa Nakamura. "Depression, Recovery, and War, 1920-1945," in Peter
Duus, ed. CAMBRIDGE HISTORY OF JAPAN, Volume 6:
THE TWENTIETH CENTURY (1988: Cambridge University Press),
451-493.

Michiko Ikeda. "Protectionism and Discrimination against Japan's Foreign Trade,
1926-1937." 1989: Ph.D. dissertation, Harvard University.

Osamu Ishii. COTTON TEXTILE DIPLOMACY: JAPAN, GREAT BRITAIN, AND THE UNITED STATES, 1930-1936. 1981: Arno.

Irvine H. Anderson, Jr. STANDARD-VACUUM OIL COMPANY AND THE UNITED STATES EAST ASIAN POLICY, 1933-1941. 1975: Princeton University Press.

Jonathan Utley. "Upstairs, Downstairs at Foggy Bottom: Oil Exports and Japan, 1940-1941," *Prologue: The Journal of the National Archives* 8.1 (1976), 17-28.

U.S. Department of State. "Economic Measures by the United States Affecting Trade with Japan," in FOREIGN RELATIONS OF THE UNITED STATES: JAPAN, 1931-1941. Pages 201-273 in volume 2 cover 1937 to 1941.

Donald J. Friedman. THE ROAD FROM ISOLATION: THE CAMPAIGN OF THE AMERICAN COMMITTEE FOR NON-PARTICIPATION IN JAPANESE AGGRESSION, 1938-1941. 1968: Council on East Asian Studies, Harvard University.

American Committee for Non-Participation in Japanese Aggression. AMERICA'S SHARE IN JAPAN'S WAR GUILT. 1938: American Committee for Non-Participation in Japanese Agression.

Philip J. Jaffe. "Economic Provincialism and American Far Eastern Policy," *Science and Society* 5.4 (1941), 289-309.

Greater East Asia War Inquiry Commission. THE AMERICAN-BRITISH CHALLENGE DIRECTED AGAINST JAPAN. 1943: Mainichi Shimbunsha.

JAPAN AT WAR: GENERAL STUDIES

Waldo Heinrichs. "World War II," KŌDANSHA ENCYCLOPEDIA OF JAPAN 8: 271-277.

John W. Dower. "Rethinking World War Two in Asia," *Reviews in American History* 12.2 (1984), 155-169.

_____. WAR WITHOUT MERCY: RACE AND POWER IN THE PACIFIC
WAR. 1986: Pantheon.

_____. JAPAN IN WAR AND PEACE: SELECTED ESSAYS. 1994:
The New Press.

Shunsuke Tsurumi. AN INTELLECTUAL HISTORY OF WARTIME JAPAN,
1931-1945. 1986: KPI.

Saburō Ienaga. THE PACIFIC WAR: 1931-1945. Frank Baldwin, transl. 1978:
Pantheon.

John Toland. THE RISING SUN: THE DECLINE AND FALL OF THE
JAPANESE EMPIRE. 1970: Random House.

John Costello. THE PACIFIC WAR, 1941-1945. 1981: Quill.

Ronald H. Spector. EAGLE AGAINST THE SUN: THE AMERICAN WAR
WITH JAPAN. 1985: Free Press.

William A. Renzi & Mark D. Roehrs. NEVER LOOK BACK: A HISTORY OF
WORLD WAR II IN THE PACIFIC. 1991: M. E. Sharpe.

Akira Iriye. POWER AND CULTURE: THE JAPANESE-AMERICAN WAR,
1941-1945. 1981: Harvard University Press.

Christopher Thorne. ALLIES OF A KIND: THE UNITED STATES, BRITAIN,
AND THE WAR AGAINST JAPAN, 1941-1945. 1979: Oxford
University Press.

_____. THE ISSUE OF WAR: STATES, SOCIETIES, AND THE FAR
EASTERN CONFLICT, 1941-1945. 1985: Oxford University Press.

Meirion Harries. SOLDIERS OF THE SUN: THE RISE AND FALL OF THE
IMPERIAL JAPANESE ARMY, 1868-1945. 1991: Random House.

David Bergamini. JAPAN'S IMPERIAL CONSPIRACY. 1971: Morrow.

Alvin D. Coox. THE UNFOUGHT WAR: JAPAN, 1941-1942. 1992:
San Diego State University Press.

Basil Collier. THE WAR IN THE FAR EAST, 1941-1945: A MILITARY
HISTORY. 1969: Morrow.

Charles Bateson. THE WAR WITH JAPAN: A CONCISE HISTORY. 1968: Ure Smith.

Christopher J. Argyle. JAPAN AT WAR, 1937-1946. 1976: Barker.

Arthur Marder. OLD FRIENDS, NEW ENEMIES: THE ROYAL NAVY AND THE IMPERIAL JAPANESE NAVY— STRATEGIC ILLUSIONS, 1936-1941. 1981: Oxford University Press.

John Sbrega. THE WAR AGAINST JAPAN. 1985: Garland.

Haywood S. Hansell. THE STRATEGIC AIR WAR AGAINST GERMANY AND JAPAN: A MEMOIR. 1986: Office of Air Force History, U.S. Air Force.

Stanley Falk. "Japanese Strategy in World War II," *Military Review* 42 (1962), 70-81.

_____. "Organization and Military Power: The Japanese High Command in World War II," *Political Science Quarterly* 76 (1961), 503-518.

Hans-Adolf Jacobsen & Arthur L. Smith, Jr., eds. WORLD WAR II: POLICY AND STRATEGY. 1979: ABC Clio.

H. P. Willmott. EMPIRES IN THE BALANCE: JAPANESE AND ALLIED PACIFIC STRATEGIES TO APRIL 1942. 1982: Naval Institute.

_____. THE BARRIER AND THE JAVELIN: JAPANESE AND ALLIED PACIFIC STRATEGIES, FEBRUARY TO JUNE 1942. 1983: Naval Institute.

_____. "A6M Zero," in CLASSIC AIRCRAFT OF WORLD WAR II (1982: Bison Books), 201-264.

Ronald L. Tarnstrom. THE WARS OF JAPAN. 1992: Trogen Books.

J. R. M. Butler. THE WAR AGAINST JAPAN. United Kingdom Military Series. 1957: Her Majesty's Stationery Office.

John J. Stephan. HAWAII UNDER THE RISING SUN: JAPAN'S PLANS FOR CONQUEST AFTER PEARL HARBOR. 1983: University of Hawaii Press.

Ronald Lewin. THE AMERICAN MAGIC: CODES, CIPHERS, AND THE DEFEAT OF JAPAN. 1982: Farrar Straus & Giroux.

Edward van der Rhoer. DEADLY MAGIC. 1978: Charles Scribner's Sons.

David Kahn, ed. MAGIC DIPLOMATIC SUMMARY. 8 volumes. 1980:
    Garland.

Alvin Coox. JAPAN: THE FINAL AGONY. 1970: Ballentine.

Louis Allen. THE END OF THE WAR IN ASIA. 1979: Hart-Davis
    MacGibbon.

Robert J. C. Butow. JAPAN'S DECISION TO SURRENDER. 1954: Stanford
    University Press.

Lester Brooks. BEHIND JAPAN'S SURRENDER: THE SECRET STRUGGLE
    THAT ENDED AN EMPIRE. 1968: McGraw-Hill.

Leon V. Sigal. FIGHTING TO A FINISH: THE POLITICS OF WAR TERMI-
    NATION IN THE UNITED STATES AND JAPAN, 1945. 1988:
    Cornell University Press.

Martin Schofield Quigley. PEACE WITHOUT HIROSHIMA: SECRET
    ACTION AT THE VATICAN IN THE SPRING OF 1945. 1991:
    Madison Books.

Ellis M. Zacharias. SECRET MISSIONS: THE STORY OF AN INTELLI-
    GENCE OFFICER. 1946: Putnam.

Sidney Forrester Mashbir. I WAS AN AMERICAN SPY. 1953: Vantage.

P. Scott Corbett. QUIET PASSAGES: THE EXCHANGE OF CIVILIANS
    BETWEEN THE UNITED STATES AND JAPAN DURING THE
    SECOND WORLD WAR. 1987: Kent State University Press.

Pacific War Research Society. JAPAN'S LONGEST DAY. 1965: Kōdansha
    International.

Otis Cary, ed. WAR-WASTED ASIA: LETTERS, 1945-46. 1975: Kōdansha
    International. Paperback version entitled FROM A RUINED EMPIRE:
    LETTERS—JAPAN, CHINA, KOREA, 1945-46.

Shannon Boyd-Bailey McCune. INTELLIGENCE ON THE ECONOMIC
    COLLAPSE OF JAPAN IN 1945. 1989: University Press of America.

U.S. Army. REPORTS OF GENERAL MACARTHUR. Four volumes prepared by MacArthur's staff in Tokyo in 1950, but not published until 1966.

    I. THE CAMPAIGNS OF MACARTHUR IN THE PACIFIC
    I. Supplement. MACARTHUR IN JAPAN: THE OCCUPATION: THE MILITARY PHASE
    II. Part 1. JAPANESE OPERATIONS IN THE SOUTHWEST PACIFIC AREA
    II. Part 2. JAPANESE OPERATIONS IN THE SOUTHWEST PACIFIC AREA.

U.S. Army, Office of the Chief of Military History. WAR IN ASIA AND THE PACIFIC, 1937-1949. 1980: Garland. A reprint edition of monographs prepared after the war primarily within the Japanese Demobilization Agency, coordinated and translated by G-2 Section of GHQ, Far Eastern Command. The project produced 184 monographs on Japanese operations and 18 studies of Manchuria. The 15 published volumes are as follows:

    1. INTRODUCTION AND GUIDE
    2. POLITICAL BACKGROUND OF THE WAR
    3. COMMAND, ADMINISTRATION, AND SPECIAL OPERATIONS
    4. THE NAVAL ARMAMENT PROGRAM AND NAVAL OPERATIONS (PART I)
    5. THE NAVAL ARMAMENT PROGRAM AND NAVAL OPERATIONS (PART II)
    6. THE SOUTHERN AREA (PART I)
    7. THE SOUTHERN AREA (PART II)
    8. CHINA, MANCHURIA, AND KOREA (PART I)
    9. CHINA, MANCHURIA, AND KOREA (PART II)
    10. JAPAN AND THE SOVIET UNION (PART I)
    11. JAPAN AND THE SOVIET UNION (PART II)
    12. DEFENSE OF THE HOMELAND AND END OF THE WAR
    13. THE SINO-JAPANESE AND CHINESE CIVIL WARS (PART I)
    14. THE SINO-JAPANESE AND CHINESE CIVIL WARS (PART II)
    15. THE SINO-JAPANESE AND CHINESE CIVIL WARS (PART III)

United States Strategic Bombing Survey. PACIFIC WAR, 108 volumes. 1945-1947. See especially the following reports:

    1. SUMMARY REPORT (PACIFIC WAR)
    2. JAPAN'S STRUGGLE TO END THE WAR
    3. THE EFFECTS OF ATOMIC BOMBS ON HIROSHIMA AND NAGASAKI

14. THE EFFECTS OF STRATEGIC BOMBING ON JAPANESE MORALE
42. THE JAPANESE WARTIME STANDARD OF LIVING AND UTILIZATION OF MANPOWER
53. THE EFFECTS OF STRATEGIC BOMBING ON JAPAN'S WAR ECONOMY
55. EFFECTS OF AIR ATTACK ON JAPANESE URBAN ECONOMY (SUMMARY REPORT)
72. INTERROGATIONS OF JAPANESE OFFICIALS (Volumes 1 and 2)
73. CAMPAIGNS OF THE PACIFIC WAR
96. A REPORT ON PHYSICAL DAMAGE IN JAPAN (SUMMARY REPORT)
97. JAPANESE MILITARY AND NAVAL INTELLIGENCE

THE SINO-JAPANESE WAR OF 1937-1945

Youli Sun. CHINA AND THE ORIGINS OF THE PACIFIC WAR, 1931-1941. 1993: St. Martin's.

John H. Boyle. "Sino-Japanese War of 1937-1945," KŌDANSHA ENCYCLO-PEDIA OF JAPAN 7: 199-202.

_____. CHINA AND JAPAN AT WAR, 1937-1945: THE POLITICS OF COLLABORATION. 1972: Stanford University Press.

_____. "An Incident Becomes a War: Konoe's *Aite ni Sezu* Declaration," *Japan Interpreter* 6.3 (1970), 309-325.

_____. "The Road to Sino-Japanese Collaboration: The Background to the Defection of Wang Ching-wei," *Monumenta Nipponica* 25.3-4 (1970), 267-301.

Frank Dorn. THE SINO-JAPANESE WAR, 1937-1941: FROM THE MARCO POLO BRIDGE TO PEARL HARBOR. 1974: Macmillan.

James C. Hsiung & Steven I. Levine, eds. CHINA'S BITTER VICTORY: THE WAR WITH JAPAN, 1937-1945. 1992: M. E. Sharpe.

Chang-tai Hung. WAR AND POPULAR CULTURE: RESISTANCE IN MODERN CHINA, 1937-1945. 1994: University of California Press.

Michael Lindsay. THE UNKNOWN WAR: NORTH CHINA, 1937-1945. 1975: Bergstrom & Boyle.

Dick Wilson. WHEN TIGERS FIGHT: THE STORY OF THE SINO-JAPANESE WAR, 1937-1945. 1982: Viking.

Lincoln Li. THE JAPANESE ARMY IN NORTH CHINA, JULY 1937-DECEMBER 1941: PROBLEMS OF POLITICAL AND ECONOMIC CONTROL. 1975: Oxford University Press.

Chalmers A. Johnson. PEASANT NATIONALISM AND COMMUNIST POWER: THE EMERGENCE OF REVOLUTIONARY CHINA, 1937-1945. 1962: Stanford University Press.

Gerald E. Bunker. THE PEACE CONSPIRACY: WANG CHING-WEI AND THE CHINA WAR, 1937-1941. 1972: Harvard University Press.

George Taylor. JAPANESE SPONSORED REGIME IN NORTH CHINA. 1939: Institute of Pacific Relations.

Kimitada Miwa. "The Chinese Communists' Role in the Spread of the Marco Polo Bridge Incident into a Full-Scale War," *Monumenta Nipponica* 18.1-4 (1963), 313-328.

_____. "The Wang Ching-Wei Regime and Japanese Efforts to Terminate the China Conflict," in Joseph Roggendorf, ed. STUDIES IN JAPANESE CULTURE: TRADITION AND EXPERIMENT (1963: Monumenta Nipponica Monographs), 123-142.

Roy M. Stanley. PRELUDE TO PEARL HARBOR: WAR IN CHINA, 1937-1941. JAPAN'S REHEARSAL FOR WORLD WAR II. 1983: Charles Scribner's Sons.

Lloyd Eastman. SEEDS OF DESTRUCTION: NATIONALIST CHINA IN WAR AND REVOLUTION, 1937-1949. 1984: Stanford University Press.

F. F. Liu. A MILITARY HISTORY OF MODERN CHINA, 1924-1949. 1956: Princeton University Press.

Arthur N. Young. CHINA AND THE HELPING HAND, 1937-1945. 1963: Harvard University Press.

William H. Chamberlin. JAPAN OVER ASIA. Revised edition. 1937: Little, Brown.

T. A. Bisson. JAPAN IN CHINA. 1938: Macmillan.

Harold J. Timperly, ed. THE JAPANESE TERROR IN CHINA. 1938:
    New York Books for Libraries.

Takeo Itō. LIFE ALONG THE SOUTH MANCHURIAN RAILWAY:
    THE MEMOIRS OF ITŌ TAKEO. Transl. Joshua A. Fogel. 1989:
    M. E. Sharpe.

Chong-sik Lee. REVOLUTIONARY STRUGGLE IN MANCHURIA:
    CHINESE COMMUNISM AND SOVIET INTEREST, 1922-1945.
    1983: University of California Press.

_____. COUNTERINSURGENCY IN MANCHURIA: THE JAPANESE
    EXPERIENCE. 1967: RAND Corporation Memorandum RM-5012-
    ARPA.

Kiyoshi Miki & Karoku Hosokawa. INTRODUCTORY STUDIES ON THE
    SINO-JAPANESE CONFLICT. 1941: Institute of Pacific Relations.

Royal Institute of International Affairs. CHINA AND JAPAN. 3rd edition.
    1941: Oxford University Press.

CHINA HANDBOOK, 1937-1945. 1947: Macmillan.

Frederick T. Merrill. JAPAN AND THE OPIUM MENACE. 1942: Institute of
    Pacific Relations & Foreign Policy Association.

Michael Schaller. THE U.S. CRUSADE IN CHINA, 1938-1945. 1979:
    Columbia University Press.

SOUTHEAST ASIA & THE CO-PROSPERITY SPHERE

John H. Boyle. "Greater East Asia Co-Prosperity Sphere," KŌDANSHA ENCY-
    CLOPEDIA OF JAPAN 3: 60-62.

Harry J. Benda. "The Japanese Interregnum in Southeast Asia," in Grant K.
    Goodman, ed. IMPERIAL JAPAN AND ASIA (1967: Occasional
    Papers of the East Asia Institute, Columbia University), 65-79.

Katsumi Usui. "Pursuing an Illusion: The New Order in East Asia," *Japan Interpreter* 6.3 (1970), 326-337.

Grant K. Goodman. "Japan and Southeast Asia in the Pacific War: A Case of Cultural Ambiguity," in The Japan P. E. N. Club, ed. STUDIES ON JAPANESE CULTURE (1973: The Japan P. E. N. Club), 2: 235-241.

————, ed. JAPANESE CULTURAL POLICIES IN SOUTHEAST ASIA DURING WORLD WAR II. 1991: St. Martin's.

Joel V. Berreman. "The Japanization of Far Eastern Occupied Areas," *Pacific Affairs* 17 (1944), 168-180.

F. C. Jones. JAPAN'S NEW ORDER IN EAST ASIA: ITS RISE AND FALL, 1937-1945. 1954: Oxford University Press.

Joyce C. Lebra, ed. JAPAN'S GREATER EAST ASIA CO-PROSPERITY SPHERE IN WORLD WAR II: SELECTED READINGS & DOCU-MENTS. 1975: Oxford University Press.

————. JAPANESE-TRAINED ARMIES IN SOUTHEAST ASIA: INDEPEN-DENCE AND VOLUNTEER FORCES IN WORLD WAR II. 1977: Columbia University Press.

————. JUNGLE ALLIANCE: JAPAN AND THE INDIAN NATIONAL ARMY IN WORLD WAR II. 1971: Asia Pacific.

Willard H. Elsbree. JAPAN'S ROLE IN SOUTHEAST ASIAN NATIONALIST MOVEMENTS, 1940-1945. 1953: Harvard University Press.

Alfred W. McCoy, ed. SOUTHEAST ASIA UNDER JAPANESE RULE. 1980: Yale University Southeast Asia Studies, Monograph Series 22.
Ten essays covering aspects of the war in Indonesia, Sumatra, Malaya, Vietnam, Burma, the Philippines, Papua New Guinea, and Siam.

William H. Newell, ed. JAPAN IN ASIA. 1981: Singapore University Press.
Seven essays on the World War II period.

Josef Silverstein, ed. SOUTHEAST ASIA IN WORLD WAR II: FOUR ESSAYS. 1966: Yale University Press.

James W. Morley, ed. THE FATEFUL CHOICE: JAPAN'S ADVANCE INTO SOUTHEAST ASIA, 1939-1941. 1980: Columbia University Press.

Eric Robertson. THE JAPANESE FILE: PRE-WAR JAPANESE PENETRA-
TION IN SOUTHEAST ASIA. 1980: Heinemann.

Iwaichi Fujiwara. F KIKAN: JAPANESE ARMY INTELLIGENCE
OPERATIONS IN SOUTHEAST ASIA DURING WORLD WAR II.
Yōji Akashi, transl. 1983: Heinemann.

Benedict R. O'G. Anderson. "Japan: 'The Light of Asia'," in Josef Silverstein,
ed. SOUTH-EAST ASIA IN WORLD WAR II: FOUR ESSAYS.
1966: Yale University Press.

Robert S. Ward. ASIA FOR THE ASIATICS?: THE TECHNIQUES OF
JAPANESE OCCUPATION. 1945: University of Chicago Press.

Hiroshi Shimizu. "From *Karayuki-san* to *Sōgō Shōsha*: The Evolution of the
Japanese Commercial Community in Pre-War Netherlands East Indies,"
Japan Forum 3.1 (1991), 37-56.

Anthony Reid. "The Japanese Occupation and Rival Indonesian Elites: Northern
Sumatra in 1942," *Journal of Asian Studies* 35.1 (1975), 49-61.

Harry J. Benda, James K. Irikura & Kōichi Kishi, eds. JAPANESE MILITARY
ADMINISTRATION IN INDONESIA: SELECTED DOCUMENTS.
1965: Yale University Southeast Asia Studies, Translation Series 6.

M. Z. Aziz. JAPAN'S COLONIALISM AND INDONESIA. 1955: Martinus
Nijhoff.

Harry J. Benda. THE CRESCENT AND THE RISING SUN: INDONESIAN
ISLAM UNDER THE JAPANESE OCCUPATION, 1942-1945. 1958:
Institute of Pacific Relations.

Benedict R. O'G. Anderson. SOME ASPECTS OF INDONESIAN POLITICS
UNDER THE JAPANESE OCCUPATION: 1944-1945. 1961: Cornell
University Press.

Barbara Gifford Shimer & Guy Hobbs, transl. THE KENPEITAI IN JAVA
AND SUMATRA (Selections from *Nihon Kenpei Seishi*). 1986:
Cornell Modern Indonesia Project, Translation Series 65.

Anthony Reid & Akira Ōki, eds. THE JAPANESE EXPERIENCE IN INDONE-
SIA: SELECTED MEMOIRS OF 1942-1945. 1986: Ohio University,
Center for International Studies, Center for Southeast Asian Studies.

Justin J. Cornfield. A BIBLIOGRAPHY OF LITERATURE RELATING TO THE MALAYAN CAMPAIGN AND THE JAPANESE PERIOD IN MALAYA, SINGAPORE AND NORTHERN BORNEO. 1988: University of Hull, Centre for South-East Asian Studies.

Ba Maw. BREAKTHROUGH IN BURMA: MEMOIRS OF A REVOLUTION, 1939-1946. 1968: Yale University Press.

Frank N. Trager. BURMA: JAPANESE MILITARY ADMINISTRATION. SELECTED DOCUMENTS, 1941-1945. 1973: University of Pennsylvania.

Maurice Collis. LAST AND FIRST IN BURMA (1941-1948). 1956: Faber & Faber.

Won Z. Yoon. JAPAN'S SCHEME FOR THE LIBERATION OF BURMA: THE ROLE OF THE MINAMI KIKAN AND THE "THIRTY COMRADES." 1973: Center for International Studies, Ohio University.

Chaiwat Khamchoo & E. Bruce Reynolds, eds. THAI-JAPANESE RELATIONS IN HISTORICAL PERSPECTIVE. 1988: Institute of Asian Studies, Chulalongkorn University.

E. Bruce Reynolds. THAILAND AND JAPAN'S SOUTHERN ADVANCE, 1940-1945. 1994: St. Martin's.

William L. Swan. JAPANESE ECONOMIC ACTIVITY IN SIAM: FROM THE 1890S UNTIL THE OUTBREAK OF THE PACIFIC WAR. 1986: Centre for South East Asian Studies, Gaya.

_____. "Thai-Japan Monetary Relations at the Start of the Pacific War," *Modern Asian Studies* 23.2 (1989), 313-347.

Thamsook Numnonda. THAILAND AND THE JAPANESE PRESENCE, 1941-45. 1977: Institute of Southeast Asian Studies (Singapore).

Clifford Kinvig. THE RIVER KWAI RAILWAY: THE STORY OF THE BURMA-SIAM RAILROAD. 1992: Brassey's.

John McAlister. VIET NAM: THE ORIGINS OF REVOLUTION. 1969: Knopf.

H. J. Lethbridge. "Hong Kong Under Japanese Occupation," in I. C. Jarvie, ed. HONG KONG: A SOCIETY IN CHANGE (1969: Praeger and Routledge & Kegan Paul), chapter 5.

Tam Yue-him, ed. HONG KONG AND JAPAN: GROWING CULTURAL
   AND ECONOMIC INTERATIONS, 1845-1987. 1988: Japan Society
   of Hong Kong.

Louis Allen. THE END OF THE WAR IN ASIA. 1976: Hart-Davis MacGibbon.

Grant Goodman. "Philippines and Japan," KŌDANSHA ENCYCLOPEDIA OF
   JAPAN 6: 183-184.

Teodoro Agoncillo. THE FATEFUL YEARS: JAPAN'S ADVENTURE IN
   THE PHILIPPINES, 1941-1945. 2 volumes. 1965: Garcia.

Hernando Abaya. BETRAYAL IN THE PHILIPPINES. 1946: A. A. Wyn.

A. V. H. Hartendorp. THE JAPANESE OCCUPATION OF THE
   PHILIPPINES. 2 volumes. 1967: Bookmark.

D. J. Steinberg. PHILIPPINE COLLABORATION IN WORLD WAR II. 1967:
   University of Michigan Press.

Elmer Lear. THE JAPANESE OCCUPATION OF THE PHILIPPINES:
   LEYTE, 1941-1945. 1961: Cornell South East Asian Studies,
   Data Paper 42.

_____. "Collaboration in Leyte: The Philippines Under Japanese Occupation,"
   Far Eastern Quarterly 11.2 (1952), 183-206.

Ma. Felisa A. Syjuco. THE KEMPEI TAI IN THE PHILIPPINES, 1941-1945.
   1988: New Day Publishers.

Inofre D. Corpuz. THE PHILIPPINES. 1965: Prentice-Hall.

Carlos P. Romulo. I SEE THE PHILIPPINES RISE. 1946: Doubleday.

THE WAR IN JAPANESE EYES

Haruko Taya Cook & Theodore F. Cook, eds. JAPAN AT WAR: AN ORAL
   HISTORY. 1992: The New Press.

Ben-Ami Shillony. POLITICS AND CULTURE IN WARTIME JAPAN. 1981:
   Oxford University Press.

_____. "Japanese Intellectuals During the Pacific War," *Proceedings of the British Association for Japanese Studies* 2 (1977), 90-99.

_____. "Universities and Students in Wartime Japan," *Journal of Asian Studies* 45.4 (1986), 769-787.

Thomas R. H. Havens. VALLEY OF DARKNESS: THE JAPANESE PEOPLE AND WORLD WAR TWO. 1978: Norton; 1986: University Press of America.

_____. "Japanese Society During World War II," KŌDANSHA ENCYCLO-PEDIA OF JAPAN 8: 277-278.

Kazuko Tsurumi. SOCIAL CHANGE AND THE INDIVIDUAL: JAPAN BEFORE AND AFTER DEFEAT IN WORLD WAR II. 1970: Princeton University Press. See especially the chapters on ideological conversion in the 1930s (29-79), the Army and the emperor system (80-98), "socialization for death" in the schools and military (99-137), and "the voice of the dead" (138-179).

Shunsuke Tsurumi. AN INTELLECTUAL HISTORY OF WARTIME JAPAN, 1931-1945. 1986: KPI.

John W. Dower. EMPIRE AND AFTERMATH: YOSHIDA SHIGERU AND THE JAPANESE EXPERIENCE, 1878-1954. 1979: Council on East Asian Studies, Harvard University. Chapters 7 and 8 deal with conservative criticism of the war and the fear of revolution in wartime Japan.

_____. WAR WITHOUT MERCY: RACE AND POWER IN THE PACIFIC WAR. 1986: Pantheon.

_____. JAPAN IN WAR AND PEACE: SELECTED ESSAYS. 1994: The New Press. See especially essays on wartime legacies (9-32), wartime cinema (33-54), Japan's atomic bomb research during World War II (55-100), and fear of popular upheaval on the part of the Thought Police (101-154).

Donald Keene. "Japanese Literature and Politics in the 1930s," *Journal of Japanese Studies* 2.2 (1976), 225-248.

_____. "Japanese Writers and the Greater East Asia War," *Journal of Asian Studies* 23.2 (1964), 209-225.

_____. "The Barren Years: Japanese War Literature," *Monumenta Nipponica* 33.1 (1978), 67-112.

_____. "War Literature," in his DAWN TO THE WEST: JAPANESE LITERATURE OF THE MODERN ERA (1984: Holt, Rinehart & Winston), 906-961.

Noriko Mizuta Lippit. "War Literature," KŌDANSHA ENCYCLOPEDIA OF JAPAN 8: 225-228.

Joseph L. Anderson & Donald Richie. THE JAPANESE FILM: ART AND INDUSTRY. Expanded edition. 1982: Princeton University Press. Chapters 7 and 8 cover the period 1939-1945.

Time-Life Books. JAPAN AT WAR. 1980: Time-Life.

S. L. Mayer, ed. THE JAPANESE WAR MACHINE. 1976: Chartwell.

Masanobu Tsuji. SINGAPORE, THE JAPANESE VERSION. 1962: St. Martin's.

Alvin D. Coox & Saburō Hayashi. KŌGUN: THE JAPANESE ARMY IN THE PACIFIC WAR. 1959: Marine Corps Association.

Hanama Tasaki. LONG THE IMPERIAL WAY. 1950: Houghton Mifflin.

Jirō Horikoshi. EAGLES OF MITSUBISHI: THE STORY OF THE ZERO FIGHTER. 1981: University of Washington Press.

Gordon W. Prange, with Donald M. Goldstein & Katherine V. Dillon. GOD'S SAMURAI: LEAD PILOT AT PEARL HARBOR. 1990: Brassey's. A biography of naval aviator Fuchida Mitsuo.

Saburō Sakai, with Martin Caidin & Fred Saitō. SAMURAI! 1991: Naval Institute Press.

David C. Evans, ed. & transl. THE JAPANESE NAVY IN WORLD WAR II: IN THE WORDS OF FORMER JAPANESE NAVAL OFFICERS. 2nd edition. 1986: Naval Institute Press.

L. D. Meo. JAPAN'S RADIO WAR ON AUSTRALIA, 1941-1945. 1968: Melbourne University Press.

Denis & Peggy Warner. THE SACRED WARRIORS: JAPAN'S SUICIDE LEGIONS. 1982: Avon.

Richard O'Neill. SUICIDE SQUADS. 1981: Ballantine.

Rikihei Inoguchi & Takashi Nakajima. THE DIVINE WIND: JAPAN'S
KAMIKAZE FORCE IN WORLD WAR II. 1958: U.S. Naval
Academy.

Ryūji Nagatsuka. I WAS A KAMIKAZE. 1973: Macmillan.

Hagoromo Society of Kamikaze Divine Thunderbolt Corps Survivors, comp.
BORN TO DIE: THE CHERRY BLOSSOM SQUADRONS.
Andrew Adams, ed. 1973: Ohara.

Mitsuru Yoshida. REQUIEM FOR BATTLESHIP 'YAMATO'. Richard H.
Minear, transl. 1985: University of Washington Press.

Shōhei Ōoka. FIRES ON THE PLAIN. Ivan Morris, transl. 1957: Knopf.
A translation of *Nobi*, the most famous Japanese recreation of a soldier's
dehumanizing experiences.

Hiroshi Noma. ZONE OF EMPTINESS. Bernard Frechtman, transl. 1956:
World.

Tetsurō Ogawa. TERRACED HELL: A JAPANESE MEMOIR OF DEFEAT
AND DEATH IN NORTHERN LUZON, PHILIPPINES. 1972: Tuttle.

Michio Takeyama. HARP OF BURMA. Howard Hibbett, transl. 1966: Tuttle.

Jirō Osaragi. HOMECOMING. Brewster Horowitz, transl. 1955: Knopf.

Masuo Katō. THE LOST WAR: A JAPANESE REPORTER'S INSIDE
STORY. 1946: Knopf.

Toshikazu Kase. JOURNEY TO THE MISSOURI. 1950: Yale University
Press.

Yoshio Kodama. I WAS DEFEATED. Robert Booth & Tarō Fukuda, transl.
1951: Tarō Fukuda.

Shigenori Tōgō. THE CAUSE OF JAPAN. 1956: Simon & Schuster.

Matome Ugaki. FADING VICTORY: THE DIARY OF ADMIRAL MATOME
UGAKI, 1941-1945. Masataka Chihaya, transl. 1991: University of
Pittsburgh Press.

Mamoru Shigemitsu. JAPAN AND HER DESTINY: MY STRUGGLE FOR PEACE. 1958: Dutton.

Gwen Terasaki. BRIDGE TO THE SUN. 1957: University of North Carolina Press.

"The War and Japan: Revisionist Views." Special issue of *Japan Echo* 11 (1984). Articles by Japanese writers.

Takeshi Matsuda. "The Coming of the Pacific War: Japanese Perspectives," *Reviews in American History* 14.4 (1986), 629-652.

THE ATOMIC BOMBS

Martin J. Sherwin. A WORLD DESTROYED: THE ATOMIC BOMB AND THE GRAND ALLIANCE. Revised edition. 1987: Knopf.

Barton J. Bernstein, ed. THE ATOMIC BOMB: THE CRITICAL ISSUES. 1976: Little, Brown.

_____. "The Perils and Politics of Surrender: Ending the War with Japan and Avoiding the Third Atomic Bomb," *Pacific Historical Review* 46.1 (1977), 1-27.

Edwin Fogelman, ed. HIROSHIMA: THE DECISION TO USE THE A-BOMB. 1964: Charles Scribner's Sons.

James West Davidson & Mark Hamilton Lytle. "The Decision to Drop the Bomb," in their AFTER THE FACT: THE ART OF HISTORICAL DETECTION (1982: Knopf), 2: 320-355.

Gar Alperovitz. ATOMIC DIPLOMACY: HIROSHIMA AND POTSDAM. 1965; 1985: Vintage. See especially the 1985 edition, with an updated introduction by the author.

_____. "The Use of the Atomic Bomb," in his COLD WAR ESSAYS (1970: Doubleday-Anchor), 51-73. A critique of the orthodox American position on the use of the atomic bombs by Feis (1966) below.

P. M. S. Blackett. FEAR, WAR, AND THE BOMB. 1949: Whittlesey. The first major criticism of the use of the bomb, by an eminent British nuclear physicist and policy adviser.

Louis Morton. "The Decision to Use the Atomic Bomb," in K. R. Greenfield, ed. COMMAND DECISIONS (1959: Harcourt Brace), 388-410.

Herbert Feis. THE ATOMIC BOMB AND THE END OF WORLD WAR II. 1966: Princeton University Press. A revision of the author's 1961 monograph entitled JAPAN SUBDUED: THE ATOMIC BOMB AND THE END OF THE WAR IN THE PACIFIC.

Otis Cary. "Atomic Bomb Targeting—Myths and Realities," *Japan Quarterly* 26.4 (1979), 506-514. On the deletion of Kyoto from U.S. atomic-bomb targets.

John Hersey. HIROSHIMA. 1946: Bantam.

George Feifer. TENNŌZAN: THE BATTLE OF OKINAWA AND THE ATOMIC BOMB. 1992: Ticknor & Fields.

Pacific War Research Society. THE DAY MAN LOST: HIROSHIMA, 6 AUGUST 1945. 1983: Kōdansha International.

Dan Kurzman. DAY OF THE BOMB: COUNTDOWN TO HIROSHIMA. 1985: McGraw-Hill.

Committee for the Compilation of Materials on Damage Caused by the Atomic Bombs in Hiroshima and Nagasaki. HIROSHIMA AND NAGASAKI: THE PHYSICAL, MEDICAL, AND SOCIAL EFFECTS OF THE ATOMIC BOMBINGS. Translated by Eisei Ishikawa & David L. Swain from the 1979 Iwanami Shoten publication *Hiroshima Nagasaki no Genbaku Saigai*. 1981: Basic Books. A basic compendium of data.

Kurt W. Tong. "Korea's Forgotten Atomic Bomb Victims," *Bulletin of Concerned Asian Scholars* 23.1 (1991), 31-37. Includes bibliography.

Robert J. Lifton. DEATH IN LIFE: SURVIVORS OF HIROSHIMA. 1967: Random House.

Betty Jean Lifton. A PLACE CALLED HIROSHIMA. 1985: Kōdansha International.

Michael J. Yavenditti. "The American People and the Use of Atomic Bombs on Japan: the 1940s," *The Historian* 36 (1974), 224-247.

Monica Braw. THE ATOMIC BOMB SUPPRESSED: AMERICAN CENSORSHIP IN OCCUPIED JAPAN. 1991: M. E. Sharpe.

Glenn D. Hook. "Censorship and Reportage of Atomic Damage and Casualties in Hiroshima and Nagasaki," *Bulletin of Concerned Asian Scholars* 23.1 (1991), 13-25.

Paul Boyer. BY THE BOMB'S EARLY LIGHT: AMERICAN THOUGHT AND CULTURE AT THE DAWN OF THE ATOMIC AGE. 1985: Pantheon.

Masuji Ibuse. BLACK RAIN. A translation of *Kuroi Ame*, by John Bester. 3rd edition. 1981: Kōdansha International.

John Whittier Treat. "Atomic Bomb Literature and the Documentary Fallacy," *Journal of Japanese Studies* 14.1 (1988), 27-57.

_____. "Hiroshima and the Place of the Narrator," *Journal of Asian Studies* 48.1 (1989), 29-49. On the semi-autobiographical works of the novelist Ōta Yōko, a survivor of the Hiroshima bombing.

Kenzaburō Ōe, ed. THE CRAZY IRIS AND OTHER STORIES OF THE ATOMIC AFTERMATH. 1985: Shūeisha.

Michihiko Hachiya. HIROSHIMA DIARY: THE JOURNAL OF A JAPANESE PHYSICIAN, AUGUST 6-SEPTEMBER 30, 1945. 1955: University of North Carolina Press.

Osada Arata, comp. CHILDREN OF HIROSHIMA. 1959; 1982: Harper.

Takashi Nagai. WE OF NAGASAKI. 1951: Duell, Sloan & Pearce.

_____. THE BELLS OF NAGASAKI. William Johnston, S. J., transl. 1984: Kōdansha International.

Tatsuichirō Akizuki. NAGASAKI 1945. 1982: Charles Rivers.

Miyao Ōhara. THE SONGS OF HIROSHIMA. 1971: Taihei Shuppansha.

David G. Goodman, transl. AFTER APOCALYPSE: FOUR JAPANESE PLAYS OF HIROSHIMA AND NAGASAKI. 1986: Columbia University Press.

Kyōko Hayashi. "Hayashi Kyōko's 'Two Grave Markers' (*Futari no bohyō*)," Kyōko Selden, transl., *Bulletin of Concerned Asian Scholars* 18.1 (1986), 23-35.

_____. "Hayashi Kyōko's 'Procession on a Cloudy Day (*Kumoribi no kōshin*)," Hirosuke Kashiwagi, transl., *Bulletin of Concerned Asian Scholars* 25.1 (1993) 58-69.

Kyōko & Mark Selden, eds. THE ATOMIC BOMB: VOICES FROM HIROSHIMA AND NAGASAKI. 1989: M. E. Sharpe. The introductory essay in this book can also be found, slightly revised, as Mark Selden's "The United States, Japan, and the Atomic Bomb," *Bulletin of Concerned Asian Scholars* 23.1 (1991), 3-13.

Kyōko Selden. "Children of Nagasaki." Translations of seven accounts of the Nagasaki bombing by children who survived. *Bulletin of Concerned Asian Scholars* 18.3 (1986), 32-38.

_____. "Poems by Atomic Bomb Survivors," *Bulletin of Concerned Asian Scholars* 19.2 (1987), 17-23.

Sankichi Tōge. "Hiroshima Poems by Tōge Sankichi," Richard H. Minear, transl., *Bulletin of Concerned Asian Scholars* 19.4 (1987), 53-54.

Richard H. Minear, ed. & transl. HIROSHIMA: THREE WITNESSES. 1990: Princeton University Press. Major works by survivors: Hara Tamiki, Ōta Yōko, and Tōge Sankichi. Includes a useful bibliography.

Sadako Kurihara. BLACK EGGS: POEMS BY KURIHARA SADAKO. Richard H. Minear, transl. 1994: Center for Japanese Studies, University of Michigan.

John W. Dower & John Junkerman, eds. THE HIROSHIMA MURALS: THE ART OF IRI MARUKI AND TOSHI MARUKI. 1985: Kōdansha International. Reviewed by Richard Minear in *Bulletin of Concerned Asian Scholars* 19.4 (1987), 58-63.

Alan Wolfe. "Toward a Japanese-American Nuclear Criticism: The Art of Iri and Toshi Maruki in Text and Film," *Bulletin of Concerned Asian Scholars* 19.4 (1987), 55-57. Discusses the book (above) and 1986 film (HELLFIRE: A JOURNEY FROM HIROSHIMA) on the Marukis by Dower and Junkerman.

Japan Broadcasting Corporation (NHK), ed. UNFORGETTABLE FIRE: PICTURES DRAWN BY ATOMIC BOMB SURVIVORS. 1977: Pantheon.

Keiji Nakazawa. BAREFOOT GEN. 3 volumes. 1979; republished in 1987 by
New Society Publishers as BAREFOOT GEN (*HADASHI NO GEN*):
A CARTOON HISTORY OF HIROSHIMA. English version of the
famous comic-strip style Japanese serial *Hadashi no Gen*, depicting the
life of a young survivor of Hiroshima and based on the artist's own
experiences.

Sadao Asada. "Japanese Perceptions of the A-Bomb Decision," in Joe C. Dixon,
ed. THE AMERICAN MILITARY AND THE FAR EAST (1980: an
American Air Force symposium; Office of Air Force History), 199-219.

John W. Dower. "'NI' and 'F': Japan's Wartime Atomic Bomb Research," in his
JAPAN IN WAR AND PEACE (1994: The New Press), 55-100.

I.M.T.F.E. & OTHER WAR CRIMES TRIALS

*John R. Lewis. UNCERTAIN JUDGEMENT: A BIBLIOGRAPHY OF WAR
CRIMES TRIALS. 1979: Clio Books.

R. John Pritchard & Sonia Zaide Pritchard, eds. THE TOKYO WAR CRIMES
TRIAL: THE COMPLETE TRANSCRIPTS OF THE PROCEEDINGS
OF THE INTERNATIONAL MILITARY TRIBUNAL FOR THE FAR
EAST IN TWENTY-TWO VOLUMES. 1981: Garland. The most
accessible version of the I.M.T.F.E. proceedings; includes an index.
The Proceedings are also available on microfilm from the Library of
Congress (37 reels).

Paul S. Dull & Michael Umemura. THE TOKYO TRIALS: A FUNCTIONAL
INDEX TO THE PROCEEDINGS OF THE IMTFE. 1957: University
of Michigan Press.

U.S. War Department. JUDGMENT OF THE INTERNATIONAL MILITARY
TRIBUNAL FOR THE FAR EAST. 7 parts in 2 volumes. 1948:
Government Printing Office.

Radhabinod Pal. THE INTERNATIONAL MILITARY TRIBUNAL FOR THE
FAR EAST: DISSENTIENT JUDGMENT. 1953: Sanyal.

B. V. A. Roling & C. F. Ruter, eds. THE TOKYO JUDGMENT: THE INTERNATIONAL MILITARY TRIBUNAL FOR THE FAR EAST (I.M.T.F.E.), 26 APRIL 1946 - 12 NOVEMBER 1948. 3 volumes. 1977: APA University Press. A convenient source for the Judgment (volume 1), and full text of Justice Pal's dissent (volume 2).

Solis Horowitz. "The Tokyo Trial," *International Conciliation* 465 (1950: Carnegie Endowment for International Peace), 473-584. A brief summary of the trial by a member of the prosecution.

Kenzō Takayanagi. THE TOKIO TRIALS AND INTERNATIONAL LAW; ANSWER TO THE PROSECUTION'S ARGUMENTS ON INTER-NATIONAL LAW DELIVERED AT THE INTERNATIONAL MILITARY TRIBUNAL FOR THE FAR EAST ON 3 AND 4 MARCH 1948. 1948: Yūhikaku.

R. John Pritchard. AN OVERVIEW OF THE HISTORICAL IMPORTANCE OF THE TOKYO WAR TRIAL. Nissan Occasional Papers, No. 5. 1987: Nissan Institute of Japanese Studies, Oxford.

Junji Kinoshita. BETWEEN GOD AND MAN: A JUDGEMENT ON WAR CRIMES. Eric J. Gangloff, transl. 1979: University of Washington Press. Historical drama on the trials and on war crimes and guilt.

Baron M. P. A. Hankey. POLITICS, TRIALS AND ERRORS. 1950: Regnery.

Richard Minear. VICTOR'S JUSTICE: THE TOKYO WAR CRIMES TRIAL. 1971: Princeton University Press.

Arnold C. Brackman. THE OTHER NUREMBERG: THE UNTOLD STORY OF THE TOKYO WAR CRIMES TRIALS. 1987: Morrow.

Chihiro Hosoya, Nisuke Andō, Yasuaki Ōnuma & Richard H. Minear, eds. THE TOKYO WAR CRIMES TRIAL: AN INTERNATIONAL SYMPOSIUM. 1986: Kōdansha International.

Bart van Poelgeest. "The Netherlands and the Tokyo Trial," *Japan Forum* 4.1 (1992), 81-90.

Saburō Shiroyama. WAR CRIMINAL: THE LIFE AND DEATH OF HIROTA KŌKI. John Bester, transl. 1974: Kōdansha International.

Philip R. Piccigallo. THE JAPANESE ON TRIAL: ALLLIED WAR CRIMES OPERATIONS IN THE EAST, 1945-1951. 1979: University of Texas Press.

A. Frank Reel. THE CASE OF GENERAL YAMASHITA. 1949: University of Chicago Press.

Arthur Swinson. FOUR SAMURAI: A QUARTET OF JAPANESE ARMY COMMANDERS IN THE SECOND WORLD WAR. 1968: Hutchinson.

Richard R. Lael. THE YAMASHITA PRECEDENT: WAR CRIMES AND COMMAND RESPONSIBLITY. 1982: Scholarly Resources.

Lawrence Taylor. A TRIAL OF GENERALS: HOMMA, YAMASHITA, MACARTHUR. 1981: Icarus.

Kurt Steiner. "War Crimes and Command Responsibility: From the Bataan Death March to the MyLai Massacre," *Pacific Affairs* 58.2 (1986), 293-298. A review of Lael and Taylor.

John Frederick Hanson. "The Trial of Lieutenant General Masaharu Homma." 1977: Ph.D. dissertation, Mississippi State University.

Edward F. Langley Russell, Lord of Liverpool. THE KNIGHTS OF BUSHIDŌ: THE SHOCKING HISTORY OF JAPANESE WAR ATROCITIES. 1958: Dutton.

MATERIALS ON THE TRIAL OF FORMER SERVICEMEN OF THE JAPANESE ARMY CHARGED WITH MANUFACTURING AND EMPLOYING BACTERIOLOGICAL WEAPONS. 1950: Moscow, Foreign Languages Publishing House. Proceedings of the December 25-30, 1949 Khabarovsk trial of 12 former Japanese military men.

John W. Powell. "Japan's Germ Warfare: The U.S. Cover-up of a War Crime," *Bulletin of Concerned Asian Scholars* 12.2 (1980), 2-17.

_____. "Japan's Biological Weapons, 1930-1945: A Hidden Chapter in History," *Bulletin of the Atomic Scientists* 37.8 (October 1981), 43-53.

Peter Williams & David Wallace. UNIT 731: JAPAN'S SECRET BIOLOGICAL WARFARE IN WORLD WAR II. 1989: Free Press.

Sheldon H. Harris. FACTORIES OF DEATH: JAPANESE BIOLOGICAL WARFARE, 1932-1945, AND THE AMERICAN COVER-UP. 1994: Routledge.

Richard Falk. "The Shimoda Case: A Legal Appraisal of the Atomic Attacks Upon Hiroshima and Nagasaki," *American Journal of International Law* 59 (1965), 759-793.

Masayo Duus. TOKYO ROSE: ORPHAN OF THE PACIFIC. Peter Duus, transl. 1979: Kōdansha International.

Russel Warren Howe. THE HUNT FOR "TOKYO ROSE." 1990: Madison Books.

Stanley Kutler. THE AMERICAN INQUISITION: JUSTICE AND INJUSTICE IN THE COLD WAR. 1982: Hill & Wang. See the chapter on Tokyo Rose.

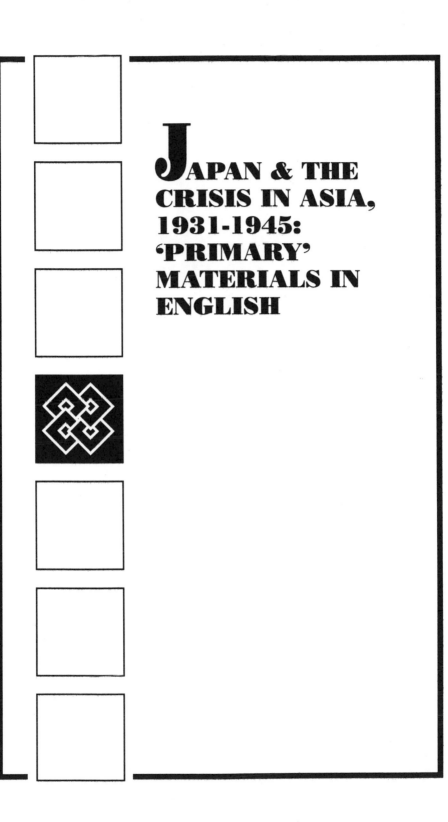

JAPAN & THE CRISIS IN ASIA, 1931-1945: 'PRIMARY' MATERIALS IN ENGLISH

Japan & the Crisis in Asia, 1931-1945: 'Primary' Materials in English

ENGLISH-LANGUAGE PRESS IN JAPAN

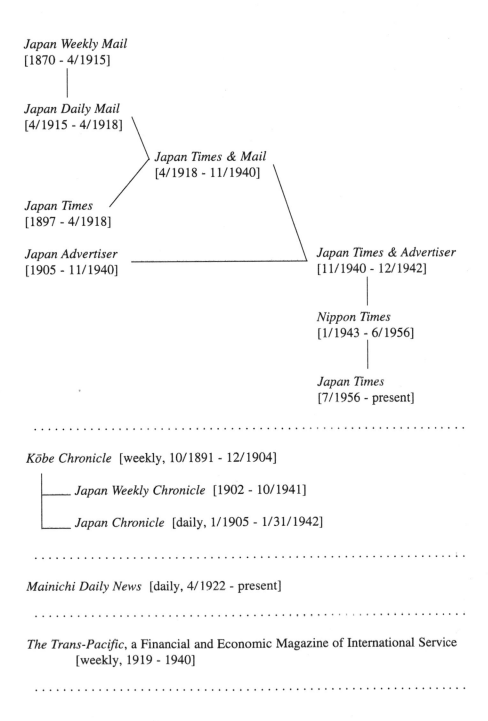

Japan Weekly Mail
[1870 - 4/1915]

Japan Daily Mail
[4/1915 - 4/1918]

Japan Times & Mail
[4/1918 - 11/1940]

Japan Times
[1897 - 4/1918]

Japan Advertiser
[1905 - 11/1940]

Japan Times & Advertiser
[11/1940 - 12/1942]

Nippon Times
[1/1943 - 6/1956]

Japan Times
[7/1956 - present]

Kōbe Chronicle [weekly, 10/1891 - 12/1904]

Japan Weekly Chronicle [1902 - 10/1941]

Japan Chronicle [daily, 1/1905 - 1/31/1942]

Mainichi Daily News [daily, 4/1922 - present]

The Trans-Pacific, a Financial and Economic Magazine of International Service
[weekly, 1919 - 1940]

Japan Times Weekly [- 3/1918; 6/1961-present]

Japan Times Weekly & Trans-Pacific [1918 - 1941]

Japan Times & Mail, Weekly Edition [4/1918 - 1942]

Nippon Times Weekly [1943 - 6/1956]

ENGLISH-LANGUAGE PRESS IN CHINA

China Weekly Review [*Millard's*], 1917 - 1953
   Title varies as follows:

6/1917 - 5/1921	*Millard's Review of the Far East*
6/1921 - 7/1922	*The Weekly Review of the Far East*
7/1922 - 6/1923	*The Weekly Review*
6/1923 - 8/1950	*The China Weekly Review*
	[suspended 12/13/1941 - 10/13/1945]
9/1950 - 1953	*China Monthly Review*

· ·

North China Herald [1850 - 3/1867]

└── *North China Herald & Market Report*
      [4/1867 - 1869]

      └── *North China Herald & Supreme Court & Consular Gazette*
            [1871-1941; weekly out of Shanghai]

· ·

North China Daily News [7/1864 - 3/1951]   daily; Shanghai

China Critic [5/1928 - 1946]   weekly; Shanghai

China Press [1925 -12/1941; 10/1945 - 3/1949]   daily; Shanghai

PERIODICALS PUBLISHED PRIOR TO 1945

Amerasia [1937 - 1947]. An essentially leftwing analysis.

American Chamber of Commerce of Shanghai, *Bulletin* [monthly]

Asia [1898 - 12/1946]
A lavishly illustrated monthly, published by the American Asiatic Association. Title varies:

1898 - 1/1917	*Journal of the American Asiatic Association*
3/1917 - 10/1942	*Asia*
11/1942 - 12/1946	*Asia and the Americas*

British Chamber of Commerce of Shanghai, *Journal* [monthly]

China At War [4/1938 - 12/1945]
A monthly propaganda journal published by the China Information Committee, Chungking.

China Today: A Monthly Magazine of Information and Opinion on the Far East [1934 - 1942]
Published by the leftwing American Friends of the Chinese People, and eventually merged with *Amerasia*.

Chinese Social and Political Science Review [1916 -]
Index to volumes 1-20 (1916 - 1937).

Communist International [1919 - 1940]
London.
5/1919 - 1924 = nos. 1-30.
1924 - 12/1940 = New Series, vols. 1-17.

Contemporary Japan [1932 - present]
Foreign Affairs Association of Japan. A valuable semi-official Japanese publication which includes chronologies and documents. Index to vols. 1-10 (6/1932 - 12/1941).

Contemporary Manchuria [4/1937 - 1/1941]
A bimonthly magazine published by the South Manchurian Railway Company.

Contemporary Opinions on Current Topics; Translated from Japanese
Magazines, Books, and Government Bulletins, Pamphlets and Reports from
Various Sources [1936 - 1941]
> Tokyo Information Bureau; Shigeyoshi Okamura, ed. Partially available
> on Library of Congress microfilm, 2 reels.

Empire Review [1901 - 1951]
> A British periodical. Monthly to 1942; quarterly thereafter. Title varies:

> | 1901 - 1914 | *The Empire Review* |
> | 1914 - 1922 | *The Empire Review and Journal of British Trade* |
> | 1923 - 1944 | *The Empire Review* |
> | 1944 - 1951 | *The Commonwealth and Empire Review* |

Far Eastern Review (*Engineering - Finance - Commerce*) [1904 - 1941]
> Shanghai commercial interests.

Far Eastern Survey [3/1932 - 2/1961]
> Weekly publication of the American Council of the Institute of Pacific
> Relations. Issued as "I.P.R. Memoranda" until volume 4.

Foreign Affairs [1922 - present]
> Monthly publication of the elite Council on Foreign Relations, N.Y.

Foreign Policy Bulletin [3/1920 - 6/1961]
> Foreign Policy Association, N.Y. A vehicle for more progressive and
> leftwing analysis.

Foreign Policy Reports [1925 - 1951]
> Foreign Policy Association, N.Y. Some variation in title.

The Fortnightly [1865 - 12/1954]
> London.

Illustrated London News [1842 - 1975]

International Affairs [1922 - present]
> Royal Institute of International Affairs, London. The R.I.I.A.'s
> voluminous publications in general are a valuable first-hand source for
> the pre-1945 period.

Oriental Economist, A Monthly Journal of Practical Finance and Economics for
Japan and Eastern Asia [5/1934 - present]
> English edition of *Tōyō Keizai Shimpo*, edited before the war by
> Tanzan Ishibashi.

Pacific Affairs [1928 - present]
    Institute of Pacific Relations.

The Round Table, A Quarterly Review of the Politics of the British Commonwealth [1910 - present]
    Index for vols. 1-25 (1910 - 1935).

Tokyo Gazette, A Monthly Report of Current Politics, Official Statements and Statistics [1937 - 1941]
    Japanese Government, Cabinet Information Bureau.

YEARBOOKS, ETC. — JAPAN

Japan Year Book [1905 - 1931]

Japan Times Year Book, 1933

Japan-Manchukuo Year Book [1934, 1938, 1939, 1940]

Contemporary Manchuria [1937, 1938, 1939, 1940]

Japan Year Book [1938/39, 1943/44, 1944/45, 1949/52]
    Foreign Affairs Association of Japan.

South Seas Handbook [1942/43, 1943/44, 1944/45]
    Foreign Affairs Association of Japan; complements *Japan Year Book.*

Japan Advertiser Annual Review: Finance, Industry, and Commerce [1931-1940]

Financial and Economic Annual of Japan [1901 - 1940]
    Department of Finance, Japan.

YEARBOOKS, ETC. — CHINA, ASIA & THE WEST

China Year Book [1912 - 1939]
    North China Daily News & Herald.
    H. G. W. Woodhead, ed.

Chinese Year Book [1935 -]
    Council on International Affairs, Shanghai.

China Handbook [1937 - 1945]
    Ministry of Information, China.

Annual Report of the National Economic Council, China.

Armaments Year-book: General and Statistical Information [1924 - 1939]
    League of Nations, 15 volumes.

Problems of the Pacific [1928 -]
    Biennial by Institute of Pacific Relations.

Survey of International Affairs [1920 - 1963]
    Royal Institute of International Affairs.
    Annual to 1938.
    Multi-volume problem focus for 1939 - 1946.
    Biennial or annual for 1947 - 1963.
    Index for 1920 - 1938.

The United States in World Affairs: An Account of American Foreign Relations
[1931 - 1970]
    Council on Foreign Relations, N.Y.
    From 1971, incorporated in *American Foreign Relations:*
        A Documentary Record.

GENERAL COLLECTIONS OF
OFFICIAL DOCUMENTS

Documents on International Affairs [1928 - 1963]
    Royal Institute of International Affairs.
    Annual volumes for 1928 - 1938.
    Two volumes cover 1939 - 1946.
    One volume for 1947/48, 1948/49.
    Annual volumes for 1950 - 1963.
    Companion to *Survey of International Affairs*,
        with consolidated index for 1920 - 1938.

Documents on American Foreign Relations [1938 - present]
>   World Peace Foundation, 1938/39 - 1951.
>   Council on Foreign Relations, 1951 - present.
>   Beginning with volume for 1971, retitled *American Foreign Relations:*
>   *A Documentary Record.*
>   Essentially companion to *The United States in World Affairs*
>   (CFR, 1931 - 1970).

Documents on British Foreign Policy, 1919 - 1939. Third Series
>   E. L. Woodward & Rohan Butler, eds. 9 volumes. See volumes 8 and 9
>   on the Far East.

*Documents on German Foreign Policy, 1918 - 1945, from the Archives of the
German Foreign Ministry*
>   U.S. Department of State. Issued in 16 volumes (1949 - 1957).

[Documents on Japanese Foreign Policy]
>   Included regularly as end matter in Foreign Affairs Association of
>   Japan's journal *Contemporary Japan* (from 1932).

LEAGUE OF NATIONS MATERIALS ON THE SINO-JAPANESE CONFLICT OF 1931 – 1933

Basic index to League materials
>   *Guide to League of Nations Publications: A Bibliographic Survey of the
>   Work of the League, 1920 - 1947.* Hans Aufricht, ed. (1951: Columbia
>   University Press).

Minutes of the Council
>   *Official Journal* [especially for December 1931 and March and
>   December 1932].

China's basic position
>   *Memoranda Presented to the Lytton Commission* by V. K. Wellington
>   Koo, assessor. 1932. 3 volumes.

Japan's basic position

>   *Document A—The Present Condition of China: With Reference to
>   Circumstances Affecting International Relations and the Good
>   Understanding between Nations upon which Peace Depends*
>   [revised edition, July 1932].

Document B—Relations of Japan with Manchuria and Mongolia
[revised edition, July 1932].

The Manchurian Question: Japan's Case in the Sino-Japanese Dispute as Presented Before the League of Nations [1932].

Report of the Lytton Commission
Report of the Commission of Inquiry [1932].

JAPANESE MATERIALS IN ENGLISH

Bank of Japan, Statistics Department
Hundred-Year Statistics of the Japanese Economy [Meiji Ikō Hompō Shuyō Keizai Tōkei, 1966: Nihon Ginkō].

Cabinet Information Bureau
Tokyo Gazette: A Monthly Report of Current Politics, Official Statements and Statistics [1937 - 1941].

Greater East Asia War Inquiry Commission
The American-British Challenge Directed Against Nippon
[1943: Mainichi Shimbunsha].

Ministry of Education

Shūshin-sho [Japanese ethics textbooks] in Robert King Hall,
SHŪSHIN: THE ETHICS OF A DEFEATED NATION
(1949: Teachers College, Columbia University), 73-234.

KOKUTAI NO HONGI: CARDINAL PRINCIPLES OF THE
NATIONAL ENTITY OF JAPAN [1937]. John Owen Gauntlett,
transl., Robert King Hall, ed. 1949: Harvard University Press.

Shinmin no Michi [The Way of the Subject, March 1941] Translation
in Otto Tolischus, TOKYO RECORD (1943: Reynal & Hitchcock),
405-427.

South Manchurian Railway Company
South Manchurian Railway Company. *Report on Progress in Manchuria, 1907 - 1928* [plus sequel and companion publications: 1930, 1932, 1934, 1936].

Minutes of the top-level Liaison and Imperial Conferences, 1941
Nobutake Ike, transl. & ed. JAPAN'S DECISION FOR WAR:
RECORDS OF THE 1941 POLICY CONFERENCES. 1967: Stanford
University Press. Based on volume 8 of *Taiheiyō Sensō e no Michi*.

Documents pertaining to the Greater East Asia Co-Prosperity Sphere

Joyce C. Lebra, ed. JAPAN'S GREATER EAST ASIA CO-PROS-
PERITY SPHERE IN WORLD WAR II: SELECTED READINGS
AND DOCUMENTS. 1975: Oxford University Press.

Harry J. Benda, James K. Irikura & Kōichi Kishi, eds. JAPANESE
MILITARY ADMINISTRATION IN INDONESIA: SELECTED
DOCUMENTS. 1965: Yale University Southeast Asia Studies,
Translation Series 6; based on Shigetada Nishijima & Kōichi Kishi, eds.
Indonesia ni okeru Nihon Gunsei no Kenkyū.

Japanese Military Administration [the Philippines]. THE OFFICIAL
JOURNAL OF THE JAPANESE MILITARY ADMINISTRATION
[published regularly in English in Manila from 1942].

Frank N. Trager, ed. BURMA: JAPANESE MILITARY ADMINIS
TRATION: SELECTED DOCUMENTS, 1941-1945. 1971: University
of Pennsylvania Press.

OFFICIAL U.S. PUBLICATIONS

Franklin D. Roosevelt.
Franklin D. Roosevelt. THE PUBLIC PAPERS AND ADDRESSES OF
FRANKLIN D. ROOSEVELT. 13 volumes. 1950: Random House.

U.S. Air Force
U.S. Air Force. THE ARMY AIR FORCES IN WORLD WAR II.
Volumes 1, 4, and 5 deal with Japan.

U.S. Congress

HEARINGS OF THE JOINT COMMITTEE ON THE INVESTIGA
TION OF THE PEARL HARBOR ATTACK. 39 parts. 1946.

REPORT OF THE JOINT COMMITTEE ON THE INVESTIGATION
OF THE PEARL HARBOR ATTACK. 1 volume. 1946.

U.S. Department of the Army

> U.S. Department of the Army. JAPANESE MONOGRAPH SERIES.
> 185 studies dealing with the war in the Pacific and originally prepared
> primarily by former Japanese military officers. Available on Library of
> Congress microfilm in 14 reels. 47 of the most important monographs
> are available in a 15-volume reprint edition by Garland Publishing Inc.:
> WAR IN ASIA AND THE PACIFIC, 1937-1945 (1980). See page 327.

> U.S. Department of the Army. JAPANESE STUDIES ON
> MANCHURIA. 13 studies originally prepared by former Japanese
> military officers. Available on Library of Congress microfilm.

> U.S. Department of the Army. REPORTS OF GENERAL
> MACARTHUR. 2 volumes in 4 books. Originally prepared by
> MacArthur's General Staff in 1950, but not published until 1966.

>> I. *The Campaigns of MacArthur in the Pacific.*
>> I. Supplement. *MacArthur in Japan: The Occupation:*
>> *Military Phase.*
>> II. Parts 1 and 2. *Japanese Operations in the Southwest*
>> *Pacific Area.*

> U.S. Department of the Army. THE UNITED STATES ARMY IN
> WORLD WAR II. This series, including various related publications,
> is published under the auspices of the Office of the Chief of Military
> History.

U.S. Department of Defense
> U.S. Department of Defense. THE ENTRY OF THE SOVIET UNION
> INTO THE WAR AGAINST JAPAN: MILITARY PLANS,
> 1941-1945. 1955.

U.S. Department of State

> U.S. Department of State. For consular reports and related materials
> pertaining to U.S. relations with Japan and China and available on
> microfilm from the U.S. government, consult *Catalog of National*
> *Archives Microfilm Publications.* See also pages 362-364 below for
> privately issued collections of official documents.

U.S., Department of State. FOREIGN RELATIONS OF THE UNITED
STATES. "Far East" volumes in this basic State Department series are:

1931	vol. 3	1937	vol. 3 & 4
1932	3 & 4	1938	3 & 4
1933	3	1939	3 & 4
1934	3	1940	4
1935	3	1941	4 & 5
1936	4		

U.S. Department of State. FOREIGN RELATIONS OF THE UNITED
STATES: JAPAN, 1931-1941. 2 volumes, published in 1943 while the
war (and debate over Pearl Harbor) was going on.

U.S. Department of State. PEACE AND WAR: UNITED STATES
FOREIGN POLICY, 1931-1941. Published in 1943 and focusing on
pre-Pearl Harbor relations with Japan and Germany.

U.S. Department of State. REPORT ON JAPANESE REPARATIONS
TO THE PRESIDENT OF THE UNITED STATES, NOVEMBER 1945
TO April 1946 DOS Publication 3174, Far Eastern Series 25. ["The
Pauley Report." See also the complementary report by Edwin W. Pauley
entitled U.S. Department of State. REPORT ON JAPANESE ASSETS
IN MANCHURIA TO THE PRESIDENT OF THE UNITED STATES,
JULY 1946.]

U.S. Department of State. UNITED STATES RELATIONS WITH
CHINA, WITH SPECIAL REFERENCE TO THE PERIOD 1944-1949.
1949. DOS Publication 3573, Far Eastern Series 30. The famous
"China White Paper" of August 1949.

U.S. Strategic Bombing Survey
    U.S. Strategic Bombing Survey. PACIFIC WAR [1945 - 1947].
    Consists of 108 reports. For the most useful general reports,
    see pages 327-8.

U.S. ARCHIVAL MATERIALS AVAILABLE IN MICROFILM FROM COMMERCIAL SOURCES

The extensive declassification of formerly confidential U.S. government documents since the 1960s has facilitated the extensive copying of both civilian and military archival materials. The following large collections, covering post-1945 as well as pre-1945 activities, are offered by University Publications of America (usually accompanied by an index):

- *Confidential U.S. Diplomatic Post Records: Japan*

    Part 1. Japan, 1914-1918. 11 reels.
    Part 2. Japan, 1919-1929. 50 reels.
    Part 3. Japan, 1930-1941. 80 reels.

- *The MAGIC Documents: Summaries and Transcripts of the Top-Secret Diplomatic Communications of Japan, 1938-1945.* 14 reels.

- *Confidential U.S. State Department Central Files*

    Japan: Internal Affairs, 1945-1949. 42 reels.
    Japan: Internal Affairs, 1950-1954. 62 reels.

- *U.S. Military Intelligence Reports: Japan, 1918-1941.* 31 reels.

- *U.S. Military Intelligence Reports: China, 1911-1941.* 15 reels.

- *Records of the Joint Chiefs of Staff*

    Pacific Theater, 1942-1945. 14 reels.
    The Far East, 1946-1953. 14 reels.

- *OSS / State Department Intelligence and Research Reports*

    Japan and Its Occupied Territories during World War II. 16 reels.
    Postwar Japan, Korea and Southeast Asia. 6 reels.
    Japan, Korea, Southeast Asia, and the Far East Generally: 1950-1961 Supplement. 7 reels.

- *CIA Research Reports*

    China, 1946-1976. 6 reels.
    Japan, Korea, and the Security of Asia, 1946-1976. 5 reels.
    Vietnam and Southeast Asia, 1946-1976. 7 reels.

• *The Special Studies Series* (reports by various "think tanks")

> *China, 1970-1980.* 8 reels.
> *Japan, Korea, and the Security of Asia, 1970-1980.* 4 reels.
> *Vietnam and Southeast Asia, 1960-1980.* 13 reels.
> *Asia, 1980-1982 Supplement.* 5 reels.
> *Asia, 1982-1985 Supplement.* 12 reels.

In addition to the preceding University Publications of America collections, the following archives are available on microfilm from Scholarly Resources, Inc., under the collective title *Official Records of the U.S. Department of State Relating to Japan* (part of Record Group 59):

19th-CENTURY RECORDS

> *Diplomatic Instructions of the Department of State Regarding Japan, 1855-1906.* 7 reels.
> *Despatches from U.S. Ministers to Japan, 1855-1906.* 82 reels.
> *Records of the U.S. Legation in Japan, 1855-1912.* 94 reels.
> *Despatches from U.S. Consuls in Japan, 1856-1906.* 41 reels.
> *Notes from the Japanese Legation in the United States to the Department of State, 1858-1906.* 9 reels.
> *Notes to the Legation of Japan in the United States from the Department of State, 1860-1906.* 2 reels.

20th-CENTURY RECORDS

> *Records Relating to Political Relations Between the United States and Japan*:
> > *1910-1929.* 9 reels.
> > *1930-1939.* 5 reels.
> > *1940-1944.* 8 reels.
> > *1945-1949.* 19 reels.
> > *1950-1954.* 11 reels.
> > *1955-1959.* 11 reels.

> *Records Relating to Political Relations Between Japan and Other States,*
>
> > *1910-1929.* 1 reel.

Records Relating to the Internal Affairs of Japan:

> *1910-1929.* 43 reels.
> *1930-1939.* 33 reels.
> *1940-1944.* 20 reels.
> *1945-1949.* 39 reels.
> *1950-1954.* 51 reels.
> *1955-1959.* 48 reels.

Records Relating to Political Relations Between China and Japan, 1930-1944. 96 reels.

Other materials relating to Japan available from Scholarly Resources, Inc. include:

- *The Pacific War, October 1940-December 1945.* 27 reels. From Record Group 59, *Official Records of the U.S. Department of State Relating to World War II, 1939-1945.*

- *Wartime Conferences of the Combined Chiefs of Staff, 1941-1945.* 3 reels.

- *Diary of the Operations Division, War Department General Staff: 1942-1946.* 4 reels.

- *U.S. Army Orders of Battle for WWII.* 1 reel. Three volumes, one on the Pacific Theater.

- *Admiral Nimitz Command Summary: Running Estimate and Survey, 1941-1945.*

- *Military Intelligence in the Pacific, 1942-1946: Bulletins of the Intelligence Center, Pacific Ocean Area, and the Joint Intelligence Center, Pacific Ocean Area.* 41 reels.

- *The History of Intelligence Activities under General Douglas MacArthur, 1942-1950: The Intelligence Series, G2-USAFFE SWPA-AFPAC-FEC-SCAP.* 8 reels.

- U.S. Army Center of Military History Historical Manuscripts Collection: *The War Against Japan.* 53 reels.

- *Intercepted Japanese Messages: The Documents of MAGIC, 1938-1945.* 15 reels.

- *Records of the U.S. Department of State Relating to Commercial Relations between the United States and Japan, 1910-1949.* 17 reels.

BRITISH ARCHIVAL MATERIALS AVAILABLE FROM COMMERCIAL SOURCES

University Publications of America. *British Documents on Foreign Affairs:*

> *Reports and Papers from the Foreign Office Confidential Print.* Offered as a counterpart to the U.S. State Department's *Foreign Relations of the United States* series, these volumes are scheduled for publication between 1985 and 1988:

> *Part I. From the Mid-Nineteenth Century to the First World War: Asia.* 30 volumes.

> *Part II. From the First to the Second World War: Asia.* 50 volumes.

Scholarly Resources, Inc. *The Japan Correspondence of the British Foreign Office, 1856-1945* (Files 46 and 371). Available in the following microfilm collections:

1856-1867.	48 reels.
1868-1875.	61 reels.
1876-1882.	59 reels.
1883-1893.	65 reels.
1894-1904.	78 reels.
1905.	57 reels.
1906-1913.	47 reels.
1914-1923.	73 reels.
1924-1929.	15 reels.
1930-1936.	38 reels.
1937-1941.	48 reels.
1939-1945.	64 reels.
1942-1945.	28 reels.
1946.	40 reels.
1947.	28 reels.
1948.	35 reels.
Registers, 1856-1905.	6 reels.

Microfilming Corporation of America. *The London Times Intelligence File: The Far East (1906-1969).* 27 microfilm reels (5 of which pertain to Japan alone).

Adam Matthew Publications. *Foreign Office Files for Japan and the Far East. Series One: Embassy and Consular Archives—Japan* (Public Record Office Class FO 262).

> *1905-1920.*   18 reels.
> *1921-1923.*   44 reels.
> *1924-1926.*   44 reels.
> *1927-1929, 1930-1931, 1932-1933, 1934-1935, 1936-1940, 1945-1952, 1953-1957.* Forthcoming.

Adam Matthew Publications. *Business and Financial Papers, 1780-1939. Selected Titles from the Bodelian Library, Oxford, and the British Newspaper Library, London. Series One: International Trade.*

> Part 1: 11 titles, including *The African Times and Orient Review, 1912-1914, 1917-1918*; *The Anglo-Japanese Gazette, 1902-1909*; *The Eastern World, 1899-1908*; *The Pacific Mail, 1873-1876.* 30 reels.

OTHER ARCHIVAL MATERIALS AVAILABLE FROM COMMERCIAL SOURCES

Scholarly Resources, Inc. *The History of the Great Patriotic War of the Soviet Union, 1941-1945.* 7 reels. Written by Soviet military officers and official military and party historians; translated by the U.S. Army and Air Force.

I. M. T. F. E. & OTHER WAR CRIMES TRIALS

See pages 342-345. The Proceedings of the Tokyo war crimes trails, long inaccessible or inconvenient to use, are now available in a 27-volume reprint edition (including a 5-volume index and guide):

> R. John Pritchard & Sonia Zaide Pritchard, eds. THE TOKYO WAR CRIMES TRIAL (Garland Publishing, Inc.).

Both the Judgment and dissenting opinions, including the famous lengthy dissent
of Justice Pal, have been conveniently reprinted in 3 volumes in:

B. V. A. Roling & C. F. Ruter, eds. THE TOKYO JUDGMENT:
THE INTERNATIONAL MILITARY TRIBUNAL FOR THE
FAR EAST (I.M.T.F.E.), 29 APRIL 1946-12 NOVEMBER 1948
(1977: APA-University Press, Amsterdam BV).

A partial guide to IMTFE records is available as:

Jarritus Wolfinger, comp. PRELIMINARY INVENTORY OF THE
RECORD OF THE INTERNATIONAL MILITARY TRIBUNAL FOR
THE FAR EAST. (n.d.): National Archives & Records Service,
PI 180/RG 238.

A 535-page English transcript of the December 1949 Soviet trial of Japanese
accused of engaging in biological-warfare research involving prisoners
of war in Manchuria (the notorious "Unit 731") is:

MATERIALS ON THE TRIAL OF FORMER SERVICEMEN OF THE
JAPANESE ARMY CHARGED WITH MANUFACTURING AND
EMPLOYING BACTERIOLOGICAL WEAPONS (1950: Foreign
Language Publishing House, Moscow).

ACCOUNTS BY PARTICIPANTS

Joseph W. Ballantine. "Mukden to Pearl Harbor: The Foreign Policies of Japan,"
Foreign Affairs 27 (July 1949), 651-664.

Ba Maw. BREAKTHROUGH IN BURMA: MEMOIRS OF A REVOLUTION,
1939-1946. 1968: Yale University Press.

Alexander Cadogan. THE DIARIES OF SIR ALEXANDER CADOGAN,
1938-1945. David Dilks, ed. 1971: Cassell.

Winston Churchill. THE SECOND WORLD WAR. Multivolume. 1948-1953:
Houghton Mifflin.

Sir Robert Craigie. BEHIND THE JAPANESE MASK. 1945: Hutchinson.

John P. Davies. DRAGON BY THE TAIL. 1972: Norton.

Herbert von Dirkson. MOSCOW, TOKYO, LONDON. 1951: Hutchinson.

Anthony Eden. THE MEMOIRS OF ANTHONY EDEN, EARL OF AVON.
    Cassell.

    Volume 1: FACING THE DICTATORS, 1932-1938. 1962.
    Volume 2: THE RECKONING. 1965.
    Volume 3: FULL CIRCLE. 1960.

Robert L. Eichelberger. OUR JUNGLE ROAD TO TOKYO. 1950: Viking.

John K. Emmerson. THE JAPANESE THREAD: A LIFE IN THE U.S.
    FOREIGN SERVICE. 1978: Holt, Rinehart & Winston.

Joseph Grew. REPORT FROM TOKYO. 1942: Simon & Schuster.

_____. TEN YEARS IN JAPAN. 1944: Simon & Schuster.

_____. TURBULENT ERA: A DIPLOMATIC RECORD OF FORTY YEARS,
    1904-1945. 2 volumes. 1952: Houghton Mifflin.

Kumao Harada. See SAIONJI-HARADA MEMOIRS below.

Herbert Hoover. MEMOIRS. 3 volumes. 1951: Macmillan. Volume 2 covers
    1920-1932.

Jirō Horikoshi. EAGLES OF MITSUBISHI: THE STORY OF THE ZERO
    FIGHTER. 1980: University of Washington Press. By engineer
    involved in designing the Zero.

Akira Yoshimura. BUILD THE MUSASHI!: THE BIRTH AND DEATH OF
    THE WORLD'S GREATEST BATTLESHIP. Vincent Murphy, transl.
    1991: Kōdansha International. Based on diaries of the engineer in
    charge.

Stanley K. Hornbeck. THE U.S. AND THE FAR EAST: CERTAIN FUNDA-
    MENTALS OF POLICY. 1942: World Peace Foundation.

Cordell Hull. THE MEMOIRS OF CORDELL HULL. 2 volumes. 1948:
    Macmillan.

Harold L. Ickes. THE SECRET DIARY OF HAROLD L. ICKES. 3 volumes.
    1953-1954: Simon & Schuster.

Kikujirō Ishii. DIPLOMATIC COMMENTARIES. William R. Langdon, transl. 1936: Johns Hopkins.

Toshikazu Kase. JOURNEY TO THE "MISSOURI." 1952: Yale University Press.

Masuo Katō. THE LOST WAR: A JAPANESE REPORTER'S INSIDE STORY. 1946: Knopf.

Kōichi Kido. THE DIARY OF MARQUIS KIDO, 1931-45: SELECTED TRANSLATIONS INTO ENGLISH. 1984: University Publications of America. Reprinted from translations prepared for the IMTFE or Tokyo war crimes trials.

Sir Hughe Knatchbull-Hugessen. DIPLOMAT IN PEACE AND WAR. 1949: John Murray.

Yoshio Kodama. I WAS DEFEATED. Robert Booth & Tarō Fukuda, transl. 1951: Tarō Fukuda.

David C. Evans, ed. & transl. THE JAPANESE NAVY IN WORLD WAR II: IN THE WORDS OF FORMER JAPANESE NAVAL OFFICERS. 2nd edition. 1986: Naval Institute Press.

Hatsuho Naitō. THUNDER GODS: THE KAMIKAZE PILOTS TELL THEIR STORY. Mayumi Ichikawa, transl. 1989: Kōdansha International.

John T. Mason. THE PACIFIC WAR REMEMBERED. 1986: Naval Institute Press.

Fumimaro Konoye. "Memoirs of Prince Konoye," Exhibit No. 173 in U.S. Congress, HEARINGS OF THE JOINT COMMITTEE ON THE INVESTIGATION OF THE PEARL HARBOR ATTACK, part 20, 3958-4029.

"The Memoirs of Prince Fumimaro Konoye, with Appended Papers," translated and reproduced by 5250th Technical Intelligence Co., 10 June 1946. Record Group 331. Washington National Records Center.

See also Library of Congress microfilm WT6 from the IMTFE.

Thomas W. Lamont. ACROSS WORLD FRONTIERS. 1951: Harcourt Brace.

Sir Frederick Leith-Ross. MONEY TALKS: FIFTY YEARS OF INTER-NATIONAL FINANCE. 1968: Hutchinson.

Sidney Forrester Mashbir. I WAS AN AMERICAN SPY. 1953: Vantage.

Frederick Moore. WITH JAPAN'S LEADERS: AN INTIMATE RECORD OF
    FOURTEEN YEARS AS COUNSELLOR TO THE JAPANESE
    GOVERNMENT, ENDING DECEMBER 7, 1941. 1942: Charles
    Scribner's Sons.

Henry Morgenthau, Jr. FROM THE MORGENTHAU DIARIES. Volume 2:
    YEARS OF URGENCY, 1938-1941. John Morton Blum, ed. (1965:
    Houghton Mifflin), 344-393.

H. G. Nichols, ed. WASHINGTON DESPATCHES, 1941-1945: WEEKLY
    POLITICAL REPORTS FROM THE BRITISH EMBASSY. 1981:
    University of Chicago Press.

Major General F. S. G. Piggott. BROKEN THREAD: AN AUTOBIOGRA-
    PHY. 1950: Gale & Polden. Piggott served as military attache in Japan
    before the outbreak of war.

Anthony Reid & Akira Ōki, eds. THE JAPANESE EXPERIENCE IN
    INDONESIA: SELECTED MEMOIRS OF 1942-1945. 1986:
    Center for International Studies & Center for Southeast Asian Studies,
    Ohio University.

Sir John Pratt. WAR AND POLITICS IN CHINA. 1943: Cape.

_____. CHINA AND BRITAIN. 1944: Hastings House.

Aisin Gioro Pu-Yi. FROM EMPEROR TO CITIZEN. 2 volumes. 1964-1965:
    Foreign Language Press, Peking. Autobiography of the last Ch'ing
    emperor, who was "restored" to the throne by the Japanese in
    Manchukuo.

Franklin D. Roosevelt. F. D. R.—HIS PERSONAL LETTERS, 1928-1945.
    Elliott Roosevelt, ed. 2 volumes. 1950: Duell Sloan & Pearce.

THE SAIONJI-HARADA MEMOIRS, 1931-1940: COMPLETE TRANS-
    LATION INTO ENGLISH. 1978 (3 microfilm reels issued by
    University Publications). The famous record kept by Harada Kumao for
    Prince Kinmochi Saionji. Also available as Library of Congress
    microfilms SP49-51 from IMTFE.

Hiroshi Saitō. JAPAN'S POLICIES AND PURPOSES: SELECTIONS FROM
    RECENT ADDRESSES AND WRITINGS. 1935: Marshall Jones.
    Ambassador to U.S., 1934-35.

Mamoru Shigemitsu. JAPAN AND HER DESTINY: MY STRUGGLE FOR PEACE. 1958: Dutton.

Mohan Singh. SOLDIER'S CONTRIBUTION TO INDIAN INDEPENDENCE: THE EPIC OF THE INDIAN NATIONAL ARMY. 1974: Army Educational Stores, New Delhi.

William Slim. DEFEAT INTO VICTORY. 1960: Cassell.

Henry L. Stimson. THE FAR EASTERN CRISIS: RECOLLECTIONS AND OBSERVATIONS. 1936: Harper.

_____ & McGeorge Bundy. ON ACTIVE SERVICE IN PEACE AND WAR. 1948: Harper.

Gwen Terasaki. BRIDGE TO THE SUN. 1957: University of North Carolina Press.

Shigenori Tōgō. THE CAUSE OF JAPAN. 1956: Simon & Schuster.

Matome Ugaki. FADING VICTORY: THE DIARY OF ADMIRAL MATOME UGAKI, 1941-1945. Masataka Chihaya, transl. 1991: University of Pittsburgh Press.

Otto Tolischus. TOKYO RECORD. 1943: Reynal & Hitchcock. Reconstructed "diary" covering January 1941 to August 1942, by the former *New York Times* correspondent in Japan.

Harry S. Truman. YEAR OF DECISIONS, 1945. 1955: Doubleday.

Masanobu Tsuji. SINGAPORE: THE JAPANESE VERSION. 1960: St. Martin's.

_____. UNDERGROUND ESCAPE. Robert Booth & Tarō Fukuda, transl. 1952: Tarō Fukuda.

Lord Vansittart. THE MIST PROCESSION. 1958: Hutchinson.

Amleto Vespa. SECRET AGENT OF JAPAN. 1938: Little, Brown.

Hugh R. Wilson. DIPLOMAT BETWEEN WARS. 1941: Longmans, Green.

W. Macmahon Ball. INTERMITTENT DIPLOMAT: THE JAPAN AND BATAVIA DIARIES OF W. MACMAHON BALL. Alan Rix, ed. 1988: Melbourne University Press.

Arthur N. Young. CHINA AND THE HELPING HAND. 1963: Harvard University Press. U.S. financial adviser to China.

Ellis M. Zacharias. SECRET MISSIONS: THE STORY OF AN INTELLI-GENCE OFFICER. 1946: Putnam.

Women's Division of Sōka Gakkai, comp. WOMEN AGAINST WAR: PERSONAL ACCOUNTS OF FORTY JAPANESE WOMEN. Richard L. Gage, transl. 1986: Kōdansha International.

Tomiko Higa. THE GIRL WITH THE WHITE FLAG. Dorothy Britton, transl. 1991: Kōdansha International. The author's story of her own experiences as a young girl in Okinawa during the war.

Haruko Taya Cook & Theodore F. Cook, eds. JAPAN AT WAR: AN ORAL HISTORY. 1992: The New Press.

OCCUPIED JAPAN & THE COLD WAR IN ASIA

Occupied Japan & the Cold War in Asia

GENERAL SOURCES

John W. Dower. "Occupied Japan as History and Occupation History as Politics," *Journal of Asian Studies* 34.2 (1975), 485-504.

_____. "The Useful War," in Carol Gluck & Stephen R. Graubard, eds. SHŌWA: THE JAPAN OF HIROHITO (1992: Norton), 49-70.

_____. EMPIRE AND AFTERMATH: YOSHIDA SHIGERU AND THE JAPANESE EXPERIENCE, 1878-1954. 1979: Council on East Asian Studies, Harvard University. See especially pages 273-492.

_____. JAPAN IN WAR AND PEACE: SELECTED ESSAYS. 1994: The New Press. See especially essays on "The Useful War" (9-32), "Yoshida in the Scales of History" (208-241), and "Occupied Japan and the Cold War in Asia" (155-207).

Carol Gluck. "Entangling Illusions—Japanese and American Views of the Occupation," in Warren I. Cohen, ed. NEW FRONTIERS IN AMERICAN-EAST ASIAN RELATIONS: ESSAYS PRESENTED TO DOROTHY BORG (1983: Columbia University Press), 169-236.

Edwin O. Reischauer & Albert M. Craig. JAPAN: TRADITION AND TRANSFORMATION (1989: Houghton Mifflin), chapter 8.

Robert E. Ward & Sakamoto Yoshikazu, eds. DEMOCRATIZING JAPAN: THE ALLIED OCCUPATION. 1987: University of Hawaii Press. Interpretations by Japanese and American scholars.

*Robert E. Ward & Frank Joseph Shulman. THE ALLIED OCCUPATION OF JAPAN, 1945-1952: AN ANNOTATED BIBLIOGRAPHY OF WESTERN-LANGUAGE MATERIALS. 1974: American Library Association.

*Frank Joseph Shulman, comp. DOCTORAL DISSERTATIONS ON THE ALLIED OCCUPATION OF JAPAN, 1945-1952. 1978, with periodic supplements. Prepared for the MacArthur Memorial Symposium.

Royal Institute of International Affairs. SURVEY OF INTERNATIONAL AFFAIRS.

   1. THE FAR EAST, 1942-1946. (Hugh Borton on Japan, 307-428).
   2. 1947-1948   (F. C. Jones on Japan, 328-346).

3. 1949-1950   (F. C. Jones on Japan, 443-466).
4. 1951   (F. C. Jones on Japan, 378-433).
5. 1952   (F. C. Jones on Japan, 355-393).
6. See also companion volumes in Royal Institute of International Affairs. DOCUMENTS ON INTERNATIONAL AFFAIRS.

Supreme Commander for the Allied Powers. POLITICAL REORIENTATION OF JAPAN, SEPTEMBER 1945 TO SEPTEMBER 1948. 2 volumes. 1949: Government Printing Office. The official history of the reformist phase of the Occupation. Volume 2 is a valuable collection of basic documents.

Peter Frost. "Occupation," KŌDANSHA ENCYCLOPEDIA OF JAPAN 6: 51-55.

Hugh Patrick. "The Phoenix Risen from the Ashes: Postwar Japan," in James Crowley, ed. EAST ASIA: ESSAYS IN INTERPRETATION (1970: Harcourt Brace & World), 298-335.

Makoto Iokibe. "Japan Meets the United States for the Second Time," in Carol Gluck & Stephen R. Graubard, eds. SHŌWA: THE JAPAN OF HIROHITO (1992: Norton), 91-106.

Ikuhiko Hata. "Japan Under the Occupation," *Japan Interpreter* 10.3-4 (1976), 361-380.

_____. "The Occupation of Japan, 1945-1952," in Joe C. Dixon, ed. THE AMERICAN MILITARY AND THE FAR EAST (1981: Office of Air Force History), 92-108.

Daizaburō Yui. "Democracy from the Ruins: The First Seven Weeks of the Occupation in Japan," *Hitotsubashi Journal of Social Studies* 19 (1987), 31-45.

Howard B. Schonberger. AFTERMATH OF WAR: AMERICANS AND THE REMAKING OF JAPAN, 1945-1952. 1989: Kent State University Press.

_____. "U.S. Policy in Post-War Japan: The Retreat from Liberalism," *Science and Society* 46.1 (1982), 39-59.

Michael Schaller. THE AMERICAN OCCUPATION OF JAPAN: THE ORIGINS OF THE COLD WAR IN ASIA. 1985: Oxford University Press.

_____. DOUGLAS MACARTHUR: THE FAR EASTERN GENERAL.
1989: Oxford University Press.

Kazuo Kawai. JAPAN'S AMERICAN INTERLUDE. 1960: University of
Chicago Press.

Richard B. Finn. WINNERS IN PEACE: MACARTHUR, YOSHIDA, AND
POSTWAR JAPAN. 1992: University of California Press.

William Chapman. INVENTING JAPAN: THE MAKING OF A POSTWAR
CIVILIZATION. 1991: Prentice Hall.

Edwin M. Martin. THE ALLIED OCCUPATION OF JAPAN. 1948: Stanford
University Press.

Robert Fearey. THE OCCUPATION OF JAPAN: SECOND PHASE, 1948-
1950. 1950: Macmillan.

Baron E. J. Lewe van Aduard. JAPAN: FROM SURRENDER TO PEACE.
1964: Praeger.

Hugh Borton. JAPAN'S MODERN CENTURY: FROM PERRY TO 1970
(1970: Ronald), chapter 20.

Edwin O. Reischauer. THE UNITED STATES AND JAPAN. 3rd edition.
1965: Viking.

Masataka Kōsaka. A HISTORY OF POSTWAR JAPAN. Originally published
as 100-MILLION JAPANESE. 1982: Harper & Row.

Andrew Gordon, ed. POSTWAR JAPAN AS HISTORY. 1993: University of
California Press. Essays grouped under the themes of "Contexts,"
"Political Economy," "Mass Culture and Metropolitan Society," and
"Democratic Promise and Practice."

Shunsuke Tsurumi. A CULTURAL HISTORY OF POSTWAR JAPAN,
1945-1980. 1987: Kegan Paul International.

Carol Gluck & Stephen R. Graubard, eds. SHŌWA: THE JAPAN OF HIRO-
HITO. 1992: Norton. Originally published as v. 119, no. 3 (summer
1990), of *Daedalus* .

Harry Emerson Wildes. TYPHOON IN TOKYO: THE OCCUPATION AND
ITS AFTERMATH. 1954: Macmillan.

John D. Montgomery. FORCED TO BE FREE: THE ARTIFICIAL REVOLU-
TION IN GERMANY AND JAPAN. 1957: University of Chicago
Press.

Harold S. Quigley & John E. Turner. THE NEW JAPAN: GOVERNMENT
AND POLITICS. 1956: University of Minnesota Press.

Paul Linebarger, Chu Djang & Ardath Burks. FAR EASTERN GOVERN-
MENTS AND POLITICS: CHINA AND JAPAN (1954: Van
Nostrand), chapters 20, 21.

Herbert Passin. THE LEGACY OF THE OCCUPATION—JAPAN. 1968:
East Asia Institute, Columbia University.

Grant Goodman, comp. THE AMERICAN OCCUPATION OF JAPAN:
A RETROSPECTIVE VIEW. 1968: Center for East Asian Studies,
Kansas University.

Justin Williams, Sr. "American Democratization Policy for Occupied Japan:
Correcting the Revisionist Version," *Pacific Historical Review* 57.2
(1988), 179-202. Followed by rejoinders by John W. Dower
(pp. 202-209) and Howard Schonberger (pp. 209-218).

Robert Ward. "Reflections on the Allied Occupation and Planned Political
Change in Japan," in his POLITICAL DEVELOPMENT IN MODERN
JAPAN (1973: Princeton University Press), 477-536.

Ray Moore. "Reflections on the Occupation of Japan," *Journal of Asian Studies*
38.4 (1979), 721-734.

_____. "The Occupation of Japan as History: Some Recent Research,"
Monumenta Nipponica 36.3 (1981), 317-328.

Harry Wray & Hilary Conroy, eds. JAPAN EXAMINED: PERSPECTIVES ON
MODERN JAPANESE HISTORY (1983: University of Hawaii Press),
331-363. Essays on "The Allied Occupation: How Significant Was It?"
by Edwin Reischauer, John Dower, Rinjirō Sodei, and Eiji Takemae.

Asahi Shimbun, ed. THE PACIFIC RIVALS: A JAPANESE VIEW OF
JAPANESE-AMERICAN RELATIONS (1972: Weatherhill & Asahi),
109-209.

D. Clayton James. THE YEARS OF MACARTHUR: TRIUMPH AND
DISASTER, 1945-1964. 1985: Houghton Mifflin. The third and final
volume of the major biography of MacArthur.

John Curtis Perry. BENEATH THE EAGLE'S WINGS: AMERICANS IN OCCUPIED JAPAN. 1980: Dodd, Mead.

Robert Wolfe, ed. AMERICANS AS PROCONSULS: UNITED STATES MILITARY GOVERNMENT IN GERMANY & JAPAN, 1944-1952. 1984: Southern Illinois University Press. Includes articles by Marlene Mayo on presurrender planning and also censorship; Ralph Braibanti on the "MacArthur Shōgunate"; Eleanor Hadley on economic deconcentration and the reverse course; and Hans Baerwald on the purge.

MACARTHUR MEMORIAL SYMPOSIA. The major extended inquiry concerning Occupied Japan was a series of conferences sponsored by the MacArthur Memorial in Norfolk, Virginia (with later joint sponsorship by Old Dominion University), under the editorship of Thomas W. Burkman. Eight published volumes of papers and discussion by both scholars and participants covered the following topics:

1. THE OCCUPATION OF JAPAN AND ITS LEGACY TO THE POSTWAR WORLD. 1975.
2. THE OCCUPATION OF JAPAN: IMPACT OF LEGAL REFORM. 1977.
3. THE OCCUPATION OF JAPAN: ECONOMIC POLICY AND REFORM. 1978.
4. THE OCCUPATION OF JAPAN: EDUCATION AND SOCIAL REFORM. 1980.
5. THE OCCUPATION OF JAPAN: THE INTERNATIONAL CONTEXT. 1982.
6. THE OCCUPATION OF JAPAN: ARTS AND CULTURE. 1984.
7. THE OCCUPATION OF JAPAN: THE IMPACT OF THE KOREAN WAR. 1986.
8. THE OCCUPATION OF JAPAN: THE GRASS ROOTS. 1991.

CONTEMPORARY ACCOUNTS (1944-1952)

W. Macmahon Ball. JAPAN: ENEMY OR ALLY? 1949: Cassell.

Thomas A. Bisson. PROSPECTS FOR DEMOCRACY IN JAPAN. 1949: Macmillan.

Hugh Borton, ed. JAPAN. 1950: Cornell University Press.

Russell Brines. MACARTHUR'S JAPAN. 1948: J. B. Lippincott.

Brookings Institution. MAJOR PROBLEMS OF UNITED STATES FOREIGN
    POLICY, 1948-49. 1949: Brookings Insitution.

Noel F. Busch. FALLEN SUN: A REPORT ON JAPAN. 1948: Appleton-
    Century.

William Costello. DEMOCRACY VS. FEUDALISM IN POSTWAR JAPAN.
    1948: Hagaki Shoten.

Miriam S. Farley. ASPECTS OF JAPAN'S LABOR PROBLEMS. 1950:
    John Day.

Carl Friedrich et al., ed. AMERICAN EXPERIENCES IN MILITARY
    GOVERNMENT IN WORLD WAR II. 1948: Holt.

Mark Gayn. JAPAN DIARY. 1948: William Sloane.

John Gunther. THE RIDDLE OF MACARTHUR. 1950: Harper.

Robert King Hall. EDUCATION FOR A NEW JAPAN. 1949: Yale University
    Press.

Douglas G. Haring, ed. JAPAN'S PROSPECT. 1946: Harvard University Press.

Institute of Pacific Relations. SECURITY IN THE PACIFIC. 1945: Institute of
    Pacific Relations.

_____. PROBLEMS OF ECONOMIC RECONSTRUCTION IN THE
    FAR EAST. 1949: Institute of Pacific Relations.

Harold Issacs. NEW CYCLE IN ASIA: SELECTED DOCUMENTS ON
    MAJOR INTERNATIONAL DEVELOPMENTS IN THE FAR EAST.
    1947: Macmillan.

W. C. Johnstone. THE FUTURE OF JAPAN. 1945: Oxford University Press.

Frank Kelley & Cornelius Ryan. STAR SPANGLED MIKADO. 1947:
    McBride.

Owen Lattimore. SOLUTION IN ASIA. 1945: Little, Brown.

_____. THE SITUATION IN ASIA. 1949: Little, Brown.

John LaCerda. THE CONQUEROR COMES TO TEA: JAPAN UNDER MACARTHUR. 1946: Rutgers University Press.

Helen Mears. MIRROR FOR AMERICANS: JAPAN. 1948: Houghton Mifflin.

Harold G. Moulton & Louis Marlio. THE CONTROL OF GERMANY AND JAPAN. 1944: Brookings Institution.

Andrew Roth. DILEMMA IN JAPAN. 1945: Little, Brown.

Royal Institute of International Affairs, ed. JAPAN IN DEFEAT: A REPORT BY A CHATHAM HOUSE STUDY GROUP. 1945: Oxford University Press.

A. Frank Reel. THE CASE OF GENERAL YAMASHITA. 1949: University of Chicago Press.

Robert B. Textor. FAILURE IN JAPAN. 1951: John Day.

Harold Wakefield. NEW PATHS FOR JAPAN. 1948: Royal Institute of International Affairs.

MEMOIRS

Dean Acheson. PRESENT AT THE CREATION: MY YEARS IN THE STATE DEPARTMENT. 1969: W. W. Norton.

John Allison. AMBASSADOR FROM THE PRAIRIE, OR ALLISON WONDERLAND. 1973: Houghton Mifflin.

James F. Byrnes. SPEAKING FRANKLY. 1947: Harper.

Theodore Cohen. REMAKING JAPAN: THE AMERICAN OCCUPATION AS NEW DEAL. Herbert Passin, ed. 1987: Free Press.

W. Averell Harriman & Ellie Abel. SPECIAL ENVOY TO CHURCHILL AND STALIN, 1941-1946. 1975: Random House.

George F. Kennan. MEMOIRS, 1925-1950. 1967: Little, Brown.

Arthur W. John. UNEASY LIES THE HEAD THAT WEARS A CROWN. 2nd edition. 1987: Gen Publishers.

Douglas MacArthur. REMINISCENCES. 1964: McGraw-Hill.

Alfred C. Oppler. LEGAL REFORM IN OCCUPIED JAPAN: A PARTICI-
PANT LOOKS BACK. 1976: Princeton University Press.

Herbert Passin. "The Occupation—Some Reflections," in Carol Gluck
& Stephen R. Graubard, eds. SHŌWA: THE JAPAN OF HIROHITO
(1992: Norton), 107-129.

Matthew B. Ridgway. SOLDIER: THE MEMOIRS OF MATTHEW B.
RIDGWAY. 1956: Harper.

Harry S. Truman. MEMOIRS. 2 volumes. 1955: Doubleday.

Tatsurō Uchino. JAPAN'S POSTWAR ECONOMY: AN INSIDER'S VIEW OF
ITS HISTORY AND ITS FUTURE. 1983: Kōdansha International.

Courtney Whitney. MACARTHUR: HIS RENDEZVOUS WITH HISTORY.
1956: Knopf.

Justin Williams. JAPAN'S POLITICAL REVOLUTION UNDER
MACARTHUR: A PARTICIPANT'S ACCOUNT. 1979: University
of Georgia Press.

Charles A. Willoughby & John Chamberlain. MACARTHUR, 1941-1951:
VICTORY IN THE PACIFIC. 1954: McGraw-Hill.

Shigeru Yoshida. THE YOSHIDA MEMOIRS: THE STORY OF JAPAN IN
CRISIS. Ken'ichi Yoshida, transl. 1962: Houghton Mifflin.

OFFICIAL SCAP (SUPREME COMMANDER FOR THE ALLIED POWERS) HISTORY

HISTORY OF NON-MILITARY ASPECTS OF THE OCCUPATION OF
JAPAN

This series comprises a total of 55 monographs, all of which contain
appendices of documents. Available on microfilm from the U.S.
National Archives, and from Scholarly Resources, Inc. (as *Supreme
Commander for the Allied Powers Historical Monographs, 1945-1951*;
13 reels). This is the basic, and by far most comprehensive, official

account of the occupation, but should be used with recognition of the fact that (1) it is a house history, which seeks to present the occupation in its most favorable light; (2) most of the monographs cover only the period up to 1950, and thus this is not an adequate source for the crucial 1950-1952 period; (3) the authors of the series (SCAP's Civil Historical Section) relied primarily on public statements and internal SCAP memoranda, and were not privileged with access to materials at the highest and most classified levels; (4) attention is devoted primarily to the formal policy process, rather than to critical analysis of the actual effects and implications of policy application and policy revisions; (5) the monographic approach adopted tends to convey a fragmented and compartmentalized impression of the occupation, rather than the broader overview that was held by key decision-makers then, and which the scholar must also recreate; (6) the approach is essentially unilinear, that is, focused on American policy and initiative, and neglects the crucial dimension of US-Japanese interaction. The series nonetheless remains of central importance to scholars of the period. The individual monographs, in their officially designated order, are as follows:

1. Introduction
2. Administration of the Occupation
3. Logistic Support
4. Population
5. Trials of Class 'B' and Class 'C' War Criminals
6. Local Government Reform
7. The Purge
8. Constitutional Revision
9. National Administrative Reorganization
10. Election Reform
11. Development of Political Parties
12. Development of Legislative Responsibilities
13. Reorganization of Civil Services
14. Legal and Judicial Reform
15. Freedom of the Press
16. Theater and Motion Pictures
17. Treatment of Foreign Nationals
18. Public Welfare
19. Public Health
20. Social Security
21. Foreign Property Administration
22. Reparations
23. Japanese Property Administration
24. Elimination of Zaibatsu Control
25. Deconcentration of Economic Power

26. Promotion of Fair Trade Practices
27. The Rural Land Reform Program
28. Development of the Trade Union Movement
29. Working Conditions
30. Agriculture Cooperatives
31. Education
32. Religion
33. Radio Broadcasting
34. Price and Distribution Stabilization: Non-Food Program
35. Price and Distribution Stabilization: Food Program
36. Agriculture
37. National Government Finance
38. Local Government Finance
39. Money and Banking
40. Financial Reorganization of Corporate Enterprise
41. The Petroleum Industry
42. Fisheries
43. Forestry
44. Rehabilitation of the Non-Fuel Mining Industries
45. Coal
46. Expansion and Reorganization of the Electric Power and Gas Industries
47. The Heavy Industries
48. Textile Industries
49. The Light Industries
50. Foreign Trade
51. Land and Air Transporation
52. Water Transportation
53. Communications
54. Reorganization of Science and Technology in Japan
55. Police and Public Safety

ECONOMIC ISSUES

Martin Bronfenbrenner. "Occupation Period Economy (1945-1952),"
    KŌDANSHA ENCYCLOPEDIA OF JAPAN 2: 154-158.

_____. "Four Positions on Japanese Finance," *Journal of Political Economy*
    58.4 (1950), 281-288.

_____. "Inflation Theories of the SCAP Period," *History of Political Economy*
    7.2 (1975), 137-155.

Edward J. Lincoln. "The Shōwa Economic Experience," in Carol Gluck & Stephen R. Graubard, eds. SHŌWA: THE JAPAN OF HIROHITO (1992: Norton), 191-208.

Jūrō Teranishi & Yutaka Kōsai, eds. THE JAPANESE EXPERIENCE OF ECONOMIC REFORM. 1993: St. Martin's.

Shigeto Tsuru. JAPAN'S CAPITALISM: CREATIVE DEFEAT AND BEYOND. 1992: Cambridge University Press.

Takafusa Nakamura. THE POSTWAR JAPANESE ECONOMY: ITS DEVELOPMENT AND STRUCTURE. 1981: University of Tokyo Press.

MacArthur Memorial. THE OCCUPATION OF JAPAN: ECONOMIC POLICY AND REFORM (proceedings of the 1978 symposium). Includes papers on the Dodge Line, land reform and labor policy, zaibatsu dissolution, economic deconcentration, banking, and trade recovery.

Hyōe Ōuchi. FINANCIAL AND MONETARY SITUATION IN POST-WAR JAPAN. 1947: Institute of Pacific Relations.

Jerome B. Cohen. JAPAN'S ECONOMY IN WAR AND RECONSTRUCTION. 1949: University of Minnesota Press.

_____. JAPAN'S POSTWAR ECONOMY. 1958: Indiana University Press.

Yutaka Kōsai. "The Postwar Japanese Economy, 1945-1973," in Peter Duus, ed. CAMBRIDGE HISTORY OF JAPAN, Volume 6: THE TWENTIETH CENTURY (1988: Cambridge University Press), 494-537.

David Halberstam. THE RECKONING. 1986: William Morrow.

Michael Cusumano. THE JAPANESE AUTOMOBILE INDUSTRY: TECHNOLOGY AND MANAGEMENT AT NISSAN AND TOYOTA. 1985: Harvard University Press.

Leon Hollerman. "International Economic Controls in Occupied Japan," *Journal of Asian Studies* 38.4 (1979), 707-719.

T. A. Bisson. ZAIBATSU DISSOLUTION IN JAPAN. 1954: University of California Press.

Eleanor M. Hadley. ANTI-TRUST IN JAPAN. 1970: Princeton University Press.

_____. "Zaibatsu" and "Zaibatsu Dissolution," KŌDANSHA ENCYCLOPEDIA OF JAPAN 8: 361-366.

_____. "From Deconcentration to Reverse Course," in Robert Wolfe, ed. AMERICANS AS PROCONSULS (1984: Southern Illinois University Press), 138-154.

Hidemasa Morikawa. ZAIBATSU: THE RISE AND FALL OF FAMILY ENTERPRISE GROUPS IN JAPAN. 1992: University of Tokyo Press.

Howard Schonberger. "Zaibatsu Dissolution and the American Restoration of Japan," *Bulletin of Concerned Asian Scholars* 5.2 (September 1973), 16-31.

_____. "The Japan Lobby in American Diplomacy, 1947-1952," *Pacific Historical Review* 46 (1977), 327-359.

John Roberts. "The 'Japan Crowd' and the Zaibatsu Restoration," *Japan Interpreter* 12.3-4 (1979), 384-415.

James F. Hilgenberg. FROM ENEMY TO ALLY: JAPAN, THE AMERICAN BUSINESS PRESS, & THE EARLY COLD WAR. 1993: University Press of America.

Kōzō Yamamura. ECONOMIC POLICY IN POSTWAR JAPAN: GROWTH VERSUS ECONOMIC DEMOCRACY. 1967: University of California Press.

Lonny Edward Carlile. "Zaikai and the Politics of Production in Japan, 1940-1962." 1989: Ph.D. dissertation in Political Science, University of California.

Hideo Ōtake. "The *Zaikai* under the Occupation: The Formation and Transformation of Managerial Councils," in Robert E. Ward & Yoshikazu Sakamoto, eds., DEMOCRATIZING JAPAN: THE ALLIED OCCUPATION (1987: University of Hawaii Press), 366-391.

Haruhiro Fukui, et al., ed. THE POLITICS OF CHANGE IN POSTWAR JAPAN AND WEST GERMANY. 1993: St. Martin's. First volume of a planned series.

William S. Borden. THE PACIFIC ALLIANCE: UNITED STATES FOREIGN ECONOMIC POLICY AND JAPANESE TRADE RECOVERY, 1947-1955. 1984: University of Wisconsin Press.

John Hunter Boyle. MODERN JAPAN: THE AMERICAN NEXUS.
    1993: Harcourt Brace Jovanovich.

Michael Schaller. THE AMERICAN OCCUPATION OF JAPAN: THE ORI-
    GINS OF THE COLD WAR IN ASIA. 1985: Oxford University Press.

Carl S. Shoup. "Japanese Taxation: The Shoup Mission in Retrospect:
    An Interview," *Japan Foundation Newsletter* 16.4 (1989), 1-7.
    An interview of Shoup by Mark Ramseyer.

Martin Bronfenbrenner. "Dr. Shoup Revisits Japan: The Shoup Tax Mission
    Forty Years Later," *Japan Foundation Newsletter* 16.4 (1989), 7-10.

Soong H. Kil. "The Dodge Line and the Japanese Conservative Party." 1977:
    Ph.D. dissertation in Political Science, University of Michigan.

Chitoshi Yanaga. BIG BUSINESS IN JAPANESE POLITICS. 1968: Yale
    University Press.

Saburō Shiomi. JAPAN'S FINANCE AND TAXATION, 1940-1956. 1957:
    Columbia University Press.

Robert S. Ozaki. THE CONTROL OF IMPORTS AND FOREIGN CAPITAL
    IN JAPAN. 1972: Praeger.

Seiichirō Yonekura. "The Japanese Iron and Steel Industry: Continuity and
    Discontinuity, 1850-1970." 1990: Ph.D. dissertation in History and East
    Asian Languages Harvard University.

William M. Tsutsui. BANKING POLICY IN JAPAN: AMERICAN EFFORTS
    AT REFORM DURING THE OCCUPATION. 1988: Routledge.

Kent E. Calder. "Linking Welfare and the Developmental State: Postal Savings
    in Japan," *Journal of Japanese Studies* 16.1 (1990), 31-59.

Warren Hunsberger. JAPAN AND THE UNITED STATES IN WORLD
    TRADE. 1964: Harper & Row.

Robert V. Roosa. THE UNITED STATES AND JAPAN IN THE INTERNA-
    TIONAL MONETARY SYSTEM: 1946-1985. 1986: Group of Thirty.

Jacques Hersh. THE U.S. AND THE RISE OF EAST ASIA, 1945-1990:
    DILEMMAS OF THE POSTWAR INTERNATIONAL POLITICAL
    ECONOMY. 1993: St. Martin's.

Mark Mason. AMERICAN MULTINATIONALS AND JAPAN: THE POLITI-
CAL ECONOMY OF JAPANESE CAPITAL CONTROLS, 1899-1980.
1992: Council on East Asian Studies, Harvard University.

Takashi Shiraishi. JAPAN'S TRADE POLICIES, 1945 TO THE PRESENT
DAY. 1989: Athlone.

Kenneth L. Bauge. VOLUNTARY EXPORT RESTRICTION AS A FOREIGN
COMMERCIAL POLICY WITH SPECIAL REFERENCE TO
JAPANESE COTTON TEXTILES, 1930-1962. 1967: Garland.

Sherwood M. Fine. JAPAN'S POSTWAR INDUSTRIAL RECOVERY. 1953:
Foreign Affairs Association of Japan.

G. C. Allen. JAPAN'S ECONOMIC RECOVERY. 1986: Greenwood Press.

Bai Gao. "Arisawa Hiromi and His Theory for a Managed Economy," *Journal of
Japanese Studies* 20.1 (1994), 115-153. On an economic theorist who
contributed greatly to policies for managing Japan's economy both
before and after 1945.

Chalmers Johnson. MITI AND THE JAPANESE MIRACLE: THE GROWTH
OF INDUSTRIAL POLICY, 1925-1975. 1982: Stanford University
Press.

_____. "The People Who Invented the Mechanical Nightingale," in Carol Gluck
& Stephen R. Graubard, eds. SHŌWA: THE JAPAN OF HIROHITO
(1992: Norton), 71-90.

Laura Hein. FUELING GROWTH: THE ENERGY REVOLUTION AND
ECONOMIC POLICY IN POSTWAR JAPAN. 1990: Council on
East Asian Studies, Harvard University.

Richard J. Samuels. THE BUSINESS OF THE JAPANESE STATE: ENERGY
MARKETS IN COMPARATIVE AND HISTORICAL PERSPECTIVE.
1987: Cornell University Press.

Edwin W. Pauley. REPORT ON JAPANESE REPARATIONS TO THE
PRESIDENT OF THE UNITED STATES, NOVEMBER 1945 TO
APRIL 1946. Department of State Publication 3174, Far Eastern Series
25. 1946. The Pauley Report.

U.S. Department of State. REPORT OF THE MISSION ON JAPANESE
COMBINES, PART I, ANALYTICAL AND TECHNICAL DATA.
Department of State Publication 2628, Far Eastern Series 14. 1946.
The Edwards Report. Part II of this report, formerly classified Top
Secret, is now also available.

U.S. Department of the Army. REPORT ON THE ECONOMIC POSITION
AND PROSPECTS OF JAPAN AND KOREA AND THE MEASURES
REQUIRED TO IMPROVE THEM. 1948. The Johnston Report.

Japanese Ministry of Foreign Affairs. BASIC PROBLEMS FOR POSTWAR
RECONSTRUCTION OF JAPANESE ECONOMY: TRANSLATION
OF A REPORT OF MINISTRY OF FOREIGN AFFAIRS' SPECIAL
SURVEY COMMITTEE, SEPTEMBER 1946. An important internal
Japanese study, translated and published in 1977 by the Japan Economic
Research Center, and again in 1992 by the University of Tokyo Press
(under the new title POSTWAR RECONSTRUCTION OF THE
JAPANESE ECONOMY).

Ōkurashō Zaiseishishitsu (Ministry of Finance, Financial History Section), ed.
SHŌWA ZAISEI SHI: SHŪSEN KARA KŌWA MADE (The
Financial History of Japan: The Allied Occupation Period, 1945-1952).
Two volumes of this important 20-volume Japanese-language history of
Occupation economic and financial policy are of particular interest.
Volume 19 (Tōkei), published in 1978, contains the most comprehensive
and authoritative statistical data pertaining to the economy; unfortunate-
ly the tables do not include English headings.Volume 20 (Eibun Shiryō),
published in 1982, is an 851-page collection of basic U.S. documents on
economic policy toward Japan, many of them drawn from formerly classified archives.

LAND & LABOR

Ronald P. Dore. LAND REFORM IN JAPAN. 1959: Oxford University Press.

Lawrence I. Hewes. JAPAN: LAND AND MEN. AN ACCOUNT OF THE
JAPANESE LAND REFORM PROGRAM, 1945-1951. 1955: Iowa
State College Press.

Tsutomu Ōuchi. "The Japanese Land Reform: Its Efficacy and Limitations,"
Developing Economies 4.2 (1966), 129-150. This issue of Developing
Economies is devoted to a general reassessment of the land reform.

Ann Waswo. "The Transformation of Rural Society, 1900-1950," in Peter Duus, ed. CAMBRIDGE HISTORY OF JAPAN, Volume 6: THE TWENTI-ETH CENTURY (1988: Cambridge University Press), 541-605.

MacArthur Memorial. THE OCCUPATION OF JAPAN: ECONOMIC POLICY AND REFORM (proceedings of the 1978 symposium). Includes papers by Frank Sackton and Hiromitsu Kaneda on land reform, and Theodore Cohen and Kōji Taira on labor policy.

Theodore Cohen. REMAKING JAPAN: THE AMERICAN OCCUPATION AS NEW DEAL. Herbert Passin, ed. 1987: Free Press.

Solomon Levine. "Labor," KŌDANSHA ENCYCLOPEDIA OF JAPAN 4: 343-349, esp. 345-347.

_____. INDUSTRIAL RELATIONS IN POSTWAR JAPAN. 1958: University of Illinois Press.

Kōji Taira. "Economic Development, Labor Markets, and Industrial Relations in Japan, 1905-1955," in Peter Duus, ed. CAMBRIDGE HISTORY OF JAPAN, Volume 6: THE TWENTIETH CENTURY (1988: Cambridge University Press), 606-653.

Joe B. Moore. JAPANESE WORKERS AND THE STRUGGLE FOR POWER, 1945-1947. 1983: University of Wisconsin Press.

_____. "Production Control: Workers' Control in Early Postwar Japan," *Bulletin of Concerned Asian Scholars* 17.4 (1985), 2-26.

Miriam S. Farley. ASPECTS OF JAPAN'S LABOR PROBLEMS. 1950: John Day.

I. F. Ayusawa. A HISTORY OF LABOR IN MODERN JAPAN. 1966: University of Hawaii Press.

Kazuo Ōkōchi. LABOR IN MODERN JAPAN. 1958: Science Council of Japan.

Kōji Taira. ECONOMIC DEVELOPMENT AND THE LABOR MARKET IN JAPAN. 1970: Columbia University Press.

Robert Scalapino. "Japan," in Walter Galenson, ed. LABOR AND ECONOMIC DEVELOPMENT (1959: Wiley), 75-145.

Andrew Gordon. THE EVOLUTION OF LABOR RELATIONS IN JAPAN: HEAVY INDUSTRY, 1853-1955. 1985: Council on East Asian Studies, Harvard University.

Sheldon M. Garon. "The Imperial Bureaucracy and Labor Policy in Postwar Japan," *Journal of Asian Studies* 43.3 (1984), 441-457.

John Price. "Valery Burati and the Formation of Sohyo During the U.S. Occupation of Japan," *Pacific Affairs* 64.2 (1991), 208-225.

Howard Schonberger. "American Labor's Cold War in Occupied Japan," *Diplomatic History* 5 (1977), 327-359.

David Halberstam. THE RECKONING. 1986: William Morrow.

Taishirō Shirai, ed. CONTEMPORARY INDUSTRIAL RELATIONS IN JAPAN. 1983: University of Wisconsin Press.

POLITICAL ACTIVITY

Supreme Commander Allied Powers, Government Section. POLITICAL REORIENTATION OF JAPAN: SEPTEMBER, 1945 TO SEPTEMBER, 1948. 2 volumes. 1949: Government Printing Office. The basic and most often cited official documentary source. As its title indicates, however, this is restricted to political matters (with a few exceptions) during the first three years of occupation only.

Justin Williams. JAPAN'S POLITICAL REVOLUTION UNDER MACARTHUR: A PARTICIPANT'S ACCOUNT. 1979: University of Georgia Press.

John W. Dower. EMPIRE AND AFTERMATH: YOSHIDA SHIGERU AND THE JAPANESE EXPERIENCE, 1878-1954. 1979: Council on East Asian Studies, Harvard University.

Harold S. Quigley & John E. Turner. THE NEW JAPAN: GOVERNMENT AND POLITICS. 1956: University of Minnesota Press.

Paul Linebarger, Chu Djang & Ardath Burks. FAR EASTERN GOVERNMENTS AND POLITICS. 1954: Van Nostrand.

Hans H. Baerwald. "Early SCAP Policy and the Rehabilitation of the Diet," in Robert E. Ward & Yoshikazu Sakamoto, eds., DEMOCRATIZING JAPAN: THE ALLIED OCCUPATION (1987: University of Hawaii Press), 133-156.

Junnosuke Masumi. POSTWAR POLITICS IN JAPAN, 1945-1955. 1985: Institute of East Asian Studies, University of California, Berkeley.

Michio Muramatsu. "Bringing Politics Back into Japan," in Carol Gluck & Stephen R. Graubard, eds. SHŌWA: THE JAPAN OF HIROHITO (1992: Norton), 141-154.

Daniel B. Ramsdell. THE JAPANESE DIET: STABILITY AND CHANGE IN THE JAPANESE HOUSE OF REPRESENTATIVES, 1890-1990. 1992: University Press of America.

Kenzō Uchida. "Japan's Postwar Conservative Parties," in Robert E. Ward & Yoshikazu Sakamoto, eds., DEMOCRATIZING JAPAN: THE ALLIED OCCUPATION (1987: University of Hawaii Press), 306-338.

Haruhiro Fukui. PARTY IN POWER: THE JAPANESE LIBERAL DEMOC-RATS AND POLICY MAKING. 1970: University of California Press.

_____. "Postwar Politics, 1945-1973," in Peter Duus, ed. CAMBRIDGE HISTORY OF JAPAN, Volume 6: THE TWENTIETH CENTURY (1988: Cambridge University Press), 154-213.

Robert Scalapino & Junnosuke Masumi. PARTIES AND POLITICS IN CONTEMPORARY JAPAN. 1962: University of California Press.

Kent E. Calder. CRISIS AND COMPENSATION: PUBLIC POLICY AND POLITICAL STABILITY IN JAPAN, 1949-1986. 1988: Princeton University Press.

Steven R. Reed. JAPANESE ELECTION DATA: THE HOUSE OF REPRE-SENTATIVES, 1947-1990. 1992: Center for Japanese Studies, University of Michigan.

_____. "The People Spoke: The Influence of Elections on Japanese Politics, 1949-1955," *Journal of Japanese Studies* 14.2 (1988), 309-339.

Kurt Steiner. LOCAL GOVERNMENT IN JAPAN. 1965: Stanford University Press.

Akira Amakawa. "The Making of the Postwar Local Government System," in Robert E. Ward & Yoshikazu Sakamoto, eds., DEMOCRATIZING JAPAN: THE ALLIED OCCUPATION (1987: University of Hawaii Press), 253-283.

William W. Kelly. "Regional Japan: The Price of Prosperity and the Benefits of Dependency," in Carol Gluck & Stephen R. Graubard, eds. SHŌWA: THE JAPAN OF HIROHITO (1992: Norton), 209-227.

Antonia Judith Levi. "Peaceful Revolution in Japan: The Development of the Nosaka Theory and Its Implementation under the American Occupation." 1991: Ph.D. dissertation in History, Stanford University.

Evelyn Colbert. THE LEFT WING IN JAPANESE POLITICS. 1952: Institute of Pacific Relations.

Eiji Takemae. "Early Postwar Reformist Parties," in Robert E. Ward & Yoshikazu Sakamoto, eds., DEMOCRATIZING JAPAN: THE ALLIED OCCUPATION (1987: University of Hawaii Press), 339-365.

A. Cole, G. Totten & C. Uyehara. SOCIALIST PARTIES IN POSTWAR JAPAN. 1966: Yale University Press.

J. A. A. Stockwin. JAPAN: DIVIDED POLITICS IN A GROWTH ECONOMY. 1975: Weidenfeld & Nicholson.

Joe B. Moore. JAPANESE WORKERS AND THE STRUGGLE FOR POWER, 1945-1947. 1983: University of Wisconsin Press.

Roger Swearingen & Paul Langer. RED FLAG IN JAPAN: INTERNATIONAL COMMUNISM IN ACTION, 1919-1951. 1952: Harvard University Press.

Robert Scalapino. THE JAPANESE COMMUNIST MOVEMENT, 1920-1966. 1966: University of California Press.

Toshio G. Tsukahira. THE POSTWAR EVOLUTION OF COMMUNIST STRATEGY IN JAPAN. 1954: Massachusetts Institute of Technology Press.

Richard L-G. Deverall. RED STAR OVER JAPAN. 1952: Temple Press, Calcutta.

George M. Beckmann & Genji Ōkubo. THE JAPANESE COMMUNIST PARTY, 1922-1945. 1969: Stanford University Press.

Chalmers Johnson. CONSPIRACY AT MATSUKAWA. 1972: University of California Press.

Benjamin C. Duke. JAPAN'S MILITANT TEACHERS: A HISTORY OF THE LEFT-WING TEACHERS' MOVEMENT. 1973: University of Hawaii Press.

Rikki Kersten. DIVERGING DISCOURSES: SHIMIZU IKUTARŌ, MARUYAMA MASAO, AND POSTWAR TENKŌ. Nissan Occasional Papers, No. 20. 1994: Nissan Institute of Japanese Studies, Oxford.

Ivan Morris. NATIONALISM AND THE RIGHT WING IN POSTWAR JAPAN. 1960: Oxford University Press.

Shunsuke Tsurumi. A CULTURAL HISTORY OF POSTWAR JAPAN, 1945-1980. 1987: Kegan Paul International.

OTHER SPECIAL SUBJECTS

Wartime Thinking & Presurrender Planning

Marlene J. Mayo. "American Wartime Planning for Occupied Japan: The Role of the Experts," in Robert Wolfe, ed. AMERICANS AS PROCON-SULS (1984: Southern Illinois University Press), 3-51, 447-474.

_____. "American Economic Planning for Occupied Japan: The Issue of *Zaibatsu* Dissolution, 1942-1945," in the MacArthur Memorial's THE OCCUPATION OF JAPAN: ECONOMIC POLICY AND REFORM (1980: MacArthur Memorial), 205-228, 252-262.

Hugh Borton. "Preparation for the Occupation of Japan," *Journal of Asian Studies* 25.2 (1966), 203-212.

_____. AMERICAN PRESURRENDER PLANNING FOR POSTWAR JAPAN. 1967: Occasional Papers of the East Asian Institute, Columbia University.

Robert E. Ward. "Presurrender Planning: Treatment of the Emperor and Constitutional Changes," in Robert E. Ward & Yoshikazu Sakamoto, eds., DEMOCRATIZING JAPAN: THE ALLIED OCCUPATION (1987: University of Hawaii Press), 1-41.

Akira Iriye. POWER AND CULTURE: THE JAPANESE-AMERICAN WAR, 1941-1945. 1981: Harvard University Press.

Christopher Thorne. ALLIES OF A KIND: THE UNITED STATES, BRITAIN,
    AND THE WAR AGAINST JAPAN, 1941-1945. 1978: Oxford
    University Press.

The Purge

Hans H. Baerwald. THE PURGE OF JAPANESE LEADERS UNDER THE
    OCCUPATION. 1959: University of California Press.

John D. Montgomery. THE PURGE IN OCCUPIED JAPAN: A STUDY IN
    THE USE OF CIVILIAN AGENCIES UNDER MILITARY GOVERN-
    MENT. 1953: Johns Hopkins.

War Crimes

See pages 342-345 for the published proceedings of the International
Military Tribunal for the Far East and key sources on the general issue
of war crimes—including the I.M.T.F.E. judgment, Justice Pal's famous
lengthy dissent, the transcript of the 1949 U.S.S.R. Khabarovsk trial of
Japanese accused of biological-warfare experiments, and pertinent writings by Richard Minear, Philip Piccigallo, John Powell, and Frank Reel.

Legal Reform & Constitutional Revision

MacArthur Memorial. THE OCCUPATION OF JAPAN: IMPACT OF LEGAL
    REFORM (proceedings of the 1977 symposium). Papers and discus-
    sions deal with local government, election reform, constitutional revi-
    sion, the supreme court, and women's rights.

Alfred C. Oppler. LEGAL REFORM IN OCCUPIED JAPAN: A PARTICI-
    PANT LOOKS BACK. 1976: Princeton University Press.

University of Washington School of Law, ed. LEGAL REFORMS IN JAPAN
    DURING THE ALLIED OCCUPATION. 1977: University of
    Washington. A special issue of the *Washington Law Review*, reprinting
    7 articles on the subject published between 1949 and 1951.

Kurt Steiner. "The Occupation and the Reform of the Japanese Civil Code,"
    in Robert E. Ward & Yoshikazu Sakamoto, eds., DEMOCRATIZING
    JAPAN: THE ALLIED OCCUPATION (1987: University of Hawaii
    Press), 188-220.

Japan, House of Representatives, Parliamentary Museum. HISTORY OF
   CONSTITUTIONALISM IN JAPAN: WITH NOTES AND RELATED
   CHRONOLOGY. 1987.

Kyōko Inoue. MACARTHUR'S JAPANESE CONSTITUTION: A LINGUIS-
   TIC AND CULTURAL STUDY OF ITS MAKING. 1991: University
   of Chicago Press.

Nanette Twine. "Language and the Constitution," *Japan Forum* 3.1 (1991),
   125-137.

Osamu Nishi. TEN DAYS INSIDE GENERAL HEADQUARTERS (GHQ):
   HOW THE ORIGINAL DRAFT OF THE JAPANESE CONSTITU-
   TION WAS WRITTEN IN 1946. 1989: Seibundō.

FRAMING THE CONSTITUTION OF JAPAN: PRIMARY SOURCES IN
   ENGLISH, 1944-1949. 1989: Congressional Information Service.

John M. Maki, transl. & ed. JAPAN'S COMMISSION ON THE CONSTITU-
   TION: THE FINAL REPORT. 1980: University of Washington Press.

Kenzō Takayanagi. "Some Reminiscences of Japan's Commission on the
   Constitution," *Washington Law Review* 43.5 (1968), 961-978.

Justin Williams. "Making the Japanese Constitution: A Further Look," *American
   Political Science Review* 59 (1965), 665-679.

_____. "Completing Japan's Political Reorientation, 1947-1952: Crucial Phase
   of the Allied Occupation," *American Historical Review* 73 (1968),
   1454-1469.

Theodore McNelly. "The Japanese Constitution: Child of the Cold War,"
   Political Science Quarterly 74 (1958), 176-195.

_____. "The Renunciation of War in the Japanese Constitution," *Political
   Science Quarterly* 77 (1962), 350-378.

_____. " 'Induced Revolution': The Policy and Process of Constitutional
   Reform in Occupied Japan," in Robert E. Ward & Yoshikazu Sakamoto,
   eds., DEMOCRATIZING JAPAN: THE ALLIED OCCUPATION
   (1987: University of Hawaii Press), 76-106.

Tatsuo Satō. "The Origin and Development of the Draft Constitution of Japan,"
   Contemporary Japan 24.4-6, 7-9 (1956), 175-187, 371-387.

Hideo Tanaka. "The Conflict between Two Legal Traditions in Making the Constitution of Japan," in Robert E. Ward & Yoshikazu Sakamoto, eds., DEMOCRATIZING JAPAN: THE ALLIED OCCUPATION (1987: University of Hawaii Press), 107-132.

Tetsuya Kataoka. THE PRICE OF A CONSTITUTION: THE ORIGIN OF JAPAN'S POSTWAR POLITICS. 1991: Crane Russak.

Shōichi Koseki. "Japanizing the Constitution," *Japan Quarterly* 35.3 (1988), 234-240.

H. Fukui. "Twenty Years of Revisionism," *Washington Law Review* 43.5 (1968), 931-960.

Dan Fenno Henderson, ed. THE CONSTITUTION OF JAPAN: THE FIRST TWENTY YEARS, 1947-1967. 1968: University of Washington Press. Includes most of the articles from the "Symposium on the Japanese Constitution" in *Washington Law Review* 43.5 (1968).

Kenzō Takayanagi, Ichirō Ohtomo & Hideo Tanaka, eds. NIHONKOKU KEMPŌ SEITEI NO KATEI (The Making of the Constitution of Japan). 2 volumes. 1972: Yūhikaku. Includes English memoranda from the papers of Milo Rowell.

Bureaucracy

T. J. Pempel. "The Tar Baby Target: 'Reform' of the Japanese Bureaucracy," in Robert E. Ward & Yoshikazu Sakamoto, eds., DEMOCRATIZING JAPAN: THE ALLIED OCCUPATION (1987: University of Hawaii Press), 157-187.

Akira Kubota. HIGHER CIVIL SERVANTS IN POSTWAR JAPAN. 1969: Princeton University Press.

Chalmers Johnson. MITI AND THE JAPANESE MIRACLE: THE GROWTH OF INDUSTRIAL POLICY, 1925-1975. 1982: Stanford University Press.

The Emperor & Emperor System

Robert E. Ward. "Presurrender Planning: Treatment of the Emperor and Constitutional Changes," in Robert E. Ward & Yoshikazu Sakamoto, eds., DEMOCRATIZING JAPAN: THE ALLIED OCCUPATION (1987: University of Hawaii Press), 1-41.

Genji Ōkubo. THE PROBLEMS OF THE EMPEROR SYSTEM IN POSTWAR JAPAN. 1948: Japan Institute of Pacific Studies.

Osamu Watanabe. "The Emperor as a 'Symbol' in Postwar Japan," *Acta Asiatica* 59 (1990), 101-125.

Kiyoko Takeda Chō. "The Dual Image of the Japanese Tennō: Conflicting Foreign Ideas About the Remoulding of the *Tennō sei* at the End of the War," *Proceedings of the British Association for Japanese Studies* 1 (1976), 110-130.

Kiyoko Takeda. THE DUAL-IMAGE OF THE JAPANESE EMPEROR. 1988: New York University Press.

Masanori Nakamura. THE JAPANESE MONARCHY: AMBASSADOR JOSEPH GREW AND THE MAKING OF THE "SYMBOL EMPEROR SYSTEM," 1931-1991. Herbert Bix, Jonathan Baker-Bates, & Derek Bowen, transl. 1992: M. E. Sharpe.

Herbert P. Bix. "The Shōwa Emperor's 'Monologue' and the Problem of War Responsibility," *Journal of Japanese Studies* 18.2 (1992), 295-363.

Andrew E. Barshay. "Imagining Democracy in Postwar Japan: Reflections on Maruyama Masao and Modernism," *Journal of Japanese Studies* 18.2 (1992), 365-406.

Education

Supreme Commander for the Allied Powers, Civil Information and Education Section. POST-WAR DEVELOPMENTS IN JAPANESE EDUCATION. 1952: Civil Information and Education Section.

Toshio Nishi. UNCONDITIONAL DEMOCRACY: EDUCATION AND POLITICS IN OCCUPIED JAPAN, 1945-1952. 1982: Hoover Institution Press.

MacArthur Memorial. THE OCCUPATION OF JAPAN: EDUCATIONAL AND SOCIAL REFORM (proceedings of the 1980 symposium). Includes papers on various aspects of educational reform, welfare policy, and the civil service.

Hideo Satō. "The Basic Source Materials on the Education Reform in Postwar Japan: Report of the Surveys Conducted by the NIER Research Group," *Acta Asiatica* 54 (1988), 75-105.

Edward R. Beauchamp & James M. Vardaman, Jr. JAPANESE EDUCATION SINCE 1945: A DOCUMENTARY STUDY. 1993: M. E. Sharpe.

Gary H. Tsuchimochi. EDUCATION REFORM IN POSTWAR JAPAN: THE 1946 U.S. EDUCATIONAL MISSION. 1993: University of Tokyo Press.

Robert K. Hall. EDUCATION FOR A NEW JAPAN. 1949: Yale University Press.

_____. "Education in the Development of Postwar Japan," in MacArthur Memorial, THE OCCUPATION OF JAPAN AND ITS LEGACY TO THE POSTWAR WORLD (proceedings of the 1975 symposium), 117-148.

Victor N. Kobayashi. "Japan Under American Occupation," in Edward R. Beauchamp, ed. LEARNING TO BE JAPANESE (1978: Linnet), 181-207.

Yōko Hirohashi Thakur. "Textbook Reform in Allied Occupied Japan, 1945-1952." 1990: Ph.D. dissertation in History, University of Maryland (College Park).

Ury Eppstein. "School Songs Before and After the War: From 'Children Tank Soldiers' to 'Everyone a Good Child'," *Monumenta Nipponica* 42.4 (1987), 431-447.

Miscellaneous Subjects

MacArthur Memorial. THE OCCUPATION OF JAPAN: ARTS AND CULTURE (proceedings of the 1984 symposium). Includes papers on the media, satire, film, literature, drama, and art.

MacArthur Memorial. THE OCCUPATION OF JAPAN: THE GRASS ROOTS (proceedings of the 1991 symposium). Articles, many of which are personal reminiscences, on topics including women, religion, educational purges, and repatriation of Japanese from overseas.

Masaru Tamamoto. "Unwanted Peace: Japanese Intellectual Thought in American Occupied Japan, 1948-1952." 1988: Ph.D. dissertation , School of Advanced International Studies, Johns Hopkins University.

Masahide Ōta. "The U.S. Occupation of Okinawa and Postwar Reforms in Japan Proper," in Robert E. Ward & Yoshikazu Sakamoto, eds., DEMOCRATIZING JAPAN: THE ALLIED OCCUPATION (1987: University of Hawaii Press), 284-305.

Susan J. Pharr. "The Politics of Women's Rights," in Robert E. Ward & Yoshikazu Sakamoto, eds., DEMOCRATIZING JAPAN: THE ALLIED OCCUPATION (1987: University of Hawaii Press), 221-252.

Meirion Harries. SHEATHING THE SWORD: THE DEMILITARISATION OF JAPAN. 1987: Macmillan.

Nisuke Andō. SURRENDER, OCCUPATION, AND PRIVATE PROPERTY IN INTERNATIONAL LAW: AN EVALUATION OF US PRACTICE IN JAPAN. 1991: Oxford University Press.

Walter Edwards. "Buried Discourse: The Toro Archeological Site and Japanese National Identity in the Early Postwar Period," *Journal of Japanese Studies* 17.1 (1991), 1-23.

William P. Woodard. THE ALLIED OCCUPATION OF JAPAN AND JAPANESE RELIGIONS. 1972: Brill.

William J. Coughlin. CONQUERED PRESS: THE MACARTHUR ERA IN JAPANESE JOURNALISM. 1952: Pacific.

Nicholas John Bruno. "Major Daniel C. Imboden and Press Reform in Occupied Japan, 1945-1952." 1988: Ph.D. dissertation in History, University of Maryland (College Park).

Sey Nishimura. "Medical Censorship in Occupied Japan, 1945-1948," *Pacific Historical Review* 58.1 (1989), 1-21.

Monica Braw. THE ATOMIC BOMB SUPPRESSED: AMERICAN CENSORSHIP IN OCCUPIED JAPAN. 1991: M. E. Sharpe.

Glenn D. Hook. "Censorship and Reportage of Atomic Damage and Casualties in Hiroshima and Nagasaki," *Bulletin of Concerned Asian Scholars* 23.1 (1991), 13-25.

Jay Rubin. "From Wholesomeness to Decadence: The Censorship of Literature Under the Allied Occupation," *Journal of Japanese Studies* 11.1 (1985), 71-103.

Akira Iwasaki. "The Occupied Screen," *Japan Quarterly* 25.3 (1978), 302-322.

Kyōko Hirano. MR. SMITH GOES TO TOKYO: THE JAPANESE CINEMA UNDER THE AMERICAN OCCUPATION, 1945-1952. 1992: Smithsonian Institution Press.

THE OCCUPATION IN GLOBAL PERSPECTIVE

Yoshikazu Sakamoto. "The International Context of the Occupation of Japan," in Robert E. Ward & Yoshikazu Sakamoto, eds., DEMOCRATIZING JAPAN: THE ALLIED OCCUPATION (1987: University of Hawaii Press), 42-75.

John W. Dower. EMPIRE AND AFTERMATH: YOSHIDA SHIGERU AND THE JAPANESE EXPERIENCE, 1878-1954. 1979: Council on East Asian Studies, Harvard University.

_____. "The Eye of the Beholder: Background Notes on the U.S.-Japan Military Relationship," *Bulletin of Concerned Asian Scholars* 2.1 (October 1969), 15-30.

_____. "Occupied Japan in the American Lake, 1945-1950," in Edward Friedman & Mark Selden, eds. AMERICA'S ASIA: DISSENTING ESSAYS ON ASIAN-AMERICAN RELATIONS (1971: Pantheon), 146-206.

_____. "The Superdomino in Postwar Asia: Japan In and Out of the Pentagon Papers," in Noam Chomsky & Howard Zinn, eds. THE SENATOR GRAVEL EDITION OF THE PENTAGON PAPERS. Volume 5 (1972: Beacon), 101-142.

_____. "Occupied Japan and the Cold War in Asia," in his JAPAN IN WAR AND PEACE (1994: The New Press), 155-207.

Akira Iriye & Warren I. Cohen, eds. THE UNITED STATES AND JAPAN IN THE POSTWAR WORLD. 1989: University Press of Kentucky.

H. W. Brands, Jr. "The United States and the Reemergence of Independent Japan," *Pacific Affairs* 59.3 (1986), 387-401.

Michael Schaller. "Securing the Great Crescent: Occupied Japan and the Origins of Containment in South East Asia," *Journal of American History* 69 (1982), 392-414.

_____. THE AMERICAN OCCUPATION OF JAPAN: THE ORIGINS OF THE COLD WAR IN ASIA. 1985: Oxford University Press.

William S. Borden. THE PACIFIC ALLIANCE: UNITED STATES FOREIGN ECONOMIC POLICY AND JAPANESE TRADE RECOVERY, 1947-1955. 1984: University of Wisconsin Press.

Roger Buckley. US-JAPAN ALLIANCE DIPLOMACY, 1945-1990. 1992: Cambridge University Press.

John K. Emmerson. THE EAGLE AND THE RISING SUN: AMERICA AND JAPAN IN THE TWENTIETH CENTURY. 1988: Addison-Wesley.

Sheila K. Johnson. THE JAPANESE THROUGH AMERICAN EYES. 1988: Stanford University Press. Fascinating survey of American attitudes toward Japan since the war.

Jitsuo Tsuchiyama. "Alliance in Japanese Foreign Policy: Theory and Practice." 1984: Ph.D. dissertation in Government and Politics, University of Maryland.

Tsuyoshi Michael Yamaguchi. "The Making of an Alliance: Japan's Alliance Policy, 1945-1952." 1990: Ph.D. dissertation, School of Advanced International Studies, Johns Hopkins University.

Gabriel Kolko. THE POLITICS OF WAR: THE WORLD AND UNITED STATES FOREIGN POLICY, 1943-1945. 1968: Random House.

Joyce & Gabriel Kolko. THE LIMITS OF POWER: THE WORLD AND UNITED STATES FOREIGN POLICY, 1945-1954. 1972: Harper & Row.

MacArthur Memorial. THE OCCUPATION OF JAPAN: THE INTERNA-TIONAL CONTEXT (proceedings of the 1982 symposium). Includes papers on the Allied Council, the peace settlement, Japan and Southeast Asia, and the Occupation as seen from Great Britain, Australia, and Canada.

Herbert Feis. CONTEST OVER JAPAN. 1967: Norton.

Hideo Ibe. JAPAN THRICE OPENED: AN ANALYSIS OF JAPAN-UNITED
STATES RELATIONS. Lynne E. Riggs & Manabu Takechi, transl.
1992: Praeger.

Roger Dingman. "Strategic Planning and the Policy Process: American Plans
for War in East Asia, 1945-50," *Naval War College Review* 32 (1979),
4-21.

Frederick S. Dunn. PEACE-MAKING AND THE SETTLEMENT WITH
JAPAN. 1963: Princeton University Press.

Michael M. Yoshitsu. JAPAN AND THE SAN FRANCISCO PEACE
SETTLEMENT. 1982: Columbia University Press.

Bernard C. Cohen. THE POLITICAL PROCESS AND FOREIGN POLICY:
THE MAKING OF THE JAPANESE PEACE SETTLEMENT. 1957:
Princeton University Press.

T. G. Fraser & Peter Lowe, eds. CONFLICT AND AMITY IN EAST ASIA:
ESSAYS IN HONOUR OF IAN NISH. 1992: Macmillan.

Meirion Harries. SHEATHING THE SWORD: THE DEMILITARISATION
OF JAPAN. 1987: Macmillan.

Martin E. Weinstein. JAPAN'S POSTWAR DEFENSE POLICY, 1947-1968.
1971: Columbia University Press.

James E. Auer. THE POSTWAR REARMAMENT OF JAPANESE MARITIME
FORCES, 1945-1971. 1973: Praeger.

Takeshi Igarashi. "Peace-Making and Party Politics: The Formation of the
Domestic Foreign-Policy System in Postwar Japan," *Journal of Japanese
Studies* 11.2 (1985), 323-356.

R. K. Jain. JAPAN'S POSTWAR PEACE SETTLEMENTS. 1979: Radiant.

George H. Blakeslee. THE FAR EASTERN COMMISSION: A STUDY IN
INTERNATIONAL COOPERATION, 1945-1952. Department of State
Publication 5138, Far Eastern Series 60. 1953.

U.S. Department of State. TREATY OF PEACE WITH JAPAN. SIGNED AT
SAN FRANCISCO, SEPTEMBER 8, 1951. Department of State
Publication 4613. 1952.

U.S. Congress, Senate, Committee on Armed Services. MILITARY SITUA-
TION IN THE FAR EAST. 82nd Congress, 1st Session. 5 parts.
The 1951 Congressional hearings upon the recall of General MacArthur.

Robin Kay, ed. THE SURRENDER AND OCCUPATION OF JAPAN, volume
2 of DOCUMENTS ON NEW ZEALAND EXTERNAL RELATIONS.
1982: Government Printer, Wellington, N.Z. A huge official collection
of almost 1,800 pages.

Gordon Daniels & Reinhard Drifte, eds. EUROPE AND JAPAN: CHANGING
RELATIONSHIPS SINCE 1945. 1986: P. Norbury Publications.

Roger W. Buckley. OCCUPATION DIPLOMACY: BRITAIN, THE UNITED
STATES, AND JAPAN, 1945-1952. 1982: Cambridge University
Press.

_____. "Joining the Club: The Japanese Question and Anglo-American Peace
Diplomacy, 1950-1951," *Modern Asian Studies* 19.2 (1985), 299-319.

Peter Lowe. "The British Liaison Mission and SCAP, 1948-1952: Exchanges
during the Latter Part of the Occupation," *Japan Forum* 5.2 (1993),
245-256.

Richard N. Rosecrance. AUSTRALIAN DIPLOMACY AND JAPAN,
1945-1951. 1962: Melbourne University Press.

Alan Rix. COMING TO TERMS: THE POLITICS OF AUSTRALIA'S TRADE
WITH JAPAN, 1945-57. 1986: Allen & Unwin.

Ann Trotter. NEW ZEALAND AND JAPAN, 1945-1952: THE OCCUPATION
AND THE PEACE TREATY. 1990: Athlone.

P. A. Narasimha Murthy. INDIA AND JAPAN: DIMENSIONS OF THEIR
RELATIONS: HISTORICAL AND POLITICAL. 1986: ABC Pub.
House.

Akira Iriye. CHINA AND JAPAN IN THE GLOBAL SETTING. 1992:
Harvard University Press.

Kurt W. Radtke. CHINA'S RELATIONS WITH JAPAN, 1945-83: THE ROLE
OF LIAO CHENGZHI. 1990: St. Martin's.

Wayne C. McWilliams. HOMEWARD BOUND: REPATRIATION OF
JAPANESE FROM KOREA AFTER WORLD WAR II. 1988:
Asian Research Service.

Sung-hwa Cheong. THE POLITICS OF ANTI-JAPANESE SENTIMENT IN
KOREA: JAPANESE-SOUTH KOREAN RELATIONS UNDER
AMERICAN OCCUPATION, 1945-1952. 1991: Greenwood Press.

Ben-Ami Shillony, ed. JAPAN THIRTY YEARS AFTER THE END OF
OCCUPATION: POLITICAL, ECONOMIC AND CULTURAL
TRENDS. 1984. Special Issue in volume 18 of *Asian and African
Studies*.

Warren Cohen & Akira Iriye, eds. THE GREAT POWERS IN EAST ASIA,
1953-1960. 1990: Columbia University Press. Essays on postwar
relations.

Diplomatic History 10.1 (1986). Special issue focusing on post-1945 U.S.
policy toward Asia. Articles include Michael Schaller on "MacArthur's
Japan"; David McLean on China policy in 1949-1950; Rosemary Foot
on "Anglo-American Relations in the Korean Crisis"; Howard
Schonberger on Japanese recognition of Nationalist China in 1951-1952;
and Yōko Yasuhara on "Japan, Communist China, and Export Controls
in Asia, 1948-52."

Kenneth B. Pyle. THE JAPANESE QUESTION: POWER AND PURPOSE IN
A NEW ERA. 1991: University Press of America.

BASIC DOCUMENTARY COLLECTIONS & OFFICIAL PUBLICATIONS

Supreme Commander Allied Powers. Government Section. POLITICAL
REORIENTATION OF JAPAN: SEPTEMBER, 1945 TO SEPTEM-
BER, 1948. 2 volumes. 1949.

_____. INSTRUCTIONS TO THE JAPANESE GOVERNMENT FROM
4 SEPTEMBER 1945 TO 8 MARCH 1952. 1952. The complete
collection of SCAP instructions on political, economic, and social
matters.

_____. SUMMATION OF NON-MILITARY ACTIVITIES IN JAPAN.
35 volumes. Useful week-by-week coverage of activities from
September 1945 through August 1948.

[For the gamut of SCAP publications, see Robert Ward & Frank Joseph Shulman, THE ALLIED OCCUPATION OF JAPAN, 114-123]

Ōkurashō Zaiseishishitsu (Ministry of Finance, Financial History Section), ed. SHŌWA ZAISEI SHI: SHŪSEN KARA KŌWA MADE. The 20th and last volume of this official history (which bears the English title *The Financial History of Japan: The Allied Occupation Period, 1945-1952*), published in 1982, is an 851-page collection of official U.S. documents pertaining to the Occupation, beginning with presurrender planning and extending to the immediate post-Occupation period. Many of these documents come from declassified U.S. archives. This is the most important single documentary source for basic economic policies.

U.S. Department of the Army. REPORTS OF GENERAL MACARTHUR. 1966. "Volume 1: Supplement" of this 4-volume publication deals with such military aspects of the occupation as repatriation, demobilization, and destruction of Japanese military stocks.

Gaimushō Tokubetsu Shiryōka, ed. NIHON SENRYŌ OYOBI KANRI JŪYŌ BUNSHO SHŪ. 4 volumes. Basic documents in English with Japanese translations, to December 1949.

Far Eastern Commission. ACTIVITIES OF THE FAR EASTERN COMMIS-SION, REPORT BY THE SECRETARY- GENERAL, FEBRUARY 26, 1946 - JULY 10, 1947. Department of State Publication 2888, Far Eastern Series 24. 1947.

_____. THE FAR EASTERN COMMISSION, SECOND REPORT BY THE SECRETARY-GENERAL, JULY 10, 1947 - DECEMBER 23, 1948. Department of State Publication 3420, Far Eastern Series 29. 1949.

_____. THE FAR EASTERN COMMISSION, THIRD REPORT BY THE SECRETARY-GENERAL, DECEMBER 24, 1948 - JUNE 30, 1950. Department of State Publication 3925, Far Eastern Series 35. 1950.

_____. RECORDS OF THE FAR EASTERN COMMISSION, 1945-1952. Scholarly Resources, 167 microfilm reels.

George H. Blakeslee. THE FAR EASTERN COMMISSION: A STUDY IN INTERNATIONAL COOPERATION, 1945-1952. Department of State Publication 5138, Far Eastern Series 60. 1953.

Japanese Diet. OFFICIAL GAZETTE and OFFICIAL GAZETTE EXTRA.
Basic English-language sources for activities in both houses of the
Japanese legislature. The OFFICIAL GAZETTE contains texts of laws,
ordinances, and government announcements from April 1946. The
OFFICIAL GAZETTE EXTRA contains translations of discussions on
the Diet floor from May 1946, including policy speeches by cabinet
members and the ensuing interpellations by Diet members.

U.S. Department of State. FOREIGN RELATIONS OF THE UNITED STATES.
See especially the annual volumes on Japan and the Far East in this
basic State Department archival series.

Thomas H. Etzold & John Lewis Gaddis, eds. CONTAINMENT: DOCU-
MENTS ON AMERICAN POLICY AND STRATEGY, 1945-1950.
1978: Columbia University Press.

Robin Kay, ed. THE SURRENDER AND OCCUPATION OF JAPAN, volume
2 of DOCUMENTS ON NEW ZEALAND EXTERNAL RELATIONS.
1982: Government Printer, Wellington, N.Z. An official collection of
almost 1,800 pages.

ACCESSIBLE DECLASSIFIED ARCHIVES

A substantial portion of the many official U.S. documents declassified since
the 1960s is accessible in commercial microfilm collections. See especially the
following:

From Scholarly Resources, Inc.:

> *SWNCC (State-War-Navy Coordinating Committee) / SANACC (State-
> Army-Navy-Air Force Coordinating Committee) Case Files, 1944-1949.*
> 32 reels.

> *The History of Intelligence Activities under General Douglas MacArthur,
> 1942-1950: The Intelligence Series, G2-USAFFE SWPA-AFPAC-FEC-
> SCAP.* 8 reels.

> *Reports of the U.S. Naval Technical Mission to Japan, 1945-1946.*
> 13 reels.

> *U.S. Administration of the Ryūkyū Islands, 1946-1972.* 7 reels.

Summation of Nonmilitary Activities in Japan and Korea, 1945-1948.
8 reels.

From University Publications of America:

Documents of the National Security Council, 1947-1977. 14 reels.

Minutes of the National Security Council, with Special Advisory Reports.
3 reels.

Records of the Joint Chiefs of Staff:

>*Pacific Theater, 1942-1945.* 14 reels.
>*The Far East, 1946-1953.* 14 reels.

Confidential U.S. State Department Central Files:

>*Japan: Internal Affairs, 1945-1949.* 42 reels.
>*Japan: Internal Affairs, 1950-1954.* 62 reels.

CIA Research Reports:

>*China, 1946-1976.* 6 reels.
>*Japan, Korea, and the Security of Asia, 1946-1976.* 5 reels.
>*Vietnam and Southeast Asia, 1946-1976.* 7 reels.

OSS/State Department Intelligence and Research Reports:

>*Japan and Its Occupied Territories During World War II.*
>16 reels.
>*Postwar Japan, Korea and Southeast Asia.* 6 reels.
>*Japan, Korea, Southeast Asia, and the Far East Generally:*
>*1950-1961 Supplement.* 7 reels.

Framing the Constitution of Japan: Primary Sources in English, 1944-1949. 420 microfiches.

Educational Reform in Japan, 1945-1952: Part 1. 461 microfiches.

From University Publications of America and Maruzen:

The Occupation of Japan

>*Part 1: US Planning Documents, 1942-1945. 490 microfiches.*

Part 2: US and Allied Policy, 1945-1952. 446 microfiches.
*Part 3: Reform, Recovery, and Peace, 1945-1952. 820 micro
fiches.*

Formerly secret executive sessions of Congressional hearings pertinent to Japan
and Asia began to be declassified as a "Historical Series" and published in the
1970s. See especially the following:

U.S. Congress, Senate Foreign Relations Committee. *Executive Sessions
of the Senate Foreign Relations Committee (Historical Series).*
Multi-volume, beginning with the 80th Congress of 1947-48.

_____. *Legislative Origins of the Truman Doctrine.* 1947.

_____. *Foreign Relief Aid.* 1947.

_____. *Foreign Relief Assistance Act.* 1948.

_____. *Vandenberg Resolution and NATO.* 1948-1949.

_____. *Economic Assistance to China and Korea.* 1949-1950.

_____. *Reviews of the World Situation.* 1949-1950.

_____. *Military Assistance Program.* 1949.

_____. *Extension of European Recovery Program.* 1949.

U.S. Congress, House Committee on International Relations. *Selected
Executive Session Hearings of the Committee, 1943-1950.* 8 volumes;
see especially volume 7 on "Policy in the Far East" and volume 8 on
"Mutual Defense Assistance Program."

THE COLD WAR IN ASIA:
COUNTRY & REGIONAL STUDIES

Harold R. Issacs. NEW CYCLE IN ASIA: SELECTED DOCUMENTS ON
MAJOR INTERNATIONAL DEVEOPMENTS IN THE FAR EAST.
1947: Macmillan.

Akira Iriye. THE COLD WAR IN ASIA: A HISTORICAL INTRODUCTION. 1974: Prentice-Hall.

_____ & Yōnosuke Nagai, eds. THE ORIGINS OF THE COLD WAR IN ASIA. 1977: Columbia University Press.

Edward Friedman & Mark Selden, eds. AMERICA'S ASIA: DISSENTING ESSAYS ON ASIAN-AMERICAN RELATIONS. 1969: Pantheon.

Noam Chomsky & Howard Zinn, eds. THE SENATOR GRAVEL EDITION OF THE PENTAGON PAPERS, volume 5: "Critical Essays." 1972: Beacon.

Japanese Association for American Studies. UNITED STATES POLICY TOWARD EAST ASIA, 1945-1950. Six essays by Japanese scholars in the maiden issue of the English-language *Japanese Journal of American Studies* (1980).

Roger W. Bowen. INNOCENCE IS NOT ENOUGH: THE LIFE AND DEATH OF HERBERT NORMAN. 1986: M. E. Sharpe.

Marc S. Gallicchio. THE COLD WAR BEGINS IN ASIA: AMERICAN EAST ASIAN POLICY AND THE FALL OF THE JAPANESE EMPIRE. 1988: Columbia University Press.

David W. Mabon. "Elusive Agreements: The Pacific Pact Proposals of 1949-1951," *Pacific Historical Review* 57.2 (1988), 147-177.

Kurt W. Radtke. CHINA'S RELATIONS WITH JAPAN, 1945-83: THE ROLE OF LIAO CHENGZHI. 1990: St. Martin's.

Chalmers Johnson. "The Patterns of Japanese Relations with China, 1952-1982," *Pacific Affairs* 59.3 (1986), 402-428.

Tang Tsou. AMERICA'S FAILURE IN CHINA, 1941-1950. 1963: University of Chicago Press.

Dorothy Borg & Waldo Heinrichs, eds. UNCERTAIN YEARS: CHINESE-AMERICAN RELATIONS, 1947-1950. 1980: Columbia University Press.

Robert M. Blum. DRAWING THE LINE: THE ORIGIN OF THE AMERICAN CONTAINMENT POLICY IN EAST ASIA. 1982: Norton.

Nancy Bernkopf Tucker. PATTERNS IN THE DUST: CHINESE-AMERICAN RELATIONS AND THE RECOGNITION CONTROVERSY, 1949-1950. 1983: Columbia University Press.

_____. "American Policy Toward Sino-Japanese Trade in the Postwar Years: Politics and Prosperity," *Diplomatic History* 8.3 (1984), 183-208.

MacArthur Memorial. THE OCCUPATION OF JAPAN: THE IMPACT OF THE KOREAN WAR. (proceedings of the 1986 symposium). Includes papers on the economy, diplomacy, the Japanese Communist Party, Toyota, and Koreans in Japan.

Bruce Cumings. "The Origins and Development of the Northeast Asian Political Economy: Industrial Sectors, Product Cycles, and Political Consequences," *International Organization* 38.1 (1984), 1-40.

_____, ed. CHILD OF CONFLICT: THE KOREAN-AMERICAN RELA-TIONSHIP, 1943-1953. 1983: University of Washington Press.

_____. THE ORIGINS OF THE KOREAN WAR. Princeton University Press.

Volume 1: LIBERATION AND THE EMERGENCE OF SEPARATE REGIMES, 1945-1947. 1981.
Volume 2: THE ROARING OF THE CATARACT, 1947-1950. 1990.

James I. Matray. THE RELUCTANT CRUSADE: AMERICAN FOREIGN POLICY IN KOREA, 1941-1950. 1985: University of Hawaii Press.

Frank Baldwin, ed. WITHOUT PARALLEL: THE AMERICAN-KOREAN RELATIONSHIP SINCE 1945. 1974: Pantheon.

Soon Chung Cho. KOREA IN WORLD POLITICS, 1940-1950: AN EVALUA-TION OF AMERICAN RESPONSIBILITY. 1967: University of California Press.

William W. Stueck, Jr. THE ROAD TO CONFRONTATION: AMERICAN POLICY TOWARD CHINA AND KOREA, 1947-1950. 1981: University of North Carolina Press.

Samuel P. Hayes. THE BEGINNING OF AMERICAN AID TO SOUTHEAST ASIA: THE GRIFFIN MISSION OF 1950. 1971: Heath.

David Wightman. TOWARD ECONOMIC COOPERATION IN ASIA: THE ECONOMIC COMMISSION FOR ASIA AND THE FAR EAST. 1963: Yale University Press.

Russell Fifield. AMERICANS IN SOUTHEAST ASIA: THE ROOTS OF COMMITMENT. 1973: Crowell.

Masaya Shiraishi. JAPANESE RELATIONS WITH VIETNAM, 1951-1987. 1990: Southeast Asia Program, Cornell University.

Thomas R. H. Havens. FIRE ACROSS THE SEA: THE VIETNAM WAR AND JAPAN, 1965-1975. 1987: Princeton University Press.

George McTurnan Kahin & John W. Lewis. THE UNITED STATES IN VIETNAM. Revised edition. 1969: Dell.

William Appleman Williams, Thomas McCormick, Lloyd Gardner & Walter LaFeber, eds. AMERICA IN VIETNAM: A DOCUMENTARY HISTORY. 1985: Anchor-Doubleday.

Robert J. McMahon. COLONIALISM AND COLD WAR: THE UNITED STATES AND THE STRUGGLE FOR INDONESIAN INDEPENDENCE, 1945-1949. 1981: Cornell University Press.

Max Beloff. SOVIET POLICY IN THE FAR EAST, 1944-1951. 1953: Oxford University Press.

Marc Gallicchio. "The Kuriles Controversy: U.S. Diplomacy in the Soviet-Japan Border Dispute, 1941-1956," *Pacific Historical Review* 60.1 (1991), 69-101.

Russell D. Buhite. SOVIET-AMERICAN RELATIONS IN ASIA, 1945-1954. 1981: University of Oklahoma Press.

Roger Swearingen. THE SOVIET UNION AND POSTWAR JAPAN: ESCALATING CHALLENGE AND RESPONSE. 1978: Hoover Institution.

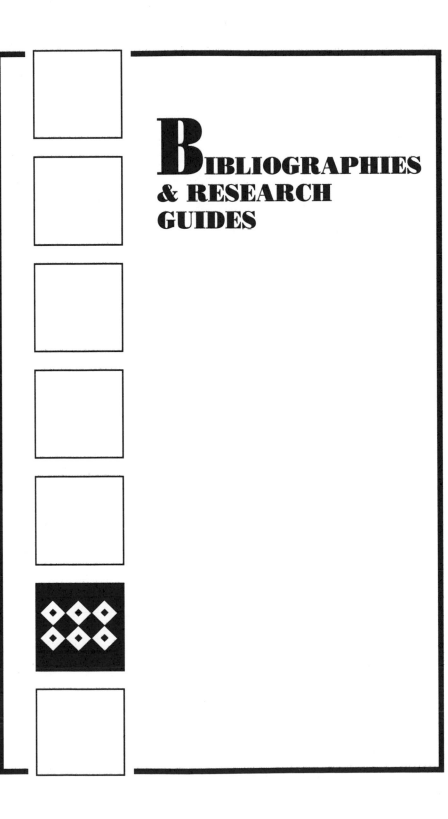

BIBLIOGRAPHIES & RESEARCH GUIDES

GUIDES TO WESTERN-LANGUAGE MATERIALS

James L. Gardner. JAPAN ACCESS: A BIBLIOGRAPHY OF BIBLIOGRA-
PHIES. 1990: Wings of Fire Press.

Frank Joseph Shulman. JAPAN. World Bibliographical Series, volume 103.
1989: Clio. Nearly 2,000 listings, focusing on the 1970s and 1980s,
many with extensive annotations.

Kenneth E. Carpenter & Raymond Lum, comp. WESTERN BOOKS ON ASIA:
JAPAN. 1992-1993: Research Publications International. Over 3,000
volumes in European languages, written from the sixteenth century to
World War II, on microfiche.

A GUIDE TO REFERENCE BOOKS FOR JAPANESE STUDIES. 1989:
International House of Japan Library.

CATALOGUE OF BOOKS IN ENGLISH ON JAPAN, 1945-1981. 1986:
Japan Foundation. Lists nearly 9,000 books published between 1945
and 1981.

CATALOGUE OF BOOKS ON JAPAN TRANSLATED FROM THE
JAPANESE INTO ENGLISH, 1945-1981. 1988: Japan Foundation.

Richard Perren, ed. & comp. JAPANESE STUDIES FROM PRE-HISTORY TO
1990: A BIBLIOGRAPHICAL GUIDE. 1992: Manchester University
Press.

International Secretariat, Institute of Pacific Relations. IPR PUBLICATIONS
ON THE PACIFIC, 1925-1952. 1953: Institute of Pacific Relations.
1,408 entries.

Library of Congress. THE JAPANESE EMPIRE: INDUSTRIES AND
TRANSPORTATION—A SELECTED LIST OF REFERENCES. 1943.
598 entries.

_____. JAPAN: ECONOMIC DEVELOPMENT AND FOREIGN POLICY—
A SELECTED LIST OF REFERENCES. 1940. 403 entries.

G. Raymond Nunn. JAPANESE PERIODICALS AND NEWSPAPERS IN
WESTERN LANGUAGES. 1979: Mansell. Lists 3,500 titles, dating
from the 1860s to 1978.

Hugh Borton, Serge Elisseeff, William Lockwood & John C. Pelzel. A
SELECTED LIST OF BOOKS AND ARTICLES ON JAPAN IN
ENGLISH, FRENCH, AND GERMAN. 1954: Harvard-Yenching
Institute. 1,781 entries.

Bernard S. Silberman. JAPAN AND KOREA: A CRITICAL BIBLIOGRA-
PHY. 1962: University of Arizona Press. 1,933 entries.

Kokusai Bunka Kaikan (Naomi Fukuda, ed). UNION CATALOG OF BOOKS
ON JAPAN IN WESTERN LANGUAGES. 1968. 543 pages.

Association for Asian Studies. CUMULATIVE BIBLIOGRAPHY OF ASIAN
STUDIES, 1941-1965 (1969). Covers both books and articles, and
consists of a 4-volume *Author Bibliography* and 4-volume *Subject
Bibliography* .

_____. CUMULATIVE BIBLIOGRAPY OF ASIAN STUDIES, 1966-1970
(1973). Consists of a 3-volume *Author Bibliography* and 4-volume
Subject Bibliography .

_____. BIBLIOGRAPHY OF ASIAN STUDIES. Annual, beginning in 1970
with books and articles published in 1969. The annual bibliographies
are published as separate volumes accompanying the *Journal of Asian
Studies* .

Thomas P. Fenton & Mary J. Heffron. ASIA AND PACIFIC: A DIRECTORY
OF RESOURCES. 1986: Orbis Books. Lists mostly small, low-budget
organizations and their publications—information often difficult to find
elsewhere.

Frank J. Shulman, comp. & ed. JAPAN AND KOREA: AN ANNOTATED
BIBLIOGRAPHY OF DOCTORAL DISSERTATIONS IN WESTERN
LANGUAGES, 1877-1969. 1970: American Library Association.

_____. DOCTORAL DISSERTATIONS ON JAPAN AND KOREA,
1969-1979: AN ANNOTATED BIBLIOGRAPHY OF STUDIES IN
WESTERN LANGUAGES . 1982: University of Washington Press.

_____. DOCTORAL DISSERTATIONS ON ASIA: AN ANNOTATED BIBLIOGRAPHICAL JOURNAL OF CURRENT INTERNATIONAL RESEARCH. Published periodically for the Association for Asian Studies by Xerox University Microfilms, beginning with volume 1, number 1 in Winter 1975.

Herbert Passin, comp. JAPANESE EDUCATION: A BIBLIOGRAPHY OF MATERIALS IN THE ENGLISH LANGUAGE. 1970: Teachers College, Columbia University. Contains 1,524 entries.

Hideo Satō. "The Basic Source Materials on the Education Reform in Postwar Japan: Report of the Surveys Conducted by the NIER Research Group," *Acata Asiatica* 54 (1988), 75-105.

James William Morley, ed. JAPAN'S FOREIGN POLICY, 1868-1941: A RESEARCH GUIDE. 1974: Columbia University Press. Contains both critical essays and bibliographies, with strong emphasis on Japanese materials up to 1970-1971.

Ernest R. May & James C. Thomson, Jr., eds. AMERICAN-EAST ASIAN RELATIONS: A SURVEY. 1972: Harvard University Press. Bibliographic essays organized by chronology rather than topical focus.

Janet Ziegler, comp. WORLD WAR II: A BIBLIOGRAPHY OF BOOKS IN ENGLISH, 1945-1965. 1971: Hoover Institution Press.

Bernd Martin. "Japan und der Krieg in Ostasien: Kommentierender Bericht uber das Schrifttum," Sonderheft 8, *Historische Zeitschrift* (1980), 79-228. A detailed bibliographic essay on World War Two in Asia.

R. John Pritchard & Sonia Zaide Pritchard, eds. GUIDE TO THE INTERNA-TIONAL MILITARY TRIBUNAL FOR THE FAR EAST, 5 volumes. Included in the 27-volume Garland reprint of the records of the International Military Tribunal for the Far East, under the series title THE TOKYO WAR CRIMES TRIAL.

Robert E. Ward & Frank J. Shulman. THE ALLIED OCCUPATION OF JAPAN, 1945-1952: AN ANNOTATED BIBLIOGRAPHY OF WESTERN-LANGUAGE MATERIALS. 1974: American Library Association. An indispensible 867-page guide.

Frank J. Shulman, comp. & ed. DOCTORAL DISSERTATIONS ON THE ALLIED OCCUPATION OF JAPAN, 1945-1952. 1978: prepared for a symposium at the MacArthur Memorial, Norfolk, Virginia.

William D. Wray. JAPAN'S ECONOMY: A BIBLIOGRAPHY OF ITS PAST AND PRESENT. 1989: Markus Wiener.

Karl Boger. POSTWAR INDUSTRIAL POLICY IN JAPAN: AN ANNOTAT-ED BIBLIOGRAPHY. 1988: Scarecrow Press.

Institute of Developing Economies. A SELECTED BIBLIOGRAPHY ON THE ECONOMIC DEVELOPMENT OF JAPAN. 1970. 1,780 entries.

Roberta Abraham. BIBLIOGRAPHY ON TECHNOLOGY AND SOCIAL CHANGE IN CHINA AND JAPAN. 1974: Committee on Technology and Social Change in Foreign Cultures, Iowa State University. 252 pages.

Rex Coleman & John Owen Haley. AN INDEX TO JAPANESE LAW: A BIBLIOGRAPHY OF WESTERN LANGUAGE MATERIALS, 1867-1973. 1975. Special issue of *Law in Japan: An Annual* .

Arcadio Schwade. SHINTŌ—BIBLIOGRAPHY IN WESTERN LANGUAGES: BIBLIOGRAPHY ON SHINTŌ AND RELIGIOUS SECTS, INTEL-LECTUAL SCHOOLS AND MOVEMENTS INFLUENCED BY SHINTŌISM. 1986: E. J. Brill.

International House of Japan Library, comp. MODERN JAPANESE LITERA-TURE IN TRANSLATION: A BIBLIOGRAPHY. 1979: Kōdansha International. Nearly 9,000 citations, covering some 1,500 authors from 1868 to 1978.

James L. Gardner. ZEN BUDDHISM: A CLASSIFIED BIBLIOGRAPHY OF WESTERN-LANGUAGE PUBLICATIONS THROUGH 1990. 1991: Wings of Fire Press.

Hesung Chun Koh et al. KOREAN AND JAPANESE WOMEN: AN ANA-LYTIC BIBLIOGRAPHIC GUIDE. 1982: Greenwood.

Kristina Ruth Huber. WOMEN IN JAPANESE SOCIETY: AN ANNOTATED BIBLIOGRAPHY OF SELECTED ENGLISH MATERIALS. Bibliographies and Indexes in Women's Studies, Number 16. 1992: Greenwood Press.

Claire Zebroski Mamola. JAPANESE WOMEN WRITERS IN ENGLISH TRANSLATION: AN ANNOTATED BIBLIOGRAPHY. 2 vols. 1989, 1992: Garland.

Yasuhiro Yoshizaki. STUDIES IN JAPANESE LITERATURE AND
    LANGUAGE: A BIBLIOGRAPHY OF ENGLISH MATERIALS.
    1979: Nichigai.

Latin American Studies Center, California State University, Los Angeles.
    LATIN AMERICA AND JAPAN: A BIBLIOGRAPHY. 1975.
    25 pages.

G. Raymond Nunn. ASIA: REFERENCE WORKS—A SELECT ANNO-
    TATED GUIDE. 1980: Mansell.

Asia/North America Communications Center [Hong Kong]. AMERICA IN
    ASIA: RESEARCH GUIDES ON UNITED STATES ECONOMICS IN
    PACIFIC ASIA. 1979.

William L. Holland. "Source Materials on the Institute of Pacific Relations,"
    Pacific Affairs 58.1 (1985), 91-97.

Peter Grilli, ed. JAPAN IN FILM: A COMPREHENSIVE CATALOGUE OF
    DOCUMENTARY AND THEATRICAL FILMS ON JAPAN AVAIL-
    ABLE IN THE UNITED STATES. 1984 (followed by supplements):
    Japan Society of New York. An excellent annotated guide to Japan-
    related films.

ENGLISH GUIDES TO JAPANESE MATERIALS

The Japan Foundation. AN INTRODUCTORY BIBLIOGRAPHY FOR JAPAN-
    ESE STUDIES. Ongoing series from 1974. Includes bibliographic
    surveys of various disciplines by leading Japanese scholars.

A GUIDE TO REFERENCE BOOKS FOR JAPANESE STUDIES. 1989:
    International House of Japan Library.

Herschel Webb. RESEARCH IN JAPANESE SOURCES: A GUIDE. 1965:
    Columbia University Press.

American Library Association. GUIDE TO JAPANESE REFERENCE BOOKS.
    1966. English version of *Nihon no Sankō Tosho* , 1965.

Library of Congress. GUIDE TO JAPANESE REFERENCE BOOKS:
    SUPPLEMENT. 1979.

Naomi Fukuda, ed. BIBLIOGRAPHY OF REFERENCE WORKS FOR JAPAN-
ESE STUDIES. 1979: Center for Japanese Studies, University of
Michigan. Covers Japanese materials published up to 1977, excluding
education, law, science and technology.

Kokusai Bunka Shinkōkai. K.B.S. BIBLIOGRAPHY OF STANDARD REFER-
ENCE BOOKS FOR JAPANESE STUDIES, WITH DESCRIPTIVE
NOTES. 1971 for "Generalia." Other volumes cover specific areas of
study.

Yasuko Makino & Masaei Saitō. A STUDENT GUIDE TO JAPANESE
SOURCES IN THE HUMANITIES. 1994: Center for Japanese
Studies, University of Michigan.

Naomi Fukuda, ed. JAPANESE HISTORY: A GUIDE TO SURVEY
HISTORIES—PART 1, BY PERIOD. 1984: Center for Japanese
Studies, University of Michigan.

_____, ed. JAPANESE HISTORY: A GUIDE TO SURVEY HISTORIES—
PART 2, LITERATURE. 1986: Center for Japanese Studies,
University of Michigan.

Masato Matsui, ed. JAPANESE PERFORMING ARTS: AN ANNOTATED
BIBLIOGRAPHY. 1981: Center for Asian and Pacific Studies,
University of Hawaii. This and the following five titles comprise a
series of useful bibliographies listing Japanese holdings in the University
of Hawaii's Hamilton Library.

_____, Tomoyoshi Kurokawa, & Minako I. Song. RYŪKYŪ: AN ANNO-
TATED BIBLIOGRAPHY. 1981: Center for Asian and Pacific
Studies, Council for Japanese Studies, University of Hawaii.

_____, Minako I. Song, & Tomoyoshi Kurokawa, eds. NAN'YŌ (SOUTH
SEAS): AN ANNOTATED BIBLIOGRAPHY. 1982: Center for
Asian and Pacific Studies, University of Hawaii.

_____, Tomoyoshi Kurokawa, & Jun Nakamura. RUSSO-JAPANESE
FRONTIER REGION: JAPANESE SOURCE MATERIALS. 1984:
Center for Asian and Pacific Studies, Council for Japanese Studies,
University of Hawaii at Manoa.

_____, Mitsugu Sakihara, & Tetsuto Umeki. SATSUMA DOMAIN:
JAPANESE RESEARCH RESOURCES. 1986: Center for Asian and
Pacific Studies, Council for Japanese Studies, University of Hawaii at
Manoa.

_____, Jun Nakamura, & Tomoyoshi Kurokawa, eds. JAPANESE ECONOMIC AND TECHNOLOGICAL DEVELOPMENTS: AN ANNOTATED BIBLIOGRAPHY. 1989: Center for Japanese Studies, University of Hawaii at Manoa.

Japan Business History Institute. JAPANESE YEARBOOK ON BUSINESS HISTORY. 1984- . Yearly summaries of "The Works of Japanese Business Historians."

Naofusa Hirai. "Studies on Shintō in Pre- and Post-War Japan," *Acta Asiatica* 51 (1987), 96-118.

Masao Terasaki. "The Study of Japanese Educational History: A Brief History and Related Problems," *Acta Asiatica* 54 (1988), 106-123.

Hideo Satō. "The Basic Source Materials on the Education Reform in Postwar Japan: Report of the Surveys Conducted by the NIER Research Group," *Acata Asiatica* 54 (1988), 75-105.

James William Morley, ed. JAPAN'S FOREIGN POLICY, 1868-1941: A RESEARCH GUIDE: Columbia University Press. Includes detailed discussion of Japanese materials up to 1970-1971.

Sadao Asada, ed. INTERNATIONAL STUDIES IN JAPAN: A BIBLIOGRAPHIC GUIDE. 1988: Japan Association of International Relations.

_____, ed. JAPAN AND THE WORLD, 1853-1952: A BIBLIOGRAPHIC GUIDE TO JAPANESE SCHOLARSHIP IN FOREIGN RELATIONS. 1989: Columbia University Press.

Cecil H. Uyehara. CHECK LIST OF ARCHIVES IN THE JAPANESE MINISTRY OF FOREIGN AFFAIRS, TOKYO, JAPAN, 1868-1945. 1954: Photoduplication Service, Library of Congress. The basic guide to archives seized after the Pacific War and microfilmed for the Library of Congress. Pages 112-146 deal with materials from the International Military Tribunal for the Far East.

John Young. CHECKLIST OF MICROFILM REPRODUCTIONS OF SELECTED ARCHIVES OF THE JAPANESE ARMY, NAVY, AND OTHER GOVERNMENTAL AGENCIES, 1868-1945. 1959: Georgetown University Press.

_____. THE RESEARCH ACTIVITIES OF THE SOUTH MANCHURIAN RAILWAY COMPANY, 1907-1945: A HISTORY AND BIBLIOGRAPHY. 1966: East Asian Institute, Columbia University.

Michiko Kiyohara, comp. A CHECKLIST OF MONOGRAPHS AND PERIOD-ICALS ON THE JAPANESE COLONIAL EMPIRE. 1981: Hoover Institution Press.

Wayne Lammers & Osamu Masaoka, comp. JAPANESE A-BOMB LITERA-TURE: AN ANNOTATED BIBLIOGRAPHY. 1977: Wilmington College Peace Resource Center. 132 pages. Followed by later updates.

Naomi Fukuda, ed. SURVEY OF JAPANESE COLLECTIONS IN THE UNITED STATES, 1979-1980. 1981: Center for Japanese Studies, University of Michigan. Surveys 29 collections.

Japan-U.S. Friendship Commission. CURRENT JAPANESE SERIALS IN THE HUMANITIES AND SOCIAL SCIENCES RECEIVED IN AMERI-CAN LIBRARIES. 1980. Published by East Asia Collection, Indiana University Library, and itemizing 4,389 serials.

Yasuko Makino. NATIONAL UNION LIST OF CURRENT JAPANESE SERIALS IN EAST ASIAN LIBRARIES OF NORTH AMERICA. 1992: Association for Asian Studies.

Thaddeus Y. Ohta. JAPANESE NATIONAL GOVERNMENT PUBLICA-TIONS IN THE LIBRARY OF CONGRESS. 1981: Library of Congress.

Philip M. Nagao. JAPANESE LOCAL HISTORIES IN THE LIBRARY OF CONGRESS: A BIBLIOGRAPHY. 1988: Library of Congress.

Library of Congress. JAPANESE GOVERNMENT DOCUMENTS AND CENSORED PUBLICATIONS: A CHECKLIST OF THE MICRO-FILM COLLECTION. 1992: Library of Congress.

Nozomu Hayashi & Peter Kornicki, eds. EARLY JAPANESE BOOKS IN CAMBRIDGE UNIVERSITY LIBRARY: A CATALOGUE OF THE ASTON, SATOW, AND VON SIEBOLD COLLECTIONS. 1991: Cambridge University Press.

Basic guides to current Japanese publications:

- *Nihon Zenkoku Shoshi* (Japan National Bibliography Weekly List). Weekly publication of the National Diet Library.

- *Shuppan Nyūsu* (Publishing News). Published 3 times per month by Shuppan News, Ltd.

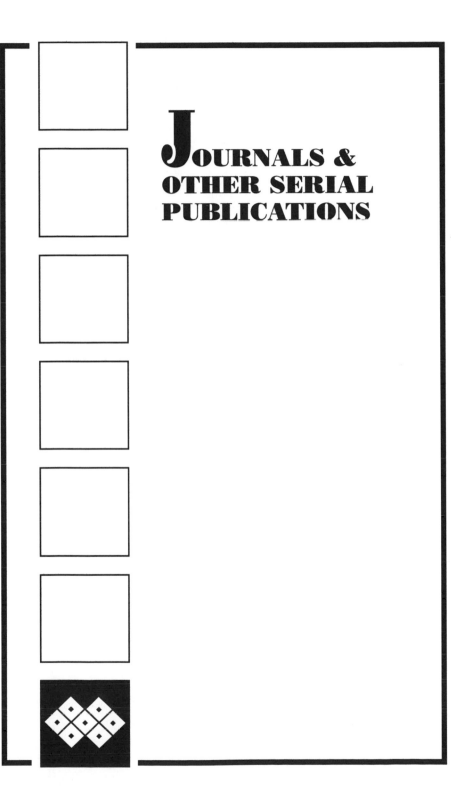

JOURNALS & OTHER SERIAL PUBLICATIONS

JOURNALS & OTHER SERIAL PUBLICATIONS

Acta Asiatica (1961-)

Amerasia (1937-1947)

Ampo: Japan-Asia Quarterly Review (1969-)

Annals of the Institute of Social Science (Institute of Social Science, University of Tokyo; 1966- ; succeeds *Social Science Abstracts*, 1953-1965)

Asia (1898-1946; from November 1942, title becomes *Asia and the Americas*)

Asian Art (1988-)

Asian Folklore Studies (1963- ; succeeds *Folklore Studies*, 1942-1962)

Asian Perspectives: A Journal of Archeology and Prehistory of Asia and the Pacific (1957-)

Asian Survey (1961- ; successor to *Far Eastern Survey*)

Asian Theater Journal (1984-)

Bulletin of Concerned Asian Scholars (1968-)

Bulletin of the European Association for Japanese Studies (1974-)

Bulletin of the Nanzan Institute for Religion and Culture (1977-)

China Today (1932-1942; merges with *Amerasia*)

Contemporary Japan (1932-)

Current Politics and Economics of Japan (1991-)

Daily Summary of Japanese Press (U.S. Embassy, Japan, from 1954; title varies)

The Developing Economies (1962-   )

The East (1964-   )

East-West Film Journal (1986-   )

Economic Survey of Japan (annual from 1950/1951 by the Economic Planning
     Agency and predecessor agencies of the Japanese Government)

Far Eastern Economic Review (1946-   )

Far Eastern Survey (1932-1961; succeeded by *Asian Survey*)

Far Eastern Quarterly (1941-1956; succeeded by *Journal of Asian Studies*)

Folklore Studies (1942-1962; succeeded by *Asian Folklore Studies*)

Harvard Journal of Asiatic Studies (1936-   )

History of Religions (1961-   )

Hitotsubashi Journal of Economics (1960-   )

Hitotsubashi Journal of Law and Politics (1960-   )

Hitotsubashi Journal of Social Studies (1960-   )

Japan Annual of Law and Politics (1952-   )

Japan Christian Quarterly (1925-   )

Japan Christian Yearbook (1903-   )

Japan Echo (1974-   )

Japan Forum (1989-   )

Japan Foundation Newsletter (1973-   )

Japan Interpreter (1970-   ; succeeds *Journal of Social and Political Ideas in
     Japan*, 1963-1967)

Japan Political Research (1990- ; succeeds *Newsletter of Research on Japanese Politics*, 1970-1989)

Japan Quarterly (1954-) Especially useful for "Recent Publications on Japan" and "Chronology" features.

Japan Review (International Research Center for Japanese Studies, Kyoto, (1990-)

Japan Socialist Review (1961-)

Japan Times (newspaper, 1897-)

Japanese Economic Studies (1972-)

Japanese Journal of Religious Studies (1974- ; replaces *Contemporary Religions in Japan*, 1960-1970)

Japanese Studies in the History of Science (1962-1979)

Journal of American-East Asian Relations (1992-)

Journal of Asian History (1967-)

Journal of Asian Studies (1956- ; succeeds *Far Eastern Quarterly*, 1941-1956)

Journal of Contemporary Asia (1970-)

Journal of Japanese Studies (1974-)

Journal of Northeast Asian Studies (1982-)

Journal of Social and Political Ideas in Japan (1963-1967; succeeded by *Japan Interpreter*)

Kyoto University Economic Review (1926-)

Law in Japan (1967-)

Memoirs of the Research Department of the Tōyō Bunko (1920s-)

Modern Asian Studies (1967-)

Monumenta Nipponica (1938-)

Newsletter of Research on Japanese Politics (1970-1989; succeeded by *Japan Political Research*)

Nichibunken Newsletter (International Research Center for Japanese Studies, Kyoto, 1988-   )

Nissan Occasional Paper Series (Nissan Institute of Japanese Studies, Oxford, 1986-   )

Occasional Papers (Center for Japanese Studies, University of Michigan, 1951-1969)

Oriental Economist (1934-   )

Pacific Affairs (1928-   )

Pacific Historical Review (1932-   )

Papers on Japan (East Asian Research Center, Harvard University, 1961-1972)

Philosophical Studies of Japan (1959-1970)

Philosophy East and West (1951-   )

Positions: East Asia Cultures and Critique (1993-   )

Sino-Japanese Studies Newsletter (1988-   )

Social Science Abstracts (Institute of Social Science, University of Tokyo; 1953-1965; succeeded by *Annals of the Institute of Social Science*)

Summaries of Selected Japanese Magazines (U.S. Embassy, Japan, from 1954; title varies)

Transactions, Asiatic Society of Japan ("Series 1" from 1872; "Series 2" from 1924; "Series 3" from 1948, "Series 4" from 1986) See Richard Wilson & June Colby, "*The Transactions of the Asiatic Society of Japan 1872-1986: Comprehensive Index,*" in *Transactions, Asiatic Society of Japan*, 4th series, 4 (1989), 87-179.

Transactions, Japan Society of London (1892-   )

Trans-Pacific (newspaper, 1919- 1940)

U.S.-Japan Women's Journal (1991-   )

INDEX

ABOUT THE
AUTHORS

JOHN W. DOWER, born in 1938, is Professor of History and Henry Luce Professor of International Cooperation at the Massachusetts Institute of Technology. He is the author of *Japan in War and Peace: Selected Essays*, *War Without Mercy: Race and Power in the Pacific War*, *Empire and Aftermath: Yoshida Shigeru and the Japanese Experience, 1878-1954* and *The Elements of Japanese Design*, and is the editor of *The Origins of the Japanese State: Selected Writings of E. H. Norman* and coeditor of *The Hiroshima Murals: The Art of Iri Maruki and Toshi Maruki.*.

TIMOTHY S. GEORGE, born in 1955, is a Ph.D. candidate in modern Japanese history at Harvard University. He is currently a Fulbright Graduate Research Fellow and a Foreign Research Scholar at the University of Tokyo's Institute of Social Science, researching a dissertation titled *Minamata: Power, Policy, and Citizenship in Postwar Japan*. He has written and translated a number of articles on modern Japan.